1959

Books by Fred Kaplan

1959: The Year Everything Changed

*Daydream Believers: How a Few Grand Ideas
Wrecked American Power*

The Wizards of Armageddon

1959

The Year Everything Changed

Fred Kaplan

WILEY

John Wiley & Sons, Inc.

Published by John Wiley & Sons, Inc., Hoboken, New Jersey
Published simultaneously in Canada

Credits appear on page 309 and constitute an extension of this copyright page.

For general information about our other products and services, please contact our Customer Care Department within the United States at (800) 762-2974, outside the United States at (317) 572-3993 or fax (317) 572-4002.

Wiley also publishes its books in a variety of electronic formats. Some content that appears in print may not be available in electronic books. For more information about Wiley products, visit our web site at www.wiley.com.

Library of Congress Cataloging-in-Publication Data:

Kaplan, Fred M.
    1959 : the year everything changed / Fred Kaplan.
      p. cm.
    Includes bibliographical references and index.
    ISBN 978-0-470-60203-4 (paper)
    ISBN 978-0-470-38781-8 (cloth)
        1. History, Modern—1945–1989.   2. Civilization, Modern—1950–   I. Title.
  II.   Title: Nineteen fifty nine.
    D842.5.K35 2009
    909.82'5—dc22

                                                                    2008045529

For Maxine & Sophie, through the next fifty years
And, as always, for Brooke

"I mean, man, whither goest thou? Whither goes thou, America, in thy shiny car in the night?"

—Jack Kerouac

I tell you, the New Frontier is here, whether we seek it or not.

—John F. Kennedy

What we in hindsight call change is usually the unexpected swelling of a minor current as it imperceptibly becomes a major one and alters the prevailing mood.

—Morris Dickstein

Contents

Timeline

January 1   Fidel Castro's revolutionaries take power in Cuba.

January 2   Soviets' Lunik 1 spacecraft breaks free of Earth's gravitational pull.

January 4   Soviet deputy premier Anastas Mikoyan visits the United States.

January 9   Federal judge orders Atlanta to integrate its buses and trolleys.

January 10   Hayden Planetarium in New York reopens with a show on space exploration called "The Sky Is the New Frontier."

January 12   Berry Gordy borrows $800 from his family to buy a studio for his new record company, Motown.

January 19   Federal judge orders Virginia to desegregate its schools.

February 5   Allen Ginsberg returns to Columbia University to give a poetry reading to a packed auditorium.

February 13   U.S. Air Force generals coin the word "aerospace" to claim military control of outer space in addition to the skies.

March 1   Martin Luther King Jr. meets with Vinoba Bhave, the Gandhian "walking saint," at the ashram in Ahmedabad, India.

March 2   Miles Davis begins to record *Kind of Blue.*

March 3   U.S. Pioneer IV spacecraft matches the feat of Lunik 1.

March 12   C. Wright Mills publishes "Culture and Politics: The 4th Epoch," inspiring an American New Left.

March 13   Herman Kahn begins his marathon lecture series on thermonuclear war.

March 17 Excerpt of William Burroughs's *Naked Lunch* appears in *Big Table* magazine.

March 18 U.S. Postmaster General seizes copies of *Big Table* for violating obscenity laws.

March 18 Barney Rosset of Grove Press announces he will publish the illegal, uncensored version of D. H. Lawrence's *Lady Chatterley's Lover*.

March 24 Texas Instruments announces the invention of the integrated circuit, or microchip.

April 5 3rd International Auto Show introduces the Datsun and the Toyota.

April 9 "Sick comic" Lenny Bruce appears on national television.

April 15 Fidel Castro visits the United States.

April 28 Grove Press sues U.S. Post Office for confiscating copies of *Lady Chatterley's Lover.*

May 4 John Coltrane records *Giant Steps.*

May 7 Philip Roth's *Goodbye, Columbus* is published.

May 22 Ornette Coleman records *The Shape of Jazz to Come.*

June 8 U.S. Navy and Post Office launch "missile mail" experiment.

June 18 Federal court overturns Arkansas school-segregation law.

June 25 Dave Brubeck starts to record *Time Out.*

June 29 U.S. Supreme Court overturns the banning of a French film of *Lady Chatterley's Lover.*

July 8 First two U.S. soldiers are killed in South Vietnam.

July 12 Malcolm X travels to the Middle East.

July 13 Mike Wallace's TV documentary *The Hate That Hate Produced*, about Malcolm X and the Black Muslims, is aired nationwide.

July 21 Grove Press wins court victory and right to publish *Lady Chatterley's Lover.*

July 23 G. D. Searle applies for FDA approval of the birth control pill.

July 24 Soviet premier Nikita Khrushchev and Vice President Richard Nixon hold "kitchen debate" in Moscow.

September 9 U.S. Civil Rights Commission releases its first report detailing racial discrimination in America.

September 15 Khrushchev visits the United States.

September 19 Philip Morrison and Giuseppi Cocconi's "Searching for Interstellar Communication" is published in *Nature*.

October 4 Allan Kaprow stages the first Happening.

October 5   IBM 1401, first practical business computer, goes on sale.

October 21   Guggenheim Museum, first U.S. art museum dedicated to non-objective art, opens.

October 30   Norman Mailer's *Advertisements for Myself* is published.

November 4   John Howard Griffin begins his trip to the Deep South disguised as a black man, for his book *Black Like Me*.

November 11   John Cassavetes' film *Shadows* opens.

November 16   François Truffaut's *The 400 Blows* opens in New York.

November 17   The Ornette Coleman Quartet debuts at the Five Spot.

November 19   Ford Motor Company shuts down production of the Edsel.

December 16   *Sixteen Americans*, the first museum show featuring Robert Rauschenberg and Jasper Johns, opens at the Museum of Modern Art.

December 31   John F. Kennedy prepares to announce that he will run for president in the 1960 election.

1

Breaking the Chains

On January 2, 1959, a Soviet rocket carrying the Lunik I space capsule—also known as *Mechta*, "the dream"—blasted off from the Baikonur Cosmodrome in Tyuratam, Kazakhstan, accelerated to twenty-five thousand miles per hour (the magical speed known as "escape velocity"), sailed past the moon, and pushed free of Earth's orbit, becoming the first man-made object to revolve around the sun among the celestial bodies. The next issue of *Time* magazine hailed the feat as "a turning point in the multibillion-year history of the solar system," for "one of the sun's planets had at last evolved a living creature that could break the chains of its gravitational field."

The flight of the Lunik set off a year when chains of all sorts were broken with verve and apprehension—not just in the cosmos, but in politics, society, culture, science, and sex. A feeling took hold that the breakdown of barriers in space, speed, and time made other barriers ripe for transgressing.

1959 was the year when the shockwaves of the new ripped the seams of daily life, when humanity stepped into the cosmos and also commandeered the conception of human life, when the world shrank but the knowledge needed to thrive in it expanded exponentially, when outsiders became insiders, when categories were crossed and taboos were trampled, when everything was changing and everyone knew it—when the world as we now know it began to take form.

1

Just two months before Lunik, "the jet age" roared into being, when a brand-new Boeing 707, owned by Pan American World Airways, took off with great fanfare on the first nonstop flight across the Atlantic to Paris. On the runway, First Lady Mamie Eisenhower declared, "I christen thee 'Jet Clipper America'!" before smashing a bottle of ocean water across the plane's nose and cheering with a crowd of thousands as the plane rolled down the runway while the Air Force band played "The Star-Spangled Banner." The *New York Times* enthused over "the possibility of hurdling an ocean from one continent to another, from one world to another, in half a dozen hours"—age-old longings that were "no longer daydreams, because the jets are here."

Now, with the New Year barely under way, the world was thrust into "the space age." The Russians and the Americans would go at it—in a "space race"—all year long, back and forth, each side trumpeting some new triumph with startling alacrity.

Outer space and lightning speed animated the popular consciousness. Mass-circulation magazines and newspapers ran lengthy articles explaining the "new geography" of solar orbits and galaxies. NASA lingo—"blast off," "countdown," "A-OK"—swooshed into the everyday lexicon. Madison Avenue picked up on the coinage with advertisements touting new products—from cars to telephones to floor waxes—as "jet age," "space age," "the world of the future," "the countdown to tomorrow."

And tomorrow promised to be not just another day but a new dawn. The era's rising young political star, John Fitzgerald Kennedy, would run for president on a slogan of "Leadership for the '60s"— the first time that the future was defined in terms of a decade, which presumed to hold out both menace and hope but in either case great change. Kennedy presented his youth as a virtue—another reversal of the norm—describing himself as a man "born in this century," keen to explore "the New Frontier."

The phrase was a reference to Frederick Jackson Turner's classic essay of 1893, "The Frontier in American History," which argued that the "American character"—its "restless, nervous energy" and "dominant individualism"—was a product of the frontier's vast emptiness, with its prospect of a continuous "expansion westward," each step siring "new opportunities" for conquest, settlement, and "perennial rebirth."

By the 1950s, this frontier had long been filled and settled. The new frontier now lay in outer space, and its prospect of seemingly infinite expansion set off a new wave—a new way of seeing and experiencing on Earth.

The space program itself, and the markets that it seemed certain to generate, spurred scientists to develop new technologies—most notably the microchip and faster, smaller computers—which would transform the fantasies of science fiction into the routines of daily life.

This enchantment with the new also galvanized a generation of artists to crash through their own sets of barriers—and attracted a vast audience that was suddenly, even giddily, receptive to their iconoclasm.

New comedians—"sick comics," some called them—satirized the once-forbidden topics of race, religion, and politics. Brazen novelists loosened the language and blurred the boundaries between author and subject, reportage and literature. Rebellious filmmakers shot improvisational movies outside the confines of Hollywood studios. Painters created a new kind of art that streaked outside the canvas. Jazz musicians improvised a new kind of music that broke through the structures of chords and pre-set rhythms. A new record label, Motown, laid down a jazz-inflected rhythm and blues that insinuated black culture into the mainstream, inspired baby-boomer rock 'n' roll, and supplied the soundtrack for the racial revolts and interminglings that lay ahead.

These currents were quickened by a series of expansive government edicts. The new United States Civil Rights Commission ordered a series of investigations on racial discrimination in voting, housing, and schools. The Supreme Court issued rulings that lifted restrictions on free speech and literature. Toward the end of the year, the Food and Drug Administration held hearings that resulted in the approval of a birth-control pill, which unleashed a revolution in women's lives and in sexual activity, unbridled and spontaneous.

Yet the thrill of the new was at once intensified and tempered by an undercurrent of dread. Outer space loomed as a frontier not only for satellites, rockets, and computers but also for missiles, H-bombs, and apocalyptic war.

And so, the year also saw panic over fallout shelters, fears of a "missile gap," and an escalation of the Cold War. Nikita Khrushchev, the Soviet premier, boasted that his defense factories were churning out nuclear-tipped missiles "like sausages." In the U.S. Congress, the Joint Atomic Energy Committee held five days of public hearings on the effects of a "limited" nuclear attack. Scientists were detecting hazardous levels of radiation in milk, as a result of H-bomb tests in the atmosphere. A mordant physicist named Herman Kahn toured the country and tantalized large crowds with marathon lectures on how to fight, survive, and win a nuclear war.

It was this twin precipice—the prospect of infinite possibilities and instant annihilation, both teetering on the edge of a new decade—that gave 1959 its distinctive swoon and ignited its creative energy.

The latter half of the preceding decade, especially from 1945 to 1947, when America created the bomb, won World War II, and emerged as a sprawling global power, also marked a vivid turning point. But the generation in control before the war remained in control just after. The most talented among them adapted well to the expansion of their domain. They devised new institutions and strategies—political, economic, and military—that rebuilt the West and allowed the emerging American superpower to advance its interests without triggering World War III. But these men tended to view nations as static pieces on a chessboard; the elites of the opposing superpower did the same, more harshly still; and the smaller pieces on the board, devastated by six years of brutal warfare, could manage little in the way of resistance—as yet. At home, these leaders saw the end of the war as a time to restore the old order—unaware that although the American homeland was physically intact, its social fabric had unraveled.

It would take another dozen years before the nation set out, or stumbled forth, in a clear new direction—before it responded to the shifting contours and redefined itself in their light and shadows. The new path was carved by the younger generation, those who grew up through depression and war—and who felt dissatisfied with the false peace that followed: bent out of shape, or spurred to revolt, by the dissonance between the new era's promised hopes and palpable fears. It was in the late 1950s that the war years' adolescents and young soldiers came into their own, approaching the ages of thirty or forty—too young to shove their elders out of power but old enough, and self-consciously so, to claim a stake in the future and to make themselves heard.

This raucousness reached a crescendo in the next decade—the sixties—with the sexual revolution, free speech, rock 'n' roll, campus uprisings, and racial riots, all erupting against the escalation of a savage war in Southeast Asia and the wondrous spectacle of landing a man on the moon. Yet all of these cataclysms sprang not from the impulses or ideals of the baby-boom generation but rather from the revolts and revelations of 1959—and many of the new instigators were well aware of their roots and took inspiration from their predecessors.

The truly pivotal moments of history are those whose legacies endure. And, as the mid-forties recede into abstract nostalgia, and the late sixties evoke puzzled shudders, it is the events of 1959 that continue to resonate in our own time. The dynamics that were unleashed fifty years ago and that continue to animate life today—the twin prospects of infinite expansion and total destruction—seem to be shifting to a new phase, crossing yet another new frontier.

A dramatic, though in some ways coincidental, parallel is the emergence of another young outsider elected on a promise of hope and change—though Barack Obama, born in the year of John F. Kennedy's inauguration, pushes the concept of outsider to new extremes. The son of a Kansan mother and a Kenyan father (whose own father was born Muslim), Obama grew up in Indonesia and Hawaii, went to college in California and New York and to law school at Harvard, then rose through politics in Chicago—he's not just a black man (extraordinary enough), he's multiracial, multinational, multiethnic, a man of the country, the city, the tropical islands, and beyond—the living embodiment of every late-fifties dream of smashing through barriers and integrating not merely black with white, but America with the world.

Yet the more significant parallels are the conditions surrounding the two young presidents' ascents—global power dispersing, cultures fracturing, the world shrinking, and science poised to spawn new dreams and nightmares—though, again, in Obama's time, our time, these trends appear monstrously magnified.

The distribution of global power—which once let American policy makers get by with a little knowledge about Russia and maybe

China—began dispersing in the late fifties to the point where ignorance of small countries like Vietnam and Cuba got us into deadly trouble. Today the collapse of power centers, brought on by the end of the Cold War, requires political elites to know about regional tribes, separatist enclaves, stateless terrorists, to say nothing of financial interdependencies, climate change, energy alternatives, and other aspects of security that have nothing to do with traditional gauges of the military balance.

Cultural power has also devolved, as the assaults that seemed so daring fifty years ago, in painting, literature, music, and film—the idea that anything can be art, anyone can be an artist, any language is permissible, one kind of artist can also be another kind of artist, and neither age nor ethnicity determines eligibility—have insinuated themselves into the mainstream. Now the next round of splintering— already under way in blogs, iTunes, eBooks, YouTube, Twitter, News Feed, Flickr, and who knows what new forums to come—is not only broadening further the boundaries of art but stands to shatter the final barriers between artist and audience, public and private, spectacle and life.

In science and technology, the trajectory from 1959 to 2009, and likely onward to the future, is one of ever-expanding expectations of what is explorable—from the galaxies to subatomic particles and everything in between—to the point where we seem on the verge of touching infinity in all directions.

The microchip, which brought forth the digital age—with its mini-computers, multipurpose cell phones, and instantaneous access to everyone, everything, everywhere—may, over the next few decades, spark revolutions in artificial intelligence, brain-augmenting nanochips, and other devices of such minuscule size yet such gargantuan processing power that their full applications can scarcely be imagined.

Advances in biological research, which in 1959 produced a pill to control human birth—with its resulting social, economic, and cultural upheavals—may in the coming years create gene therapies and synthetic organs that long postpone human death, with still more tumultuous consequences.

There was, is, and always will be a dark side of this juggernaut to tomorrow. Just as the flip side of rockets and satellites was H-bombs and missiles, so biotechnology can also yield biohazards and bio-weapons, brain-augmentations might dehumanize the soul, the omni-presence of online networks could warp community and erode the sense of self, while the infinite fracturing of culture threatens to wipe out the concept of a shared culture, nation, or world.

In the summer of 1959, Allen Ginsberg, the generation's vision-ary poet of exuberance and doom, wrote in the *Village Voice*: "No one in America can know what will happen. No one is in real con-trol. America is having a nervous breakdown. . . . Therefore there has been great exaltation, despair, prophecy, strain, suicide, secrecy, and public gaiety among the poets of the city."

He might as well have written it today.

2

A Visitor from the East

On January 4, 1959, two days after the Lunik launch, came another Soviet sensation. Anastas Mikoyan, the Kremlin's number-two man, landed at New York's Idlewild Airport for what he called "a fortnight's holiday," and he wound up reshaping the concept and practice of superpower diplomacy.

The biggest novelty was the journey itself. No Soviet official of such high rank had ever set foot in the United States. Hardly less remarkable was how the trip came about. For the previous two years, Nikita Khrushchev, the Soviet premier, had tried to arrange face-to-face talks with the American president, Dwight Eisenhower, to no avail. The two leaders had met four years earlier at the multinational disarmament conference in Geneva, but as Eisenhower himself complained, those sessions were by nature "sterile" set pieces, too large and formal to be useful. So, on December 17, 1958, with no advance notice, Mikoyan sent the U.S. Embassy in Moscow a routine request for a visa, explaining that he wanted to visit his friend Mikhail Manshikov, the Soviet ambassador in Washington.

Word of the impending trip quickly leaked out, and a dozen elite organizations across the United States—the Council on Foreign Relations, the Economic Club of New York, the Union Club of Cleveland, among others—cabled the embassy or the Kremlin, inviting Mikoyan to come talk at their forums while he was in the country. The *New York Times* reported that the trip had "aroused more excitement and anticipation . . . than any similar visit by a foreign dignitary in many years."

The visit caught Eisenhower off guard. His secretary of state, John Foster Dulles, scrambled to set up a meeting. The day before Mikoyan's arrival, Dulles, having just returned to Washington from a vacation in Jamaica, grumbled to reporters that the whole business was highly irregular—no appointments had been made, no agenda had been set. "But," he said, "I will certainly try to see him."

Mikoyan wound up meeting twice with Dulles—once at the State Department toward the start of the trip and once more, at the White House with President Eisenhower, toward the end. In between, Mikoyan hit the road by motorcade and plane, trailed by a pack of reporters who covered his every move as they would a celebrity. Newspaper readers learned that while stopping for breakfast at a Howard Johnson's on the New Jersey Turnpike, Mikoyan chatted with the waitress and admired the Formica countertop. He strolled through downtown Washington, eyeing a bookstore window display of Boris Pasternak's *Doctor Zhivago*, the new best seller that was banned in his homeland. In Manhattan, he traipsed through the aisles of Macy's and lunched with Wall Street bankers. Touring a Hollywood studio, he kissed Jerry Lewis on both cheeks and chatted with Sophia Loren.

Mikoyan delivered speeches to workers at Detroit Edison's River Rouge power plant, to furniture salesmen at the Chicago Merchandise Mart, and to industrialists in San Francisco— everywhere talking peace and drawing vigorous applause. He told rapt audiences that he now realized American capitalists didn't want war because it would destroy their factories. "We are all tired of the Cold War and would very much like to have a hot peace," he said to a crowd of auto executives at the prestigious Detroit Club. To a packed ballroom of 1,100 businessmen at New York's Waldorf-Astoria, he complained that the U.S. government had met Moscow's peace proposals with "a *nyet, nyet, nyet*," and pleaded, "Let us now make an effort to have a *da, da, da* in our relations." Harrison Salisbury, the *New York Times*'s foreign correspondent, who rode along with the press pack, likened Mikoyan's tour to "a presidential campaign" and admired his "outstanding gift of public relations." His "blunt words, crackling wit, and unfailing good humor," Salisbury wrote, were sure to have a "deepening impact."

Mikoyan was the ideal emissary for this PR blitz. Dapper, soft-spoken, and self-assured, he seemed more like a European businessman than a Red apparatchik, and in a way, he was both. At sixty-three, he was an authentic "Old Bolshevik" who had joined Lenin's Communist party before the 1917 Revolution—one of just two such men still alive after the scourge of war and Stalin's purges.

Back in 1926, Mikoyan was named commissar for internal and external trade, and he spent the next three decades keeping the Soviet state financially afloat. He had traveled to the United States once before, in 1936, and came away impressed with the American worker's standard of living, even during the Great Depression. He was especially taken with such treats as Corn Flakes, Puffed Wheat, canned food, and, above all, ice cream. Upon his return to Moscow, he ordered the construction of a meat-canning plant to U.S. standards and set up Russia's first ice-cream factory with machinery bought from American companies. During World War II, he served as the Red Army's grand quartermaster, mobilizing the eastward retreat of factories from Moscow and Leningrad and processing delivery of Lend-Lease aid from America. After the war, he devised the economic policy that tightened Soviet control of Eastern Europe, wresting away the region's natural resources—including uranium from East Germany and Czechoslovakia—and setting up front-companies that funneled the revenue to Moscow. Unlike any of Khrushchev's other men, he could speak the language of Western financiers, almost to the point of passing as one of them.

But Eisenhower's intelligence officials were suspicious. Mikoyan was also known to be loyal to the regime and hard as nails. Two years earlier, a *Time* magazine cover story about Mikoyan was aptly headlined "The Survivor." During the purges and show trials of the thirties, he was a member of Stalin's dinner-table clique. As the winds shifted after Stalin's death, so did he. At the Twentieth Party Congress in 1956, where Khrushchev catalogued the late dictator's crimes, Mikoyan stood and delivered the first anti-Stalin speech. But the same year, when Khrushchev wanted to crush the rebellion in Hungary, he sent Mikoyan to oversee the crackdown. (It was for this reason that during his American trip, he was followed not only by cheering crowds yearning for peace, but also by Hungarian émigrés shouting, "Mass murderer!") In 1957, when a group of high-ranking party members conspired to oust Khrushchev, Mikoyan alone stood by his side. Khrushchev sent the conspirators off to small factories in the provinces; one of them, the experienced diplomat Vyacheslav Molotov, was named ambassador to Outer Mongolia. Mikoyan, on the other hand, was promoted to deputy premier. Khrushchev affectionately called him "my Armenian" and "my rug merchant." It was only natural that Mikoyan would be sent on this trip to America; there was literally no other choice.

To a degree that no one in the West understood at the time, Khrushchev was under tremendous pressure at the start of 1959. For all his bluster about churning out missiles, he had nothing; his ICBM program was in a rut; he was bluffing, in an attempt to deter an attack by the United States, which was encircling Soviet borders with military bases and deploying medium-range missiles within striking distance of Russian bases and cities.

Khrushchev was also panicked by a deepening crisis in Berlin. Berlin was the Cold War's hot spot, an unsettled anomaly of the armistice ending World War II. After their victory, the Allied powers divided Germany into four zones—separately occupied by the United States, England, France, and the USSR—corresponding to the position of each nation's army at the time of the Nazis' surrender. The Allies also divided the capital city of Berlin into four sectors. As East-West relations deteriorated into Cold War, Germany was divided into two nations—Communist-ruled East Germany in what had been the Soviet zone and West Germany as the merger of the three Western sectors. Berlin also remained divided, but the city was trapped a hundred miles inside East German territory. In 1948, Stalin ordered a blockade of all roads leading into West Berlin. The United States mounted a massive airlift, dropping and delivering packages of aid into the city for more than three hundred days. Finally, Stalin halted the blockade, and the four powers signed an agreement guaranteeing permanent Western access to the enclave.

Over the next decade, as West Germany grew free and prosperous while East Germany stagnated under the Soviet boot, Easterners immigrated to the West in droves, using West Berlin as the transit point. By the fall of 1958, East Germany had lost two million people, with continued losses of more than ten thousand per month, including some of its best-educated youth.

In November, a desperate Khrushchev announced that, within six months, he would sign a "peace treaty" with East Germany, declaring the agreement of a decade earlier "null and void," and placing all of Berlin under East German sovereignty, which essentially meant Moscow's control. If the United States resisted and tried to retain free access to West Berlin, there would be war.

The launching of Lunik was deliberately timed. To Sergei Korolev, the visionary director of the Soviet Union's space program, it marked a grand first step toward exploring the moon, the planets, and the stars. To Khrushchev, the feat was meant to reinforce his great bluff—that he had an advanced missile program that could threaten the Americans and perhaps pressure them into surrendering Berlin.

Lunik was a massive capsule—seventeen feet long, eight feet in diameter, weighing over three thousand pounds and carrying nearly eight hundred additional pounds of instruments. During the previous fall and winter, the United States had tried three times to launch much smaller capsules toward the moon. None of them covered even half the distance before tumbling back to Earth.

Two days after Lunik went up, on the same day as Mikoyan's visit, the *New York Times* called the launch "unquestionably the greatest achievement of the Space Age" but also a sign "that the Russians have more powerful rockets and therefore greater capacity to deliver intercontinental ballistic missiles." The "big question as the New Year begins," the story concluded, was "whether Moscow will press her challenge to the point of war."

What no American knew—what remained secret until decades later, after the Soviet Union collapsed and the Kremlin's archives were opened—was that Khrushchev's threats against Berlin touched off a political battle inside the Kremlin and that Mikoyan, normally the premier's top ally, led the dissent.

Mikoyan had been in Germany during the Berlin blockade; he knew how much the Americans valued West Berlin as a banner of freedom and as a token of their commitment to the defense of Europe. He had never bought the Communist doctrine that deemed war with the capitalist nations "inevitable." More than this, he knew, as did his boss, that the Soviet Union was far from ready for a war with the United States. He feared that if Khrushchev pushed his ultimatum, there might really be a war and the outcome would be disastrous.

And so Mikoyan proposed a trip to America, as a vehicle for softening Khrushchev's provocation. Before leaving, he'd persuaded the premier to modify his Berlin policy, but the compromise was lame. Khrushchev agreed to let West Berlin exist as a "free city" but under East German auspices—that is, free in name only. When Mikoyan presented the notion to Eisenhower and Dulles, they replied that it still sounded like an ultimatum, and he must have known they were right. What Khrushchev allowed him to say would not be enough to undo the diplomatic damage. So, Mikoyan set out to alter the broader climate, taking to the American road and making his case—that the Soviet Union did not want war, that the Cold War should end, and that the two nations should resume active trade—directly to the American people and their captains of industry.

On those terms, Mikoyan's mission was a stunning success. James Reston, the *New York Times*'s diplomatic correspondent, wrote in his analysis of the Soviet visitor: "He brought nothing new as a solution to the Cold War. He changed nothing of substance. And yet his performance stands as a reminder that the old diplomacy with its rigid forms and courtesies is gone, and the new diplomacy, part tourism, part missionary zeal, part propaganda, is here to stay." Mikoyan pursued an approach, Reston wrote, for which Americans once had a knack—"avoiding old forms and adopting new."

At the start of his seventh year as president, Dwight Eisenhower— the supreme allied commander during World War II—was the very embodiment of old form. He was sixty-eight, up till then the oldest man ever to hold the office. He had recently suffered a heart attack. John Foster Dulles, his notoriously belligerent secretary of state, was terminally ill with cancer and would die before the summer. After prolonged postwar prosperity, the American economy was in recession; the country seemed rudderless, stagnant, its world position in decline, its people suffering a crisis of self-confidence. As a result, Eisenhower's Republican Party lost a record sixteen Senate seats in the 1958 midterm elections and forty-eight seats in the House, turning the Democrats' slight edge, which they had picked up just two years earlier, into an indomitable majority for the subsequent two decades.

Eisenhower was shrewder than he seemed; he had quietly stood up to Soviet pressures and staved off the war hawks in his own

military and in Congress. But he was not only losing the global battle for image, he was failing to see that it had suddenly become a key
battleground. The world had grown suddenly smaller, through the
revolutions of jet travel and, more perilously, nuclear-tipped missiles
capable of destroying civilizations in a matter of minutes. Foreign
crises could no longer be the exclusive province of hidebound diplomats attending leisurely summits in neutral capitals. Crises had to
be engaged, on the spot, in the moment, by and between the leaders
who really had power.

At the end of 1959, John F. Kennedy, the young Democratic senator from Massachusetts, would launch his campaign for the presidency on a promise to "get the country moving again." This theme
was no less crisply articulated at the start of the year, as the new session of Congress opened, by Lyndon Baines Johnson of Texas, the
Senate majority leader, who was planning his own run for the White
House. Emboldened by his party's swollen ranks, Johnson lambasted
the Republican administration for a "deficit of vigor," a tendency to
"exalt the static," and a failure to meet the challenges of "a new age,"
adding, "Free men can afford much," but they "can never afford the
price of inertia."

3

The Philosopher of Hip

At the start of 1959, Norman Mailer was restless. He'd been in a funk for over a year, but felt that he was about to rouse himself out of it. He and his wife, an almost equally temperamental artist named Adele Morales, had just moved back to New York City after spending two years in the Connecticut suburbs. They'd bought an apartment in Greenwich Village, the center of bohemia and jazz and festive boozing. Maybe the rush would reenergize him. And he was embarking on a new book—he would call it *Advertisements for Myself*—reflecting a new kind of writing; he didn't quite know where it was taking him, but anything new was welcome.

Twelve years had passed since Mailer wrote *The Naked and the Dead*, his first novel and, by general acclaim, the best American novel to come out of World War II. He was only twenty-five when the book was published, and it made him a literary celebrity. It was not only a commercial hit—soaring to the top of the best-seller list and selling two hundred thousand copies in hardcover—but a critical success as well, its raw realism likened to that of Ernest Hemingway. The *New York Herald Tribune*'s review was typical, hailing it as an "astonishing book . . . a major war novel" and Mailer himself as having joined "the ranks of major American novelists." Since his freshman year at Harvard, Mailer had been obsessed with becoming a great writer, the greatest writer of his generation. With *The Naked and the Dead*, the dream seemed in sight.

But now, Mailer was thirty-six. His second novel, *Barbary Shore*, had drawn scathing reviews and meager sales; his third, *The Deer Park*, received mixed notices and sold well by most standards—fifty thousand copies in hardcover, enough to make the best-seller list—but fell far short of the mark set by his debut. Mailer feared failure as deeply as he craved success, and he wondered if his force was spent—if the novel itself might be a spent force, and he set about devising a style and, with it, an identity, more suitable to a great writer of his time.

He set out on this new path gradually and hesitantly. He had started to write another novel, but by the spring of 1958 he'd completed only sixty pages and felt nothing more coming. He felt run-down, short on energy, middle-aged.

So he put the novel aside for a moment (in fact, he would never resume it) and began to compile a collection of his shorter pieces—essays, reviews, stories, some published, some not—and to write prefaces to each piece that he hoped would stitch the book together. He had modest expectations for this book, as did his publisher, G. P. Putnam, which advanced him a mere $3,500. But Mailer was keen to do it, in part to be doing *something*, in part to explore some ideas that he had thrown on the table a couple of years ago and had since lacked a forum to elaborate, ideas that probed the depths of his spiritual, moral, and intellectual crises—which he saw as reflecting the crises of American society in the age of Eisenhower—and his vague sense of "an underground revolution on its way."

If much of the decade was a deadening, fearful time for America, it was also such a time for Mailer personally. His first novel's success, so early in his life, opened up opportunities, but it also imposed frightful pressures. He told friends that his second novel had to be at least as successful—had to be "perfect." *The Naked and the Dead* was inspired by his own experiences during the war in the Pacific; Mailer, in fact, had joined the Army and gone to war precisely in order to write a novel about it afterward. But he'd had no notable experiences since, nothing else to fill up another great novel. Still, he felt obligated to write one; that's what writers did. He and his first wife, Bea, were in Paris when *Naked* came out. They'd sailed over in the fall of

1947, after it had gone to press but before it was published. News of its success swiftly crossed the Atlantic and gave him instant status in café society. A left-wing existentialism was in fashion, and Mailer soaked it up. When he returned to the States, he wrote a novel called *Barbary Shore*—a dry, didactic treatise about capitalism, socialism, and the oppressive state. It came out in 1951, and the reviews were uniformly savage ("this evil-smelling novel," "paceless, tasteless, and graceless," "this confused charade," "a monolithic flawless badness").

His publisher rejected the draft of his next novel, *The Deer Park*, as did six others that Mailer canvassed. They all feared that it might be banned for obscenity; it contained a few salacious scenes of extra-marital sex, and Mailer refused to alter them. Beyond that, they just didn't like it. Putman finally gave him a contract, though even its editors admitted that the book wasn't to their taste and that they'd bought it hoping Mailer would soon return to form.

All this sent Mailer into depression, spiked by heavy drinking, followed by an ailing liver. In the spring of 1954, he and his second wife, Adele, went down to Mexico for a rest. There he experienced two new sensations. The first was an angry, rebellious attitude toward the publishing world and the larger society that it represented. The second was the purring fuel of marijuana.

"I was out of fashion, and that was the score," Mailer would later write in a long chunk of *Advertisements for Myself*, recounting his troubles with *The Deer Park*. "All I felt then was that I was an outlaw, a psychic outlaw, and I liked it, I liked it a good night better than trying to be a gentleman."

After he came back home from Mexico, Mailer paved a new path, to the alarm or curiosity of his literary friends, most of them other novelists as well as critics who wrote for the New York intellectual journals—*Dissent*, *Commentary*, and the *Partisan Review*. He and Adele remained friendly with this circle, but they also started going to parties in Harlem, an exotic thing to do in that uniformly segregated time. Their new uptown friends introduced them to jazz, and Mailer started prowling the city's jazz clubs, a different one each weekend.

All these new sensations—jazz, marijuana, and a sexual energy that he found aroused by both—inspired Mailer to start keeping a journal to keep up with all the ideas ricocheting in his brain, and to write it while smoking his magic weed. It was a frantic document, 248 double-spaced typewritten pages in all, hammered out sporadically over a three-month period from December 1, 1954, to March 4, 1955.

He wrote it mainly as an act of therapy, a self-administered form of the psychoanalysis that had come into fashion. It was, as might be expected, a wild mishmash, rife with loopy ramblings and drug-addled revelations, some profound, many bizarre, a few both. The existentialism of sex was a recurring theme—its power to suspend time and implant the sensation of being a god. He mused on the notion that southern racism stemmed from a fear that black men were better at sex and that, therefore, to give them social and political equality would tip the playing board in their favor. He celebrated the hipster as the subterranean risk taker who, in an age when socialism was passé but cultural revolts were rumbling, might play the same role that Marx once credited to the proletariat—the spark of the revolution. And he waxed lyrically on modern jazz as the language of this revolt, likening the soloist's spontaneous effort to craft something new and thrilling from a familiar line of music to the thrill of a bullfighter dodging death or a driver racing into traffic, insouciant of the dangers, confident of swerving at just the right second.

Mailer would later look back on the journal as a set of ravings—but also as "the start of more ideas than I will ever have again." In fact, most of the ideas that he would develop in articles and books through the end of the decade, and some beyond, first took form in its pages.

Above all, it was in these journals that he envisioned his next phase as a writer. Just as he had to break away from the standard persona of a literary gentleman to experience the dark and wild side of urban life, so he also had to break through standard literary forms to describe and analyze the new era's sensations. "What terrifies me," he wrote in one entry, "is exactly this: I am shoving off into a total reevaluation of everything."

In the spring of 1955, he found a forum for his new iconoclasm. He got a call from two friends, Dan Wolf and Ed Fancher, who were starting a weekly newspaper in Greenwich Village aimed at the neighborhood's young bohemians. It would be called the *Village Voice*, and they asked Mailer to come in as a co-owner. He invested $5,000, thinking it might be a lark. The first issue came out in late September. It was drab, as was the next one and the one after that. The paper was losing money at a rapid clip. In part to save his investment, in part to have something to do, Mailer decided to write a regular column.

The Deer Park came out at about the same time. The reviews weren't as grim as those for Barbary Shore, but several were bad. As an up-yours gesture, Mailer took out a full-page ad in the Voice, reprinting excerpts from the most damning reviews: "The year's worst snake pit in fiction," "Sordid . . . crummy," "Moronic mindlessness," "Golden garbage heap," "Nasty," "Silly," "Dull."

It was his way of appearing to laugh off the critics, but in fact they revived his anger and sent him into a postpartum gloom. He was in the mood for war. The column would be his battlefield.

In the beginning, he didn't know where to aim his fire. His first column, in mid-January 1956, headlined "A Column for Slow Readers," insulted his own audience as frustrated, dim-witted, and envious of those more talented, like himself. The hate mail poured in. (One letter, printed in the following week's issue, read: "This guy Mailer. He's a hostile, narcissistic pest. Lose him.") For a while, Mailer reveled in the fury. He was getting "slightly punch-drunk," as he later described himself in those days—literally. Most parties thrown by the Voice ended with Mailer starting a fistfight with somebody.

Two months into writing his columns, his good friend, Robert Lindner, died of a heart ailment at the age of forty-one. Lindner, a renegade psychoanalyst, had written several books, including Prescription for Rebellion, Must You Conform? and Rebel without a Cause (Warner Brothers paid Lindner to use the title of the last book for a movie with James Dean, but it otherwise had little to do with the text). His broad thesis was that man has an "instinct for rebellion." In this sense, the decade's bland conformity was not only deadening the culture but perverting human biology. Lindner gave scientific sanction to Mailer's own fitful rebelliousness, not only in his ideas but personally. He was the one who'd urged Mailer to keep the marijuana journal as a sort of therapy; Mailer would mail him a copy of each entry for his comment.

Lindner's death may have driven Mailer to take another look at the journal. In any case, a few weeks later, he wrote a column called "The Hip and the Square," the ideas of which came straight from the journal's pages. "Hip," he wrote, "is an American existentialism" found most authentically in blacks, soldiers, psychopaths, drug addicts, and jazz players—all those who possess an "intense awareness of the present tense in life."

A couple of weeks later, in mid-May, he continued the theme, wondering if the worst of the decade was over. He himself had passed through "years of intense pessimism," but now, he wrote, "I feel the hints, the clues, the whispers of a new time coming. There is a universal rebellion in the air," in which "the destructive, the liberating, the creative nihilism of the Hip, the frantic search for potent Change may break into the open with all its violence, its confusion, its ugliness and horror, and yet . . . if we have courage enough, there is beauty beneath."

Soon after that piece, Mailer quit the *Voice*, frustrated by sloppy copyediting and by his growing awareness that Wolf and Fancher didn't want to make the paper as radical as he did. When he started writing for the *Voice*, Mailer regarded the column as personal therapy. By the time he quit, he saw it as "the first lick of fire in a new American consciousness," his rediscovered yearning to be "a hero of my time." This was classic megalomania, but there was also something to it. Somehow, through his own obsessions, hang-ups, and drug-soaked revelations, Mailer had glommed on to the cultural revolution in the making.

In April 1957, he wrote an article for his friend Irving Howe, the editor of *Dissent*, one of the leading small journals—circulation about five thousand—by and for left-leaning intellectuals who were disillusioned by Stalin and sought new grounding in democratic socialism and high modernism. Mailer titled the article, which was published in the summer issue, "The White Negro: Superficial Reflections on the Hipster."

In one of the early entries of his marijuana journal two years earlier, when he was first musing on the hipster as the new proletariat, Mailer wrote: "Wild thought. The atom bomb may actually have kicked off hipsterism." This became the central idea of "The White Negro."

"Probably," the article began, "we will never be able to determine the psychic havoc of the concentration camps and the atom bomb upon the unconscious mind of almost everyone alive in these years." Arising from this bleakness, he continued, is a new type of human being, the hipster—"the American existentialist," "the white Negro"—as a brave response to the prospect of instant holocaust. "If the fate of twentieth-century man is to live with death from adolescence to premature senescence," Mailer went on, then the "only life-giving answer is to live with death as immediate danger, to divorce oneself from society, to exist without roots, to set out on that uncharted journey into the rebellious imperatives of the self."

This line would serve as an anthem of sorts to a generation of rebels in the wings.

It was a wild-eyed essay, unlike anything in style or substance that Mailer or anyone in his circle had written or read in their time. Much of it was misguided, overly romanticized, entangled more with Mailer's own obsessions and insecurities than with the real-life hipsters and black men that he depicted and with whom he so clearly yearned to identify. He glorified violence to a degree that disturbed hipsters and squares alike. His understanding of jazz was, in a sense, comically shallow. "Jazz is orgasm," he wrote in one passage, seemingly unaware of the deep grounding in musical theory, technique, and sheer discipline that great jazz musicians pour into their compositions or solos. (At one point, Mailer rented a saxophone and blew along with his jazz records, thinking that he, too, could be a hipster—a white Negro—through sheer passion and osmosis.)

James Baldwin, who'd met Mailer in Paris in the summer of 1956 and who endured a rocky friendship with him for the rest of his life, would write a few years later that the black jazz musicians whom they both knew "really liked Norman" but "did not for an instant consider him remotely 'hip.' . . . They thought he was a real sweet ofay, but a little frantic."

And yet, perhaps because his own frantic swings matched those of the decade, Mailer managed to capture a spirit of the time, the rumblings of an undercurrent, the risk and adventure of rattling the cages and breaking through the bars.

Similarly, he may not have understood the depths of modern jazz, but he did grasp its essential appeal: its fierce energy, its motion, and, above all, its freedom, its explicit apartness from—and heroic indifference to—the norms of square society.

Though he rarely if ever admitted as much to others, Mailer knew that he wasn't a real hipster. In a notebook that he kept in 1959,

he acknowledged as much, admitted that though he was intellectually hip, he remained a square in action. Or, as he put it in one of the
first prefaces in *Advertisements for Myself*, "I have a fair chance to
become the first philosopher of Hip."

Writing "The White Negro" emboldened Mailer to put everything
on that gamble. He later recalled thinking that if he "had any chance
of being a great writer," it would be by navigating the currents that
he'd barreled through in that essay. "They," he said, "were going to
be my frontier."

"The White Negro" and the other essays about hip and square
would form the center of *Advertisements for Myself*, and their
themes would pervade the whole book; he wanted to put out such a
book precisely to give the ideas more prominence, to put them in the
context of his entire intellectual development.

At the start of 1959, he was getting the book in shape but still
having trouble with the prefaces to the individual pieces. He wondered whether to write prefaces at all; they were giving him so much
trouble, maybe he should just slap together the collected works and
let them speak for themselves.

One evening, soon after moving back to the city, the Beat poet
Allen Ginsberg came over to his apartment, bringing along his
friend Jack Kerouac. Mailer had befriended Ginsberg a few years
earlier; he'd never met Kerouac. When *On the Road*, Kerouac's
stream-of-consciousness, semi-autobiographical novel about a road
trip across America, was published two years earlier, Mailer, like
many in the literary establishment, laughed it off, calling the book
"pretentious" and "sentimental as a lollipop." But years later, Mailer
would admit that, in fact, he'd read the novel "with a sinking heart,"
thinking, "Oh, shit, this guy's done it. He was there, living it, and I
was just an intellectual writing about it."

For their part, Ginsberg and Kerouac had some problems with
Mailer's "The White Negro," which was published a couple of
months before *On the Road*. They thought Mailer's macho swagger
was risible. But they liked the fact that he *got* the apocalyptic tenor
of the times, that this giant of literary realism had essentially joined
their side in the emerging culture war. They, especially Ginsberg,
saw Mailer, for all his bluster, as a kindred spirit. And when they all
met, Mailer liked both of them.

Over the next couple of months, as Mailer fiddled with the introductions for *Advertisements*, banging out one false start after another, he finally hit on taking his cue from Kerouac—to write about *living* the essays, to make the book *about* the merging of his life and his art, his life *as* art. He saw that the prefaces to the various pieces might form the threads of a new kind of book, in which he would not only celebrate society's transgressors but also join their ranks. He would lay down fiction and essays and his own commentary on both all together, as if they were indistinguishable, or at least indivisible, unified by the common thread of its protagonist, who was Mailer himself, at once the tale's hero, antihero, creator, biographer, and critic. Throughout the book—before, after, sometimes in the middle of each essay or story—he would interrupt the narrative, recount how he came to write the piece, what was on his mind and how he felt at the time, appraise its merits in retrospect, and often reprint the most blistering judgments of others, with total transparency and lack of shame.

Others had written essays or memoirs or literature; but nobody had combined all three; nobody had ever created anything like this.

"Unconsciously," Mailer said many years later, "I was trying to take inventory. I was trying also to end a certain part of my literary life and begin anew."

He wanted above all to declare himself an outsider—a "psychic outlaw," as he put it—a different sort of outsider from his new Beat friends but still as much an outsider as they were.

Mailer had always been an outsider, after all—a scrappy Brooklyn Jew at Harvard, an Ivy Leaguer in the Army, a politically unschooled American among the café leftists in Paris after the war, a white boy in the Harlem lofts, an aspiring hipster in the jazz clubs. Yet he possessed a brilliant eye and ear. He could go deep inside, homing in on the essence of these scenes and sensations. But he needed to find his own voice to do that. That new voice first emerged in *Advertisements for Myself*.

In her review of the book, Diana Trilling—a prominent literary critic in her own right as well as the wife of Lionel Trilling, the celebrated moral conscience of Columbia University's English department—complained that Mailer was "posturing" and advised him to return to the realism of *The Naked and the Dead*.

Mailer wrote Trilling a letter explaining what he was up to. They were casual friends, and they were both Jewish in a WASP-dominated world, so he thought she would understand what he had to say. There had been no major Jewish novelists before World War II, he observed, because the novel is a literary genre that taps into the roots of a society and Jews had no such roots. The war—with the social leveling of conscription, then the psychic havoc wreaked by the Holocaust and the atom bomb (the premise of "The White Negro")— tore up those roots, everywhere. Everyone was free to create a new voice, a new persona, and the Jews had been expert at that for centuries. The "realism" to which Trilling wanted Mailer to return—*that* was posturing. The voice he was tapping now was his true voice, or at least *a* true voice—not some homage to someone else's past, but a reflection of his present state of mind.

Philip Roth, another Jewish novelist, ten years younger and less blustering than Mailer, made a similar point in defending his first novel, *Goodbye, Columbus*, which was also churning great controversy in 1959. Roth's book was about loud Jews and sexual desire and other provocations that sophisticated novelists—especially Jewish novelists—were not supposed to write about. One critic chided Roth's style, and that of a few other Jewish writers of the day, as "bouncy." In a speech at Stanford, Roth shot back, "When writers who do not feel much of a connection to Lord Chesterfield begin to realize that they are under no real obligation to try and write like that distinguished old stylist, they are likely enough to go out and be bouncy"— not to dazzle the reader, "but to incorporate into American literary prose the rhythms, nuances, and emphases of urban and immigrant speech," which itself might produce "a language of new and rich emotional subtleties."

When *Advertisements for Myself* was published to much acclaim at the end of October 1959, Mailer sold an excerpt not to *Dissent* or *Partisan Review*, the niche journals of his intellectual clique, but to *Esquire*, a literary but thoroughly commercial magazine, available at newsstands and supermarket bins.

The book, in this sense, was the first serious postmodern book—a major whack at the distinction between "high culture" and "mass culture." And it marked the beginnings of two literary genres that would transform American writing through the rest of the century and beyond:

the confessional memoir and the New Journalism. Mailer would emerge in the next decade as the pioneer and master of both, with such books as *The Armies of the Night* (subtitled "History As a Novel, The Novel As History"), about the antiwar march on the Pentagon, and *Miami and the Siege of Chicago*, about the rebellion at the 1968 political conventions. These books, which grew out of magazine articles, recounted major events of their time, but Mailer made no bones about his participation in them, no apologies for putting himself at the center of his accounts, since he, after all, was the one observing and analyzing the action, and any disguise of this premise would corrupt the search for truth. The New Journalism, especially as Mailer practiced it, was a technique but, even more, an attitude that broke through—at once fusing and transcending—the barriers between the artistry of literature and the legwork of reporting, between substance and style, between artist-journalist and the world all around him.

4

Generations Howling

On the night of February 5, 1959, Allen Ginsberg gave a poetry reading in the McMillin Theater at Columbia University before fourteen hundred spectators, nearly all of them students, with hundreds more turned away for lack of space. It was a triumphant night for Ginsberg, his first return to the college that had suspended him a decade earlier under sordid circumstances, and he was returning as a literary celebrity, almost a pop star.

A few years earlier, Ginsberg had been living in the Bay Area of California. Kenneth Rexroth, a local poet-impresario, sponsored weekly poetry readings at art galleries and coffee shops in San Francisco's North Beach district, a scruffy neighborhood that was attracting a growing number of young bohemians. On October 7, 1955, Ginsberg appeared at one of these readings, at the Six Gallery on Fillmore Street, and recited the first part of a poem, which he'd started writing two weeks earlier, called *Howl*. It was a brash, profane, apocalyptic meditation, with long, syncopated lines and turbulent imagery ("I saw the best minds of my generation destroyed by madness, starving hysterical naked /. . . angelheaded hipsters burning for the ancient heavenly connection to the starry dynamo in the machinery of night."), and Ginsberg read it with what even he later described as "a strange ecstatic intensity." The event caused an instant sensation. It was widely written up, hailed (though in some quarters mocked) as a new kind of poem and, more, as the cry of a new generation alienated by crass materialism and conformity.

Ginsberg publicly credited Jack Kerouac with coining the poem's title and inspiring its style of phrasing—"a spontaneous bop prosody," as Ginsberg put it, referring to the cadences of Charlie Parker's bebop jazz. As a result, *Howl* made Kerouac famous, too, and Viking Publishers, which had laid aside a proposal that he'd submitted months earlier, gave him a contract for *On the Road*, the most ambitious of eleven novels that he'd written in the previous six years, only one of which, *The Town and the City*, had ever been published (and it was largely forgotten). To the extent Kerouac was known at all until then, it was for a remark that he'd made back in the early fifties to a friend and fellow writer named John Clellon Holmes. They were talking about contemporary parallels with the "Lost Generation" after World War I and the philosophy of existentialism that followed. Kerouac said, "You know, this is a really *beat* generation." Holmes leapt up and said, "That's it, that's right!" Inspired by the line, Holmes wrote an article in 1952 for the *New York Times Magazine*, called "This Is the Beat Generation," in which he credited "John Kerouac" for the phrase.

Soon after the reading at the Six Gallery—at which Kerouac passed around jugs of wine—the "Beat" label was applied to a whole group of North Beach poets, including Rexroth, Michael McClure, Gary Snyder, and Lawrence Ferlinghetti, who also owned the City Lights Bookstore and had just started an imprint to publish many of these poets' works, including *Howl*.

When *On the Road* appeared in bookstores in September 1957, a review in the *New York Times* declared it an "authentic work of art," a "major novel," even a "historic occasion," proclaiming, "Just as Hemingway's *The Sun Also Rises* came to be regarded as the testament of the Lost Generation, so it seems certain that *On the Road* will come to be known as that of the 'Beat Generation.'"

The review was a fluke. The *Times*'s regular book critic, a thorough square named Orville Prescott, was on vacation when Kerouac's novel came in. An editor assigned it to a staff writer named Gilbert Millstein because he seemed to know something about the subject. Five years earlier, Millstein was the editor who'd commissioned Clellon Holmes to write the *Times Magazine* article about the "Beat

Generation." Millstein had favorably reviewed Holmes's novel, called *Go*, whose main characters were based in large part on Kerouac and Ginsberg, whom Holmes had known when they all lived in New York. And so the links came full circle.

When Prescott returned from vacation, he panned Kerouac's novel in the Sunday *Book Review* section, as expected. But Millstein's rave in the daily paper had made its impact. *On the Road* was the book of the moment; it climbed the best-seller charts, and attracted a vast following among restless young men for decades to come.

Ferlinghetti had published Ginsberg's *Howl and Other Poems* a year earlier, but Customs officials declared it "obscene" and seized copies. (One official was quoted in the press as saying, "You wouldn't want your children to come across it.") The U.S. Attorney's office in San Francisco declined to pursue the case. So the feds tried again, this time sending undercover agents into the City Lights Bookstore to buy a copy and then to arrest Ferlinghetti for publishing, and his poor cash-register clerk for selling, obscene materials.

At the ensuing trial, which was heavily publicized, provocative passages from the poem were read aloud, and a stream of eminent critics testified that it was a masterpiece. The federal judge, Clayton Horn, ruled that the book was not obscene. Before the trial, only a thousand or so copies of *Howl* had been in print. After the ruling, Ferlinghetti couldn't print copies quickly enough to sate the mass hunger for this once-forbidden fruit.

Judge Horn's ruling came down on October 3, 1957, just a few weeks after Millstein's rave review of Kerouac's novel. To most of the book-buying public, then, *Howl* and *On the Road* appeared at the same time. And so, the two works, along with Kerouac and Ginsberg themselves, were forever linked as the essential artifacts and heroic figures of the Beat movement.

Then came another wrinkle. On October 4, the day after Ginsberg's legal victory, the Soviets launched Sputnik, the first satellite, into orbit. Herb Caen, a prominent columnist for the *San Francisco Chronicle*, wrote that the bohemians hanging out on the North Beach were as "far out" as Sputnik—and so dubbed them "beatniks." The term stuck.

By 1959, newspapers and magazines were filled with stories about beatniks, who tended to be portrayed as either morally dangerous or eccentrically dimwitted. Hollywood B-movies, like *High School Confidential*, *The Wild Party*, *The Subterraneans*, and *The Beatniks*, hit screens across the country. *The Dobie Gillis Show* premiered on television that year, with Bob Denver playing Dobie's bongos-slapping beatnik friend, Maynard G. Krebs. *Life* magazine published a story called "Squaresville U.S.A. vs. Beatsville," about three teen-age girls in the small town of Hutchinson, Kansas, who wrote a letter to Lawrence Lipton, self-described leader of the beatniks in Venice, California, inviting him and his friends to come visit. "This town is Squaresville itself," the letter read, "so we as its future citizens want to be cooled in." The plan was squelched when Hutchinson's police chief put out the word that any beatniks would be arrested on sight. A "beatnik doesn't like work," the officer said. "Any man that doesn't like work is a vagrant, and a vagrant goes to jail around here."

The beatnik craze annoyed Kerouac, who had always been shy and now retreated to isolation. The term angered Ginsberg, too, who publicly called it "a foul word." But Ginsberg was also a flamboyant showman—he declaimed his poems with high drama, sometimes gleefully disrobing in his passion, as if to bare his body along with his soul—and he played on the PR possibilities. He scribbled, in a letter to Kerouac, "The general public image of beatnicks built up from movies, *Time*, TV, *Daily News, Post*, etc., is among the hep a fake and among the mass Evil and among the liberal intellectuals a mess—but that is weirdly good, I dig that we are still so purely obscure to philistines that it's inevitable that it be misunderstood. . . . Mockery is inevitable compliment."

But the Beats were getting at something disturbingly stagnant about American society, and mockery was the easiest way to dismiss the messengers out of hand.

Kerouac and Ginsberg met in 1944, when they were studying literature at Columbia. Kerouac had started college as a football player but injured his leg during the first semester and, with some relief, rekindled his longtime love of books. Ginsberg started out wanting to be a labor lawyer, but turned to poetry after taking Columbia's mandatory freshman Humanities course. The university's English department valued high modern poetry with irony, tight stanzas, and clear meters, usually iambic pentameter. Ginsberg was very good at this form. He won several college prizes for his poems and often discussed his work with his professor, the famous critic and novelist Lionel Trilling.

That same year, through a mutual friend, Ginsberg and Kerouac met William Burroughs, who was doing postgraduate work in psychology. Burroughs was a decade older and had an aristocratic bearing. He came from a wealthy St. Louis family—his grandfather had invented the adding machine—and he was living on a trust fund, which allowed him to get by well enough without working. Burroughs also had a broad grasp of literature and a penchant for authors that no one was teaching at Columbia—romantic poets, like William Blake, Arthur Rimbaud, and Hart Crane, who glorified individual expressiveness above obeisance to formal rules. The two students spent many hours in Burroughs's living room, discussing ideas and books.

Burroughs had a very dark streak and a cynical detachment. He once told Kerouac, "I'm apparently some kind of agent from another planet, but I haven't got my orders decoded yet."

When Burroughs was an adolescent, one concerned neighbor called him "a walking corpse." Burroughs agreed, wondering only whose corpse it was. A classic problem child, extremely bookish but anti-social, he was fascinated by con men. His parents sent him to the Los Alamos Ranch School in New Mexico, where the government later built the atom bomb—a connection (Burroughs didn't believe in coincidences) that haunted him the rest of his life. In the thirties, an uncle named Ivy Lee had worked as Hitler's publicist in America—another blood tie to death and sin.

By the time Ginsberg and Kerouac met him, Burroughs was experimenting with drugs and hanging out with thieves and hustlers from Times Square. The fascination rubbed off on the impressionable students. In August 1944, a fellow student named Lucien Carr, who was also a member of this circle, got into horrible trouble. A friend of Burroughs named Dave Kammerer was infatuated with Carr (everyone in this group had at least leanings toward homosexuality), stalked him incessantly and one day followed him into Riverside Park, demanding sex. Carr stabbed him repeatedly with a pocketknife. Carr confessed to Burroughs, who advised him to go to the police. Instead he went to Kerouac, who helped him dispose of the weapon. The next day, both were arrested, Kerouac as a material witness to homicide. They were also expelled from Columbia. The crime made the front pages of local papers. Kerouac was bailed out of jail by his girlfriend, and the two fled to Michigan.*

Several months later, Kerouac returned to New York and stayed in Ginsberg's dorm room, spending all his time reading. Ginsberg then caused a campus scandal. As a prankish protest, he traced the words "Fuck the Jews" on his dusty windowpane. A maid reported the deed to the dean of students, along with the tidbit that, when she entered Ginsberg's room, he was in bed with Kerouac. Some took Ginsberg's scrawling as self-hatred (he was Jewish), others as homoerotic double-entendre. In any case, he was suspended.

At that point, Ginsberg worked at a few menial jobs, to get a taste for ordinary life, then took a seven-month voyage as a merchant marine on a freighter ship. Meanwhile, Burroughs and his wife moved to Texas. Kerouac went home to Lowell, Massachusetts, where his father, a French-Canadian immigrant who owned a small printing press, was dying. He was rescued the following summer by a call from a friend named Neal Cassady, who asked him to come along for a car ride across the country, the first of several such journeys that would provide the material for *On the Road*. (Cassady was the real-life model for the character Dean Moriarty.)

Ginsberg came back to Columbia in the spring of 1947 and resumed writing the stiff poetry that his professors encouraged. One day in the spring of 1948, he was sitting on his bed, reading "Ah! Sunflower" by William Blake, one of the romantic poets that he'd learned about from Burroughs, and suddenly he had a mystical vision, an out-of-body experience, a touch of Nirvana. He later interpreted the sensation as a psychological revelation, a message from his inner self that this was the kind of poetry—intensely personal, nakedly emotional, magically prophetic—that he should be writing.

Around this time, Ginsberg found himself attracted to the outlaw derring-do of a hustler, and another friend of Burroughs, named Herbert Huncke. One night, Huncke enticed Ginsberg to join him and his pals for a cruise through the city in a stolen car. The pal who was driving took a wrong turn on a one-way street, sped away from an

---

*Carr served two years in prison, then cleaned up his act, eventually becoming a reporter, then a top editor, for United Press International. The military historian and novelist Caleb Carr is his son.

approaching police car, and crashed into a telephone pole. They were all arrested.

Ginsberg was saved by the intervention of Lionel Trilling, who brought in a professor from Columbia Law School, who in turn convinced prosecutors to commit the young poet to the Columbia Presbyterian Psychiatric Institute, free of charge, instead of sentencing him to prison.

After eight months in the hospital, Ginsberg went home to his father, a high-school teacher and poet, in Paterson, New Jersey. (His mother, who had gone insane when he was in high school, lived in an asylum up in the Bronx.) Allen wrote some articles for a local labor newspaper and asked for an assignment to interview the poet William Carlos Williams.

Williams, who was in his sixties, lived in Paterson, toiling in relative obscurity. Certainly nobody at Columbia, or most other colleges, was teaching his work. Williams took a liking to Ginsberg, and met with him several times after their first talk. Williams came out of the Black Mountain school of poets, former teachers or students at Black Mountain College, an avant-garde school set up in the thirties in Asheville, North Carolina, where artists and writers were encouraged to take their inspiration from materials and objects found in their surroundings.

Once, when Ginsberg and Williams went for a walk through the woods, they sat and wrote poems about things lying on the ground—a sliver of tin, a chunk of concrete, a hairpin.

Williams also felt strongly that a poet shouldn't be confined by arbitrary rules about the length of a line or regularity of a meter. He should write in his natural voice, constructing phrases that matched the rhythms of his own breath. This wasn't easy. In fact, done well, it was harder than conventional poetry. You couldn't just fill in the blank spaces of the metronome's ticktocks. You had to *listen* to your voice, very carefully, and devise ways to capture that rhythm, a rhythm that might not ever have been written down before.

Kerouac was thinking along the same lines; he and Ginsberg remained in frequent contact, either in person or through correspondence. But they both needed a voice before they could figure out how to transcribe it, and the voice they aimed for, the voice that most appealed to their desire for speed and risk and transcendence, a sound at once hot and cool, was modern jazz—"a spontaneous bop prosody," as Ginsberg described Kerouac's phrasing.

While they were studying at Columbia, the two often went to the jazz clubs in nearby Harlem and got to know some of the musicians, including the trumpeter Dizzy Gillespie, who along with Charlie Parker invented the style of bebop. At one set, which a fellow Columbia student was recording, Gillespie improvised a melody, based on the popular song "Exactly Like You," and titled it "Kerouac." (He thought about calling it "Ginsberg," but that wasn't as jazzy a name.)

Kerouac set down the idea of his poetic phrasing in a short essay called "The Essentials of Spontaneous Prose," in which he likened the act of writing to playing jazz. Sentences should be punctuated not by periods but only by "the vigorous space dash separating rhetorical breathing (as jazz musicians drawing breath between outblown phrases)." This was how he wrote the original draft of *On the Road*, all of it in one unindented paragraph, typed on sixteen-foot rolls of Japanese drawing paper, which he taped together as a massive scroll. That was the ideal way to capture the vista of the landscape, the whoosh of motion, the immediacy of experience.

To Kerouac, it was cheating even to revise a first impulse (though he did rewrite *On the Road*, adding punctuation, to make the book publishable). Ginsberg wasn't such a purist. He sought to convey the *impression* of spontaneity, but he relied on craft and artistry to get there.

A year before he wrote *Howl*, Ginsberg wrote to a friend, "I have been looking at early blues forms and think will apply this form of elliptical semisurrealist imagery to rhymed blues type lyrics. . . . Blues forms also provide a real varied syncopated meter, with many internal variants and changes of form in midstream like conversational thought." He later told a critic that *Howl*'s cadences were inspired in part by a recording of Dizzy Gillespie's trumpet solo on "I Can't Get Started."

Ginsberg and Kerouac were inspired, then, by several diverse influences: Burroughs's reading list of romantic visionaries like Whitman, Blake, and Rimbaud; William Carlos Williams's veneration of natural objects over lofty ideals and human breath over preset meter; and the frantic, jagged cadences of blues and bebop.

Jazz inspired Ginsberg to extend his lines much longer than any poet—even Whitman—had ever attempted. He explained later to one critic that his earlier attempts at free verse were "not expressionistic enough, not swinging enough," adding, "I have to let off steam by building a longer climactic line . . . a jazzy ride . . . to ride out on the break-rhythm without any artificial built-in guides or poles or diving boards . . . no forcing the thoughts into a straitjacket—sort of a search for the rhythm of the thoughts and their natural occurrence. . . . It's a jump up forward into life, unknown future."

The poem's long, jangling lines were what gave *Howl* its drive and power. But they were also what led many writers and critics of the day to dismiss it as unserious, not a real poem.

Not least among those who dismissed it was Lionel Trilling. Ginsberg had stayed in touch with his former mentor and savior from Columbia days. When *Howl* was published, he sent Trilling a copy, along with a cover note. "I think what is coming is a romantic period . . . a reassertion of naked personal subjective truth," he wrote. "Perhaps Whitman will be seen to have set the example," after having "been bypassed for half a century."

Though the letter was cordial, Trilling no doubt read it as a personal jab, and correctly so. (He wrote back, saying that he didn't like the poems at all.) Trilling had never regarded Whitman or any of Ginsberg's other idols as great writers. He distrusted literature that celebrated passion, transcendence, or the liberation of the self from society. Like most members of his intellectual circle, who lived in New York and wrote for the *Partisan Review*, Trilling was an ex-Marxist (some were still Marxists but anti-Stalinists) who cherished the tradition of high modernism—with its canon of works, formalist theory, and critical method—as a civilizing tool, grounded in a sense of history, to ward off the pressures of ideology and totalitarianism.

Strict form was important because it represented the elevation of rationality, which Trilling saw as "a principle of control." Back when Ginsberg first met Burroughs, and especially after his mystical experience while reading Blake, he urged his teacher to reconsider Rimbaud in particular. Trilling gave him a read, but he was repelled. Rimbaud's "rejection of the ordinary social values," he told Ginsberg, amounted to "an absolutism which is foreign to my nature and which I combat."

Later, Trilling wrote an essay, perhaps with Ginsberg in mind, noting that he understood why some of his students "have become excited over their discovery of the old animosity which Ezra Pound and William Carlos Williams bear to the iamb, and have come to feel that could they but break the iambic shackles, the whole of modern culture could find a true expression." But, Trilling went on, he found this notion illusory—and, more than that, dangerous, because unshackling formal structure could unravel the underlying social thread. In a sense, Trilling was right. Ginsberg, too, saw the connection between freedom from structures in poetry and freedom from structures in all of life. The difference was that Ginsberg yearned for both freedoms.

Back when Ginsberg was a student, Burroughs advised him to veer away from Trilling, warning, "He's got no orgones, no mana, no charge to him."

The irony was that, deep inside, Trilling might have agreed, if not in those terms. In 1985, a decade after Trilling's death, *Partisan Review* published excerpts from his private journals, which revealed a very unhappy man who loathed his own sense of seriousness and responsibility, and who envied those capable of cutting loose and expressing themselves openly.

He appeared to feel this inadequacy as far back as 1933, when his friend Clifton Fadiman showed Trilling a letter that he'd received from Ernest Hemingway. It was "a crazy letter," Trilling recounted, "written when he was drunk—self-revealing, arrogant, scared, trivial, absurd: yet I felt from reading it how right such a man is compared to the 'good minds' of my university life—how he will produce and mean something to the world . . . how his life which he could expose without dignity and which is anarchic and 'childish' is a better life than anyone I know could live. . . . And how far-far-far I am going from being a writer—how less and less I have the material and the mind and the will."

Similarly, in 1948, around the time Ginsberg urged him to read Rimbaud, Trilling wrote in his journal of coming back from a dinner party where someone had praised him for leading a life of "equilibrium," a comment that gave him "a twinge of pain" and "the sense of some awful doom" that, at age forty-two, he had "no more time, no more time" to do something creative. Not long after, he wrote, "I have only a gift of dealing rather sensibly with literature," which he regarded as "a great hoax."

In 1949, while still convalescing at the psychiatric institute, Ginsberg came to see Trilling and told him that Harcourt, Brace was about to publish Kerouac's first novel, *The Town and the City*. "I predicted that it would not be good & insisted," Trilling wrote afterward in his journal. "But later I saw with what bitterness I had made the prediction—not wanting K's book to be good because if the book of an accessory to a murder is good, how can one of mine be?"

Trilling despised the notion, popular in some avant-garde circles, that an artist had to be pathological. But he also wanted to believe in the opposite idea—that a real artist *couldn't* have a streak of "wickedness"—and he feared that he might be wrong.

The tensions between institutional order and instinctual gratification racked many among the generation that came to maturity after the war, but Trilling's sense of decorum and dignity—his ideas about the moral grounding of literature—kept his inner bohemian under wraps.

Diana Trilling, his wife and fellow critic, would later wonder, in her memoir of their marriage, whether any of Lionel's friends knew "how deeply he scorned the very qualities of character—his quiet, his moderation, his gentle reasonableness—for which he was most admired in his lifetime and which have been most celebrated since his death."

When Ginsberg returned to Columbia for his poetry reading on a cold Thursday night in February 1959, it was at the invitation not of the English Department but of a student group, the John Dewey Society. Almost no professors showed up for the event; they didn't want to grant him the legitimacy that their attendance might convey.

Lionel Trilling stayed home, too. Some of his colleagues were coming over to discuss an intellectuals' book club that they were trying to get off the ground.

But Diana Trilling—who, later that year, would chide Norman Mailer for abandoning his earlier style of literary realism—did go, along with two other faculty wives, who all nervously mapped out ahead of time where and when to meet, as if they were conspiring to commit a crime.

She wrote an essay about the event afterward for the *Partisan Review* (whose editor, Philip Rahv, accepted it after expressing misgivings about giving the Beats the implicit credibility). In her essay, she recounted her husband's turbulent past with Ginsberg and how she had chided Lionel at the time for giving his brilliant but clearly disturbed student too much attention and leniency.

Like everyone else, she had read the recent magazine stories about the now-celebrated poet, his beatnik friends, and their antics. (The issue of *Time* that was then on the newsstands described a cocktail party in Chicago, where Ginsberg introduced himself by saying, "I'm crazy like a daisy," to which his lover and fellow poet, Peter Orlovsky, replied that *he* was "crazy as a wild flower.")

As Mrs. Trilling walked into the already-packed auditorium, she noticed that the audience was "crazily young." She sighed at the girls with their "blackest black stockings" and the boys in their checked shirts and blue jeans ("standard uniforms in the best nursery schools," she would cluck). But she was also surprised. She'd expected the kids to smell bad, but they didn't. "These people may think they're dirty inside and dress up to it," she wrote in her essay, but they were "clean"—as, it turned out when they came onstage, were Ginsberg and his friends.

Ginsberg read a long poem, called "Kaddish," about his mother, who had died three years ago; he choked and cried as he read it, yet, Trilling wrote, no one "tittered or showed embarrassment at this public display of emotion." Then he read "Lion in the Room," after announcing that it was "dedicated to Lionel Trilling." She misinterpreted the poem. It was about Ginsberg's vision while reading Blake back in 1948. His dedication was ironic, as he'd criticized his old teacher for failing to see the lion himself, for resisting sensory experience.

Perhaps because of her misunderstanding, Trilling found herself liking the poem. "I was much moved by it, in some part unaccountably," she wrote. "It was also a decent poem, and I am willing to admit this surprised me." She was also struck that all of Ginsberg's poems dealt with "serious subjects" and that he read them in a poetic meter. It seemed he *was* a poet after all. During the question-and-answer period, he even led a discussion of the meaning of prosody and the influence of William Carlos Williams. Suddenly, she saw that Ginsberg and his friends had "earned . . . their right to be heard in the university"—not because of "their whackiness and beat-upness," but by "their energy of poetic impulse . . . their studious devotion to their art."

When Diana Trilling arrived back home, her husband's meeting was still going on. It was a meeting, she wrote, "of the pleasant professional sort," like "the comfortable living room" in which such meetings usually take place "at a certain point in a successful modern literary career," confirming the writer's "sense of disciplined achievement and well-earned reward." This comfort was "not ever to be spoken of except with elaborate irony," she continued, "lest it propose a life without risk and therefore without virtue."

W. H. Auden, the legendary poet, and the only one of the men at the meeting who was not dressed in a suit (he wore an old brown leather jacket), asked her what she thought of the reading.

She replied that she'd been moved by it.

"I'm ashamed of you," Auden said.

"It's different," she responded, "when it's human beings and not just a sociological phenomenon."

She left the men with their drinks and their discussion. She concluded her *Partisan Review* essay by noting an "unfathomable gap that was all so quickly and meaningfully opening up between the evening that had been and the evening that was now so surely reclaiming me."

For an inkling, she sensed that Ginsberg's poetry reading at Columbia and the intellectual establishment's hostile indifference to it, both on campus and now in her living room, marked the first crack in a sociocultural breakup that would grip the coming decade—the opening fissure of the Generation Gap.

5

The Cosmonaut of Inner Space

On March 17, 1959, a thirty-five-page excerpt of *Naked Lunch*, an unpublished novel by William Burroughs, appeared in the debut issue of a Chicago-based literary journal called *Big Table*. The next day, the United States Postmaster General seized all copies mailed out to bookstores and subscribers, declaring that the magazine was obscene.

After he left New York, more than a decade earlier, Burroughs had moved to the southwest, then to Mexico, living off the land, raising a son, but also indulging in drug addiction, buggery, and violence. One afternoon in 1951, after he and his wife, Joan, had been drinking, she dared him to shoot a champagne glass off her head, à la William Tell. He fired his pistol, missing the glass and killing her. A Mexican court found him guilty only of "criminal imprudence;" he served a mere thirteen days in jail.

Drenched in guilt, he immersed himself in writing two thinly autobiographical novels, *Queer* and *Junky*, graphic tales of hustlers, addicts, pushers, and pimps. (Burroughs was always aware of his homosexuality; his marriage was a rare bow to convention.) *Queer* stayed in the drawer for many decades. He sold *Junky* to Ace Books, one of the pioneering publishers of cheap paperbacks, under the pseudonym William Lee, the name that he later gave his alter-ego protagonist in *Naked Lunch* and that Kerouac gave the character based on Burroughs—Old Bill Lee—in *On the Road*. *Junky* sold over 100,000 copies and made the author an alluring figure of mystery among the Beat cognoscenti.

In 1955, Burroughs moved to Tangier, Morocco, an "international zone" rife with corruption, outlaws, easy drugs, and wild boys. Settling in a hotel called the Villa Muniria, which visiting friends called "Villa Delirium," he started writing the novel that would become *Naked Lunch* (his original title, a play on the city's status, was *Interzone*), a frenzied pastiche of hair-raisingly vivid imagery that wasn't so much *about* an addict as it was the hallucinogenic projection of his junk-zapped brainwaves.

"There is only one thing a writer can write about: *what is in front of his senses at the moment of writing*," Burroughs wrote in one of his many prefaces. "This novel is about transitions, larval forms, emergent telepathic faculty, attempts to control and stifle new forms," he wrote in another. "I am trying, like Klee, to create something that will have a life of its own, that can put me in real danger . . . some excess of feeling or behavior that will shatter the human pattern. . . . This book spills off the page in all directions, kaleidoscope of vistas, medley of tunes and street noises, farts and riot yipes and the slamming steel shutters of commerce, screams of pain and pathos."

After finishing the book, in the wake of Sputnik and Lunik, he described himself as "a cosmonaut of inner space," adding, "If writers are to travel in space time and explore areas opened up by the space age, I think they must develop techniques quite as new and definite as the techniques of physical space travel."

Soon after starting the novel, Burroughs went to London to see a doctor who had devised a cure for heroin addiction. He came back to Tangier reasonably clean, and resumed writing at a mad pace, sometimes while munching *majoun*, a local candy made of honey, spices, and marijuana. Paul Bowles, the American writer, was also living in Tangier and would often visit, each time startled by the messily typed pages scattered all over the room, the floor scuffed with heel marks, and Burroughs pacing from one ashtray to another, puffing on *kif* cigarettes, and laughing hysterically while reading aloud from his manuscript.

Burroughs had been mailing Ginsberg snippets of the book from the beginning. On the dedication page of *Howl*, Ginsberg had thanked not only Kerouac but also "William Seward Burroughs, author of *Naked Lunch*, an endless novel which will drive everybody mad."

Ginsberg and Kerouac visited Burroughs in the spring of 1957 and helped him collate and edit the pages. Ginsberg wrote a friend back in the States, describing the evolving book as a string of "unpublishable mad routines" about conspiracy theories, talking assholes, and hanged men who ejaculate when their necks snap. He likened its imagery to the grotesque-beautiful paintings of Francis Bacon, who was also in Tangier that season. Kerouac, who was typing a clean copy, would later recall that he had to stop because it was giving him "horrible nightmares."

Later that year, Ginsberg got a letter from Irving Rosenthal, a graduate student at the University of Chicago who had just become editor of the *Chicago Review*, an unusually reputable student-run literary journal. Rosenthal was enamored of the "San Francisco Renaissance," as the Beat poetry movement had come to be called, and he wanted to devote the entire spring 1958 issue to its writers. Ginsberg rounded up the usual gang, including himself and Kerouac, and suggested that Rosenthal add Burroughs to the roster. Burroughs was "the only one unpublished in US so far," Ginsberg wrote, but added that he "is equal to Jack K. in prose strength."

Two weeks later Ginsberg sent Rosenthal a batch of poems. "Don't worry about what people will say if you turn out a screwy magazine," he wrote in a cover letter. "Do you want to die an old magazine editor in a furnished room who knew what was in every cup of tea? Put some arsenic in the magazine!" In a P.S., he added, "Ah! I forgot—I also enclose some final poison for your pot—Burroughs! He sent me this excerpt this week!"

The excerpt was fairly mild and, mixed in with the poems by Ginsberg and Kerouac, stirred little notice. Shortly after the issue appeared, Ginsberg sent Rosenthal the entire manuscript of *Naked Lunch* from Paris, where Burroughs had moved and much of the Beat gang was visiting. The document was a mess—four hundred pages of discontinuous, overlapping fragments.

Rosenthal loved it, wrote Burroughs directly about possible ways to edit it, and published the entirety of the book's third chapter in the autumn 1958 issue. This excerpt was much more hard-core. One passage read: "She seized a safety pin caked with blood and rust, gouged a hole in her leg which seemed to open like an obscene festering mouth waiting for unspeakable congress with the dropper which she now plunged out of sight into the gaping wound." There were sentences about pus, miasma, bugs, cocaine, bats, pimps, and schizophrenic detectives. At the end of the ten-page excerpt, Rosenthal tacked on: "To be continued."

On October 25, a few weeks after the issue came out, Jack Mabley, a popular columnist for the *Chicago Daily News* and a self-described "bluenose," wrote a front-page article headlined "Filthy Writing on the Midway." It began: "Do you ever wonder what happens to little boys who scratch dirty words on railroad underpasses? They go to college and scrawl obscenities in the college literary magazine." Mabley concluded, "I don't put the blame on the juveniles who wrote and edited this stuff, because they're immature and irresponsible. But the University of Chicago publishes the magazine. The Trustees should take a long hard look at what's circulated under their sponsorship."

And so the trustees did. The university chancellor, Lawrence Kimpton, came under pressure to shut the magazine down. A memorandum from the university's legal department warned of "a very serious effect upon fundraising, enrollment and our public relations generally." The Chicago city council was about to vote on an urban-renewal project in which the university had an interest; the Catholic Church had been scrutinizing the plan as well. Kimpton told the faculty senate that "some remedial action" needed to be taken because he'd heard that the journal's next issue was going to be "gamier" still. "To publish such copy under present conditions," he advised, might "result in further attacks by the press."

Rosenthal was told that the magazine would be shut down unless he met three conditions. The next issue had to be "non-controversial;" the *Review* would be subject to an annual appraisal by its faculty committee; and in the future, the editor must check with the committee before publishing anything that might be objectionable.

Rather than comply, half the staff quit. Rosenthal left graduate school altogether. He and his poetry editor, Paul Carroll, decided to start a new magazine and took with them all the manuscripts that had been scheduled for the next issue, including the latest Burroughs installment. He asked Kerouac, who had come up with the titles for *Howl* and *Naked Lunch*, to suggest a name for the magazine. Kerouac had recently written himself a note: "Get a bigger table." So he suggested that they call it *Big Table*. Ginsberg, Kerouac, and some other poets drove from New York to Chicago to attend a fundraiser for the magazine. They were greeted with huge crowds and enormous press coverage. Nobody had seen a beatnik before. It seemed that everybody wanted to.

The first issue of *Big Table* came out in mid-March. It was emblazoned with a red, white, and blue cover boasting "The Complete Contents of the Suppressed Winter 1959 *Chicago Review*."

The next day, the Post Office seized all the copies—and at that point, Burroughs's fortunes took their first big upward turn.

He and Ginsberg had been trying to get several book publishers interested in *Naked Lunch*, with no luck. Even Ferlinghetti had rejected it as "disgusting." Maurice Girodais of the Olympia Press in Paris turned it down, too.

But the press attention over the seizure of *Big Table* aroused Girodais's interest. The American Civil Liberties Union took on the magazine's case and announced it was suing the U.S. Post Office. John Ciardi, the poetry editor of the *Saturday Review*, wrote an article denouncing the University of Chicago and the Post Office as "book burners" and hailing Burroughs as "a writer of great power and artistic integrity engaged in a profoundly meaningful search for true values." The excerpt of *Naked Lunch* in *Big Table*, Ciardi wrote, was "a masterpiece of its own genre."

In early June, Girodais offered Burroughs an $800 advance, on the condition that he have the manuscript ready for the printers within ten days. Burroughs agreed, figuring that it was the best deal he could get. He'd seen Kerouac hassling with American publishers for five years before *On the Road* was finally bought, and then it took another year to hit the bookstores. Girodais said he'd have the book out in Paris the following *month*—in an edition of five thousand copies with another five thousand soon to follow—as part of his Olympia Press's Travellers' Companion Series, an English-language series, including volumes ranging from unvarnished porn to Henry Miller's *Tropic of Cancer*, that was marketed to American and British tourists who couldn't buy such books back home because they were banned.

Suddenly, Burroughs was a celebrity, receiving requests for interviews from *Time*, *Life*, and other mass-market magazines.

The commotion piqued the interest of Barney Rosset, the publisher of Grove Press, who had already printed several works by the Beats. Rosset bought the American rights to *Naked Lunch* in November 1959, but the manuscript sat on the shelf for three years. Before Rosset could publish it, he had to survive a court battle over another book that the Post Office had seized as obscene. The trial over that book would pave the way not only for the survival of Grove Press and the American publication of *Naked Lunch*, but also for a breakthrough in free expression.

6

The End of Obscenity

In March 1959, shortly before the copies of *Big Table* were seized, Barney Rosset, the owner of Grove Press, approached a lawyer named Charles Rembar with a proposition. Rosset was about to publish the uncensored version of D. H. Lawrence's *Lady Chatterley's Lover*, and he wanted Rembar to defend him in court when—not if, but when—federal agents confiscated the copies and came to arrest him.

Lawrence had written three versions of the novel in the late twenties, but the third version—the one that he regarded as definitive—had never been published in the United States or Britain because it was rife with four-letter words and graphic sexual descriptions, all of which were excised in existing editions. The uncut *Lady Chatterley* had long been on the list of officially banned books, to be seized by postal or customs officials if anyone tried to mail or import them. Rosset now wanted to change that situation, wanted to challenge the whole set of laws that allowed the practice of censorship.

Rosset was thirty-seven. He was born in Chicago to a Jewish father and an Irish mother. His maternal grandparents had been terrorists for the cause of Irish independence, and Rosset always felt that he inherited their sensibility. He attended a progressive high school, where he was captain of the football team, class president, and, along with Haskell Wexler, who later became a celebrated left-wing filmmaker, editor of a student magazine that they called *The*

Anti-Everything, dedicated to the proposition that they should be allowed to print and say whatever they felt like.

The war started a year after Rosset graduated, and he managed to get into the Army signal corps' film branch, shooting footage in China. Afterward, back in the States and shocked by the prevalence of racism and anti-Semitism, he made a documentary called *Strange Victory*, which blasted the U.S. government for oppressing blacks and Jews at home even after liberating the victims of fascism abroad. The film was shown at one theater, in New York City.

In 1949, he married Joan Mitchell, the abstract expressionist painter, and through her met the group of modern artists—Jackson Pollock, Willem de Kooning, Franz Kline, Robert Motherwell, and others—who hung out at the Cedar Bar in Greenwich Village. The marriage lasted for only three stormy years, but they remained friends, and so she told Rosset about a small publishing house on Grove Street that some friends of hers were abandoning. Rosset always loved literature. He bought the company, and so began Grove Press.

At first, he published reprints of Henry James novels. Then in 1954 he made a bold move. He'd read an article in the *New York Times* about a new play by Samuel Beckett called *Waiting for Godot*. He obtained a French edition, read it, traveled to Paris to meet Beckett, got along with him famously, and offered him a $200 advance for the English-language rights. The play became a major literary work and a surprise commercial success.

The book that Rosset really wanted to publish, though, was Henry Miller's *Tropic of Cancer*. Miller, who had emigrated from America to France, was a celebrated author in Europe, but most of his books, including *Tropic*, which he wrote in 1934, were banned in the United States. It was a very salacious book that made *Chatterley*, or just about any other serious novel, seem tame by comparison. Rosset had read it during his freshman year of college at Swarthmore, after learning that copies could be bought under the table at the Gotham Book Mart in midtown Manhattan. He loved the book (though more for Miller's anger at the United States than for its sexual content), wrote a term paper on it (the professor gave him a B-minus), and now, years later, as a publisher, he was calculating how to get it into bookstores on the shelves.

Around the time that Rosset bought *Godot*, Mark Schorer, an English professor at the University of California at Berkeley, wrote him to suggest that he try to publish the unexpurgated version of *Lady Chatterley*. Lawrence was a much more respectable author than Miller. Rosset figured that getting *Chatterley* legalized might serve as a precedent for *Tropic of Cancer*.

In the spring of 1954, Rosset hired a lawyer named Ephraim London, who had won a censorship case before the U.S. Supreme Court involving Roberto Rossellini's film *The Miracle*, in which Anna Magnani played an Italian peasant girl who claims that her infant was immaculately conceived by St. Joseph. The Catholic Church denounced the film as blasphemous. The New York Board of Regents, which had licensing authority over film distribution in the state, banned its release. London successfully argued before the Supreme Court that the ban violated the First Amendment's guarantee of free speech.

Rosset's plan for *Lady Chatterley* was to provoke the censors deliberately. He asked a friend in Paris to mail him four copies of the unexpurgated book, which had long been legally available there as a part of Olympia Press's Traveller's Companion Series. He then called the U.S. Customs office to make sure the book was still listed as forbidden; it was. So he notified the official that a package containing four copies of the book was en route and that he was planning to resell them. In August, Customs notified him that the books had arrived and were seized as obscene. Rosset told London to file a suit against the federal government.

At this point, the plan went awry. Alfred A. Knopf, the publisher of the censored version of the novel, threatened to sue Rosset (even though the book's copyright had lapsed) and to publish the unexpurgated text himself if Rosset won his case. This latter threat alarmed Rosset; he couldn't compete with a powerhouse like Knopf; it seemed pointless to incur the expenses of a lawsuit if he couldn't reap the rewards of a victory. Meanwhile, the publication of *Godot* was attracting many other authors to Grove, including several of the Beats. So Rosset set the matter aside for the moment.

In 1957, the New York Board of Regents, which had blocked the release of *The Miracle*, banned the showing of a French film adaptation of *Lady Chatterley's Lover*. Ephraim London took on the case, filing a lawsuit against the Regents on behalf of the distributor, Kingsley Pictures. The state courts upheld the ban, as they had done with the Rossellini film, but at the end of 1958, the U.S. Supreme Court agreed to hear the case. London told Rosset that a favorable decision, which he considered a near certainty, might provide an opening for his own long-dormant lawsuit to legalize the book. And, in the interim few years, the threats from Knopf had died down.

So, on March 18, 1959—the same day that the Post Office seized the copies of *Big Table* containing excerpts from Burroughs's *Naked Lunch*—Rosset announced that he was going to publish the uncut version of Lawrence's novel.

Very soon after this, Rosset and London had a falling-out. London bluntly challenged a comment that Rosset made about Lawrence, in the presence of some Lawrence scholars. Rosset, besides knowing that London was wrong, felt humiliated and fired him on the spot.

This put Rosset in a bind. He was about to take a huge legal risk, and he didn't have a lawyer. In fact, he personally knew only two lawyers. He called both of them. The one who called back was Charles Rembar.

Rosset knew Rembar from the Hamptons, on the eastern shore of Long Island, where they both had summer houses. Many artists rented huts or cottages in the Hamptons, and some took to playing softball on Sunday afternoons. Joan Mitchell, who was a very good athlete, played in these games, as did Pollock, de Kooning, Larry Rivers, and the art critic Harold Rosenberg. Several of the artists were émigrés who didn't know the game, so when he and Mitchell were still married, Rosset was allowed to play, as was "Cy" Rembar, one of the neighbors, who turned out to be the best hitter in the lot. The two became friends, playing tennis as well. So after Rosset fired London, he asked Rembar to take his place.

Rembar had never tried a case in court before, but he was an experienced and talented attorney. He was also the lawyer for several writers, among them his first cousin Norman Mailer (their mothers were sisters). Growing up, Mailer worshiped Rembar, who was eight years older. As an adult, Mailer still admired him enormously—for his athletic prowess, his judgment, his moral force, and his preternatural self-confidence, his inspiring belief that it was natural to win.

When Mailer was writing *The Naked and the Dead*, he asked Rembar whether it was legal to put "fuck"—a word commonly uttered by soldiers—in the dialogue. Rembar advised him to spell it "fug," which had the added virtue of more closely resembling GI guttural. Mailer followed his advice, and his editors at Rinehart had no problems. Six years later, when the same editors rejected *The Deer Park*, claiming it was obscene, and tried to back out of giving Mailer the second half of his advance, Rembar threatened to sue and made them pay in full.

Still, Rosset's challenge was in another league. State and federal courts had been very specific in their definitions of "obscenity," and by those standards, the uncut *Lady Chatterley*, whatever its literary merits, clearly met the test.

The standard had been set in England nearly a hundred years earlier, in 1868, when Lord Chief Justice Alexander James Edmund Cockburn, in a case called *Queen v. Hicklin*, defined obscenity as material that tended "to deprave and corrupt those whose minds are open to such immoral influence and into whose hands a publication of this sort may fall." Five years later, across the ocean, a young crusader named Anthony Comstock, who had founded a lobbying group called the New York Society for the Suppression of Vice, persuaded the U.S. Congress to pass a law—which became known as the Comstock Act—outlawing obscenity under Lord Cockburn's definition. Over the years, state and federal courts refined the standard, condemning a work as obscene if it was "lustful," "lewd," "lascivious," or if it aroused the typical reader's "prurient" interests.

The underlying purpose of these statutes and rulings was not so much to ban "dirty words" as to suppress sexual impulse—to put a social straitjacket on the libido.

And so, in the thirties and for many years after, it was a crime in Massachusetts to publish or sell Theodore Dreiser's *An American Tragedy*. As recently as 1948, the U.S. Supreme Court upheld a New York State court's conviction of Doubleday for publishing Edmund Wilson's novel *Memoirs of Hecate County*, because it described an extramarital entanglement.

There were some cases that ran contrary to the rule. In 1934, a federal court in New York ruled that James Joyce's *Ulysses* was not obscene. But that wasn't likely to be regarded as relevant to this case.

Only a short section of *Ulysses* was about sex, and the federal judge had ruled that it did not "excite lustful thoughts." The same could not be said of *Lady Chatterley*, which was *about* passionate, adulterous sex; the unedited version was rife with detailed descriptions, written in profane language; and, *because* Lawrence was a great writer, it was indisputably, intentionally, arousing.

More discouraging, as recently as 1957, in *Roth v. United States*, a case involving a bookseller convicted for mailing obscene materials, the U.S. Supreme Court had ruled that the First Amendment's guarantee of free speech did not apply to obscenity. *Roth* marked the first time that the Court had addressed the question explicitly. The Justices' clear verdict—the decision was 6–3—emboldened government censors and seemed to sound the death knell for civil libertarians.

Rembar could have mounted a purely procedural case on Rosset's behalf, challenging the U.S. Post Office's competence to assess literary works as obscene. But his client had more ambitious aims. Rosset's ultimate goal was still to publish Henry Miller. So, he needed to challenge the proposition that *Lady Chatterley* was obscene—and to torpedo the laws governing obscenity. He saw Grove Press as "a valve for pressurized cultural energies, a breach in the dam of American Puritanism—a whip-lashing live cable of Zeitgeist." Rembar gave it a shot.

At first glance, the Court's ruling on *Roth* seemed straightforward. The First Amendment, Justice William J. Brennan wrote in the majority decision, was never intended to allow "absolute protection for every utterance." Most states had always outlawed blasphemy and libel in addition to obscenity; in some cases, these bans dated back to the time of the Constitution's ratification. Thus, Brennan concluded, "We hold obscenity is not within the area of constitutionally protected speech or press." He went on to modify *Hicklin's* standard of obscenity—that it must have "a tendency to excite lustful thoughts." Brennan's test was "whether to the average person, applying contemporary community standards, the dominant theme of the material, taken as a whole, appeals to prurient interest."

In the two years since the *Roth* decision, most lawyers who commented on the case had emphasized the phrases "prurient interest" and "community standards." In all other respects, the ruling was seen as affirming the exclusion of obscenity from constitutional protection.

But reading and rereading the decision, Rembar noticed a loophole—a possible way out for Rosset and for every other publisher like him. As an aside, to distinguish obscenity from other kinds of expression, Brennan had written:

> The protection given speech and press was fashioned to assure unfettered interchange of ideas. . . . All ideas having even the slightest redeeming social importance—unorthodox ideas, controversial ideas, even ideas hateful to the prevailing climate of opinion—have the full protection of the guarantees, unless excludable because they encroach upon the limited area of more important interests. But implicit in the history of the First Amendment is the rejection of obscenity as utterly without redeeming social importance.

Rembar saw a weakness in this argument. What if a book was considered obscene yet also presented *ideas* or possessed even the slightest bit of "redeeming social importance"? By Brennan's logic, wouldn't it qualify for the First Amendment's protections after all?

On a sheet of paper, Rembar drew two circles that slightly overlapped. He labeled one circle, "Material appealing to prurient interest." He labeled the other, "Material utterly without social importance." By Brennan's reasoning, only material that fell in the overlapping space of both circles—that was prurient *and* worthless—could be denied the privileges of free speech.

It wouldn't help Rosset much to argue that *Lady Chatterley* was a great work of literature, not if its merits were outweighed by its lustfulness. However, it *would* help Rosset—it might save him—to argue that *Chatterley* was a novel of socially important ideas.

On April 28, 1959, Rosset filed a motion calling for the release of the impounded books. On May 14, an administrative hearing was held inside the Department of the Post Office, which at the time had a formal judiciary branch. The motion was denied.

So, on May 15, he went further up and sued the Post Office. The trial took place in the federal courthouse in Lower Manhattan, before U.S. District Judge Frederick van Pelt Bryan.

In his opening statement, Rembar said that he was challenging not the Comstock Act's general validity but rather its application to *Lady*

Chatterley's Lover. He laid out his interpretation of the *Roth* ruling, the two circles, and his inference that a work could not be obscene if it had, as he put it, "ideas of even the slightest social importance." Then he waxed on about the social importance of this book.

"Whether you agree with Lawrence or not," Rembar said, "he had something to preach to the public. He inveighed against sex without love. He preached against the mechanization of the lives of individuals that he felt came from the increasing industrialization of society. He was waving a banner in favor of an honest approach to emotional and sexual problems, as against a hypocritical one. Finally, he was, it seems to me, arguing very strongly that the approach to sex should be wholesome, natural, healthy—and not morbid."

This was in fact an accurate summary of Lawrence's philosophy, and Rembar called several prominent literary critics to say so on the witness stand.

The U.S. attorney representing the Post Office, S. Hazard Gillespie Jr., thought that Rembar had fallen into a trap. Turning to the same section of the *Roth* ruling, he recited a clause that Rembar had omitted. Yes, Justice Brennan had written that controversial ideas "have the full protection" of the First Amendment—"*unless*," Gillespie emphasized, these ideas were "excludable because they encroach upon the limited area of more important interests." One of those interests, surely, was keeping obscenity under wraps. Hence Rembar's argument was irrelevant.

But it was Rembar who had laid the trap. He drew Judge Bryan's attention to a footnote by Brennan that elaborated on what kind of "more important interests" were "excludable." The footnote listed a series of cases, all of which involved some form of *conduct*— peddling, picketing, hiring minors to sell newspapers on the streets, parading without a license, amplifying loud music from a truck. The First Amendment doesn't protect *those* kinds of controversial speech. But none of Brennan's examples concerned *writing*—expression unattached to conduct. Pure expression could be forbidden, Rembar argued, only if it was "utterly without social importance."

Gillespie fired back, arguing that the defendant could not take refuge in the book's ideas because its ideas were immoral. This was a loose argument to begin with, but before the trial was over, it would be completely invalidated by a separate case.

This was Ephraim London's case, involving the French film of *Lady Chatterley's Lover*, which happened to come before the U.S. Supreme Court in the middle of Rosset's trial, just as London had foreseen. The New York Board of Regents was refusing to let the film be distributed on the grounds that, as the Board argued, its "theme is the presentation of adultery as a desirable, acceptable and proper pattern of behavior." The Regents were enforcing a New York State law that prohibited the distribution of a film that is "obscene, indecent [or] immoral." A recent amendment to that law expanded the definition of "immoral" to include any film that "portrays acts of sexual immorality, perversion, or lewdness"—*or* that "presents such acts as desirable, acceptable or proper patterns of behavior." Nobody was charging that the film was obscene. But it did present adultery as desirable and acceptable. Hence the Regents denied the film a license.

In a unanimous verdict, the Supreme Court overruled the ban. It may well have been the easiest decision the Court had ever reached on an issue of free speech, because the principle was so clear. Justice Potter Stewart wrote in his decision, "What New York has done . . . is to prevent the exhibition of a motion picture because the picture advocates an idea—that adultery under certain circumstances may be proper behavior. Yet the First Amendment's basic guarantee is of freedom to advocate ideas." The Board of Regents, "has thus struck at the very heart of constitutionally protected liberty." Stewart went on:

> It is contended that the State's action was justified because the motion picture attractively portrays a relationship which is contrary to the moral standard, the religious precepts, and the legal code of its citizenry. This argument misconceives what it is that the Constitution protects. Its guarantee is not confined to the expression of ideas that are conventional or shared by a majority. It protects advocacy of the opinion that adultery may sometimes be proper, no less than advocacy of socialism or the single tax. And in the realm of ideas it protects the expression which is eloquent no less than that which is unconvincing.

The case, *Kingsley International Pictures Corp. v. Regents of the State University of New York*, was argued before the Supreme Court on April 23, 1959. The unanimous opinion was issued on June 29.

Three weeks later, on July 21, in the federal courthouse in Lower Manhattan, Judge Bryan ruled in favor of Grove Press and ordered the Post Office to lift all restrictions on sending copies of *Lady Chatterley's Lover* through the mail.

Never again would the Post Office assume the authority to declare a work of literature obscene or to impound copies of a book or to prosecute the shipper. The ruling didn't quite mark the end of obscenity; over the next several years, Rosset would wage further legal battles, in several state courts, over *Naked Lunch* and, finally, *The Tropic of Cancer*. But the *Chatterley* cases marked the beginning of the end. They established the principle that would pave the way to the end. And prior to 1959, this principle had not even been recognized as a valid legal argument.

The week after the *Kingsley* ruling, the editors of *Time* ridiculed Justice Stewart's decision with a sarcastic headline: "Adultery Is an Idea." But the winds were shifting, the culture changing. That summer, *Lady Chatterley's Lover* soared to the number-two slot on the *New York Times* best-seller list, topped only by Leon Uris's *Exodus*. By the fall, the Grove Press edition had sold 110,000 copies in hardcover. The paperback, when it came out, would sell nearly 2 million. Other publishers, riding piggyback on the court ruling but paying Grove no royalty, put out their own public-domain editions, which sold a total of 4 million more. Rembar later wrote in his memoirs, "The average man, it was pretty clear, was buying, because it was a dirty book." And more and more average men—and women—believed that the government shouldn't be controlling what they read.

Other novels on that summer's top-ten list included Vladimir Nabokov's *Lolita*, which was also outraging the nation's moral guardians, and Boris Pasternak's *Dr. Zhivago*, a Russian novel—unusual enough—that had been banned for political reasons by the cultural commissars in Moscow. There was an appetite for forbidden fruit, wherever it was growing—and an audience for anyone who spat its seeds in the faces of authority.

7

Sickniks

On April 9, 1959, Steve Allen, the host of his own weekly prime-time variety show on NBC-TV, introduced his first guest of the evening: "Ladies and gentlemen, here is the very shocking comedian, the most shocking comedian of our time," Allen called him, "a young man who is skyrocketing to fame—*Lenny Bruce!*"

The very appearance of Lenny Bruce on a national network television program was as striking a sign as any that something in the air was changing. Bruce was one of a handful of rebel nightclub comedians that much of the press had dubbed "sick comics" or "sickniks"—others included Mort Sahl, Jonathan Winters, and Tom Lehrer—and Bruce wore the moniker with relish.

Most of the era's big comedians, headliners on the Vegas strip or the Catskills circuit, told jokes—snappy setups and rim-shot punch lines—about wives, kids, mothers-in-law, or, at their most daring, psychiatrists. Bruce uncorked elaborate monologues about sex, drugs, religion, and politics—topics that no one was supposed to talk about in "mixed company," much less on a public stage.

Bruce's other novelty was his delivery. He loosened the language, sprinkling his bits with hipster lingo, Yiddish slang, and the syncopated cadence of jazz. Ralph J. Gleason, a leading jazz critic of the day, likened Bruce's "improvisations" to those of Charlie Parker and John Coltrane.

At the start of the year, Fantasy Records, a small Berkeley-based jazz label, released a Lenny Bruce album, which had been recorded before live audiences at various San Francisco nightclubs. Called *The Sick Humor of Lenny Bruce*, it sported a cover photo of Bruce having a picnic on the grounds of a cemetery. Later in the year, Fantasy would release a second album called *"I Am Not a Nut, Elect Me!"* Bruce was shown on its cover hugging a black woman and an Asian woman while white-hooded Klansmen hovered in the background.

On both albums, half of the material was straightforward sick humor, like something out of *Mad* magazine—a riff on a news story about a man arrested for trying to blow up an airplane with forty people and his mother on it ("which just goes to show, people lack a sense of humor"), another about the fuss made over a boy who was killed by a shark at a nearby beach ("This town is bum-rapping sharks—you don't know, maybe that kid was *snotty* with the shark").

But the other half was like nothing else around. In one long bit, called "Religions, Inc.," Bruce imagined the big TV evangelists sitting in a Madison Avenue boardroom. "Ah jus' was talkin ta Billi this aftuhnoon," Bruce says in the flamboyant southern voice of H. A. Allen addressing the group. "Ah said, 'Billi, we come a lawng way, sweetie, lawng way.' Who woulda thawt back in '31—we were hustlin' baby pitchures then, an' shingles an' siding, we were swingin', ya know. . . . An' jus like *that*, we came on it, the Gideon, an' *Bop!* there we were. Hah! The graph tells the story—Catholicism up nine points, Judaism up fifteen." In the middle of the meeting, Oral Roberts—again, Bruce imitating his voice—takes a phone call from the pope. "Hello, Johnny! What's shakin', baby? . . . Ah meant to congratulate you on the election . . . yeah. . . . That puff of white smoke was a genius stroke. . . . We got an eight-page layout with Viceroy—'The New Pope Is a Thinking Man.'"

This was daring enough; nobody made fun of the Church. Then came the hammer. "Listen," Bruce goes on in the voice of Oral Roberts talking to the pope, "Ah hate to bug ya, but they're buggin' us again with that dumb integration. . . . No, I dunno why the hell they wanna go to school either. . . . They keep saying, 'Integration, make the religious leaders talk about it.' . . . They want us to come out an' *say* things, say 'Let them go to school with *them*.' . . . Yeah, an' the 'Stop the War' scene. They say, 'Thou shalt not kill' means just that, it doesn't mean 'Amend section A.'"

In another bit, Christ and Moses come back to St. Patrick's Cathedral. "And Christ," Bruce says, "is confused, because his route took him through Spanish Harlem, and he was wondering what the hell fifty Puerto Ricans were doing living in one room when that stained glass window is worth ten G's a square foot." Bishop Sheen runs up to Cardinal Spellman and whispers, "*Pssst!* Spellman, c'mon down here, I gotta talk to you! They're *here!*" Lepers start streaming into the church, to touch Christ's hem. Spellman calls the Vatican in a panic. "This place is filling up," he screams. "What are we paying protection for? . . . Look, all I know is, I'm up to my ass in crutches and wheelchairs here!"

In a track called "How to Entertain Colored People at Parties," Bruce plays a dim-witted white man at a party in a newly integrated neighborhood, not knowing how to talk to his educated black neighbor. "You know, that Joe Louis was a hell of a fighter," he finally ventures. "What a man, boy! He's a credit to your race, don't you ever forget that, you sonofagun." The black man, trying to be polite, replies, "Well, thank you very much." "You know, you're OK, you're really a good guy," the white man says. "Well, here's to Stepin Fetchit. . . . I guess you know a lotta people in show business, eh? You know Aunt Jemima?" "No, I'm sorry, I don't know her." "That guy on the Cream of Wheat box?" "No." "Well, here's to Paul Robeson."

White people in the audience tended to freeze when Bruce did this bit; but black people, especially black actors and musicians, cracked up. They'd met white people like that, over and over; this was the story of their lives.

Lenny Bruce was born Leonard Alfred Schneider in Mineola, Long Island, in 1925. His parents divorced before he was born. His mother was a stripper-comic named Sally Marr (real name Sadie Kitchenberg), who sometimes brought Lenny with her on the road but usually dropped him off for months at a time with relatives. At seventeen, he joined the Navy. When he came back, he did routine stand-up comedy at a spaghetti joint in Brooklyn. At twenty-three, he won a talent contest on Arthur Godfrey's TV show and moved to Los Angeles, then up to the Bay area.

San Francisco was a Mecca for stand-up comics in the fifties, in much the same way that New York was for jazz. The younger, hipper comics set their sights on the hungry i (the *i* stood for "id"), a nightclub in a dingy cellar in the North Beach district—just down the street from Lawrence Ferlinghetti's City Lights Bookstore, not far from the Six Gallery, where Allen Ginsberg gave his first reading of *Howl*. The hungry i, which served wine, espresso, and cheap sandwiches, was run by Enrico Banducci, an expansive impresario who indulged the talent but not the customers, evicting anyone who heckled or talked during the acts, refunding their money, and muttering, "Please don't grace us with your presence again."

It was Mort Sahl who put the hungry i—and San Francisco—on the comedy map. He came there on Christmas night, 1953, looking for a place to do his routines, and stayed for the next three years, packing in customers and becoming famous and rich.

The son of a failed playwright, Sahl was born in Montreal in 1927 and moved to Los Angeles at the age of seven, in the middle of the Depression. After a stint in the Army, he got an engineering degree from the University of Southern California, though he often skipped classes to sleep in after late-night carousing at jazz clubs. His girlfriend was admitted to the University of California at Berkeley. He followed her up north and hung around the local coffee shops, debating politics, literature, and music. He wrote one-act plays, couldn't get them produced, so rewrote them as monologues and tried them out at the hungry i, knowing only that North Beach was where the beatniks hung out and figuring that they might like his attitude.

Unlike Bruce and most of the other comics, Sahl had never worked a room, never tried to break into the business through the conventional route. He dressed like a collegiate, in a sweater vest with rolled-up sleeves, never in a tie, much less a suit. He got up on the stage and talked, the way he'd talked at the coffee clubs, at breakneck speed, with a broad smirk. He once told a reporter that he talked so fast because, at the start of his career, he was afraid to pause; he didn't want the audience to think that he was waiting for a laugh. So he kept talking, to fill the gaps, throwing in brief asides—many of them about current events—and he soon realized that the asides were getting the biggest laughs.

If Lenny Bruce had a jazz inflection, Mort Sahl was jazz incarnate. One of Sahl's best friends was Paul Desmond, who played alto saxophone in Dave Brubeck's popular quartet. Once, in the mid-fifties, when the quartet toured college campuses, Sahl went with them as the opening act. He did the same thing, for a while, with Stan Kenton's experimental big band. Sahl saw himself as a jazz-man who blew words. "What I do," he once told an interviewer, "is improvise with a theme. . . . I often wander away from the theme and sometimes violate the chord structure, but I usually come back and resolve it, and always I try to keep a beat."

He would amble up to the stage, carrying an armload of newspapers and magazines, read marked-up passages out loud, punctuating the hypocrisies with a smirk and a snarky comment, and, at the end of some particularly savage stab, a cackle.

Sahl also talked about women, fast cars, sleek hi-fi gear, and intellectuals. In one of his jokes, three armed men holding up the Fairmont Hotel give the desk clerk a note that reads, "This is a hold-up. If you act normal, you won't get hurt." The clerk, a UC student working nights, writes back, "Act normal? Define your terms."

But Sahl made his name by going after the political powers. When the Red Scare was at its high point, Sahl would say, "Joe McCarthy doesn't question what you say so much as your right to say it." And "Every time the Russians throw an American in jail, the House Un-American Activities Committee retaliates by throwing an American in jail, too." He attacked left and right, mainly for being so bland. "Eisenhower is for integration, but gradually; Adlai Stevenson, on the other hand, is for integration, but moderately," he said in one routine. "It should be possible to compromise between those extremes." He usually ended his sets by asking, "Is there any group here that I haven't offended?" Another of his favorite lines: "I wish I had a cause because I've got a lot of enthusiasm."

He was making $5,000 to $7,500 a week working clubs around the country at a time when the average American household was earning that much per year. In the spring of 1958, he wrote and starred in a one-man show called *The Next President* at the Bijou Theater on Broadway. (The opening act was a folk-singing group called the Chorus of the Collective Conscience.) Walter Kerr, the theater critic for the *New York Herald Tribune*, wrote a mixed review but lauded it overall as "an indication that something in our society has begun—after too many muddy and fearful years—to change. First thing you know, irreverence will be in vogue again, and even satire may wear its old outrageous and becoming smile. It's nice to know improper things can once more be said in public."

Senator John Kennedy asked Sahl to write jokes for him when he began his run for the presidency. Sahl was smitten with Kennedy. He was so glamorous, witty, and intellectual. But then he started telling jokes about Kennedy in his nightclub act. After Kennedy won the election in 1960, Sahl was kicked out of the circle. Nobody expected him to jab at Kennedy as irreverently as he'd gone after Eisenhower. "I attack everybody, that's my job," Sahl often said. The falling-out with Kennedy embittered him for years.

Lenny Bruce steered clear of politicians, and they stayed away from him, too. His edges were always too rough, even before he started sprinkling dirty words into his act. Once he became well known, Bruce played the hungry i several times, but his first big break came at a club called Ann's 440, which featured as many drag queens as it did comedians. Herb Caen, the *San Francisco Chronicle* columnist who coined the term "beatnik" and who wrote the first enthusiastic notice of Mort Sahl at the hungry i, caught Bruce at Ann's 440. When Hugh Hefner, the publisher of *Playboy*, came to town, Caen took him for a look. Hefner got Bruce booked at the Cloister, a club in Chicago that paid $850 a week. The Fantasy albums followed, and he was off, soon making almost as much money as Sahl.

Neither of them had much luck with television. NBC gave Sahl a $25,000 retainer for exclusive TV appearances. In 1958, he went on one show, hosted by the singer Eddie Fisher, who, at a loss, asked Sahl to "say something funny." Sahl responded, "John Foster Dulles." The audience cracked up, but the producers were nervous. He was booked on two more shows but didn't make it past rehearsals; he was too dangerous. In frustration, Sahl told one booking agent, "You can't be afraid of *everything*." The agent replied, "But we *are*."

Bruce's appearance on Steve Allen's show was lame. The censors demanded prior approval of every word. He was going to tell one fairly mild joke about his grandmother's horror at seeing a tattoo on his arm after he got out of the Navy. "*Vaghhhhh!*" she screams. "Vhy'd you do that? You can't be buried in a Jewish ceremony!" Lenny tells her, "So what are you buggin' me? They'll cut this arm off, they'll bury *it* in a *Gentile* ceremony."

Allen's producer worried that the joke might offend Jewish viewers. Bruce told him he was being ridiculous. After conferring with the network people, the producer came back and said it might offend Gentiles, too. "It suggests," he said, "that they don't care *what* they bury." Bruce ended up doing a maudlin bit about ex-wives.

Seven years later, Bruce would be dead from a drug overdose at the age of forty. In 1961, he started to use profanity in his bits, and the police started to arrest him on charges of obscenity. The first bust came at the Jazz Workshop in San Francisco on October 10 when he said "cocksucker." As if consumed with self-destruction, Bruce escalated the culture fight, using forbidden words more and more often; local prosecutors often sent undercover cops to the clubs, in anticipation of a good night's bust.

The freedom of language unleashed by the court decisions on once-obscene books that could be read in American homes—*Lady Chatterley's Lover*, *Naked Lunch*, *The Tropic of Cancer*—did not yet apply to words spoken in a nightclub.

Bruce always thought, as did many of his champions, that the district attorneys and judges wanted to get him not so much for his profanities but for his satirical bits about the Church; many of them were Catholic. In any case, from 1962 on, he found it hard to get work. Few club owners wanted to get in trouble with the law. Then he started getting arrested for drug possession. In his last few years, his stage bits consisted almost entirely of detailed, sometimes-groggy accounts of the legal arguments at his trials.

Sahl's fortunes declined after the assassination of President Kennedy. He became obsessed with conspiracy theories and the inconsistencies in the Warren Commission's report. He devoted whole sets to reading from its transcripts.

In short, by the mid-sixties, Bruce and Sahl, who had not merely advanced but redefined the art of stand-up comedy, descended into the comic's ultimate nightmare—they were no longer funny.

The typical Borscht Belt comic didn't think Bruce and Sahl were ever funny. They didn't tell jokes, they were *just talking*—what kind of act was that?

But if both men were consumed and destroyed by martyr's complexes, at least they fulfilled the authentic martyr's role—they suffered so that their acolytes could live and thrive.

In the decades to come, there would still be comedians who told vaudevillian jokes, but there would also be many successful political and social satirists. There would still be TV shows that avoided topical themes, but there would be others—especially on the cable channels, which were immune to FCC regulations—that plunged in, with characters that talked the way real people did, profanity included. Comics like George Carlin, Richard Pryor, and Chris Rock—whole networks like HBO, Showtime, and Comedy Central—owed their livelihood, their existence, to Mort Sahl and Lenny Bruce.[*]

Even during the sickniks' heyday, some of the old-timers knew things were changing. At the end of 1958, the *New York Times* asked five comic writers to comment on "the state of the nation's humor today." James Thurber, who was sixty-six and had been drawing and writing popular, droll sketches for the *New Yorker* since the thirties, replied that America had become a "jumpy" nation, "afflicted with night terrors," living "under the threat of total demolition," perched not on the brink of war but, as he put it, on "the Brink of Was"—the brink of extinction.

At their peaks, Bruce and Sahl roamed this jumpy terrain, the same subterranean landscape as the Beats and Burroughs and Mailer's "White Negro." Their fans felt like members of a secret club, an underground movement, rendered hip by their knowing grasp of the era's surreal contradictions. Sahl put it this way: whenever he saw an airplane approaching, he never knew whether it was going to drop a hydrogen bomb or spell out "Pepsi-Cola" in skywriting.

---

[*] The shift in attitude Lenny Bruce spawned has made his own comedy and language not just permissible but respectable. Two days before Christmas 2003, George Pataki, New York's very square Republican governor, posthumously pardoned Bruce for an obscenity conviction dating from 1964 and said that he was doing so as "a declaration of New York's commitment to upholding the First Amendment."

8

Thinking about the Unthinkable

All through the spring of 1959, a thirty-seven-year-old physicist named Herman Kahn traveled across the country, delivering marathon public lectures—three-part extravaganzas lasting five hours or longer—about the art and science of fighting, surviving, and winning a nuclear war.

Kahn cut a massive profile, standing before packed auditoriums—he was just five feet eight but weighed 350 pounds—pacing, sweating, talking at a frenetic pace in a staccato Bronx accent, tossing in jokes and chuckles between his calculations and scenarios, flipping through a hundred slides stacked on two projectors, aiming his pointer at the screens displaying charts, tables, and graphs beneath such captions as "Tragic but Distinguishable Postwar States" and "Will the Survivors Envy the Dead?"

Had he taken a different path, Kahn might have been a stand-up comic, one of the "sickniks." His delivery was similar to Mort Sahl's, his brazen provocations not unlike Lenny Bruce's. In substance, though, he seemed more like a character in a William Burroughs novel—an oddly jolly paragon of linear logic run amok.

Kahn had spent most of the decade at the RAND Corporation, an Air Force–sponsored think tank on the beach of Santa Monica,

California, where intellectuals—mainly economists, mathematicians, political scientists, and physicists—spent their workaday lives pondering the imponderables of the bomb. Toward the end, Kahn was irritating RAND's management. The corporation's mission was to provide doctrinal support for Air Force budgets and weapons systems. Yet Kahn had become obsessed with evacuation plans, mineshaft shelters, and radiation detectors—which had nothing to do with the Air Force and were, therefore, distractions from the sponsor's vital concerns.

So in the spring of 1959, Kahn took a leave of absence from RAND and won a fellowship at Princeton University's Center for International Studies, where he started putting together the three-part lectures, which would form the basis of a 652-page tome called *On Thermonuclear War*.

It was the year of the "missile gap"—the belief, based on U.S. intelligence estimates (which turned out to be wrong), that the Soviet Union was way ahead of America in the race to build intercontinental ballistic missiles. One of Kahn's RAND colleagues, Albert Wohlstetter, published a widely read article in the January issue of *Foreign Affairs* called "The Delicate Balance of Terror," which concluded (on the basis of the same faulty intelligence reports) that the Soviets could launch a disarming nuclear strike of such devastation that the United States might be unable to retaliate. RAND itself was attracting public notice, thanks to a long photo essay in *Life* magazine called "Valuable Batch of Brains," featuring, as one of the captions put it, "the first look ever taken at RAND scientists deep in thought about the nation's security."

Around the same time, federal civil-defense officials testified in open congressional hearings that a "moderate-sized" nuclear attack, in which the Soviets dropped 263 H-bombs on 70 cities and 151 air bases, would instantly kill 23 million Americans and fatally injure another 26 million, as well as irradiate half the nation's available housing. Meanwhile, the U.S. Public Health Service announced that as a result of U.S. and Soviet nuclear weapons tests in the atmosphere, radioactive strontium-90 was rising to dangerous levels in milk.

Nelson Rockefeller, the governor of New York, introduced legislation requiring that all homeowners build fallout shelters, and at a conference of governors, urged that a similar program be started nationwide. The idea went nowhere; it was mainly laughed off.

Herman Kahn waddled into this cauldron of nervousness, declaring that not all was hopeless. Sure, nuclear war might happen, it probably *will* happen; but most of us, he proclaimed, can live through it; with enough foresight and perseverance, it won't be that bad.

Let's imagine, Kahn would say in his lectures, that the Soviets launch the most devastating attack imaginable, wiping out all fifty-three of America's major metropolitan areas. You might think that would destroy the whole country, but it just wasn't so. Less than 40 percent of the population lives in these metropolitan areas. That means more than 60 percent of the population would survive.

"Can you live with that?" Kahn would ask his audience in his clipped voice. "The answer is yes. Particularly the kind of tragedy this is, it's actually easy to take. It isn't like the Blitz in London, where everybody saw the little girl's hand or something like that, the kind of experience to carry around the rest of his life. People are over-killed in the *target* areas. *You* don't get to see the dead, you understand. It's a little bit distant. You hear that New York is destroyed, but you're in Princeton. You know about it, but it isn't quite the same."

Much about the postwar world will be unfamiliar; you'll be eating strange foods. "Under these circumstances," Kahn would go on, "some percent of the population is going to be nauseous. Nausea is also catching. One guy vomits, everybody vomits. Your morale is going to be low under those circumstances, believe me. It just wouldn't surprise you if people just refused to do anything." This was why people have to be equipped with radiation meters, so they can tell their vomiting neighbor, "The meter says you only got ten roentgens. What are you throwing up for? Shut up!"

When a reporter for the *San Francisco Chronicle* asked him to elaborate on his remark that nuclear war "would not preclude normal and happy lives for the majority of survivors," Kahn replied, "Who's happy and normal right now?"

Over five thousand people came to see these lectures; over thirty thousand would buy his book in hardcover when it came out the following year. There was a morbid fascination with the bomb. "Now I become death, the destroyer of worlds," J. Robert Oppenheimer famously uttered while gazing at the giant mushroom cloud rising from the explosion of the first atom bomb at the Trinity test site in Los Alamos, New Mexico. Now, fourteen years later, as the two superpowers possessed whole arsenals of these bombs and seemed poised to pack them into the nose cones of long-range missiles, the Ultimate Weapon was still the stuff of taboo.

Yet here was Kahn, this odd, seemingly genial figure with an astronomical IQ and unflappable self-confidence, staring wide-eyed into the abyss, talking insouciantly, even flippantly, about wars that might kill tens or hundreds of millions of people in a flash. One reviewer of his book would write, "Kahn does for nuclear arms what free-love advocates did for sex: he speaks candidly of acts about which others whisper behind closed doors." A staff writer for NBC News sent Kahn a fan letter, calling *On Thermonuclear War* "the most fascinating thing I have read since *Lady Chatterley.*"

RAND had its origins in the American labs and planning staffs of World War II, a war in which scientists played an unprecedented role, developing not just the atom bomb but also radar, infrared sensors, long-range rockets, torpedoes with depth charges—and a new field of intellectual endeavor called "systems analysis" or "operations research," which provided the tools with which strategists could calculate the optimal way of using these new weapons. How many tons of explosive force must a bomb release to damage various types of targets? In what sorts of formations should bomber aircraft fly? Should a plane be heavily armored, or should it be stripped of defenses so it can fly faster?

Toward the end of the war, General Henry "Hap" Arnold, commander of the U.S. Army Air Forces, started to worry. He saw the future as an age of missiles, robots, and weapons of super-destructiveness. When the war was over and the nation demobilized, how could the military retain a pool of talented scientists? The answer was Air Force Project RAND, which started as a four-man outfit in a walled-off section of the Douglas Aircraft headquarters in downtown Santa Monica. In the beginning, they worked on technical problems: comparisons of rockets and ramjets, the use of titanium alloys on supersonic planes, nuclear propulsion, upper-atmospheric physics. RAND's first report, dated May 2, 1946, was titled *Preliminary Design of an Experimental World-Circling Spaceship*, and it predicted that the launching of such a spaceship—or a satellite, as it would come to be called—"would inflame the imagination of mankind and . . . probably produce repercussions in the world comparable to the explosion of the atomic bomb." Eleven years later, the Soviets' Sputnik did just that.

Herman Kahn joined RAND in 1950 and, as his first assignment, worked on a team that was analyzing the feasibility of a nuclear-powered airplane. It was then, as he later recalled, that he "first came into contact with the philosophy which is willing to ask any question and tackle any problem."

As RAND expanded, social scientists joined the staff and performed calculations on broader questions of strategy: how best to deploy the bomber fleet, so the Soviets couldn't easily destroy it in a sneak attack; what kinds of Soviet targets to hit if nuclear war broke out. Kahn was supposed to stay put in the physics department, which had compartmentalized security clearances, but he roamed the corridors and sat in on the strategy sessions, too.

At one of these sessions, several analysts were debating whether it made sense to avoid hitting the Soviet Union's cities in the first round of a nuclear war and, instead, to attack only its military targets. Bernard Brodie, a pioneer in the arcane field of nuclear strategy, found the idea appealing but dismissed its feasibility; calculations suggested that the radioactive fallout from such a "limited" attack would still kill 2 million Russians, so sparing cities wouldn't make much difference.

Kahn put a novel twist on this calculation. The way Kahn saw it, *only* 2 million people would die. That was a lot better than 10 million or 20 or 50 million. This was the image Kahn was fashioning for himself: the fearless defense intellectual, asking the questions that everyone else ignored. He titled one of his later books, published in the sixties, *Thinking about the Unthinkable*.

The U.S. Strategic Air Command's war plan all through the fifties was hair-raising. If the Soviet army invaded Western Europe, even if it didn't set off a single nuclear weapon, SAC's plan was to unleash every bomber in the fleet and drop every nuclear bomb on every target in the USSR and Red China. In 1959, that amounted to 3,423 nuclear bombs, with the power of 7,847 megatons (nearly 8 *billion tons* of explosive), which would probably kill 285 million Russians and Chinese and severely injure 40 million more, with incalculable casualties in Europe and elsewhere from fallout.

Once, when talking about this plan during a classified briefing to the top officers at SAC headquarters in Omaha, Nebraska, Kahn said, "Gentlemen, you don't have a war plan, you have a war orgasm."

The generals laughed, but didn't take him seriously; maybe they didn't understand his critique. To drive home the point, Kahn proposed with mock sincerity that they create a "doomsday machine." It would consist of a huge stockpile of large hydrogen bombs, wired to sensors and a vast computer. When the sensors detected that the Soviet Union had committed an intolerable act, such as exploding one nuclear weapon, the machine would automatically detonate all the doomsday bombs, covering Earth with enough radiation to kill hundreds of millions, maybe billions, of people. Assisted by a RAND engineer, Kahn went so far as to draw up the blueprints for such a machine, proving it could be built. As expected, not a single SAC officer liked the idea. And yet, Kahn told them, the doomsday machine was only a slight exaggeration of SAC's actual nuclear policy: the Soviets do something provocative; we blow up most of their people; in retaliation, they blow up most of ours.[*]

The problem, Kahn often said, was that nobody—not even the commanders at SAC—took nuclear war seriously. Beneath it all, nobody really thought it would happen. But what if it did? Would the president of the United States—would any sane person—really wreak so much destruction, especially if there was a chance that the Russians would shoot back? If *we* didn't take our threat seriously, why would the Russians? What if they called our bluff? Would we surrender—or commit mass murder and suicide? And which choice was worse?

Others at RAND were mulling this same problem. That's why Bernard Brodie was thinking about a "no-cities" attack plan. William Weed Kaufmann, another strategist (and a former student of Brodie's at Yale before the war), wrote a briefing on such a plan, which he called a "counterforce" strategy. The idea was that if the Soviets invaded Western Europe, the United States should drop a

---

[*] Stanley Kubrick would borrow the concept of a "doomsday machine" as the plot device that sets off a nuclear war in his 1964 black comedy, *Dr. Strangelove*. During his research for the film, Kubrick became friends with Kahn, and it is clear that the Dr. Strangelove character is very much based on Kahn—not physically, but intellectually. Whole lines of dialogue—about mineshaft shelters and postwar survival—are taken almost verbatim from Kahn's book *On Thermonuclear War*.

small number of nuclear weapons on their strategic military targets (bomber bases, nuclear-missile sites, submarine pens, and so forth). Then the president should tell the Russians that if they didn't halt their aggression, he would pick off their cities with a "reserve force" of nuclear weapons, which hadn't yet been fired and which were invulnerable to attack, deployed either in underground missile silos or on bombers flying on constant airborne alert. A few of the Soviets' nuclear bombers might survive our counterforce strike, but—the logic went—they wouldn't dare attack our cities, for fear that we would fire our remaining weapons against theirs.

Kaufmann and some of the others at RAND who were pushing counterforce weren't enthusiastic about it. They knew that putting it in motion would be a terrible gamble. The Soviet leaders might not pick up on our finely tuned signals, or they might not be interested in playing the same game. The fallout from a counterforce attack would kill a few million Russians, and that might provoke the Kremlin to fire back in full force—regardless of the RAND calculations that deemed such a move "irrational," and regardless of Herman Kahn's spin that we would have killed *"only"* a few million. Counterforce was, at best, a desperation strategy in case nuclear war couldn't be avoided—something that a president *might* be able to do, that might bring the war under control, before all hell broke loose.

Kahn, however, was never one for halfhearted proposals. If a plan was worth doing, then it should be pursued with gusto, its logic pushed to the extreme. So there had to be the means to launch a counterforce attack. And even that wouldn't be credible unless the American people could be protected in case the Russians struck back. So we would also need a strong civil-defense program that included evacuating cities, storing supplies underground, putting people in shelters—basements would do, mineshafts would be better.

The point wasn't so much to protect the population from a Soviet attack as to give the president the leverage to threaten a counterforce first-strike with credibility. Let's say the Russians provoke another crisis over Berlin. "What do you do?" Kahn would say in his lectures. "You can evacuate the cities," he would answer himself. "Now you are talking from the so-called position of strength." Kahn figured that the American president might have to evacuate cities every few years or so, just to show the Russians that he was serious.

And if you're going to do all this and make it believable, you have to go all-out. You need the accurate weapons, deeply dug shelters, robust communications systems, and so forth, that allow you to stretch out a nuclear war for weeks, maybe a couple of months—to give you the bargaining power to coerce the Russians into surrendering, and to prevent the Russians from coercing us, *after* the initial "nuclear exchange." Kahn worked up a whole vocabulary for these scenarios. He posited three types of nuclear deterrence: Type I was simply the threat to destroy the Russians if they attack; Type II was counterforce plus civil defense, which he said added up to a "Credible First-Strike Capability"; Type III was the ability to engage in prolonged "tit-for-tat" nuclear "exchanges." He argued that a president needed all three types of deterrence to keep the Soviet threat at bay.

Another thing you needed to do, in order to pull this off, was to avoid taking steps that might relax Cold War tensions. "Relaxing tensions is dangerous," Kahn would say in his lectures, maybe half-joking but no more than half. "It's very hard to believe that any American government in a period of no-tension will keep up a large defense budget." If the United States and the USSR signed an arms-control treaty, the nation's two leading nuclear-weapons labs—Los Alamos and Lawrence Livermore—would probably collapse because first-rank physicists would be reluctant to work there. "If you had a moral onus to working on weapons," Kahn said, "you just ain't going to get people, it's just that simple."

Kahn's intention in these briefings was to stir the American people, including their political and military leaders, out of their complacency, to show them that nuclear war was possible and feasible—that reasonable people might be driven to start one. Therefore, it would be useful, as he wrote in his book, "to create a vocabulary" in which people can discuss these issues "comfortably and easily" and, on that basis, discover "more reasonable forms of using violence."

But the attempt was futile. Hydrogen bombs were so much more destructive than anything ever devised that, once the fireballs started exploding, they defied rational control.

Sometimes Kahn hinted that he realized this. At one of his first lectures, in March 1959 at Princeton, when he was talking about a "long war"—which he defined as a nuclear war lasting between two and thirty days—someone in the audience interrupted with a question:

So much would be destroyed, how would either leader, the American president or the Soviet premier, know who's won? How would either of them know who's supposed to surrender to whom? Wouldn't it be the case that neither of them would even know who's ahead, much less what to do about it?

Kahn replied, "I think that is correct."

Another hint came that same month, when Kahn gave a lecture called "Why Go Deep Underground?" at a symposium back at RAND on the topic of "protective construction." The audience consisted of structural engineers. These were the professionals who would actually design and build the bomb shelters that Kahn was advocating. They were interested in hard facts, not fanciful theories. In his lecture, Kahn advised them to overdesign the structures as much as they could, to try to compensate for all known effects of nuclear weapons—"and then," he said in conclusion, "hope for the best. . . . All we can do is just face the fact that, to some extent, the working of our installations depends upon faith."

A few years later, Allen Ginsberg would describe the Cold War as "the imposition of a vast mental barrier on everybody, a vast anti-natural psyche." In his own way, Herman Kahn was trying to break out of that barrier by maneuvering around it, hoping that along that path he might find a way to *win* the thermonuclear chess game. But at the end of each road, he confronted only steeper barriers. The bomb's destructiveness allowed no evasion, no breakthrough. For the think-tank physicist, no less than the Zen Beat poet, the only outcome was stalemate.

9

The Race for Space

In the spring of 1959, the United States got into the space race. On March 3, the Pioneer IV spacecraft blasted off from Cape Canaveral, Florida, and matched the feat of Russia's Lunik two months earlier, soaring past the moon and locking into orbit around the sun. The Pioneer capsule was much lighter (13¼ pounds, compared with Lunik's 769 pounds), and it missed the moon by a greater distance (37,000 miles off course, as opposed to 25,000). Still, after four failed attempts since the previous summer, America, too, had broken free of Earth's gravitational pull.

Until this success, Project Mercury, NASA's ambitious program to launch a manned capsule into outer space, had been languishing. The Pentagon's Defense Advanced Research Projects Agency, which controlled the budgets for all space programs, had recently given Mercury a "priority rating" lower than that of the military's missile and satellite programs, so it was suffering grave shortages in supplies and spare parts. Just before the Pioneer IV launch, Roy Johnson, a top DARPA official, dismissed Mercury as a "very screwball" project. After Pioneer, he admitted, "It looks a little less screwball now." NASA and DARPA joined forces to give Mercury "brickbat" status—the highest priority—allowing the project's managers the same access as the military to critical components. President Eisenhower approved the upgrade.

On April 9, NASA held a press conference to introduce the 7 men who would fly the first several manned missions. The space agency had started with a roster of 110 military test pilots who were physically qualified. In February, the list was pared down to 69, then 56, before a battery of physical, mental, and psychological exams whittled it down to the winners.

The press initially called them "spacemen," but NASA's public-relations specialists came up with "astronauts," a play on the Argonauts of Greek mythology who sailed into uncharted waters in search of the Golden Fleece. The astronauts—Scott Carpenter, Gordon Cooper, John Glenn, Gus Grissom, Wally Schirra, Alan Shepard, and Deke Slayton—were lionized as pioneers and moral exemplars, their names committed as indelibly to memory as those of movie stars or baseball players.

It would be another decade before another group of astronauts landed on the moon. But in both the American and Soviet space programs, the moon was always the goal—and the gateway to exploring the universe. (Soviet engineers had actually aimed Lunik 1 to *hit* the moon; the capsule missed but then flew on to achieve, at least as dramatically, "escape velocity.") The shining sphere in the night sky had been the object of flight fantasy for nearly a century, starting with Jules Verne's *From the Earth to the Moon* in 1865 and H. G. Wells's *The First Men in the Moon* in 1901, which a year later inspired the first science-fiction film, Georges Méliès's *A Trip to the Moon*, followed by hundreds, if not thousands, of similar stories, novels, and movies through the decades.

No one was immune to the dreamy thrill of escaping the planet. In October 1957, a few days after the launch of Sputnik, Allen Ginsberg giddily wrote to Jack Kerouac from Paris, "Do you realize we'll soon (10 years) be on the moon, and in our lifetime get high with brother Martians? They'll be others out there & we'll reach them, I'm certain—and our poems, too." Ginsberg wrote one such tribute, the following year in Amsterdam, called "Poem Rocket," which captured the flush of romance with space travel: "Scientist alone is true poet he gave us the moon / he promises the stars he'll make us a new universe if it comes to that / O Einstein I should have sent you my flaming mss. / O Einstein I should have pilgrimaged to your white hair! /. . . I send up my rocket to land on whatever planet awaits it / preferably religious sweet planets no money / fourth dimensional planets where Death shows movies / plants speak (courteously) of ancient physics and poetry itself is manufactured by trees."

Back on Earth, the top brass of the U.S. Air Force moved to quash any such flights of fancy. In February 1959, a few weeks before the launching of Pioneer IV, General Thomas White, the Air Force Chief of Staff, told a House committee about the coining of a new word—"aerospace." The general explained, "Air and space comprise a single continuous operational field, in which the Air Force must continue to function. This area is 'aerospace.' . . . There can be no operational boundary between them."

The committee's chairman, Democratic congressman John McCormack, suspected—correctly—that a power grab was in the works. Space was still new territory for the federal government; there were multiple and overlapping space czars, space agencies, and space commands. "Aerospace" was a key device in the campaign to put them all under Air Force control. By statute, the Air Force, which had become an independent service only a dozen years earlier (before, it was the air wing of the Army), controlled security of the air. If there were "no operational boundary" between air and space, it would control the heavens as well.

The military's three services—Army, Navy, and Air Force—bitterly distrusted one another. Eisenhower, himself a decorated Army general, was suspicious of military bureaucracies—in his farewell address, he would warn of the rapacious appetites of the "military-industrial complex"—and, all through his presidency, he kept a tight lid on the Pentagon's budget. As a result, each of the service chiefs fought for every dollar, and that often meant swiping dollars from the other chiefs.

A week after General White testified, the House committee heard from the Army's director of air defense and special systems, Major General Dwight Beach. McCormack asked General Beach about this term "aerospace." Beach replied, "I never heard of that term before. I always heard of 'armo-space'"—thus revealing that the Army, too, had parochial ambitions.

McCormack said, "Well, we encountered it the other day, a very sweet term, a very all-embracing term. Whoever coined it ought to be made a full general." McCormack asked which service should have responsibility for military space programs. Beach replied, "It should be a *national* effort," beyond the control of any one service—a fitting answer for a service chief finding himself on the ropes.

Pioneer IV put the Air Force back on the defensive. The space capsule had been boosted into space by a Juno rocket, a modification of the Jupiter intermediate-range ballistic missile, which was an Army program. Before this, three of the four failed attempts to put a capsule into space had involved Air Force rockets.

In reaction, the Air Force upped the pressure. Major General Bernard Schriever, commander of the Air Force's ballistic missile division, called for an overhaul of the space program and the abolition of DARPA. He, too, invoked the word "aerospace," portraying outer space as merely a logical extension of the Air Force's realm. The names of various Air Force divisions were changed from "Air Command" to "Aerospace Command." The Aircraft Industries Association changed its name to the Aerospace Industries Association. The Air Force adopted a new slogan—"Aerospace Power for Peace"—and the director of information sent out a directive to all commands and bases that this slogan "should be used wherever appropriate to keep Air Force members and the general public aware of the Air Force's primary . . . responsibility in the Nation's land-sea-aerospace military team."

The battle was on, not only within the Pentagon, where the maneuvering was but one skirmish in a vast arena of interservice rivalry, but, more broadly, over whether outer space would be a new frontier that might, like earlier frontiers, spark America's renewal—or whether the planets and stars would become a mere extension of ancient terrestrial conflicts.

10

Toppling the Tyranny
of Numbers

On March 24, 1959, at the Institute of Radio Engineers' annual trade show in the New York Coliseum, Texas Instruments, one of the nation's leading electronics firms, introduced a new device that would change the world as profoundly as any invention of the twentieth century—the solid integrated circuit, or, as it also came to be called, the microchip.

Without the chip, the commonplace conveniences of modern life—personal computers, the Internet, anything involving digital technology and displays, even something as simple as the handheld calculator—would be the stuff of fantasy.

It was invented not by a vast team of physicists but by one man working alone, a self-described tinkerer—not even a physicist, but an engineer—named John St. Clair Kilby.

Jack Kilby grew up on the plains of Great Bend, Kansas. His father was an electrical engineer and the president of the Kansas Power Company. In 1938, a ferocious blizzard shut down power across the western half of the state. Phone lines were knocked down, and the roads were impassible. So Hubert Kilby kept in touch with his stations and work crews, spread out across dozens of miles, through a neighbor's ham radio. Jack, then fourteen, watching his father working the dials and the microphone, marveled at the obliteration of time and distance through technology. He would later say that his lifelong interest in electronics began with that storm.

In 1941, just out of high school, Kilby took the entrance exam for the Massachusetts Institute of Technology, but he fell three points short of passing. War soon broke out, in any case. He joined the Army and was assigned to a radio repair depot in northeastern India. The Army was airlifting small guerrilla teams to Burma to organize resistance against the Japanese. The teams' radios weighed sixty pounds and frequently broke down in the jungle heat. Kilby bought spare parts on the black market in Calcutta and used them to build transmitters that were lighter and more reliable.

After the war, he studied engineering at the University of Illinois and earned a master's degree at the University of Wisconsin, but learned little that he didn't already know. In 1947, he got a job at the Centralab division of Globe Union in Milwaukee, working on miniaturizing circuits. That year, William Shockley invented the transistor at Bell Laboratories, revolutionizing the world of electronics.

Before transistors, electrical devices were powered by vacuum tubes, which were big, heavy, fragile, and very hot. By contrast, transistors were compact and light; they had no moving parts, they ran cool, and the switching and amplifying were handled by a semiconductor, not a glass bulb. Over the next decade, engineers at a growing number of firms tweaked the new technology to make it still faster, lighter, and smaller. By Christmas 1954, the first transistor radio, small enough to fit in a pocket, hit the market at a retail price of $49.95 and quickly became the biggest-selling consumer product the country had ever seen.

Science-fiction writers and several mass-magazine journalists took to predicting the imminent invention of wristwatch telephones, spaceships flying across the solar system, "thinking machines" that performed all the functions of the human brain, and computer-guided missiles that exploded right on target.

Like most real scientists, Kilby laughed at these notions. As rapidly as transistor products were advancing, there remained an enormous barrier that blocked much further progress. The barrier was called "the tyranny of numbers."

The problem was this. If you wanted a computer or some other electronic device to perform more complex operations more quickly, you would need an extra set of components—transistors, resistors, capacitors, diodes, rectifiers, and the wires to connect them all into a circuit—for each increment in speed, memory, or storage space. The futuristic miracle machines of science fiction would require so many extra components—and so much wiring, all connected precisely by hand—that, as a practical matter, they could not be built.

Already, by the late fifties, the labor costs of the electronics on board the U.S. Navy's latest aircraft carrier exceeded the hardware costs. NASA calculated that guiding a manned spacecraft to the moon would involve ten million components. Simply wiring these components together would be wildly expensive and time-consuming. The resulting system would also be unreliable; a loose solder on a single joint could stop the flow of current and shut the machine down.

Miniaturization was every electronics firm's mantra. Rockets, missiles, and spaceships were seen as the jackpot markets of the future, but if the computers guiding them couldn't get smaller, lighter, and cheaper, the future wouldn't take off. So companies competed strenuously to invent the smallest solution fastest.

Still, miniaturization alone wouldn't topple the tyranny of numbers. In some ways, because smaller components were more difficult to wire, it only intensified the problem. To break through the barrier would require a whole new approach. But what was it?

In May 1958, Kilby moved from Milwaukee to Dallas to take a job with Texas Instruments, which had just opened a new building devoted to semiconductor research. In July, most employees took their two-week summer vacation, but Kilby hadn't been with the company long enough to earn the time off. So he stayed at the new lab and thought about the problem, all alone.

Texas Instruments had made a big investment in silicon, so he focused on that as his basic material. Typically, silicon would be purified for the manufacture of transistors. But if it were treated with certain impurities, it could be used as a conductor. Treated and molded in another way, it could serve as a resistor. It could be the material for any component in a circuit—not the ideal material, but good enough.

This was Kilby's initial insight, an insight that grew out of his experiences in the Army and at Centralab, where he had developed a talent for squeezing efficiencies out of every gizmo that he grappled with: maybe all or most of the parts of a circuit could be made from the same material. In the world of electronics, even slight reductions in the cost of a circuit could yield huge savings on the production line and, therefore, a competitive advantage in the marketplace. In his thinking about silicon, Kilby seemed to have stumbled onto a way of achieving huge savings at the outset of the production process.

But this realization sparked a much larger conceptual breakthrough, the basis for a solution to the fundamental problem, the tyranny of numbers: If all the parts of a circuit could be made from the same material, maybe they could all be manufactured on a single monolithic slab. If you wanted more complexity, you wouldn't need more components or more wiring and soldering to connect them.

On July 24, Kilby drew a rough sketch of the idea in his lab notebook and wrote, "The following circuit elements could be made on a single slice: resistors, capacitor, distributed capacitor, transistor." Thus was born the integrated circuit.

When Kilby's bosses got back from vacation, he briefed them on the idea. They were skeptical but intrigued, and asked him to put together a demonstration. Kilby scrounged the lab for spare parts and supplies and, within six weeks, managed to prepare a crude experiment. The device he improvised consisted of a tiny sliver of a conductive grayish metal called germanium, not quite a half-inch wide and one-sixteenth of an inch thick, protruding with thin wires and glued to a glass slide.

On September 12, 1958, Texas Instruments' executives gathered around Kilby's lab table. Kilby hooked up his device to an oscilloscope, pulled a switch, and the curve of a sine wave undulated endlessly across the oscilloscope's screen. The circuit was complete; it was generating an electrical signal. Kilby's invention worked. The tyranny of numbers suddenly went wobbly.

When the executives displayed Kilby's new circuit at the radio engineers' trade show in March 1959, they also called a press conference in the boardroom of the New York Athletic Club around the corner on Central Park South. There they demonstrated two different types of integrated circuits, each a quarter-inch long, an eighth of an inch wide, and one thirty-second of an inch thick—about the size of a match head—and each containing the equivalent of nearly a dozen transistors, resistors, and capacitors.

TI's president, Patrick Haggerty, put the achievement in context. Commercial products that used conventional circuits could stack a few thousand components into a cubic foot. Some military hardware was designed to accommodate fifty thousand components in a space that size; with the Army's most recent micro-miniaturized circuits, the number could be stretched, in theory, to half million. But the new TI integrated circuits were so thin, you could squeeze in 34 *million* components.

Haggerty proclaimed that this new solid circuit was the most significant development in electronics since the invention of the transistor itself. He told the gathered reporters that its greatest potential lay in the rapidly growing fields of computers, rockets, missiles, satellites, and space-vehicle instrumentation, where weight, size, and reliability were critical. But, he added, with remarkable prescience, that it might also revolutionize telephones, televisions, radios, radar, hearing aids, medical instruments, any and all machines involving automation.

The press corps didn't bite, or not very hard. Neither did many of his competitors' engineers milling along the corridors at the Coliseum. Extravagant claims were common at these trade shows; everyone had long ago learned to take them with a shaker of salt.

A story in the next day's *New York Times*, about the trade show in general, highlighted three new inventions on display. The integrated circuit was one of them, but it was mentioned last and took up just two paragraphs. The bulk of the story was devoted to a radar system designed by Westinghouse that would allow motorists to drive coast to coast with their hands off the steering wheel. Thin foil strips, coded in dots and dashes, would line the nation's highways; transmitter receivers, placed on every car's front bumper, would read and decode the strips, signaling the steering wheel to keep going straight or to turn. On paper, at a time when the interstate highway system was still in the early stages of construction, the idea seemed appealing, very futuristic. In the real-world future, it went nowhere.

There was no guarantee that the integrated circuits would get off the ground, either. In the beginning, they were very expensive. To make a dent in the marketplace, they'd have to be much cheaper; but to be cheaper, they would have to have made a big dent in the marketplace—there would have to be high demand, so that they could be produced in mass quantity. That wouldn't happen until the beginning of the sixties, when President John Kennedy ordered production of the Minuteman II missile—which required tiny, reliable circuits for its guidance system—and, especially, when he set the goal of putting a man on the moon by the end of the decade. Missiles and space created the large demand. In 1961, a single chip cost $32. By 1971, thanks to the economies of large-scale production, the cost would plunge to $1.25. (By 2000, after the consumer market had vastly expanded, the price of a much more powerful chip would be less than a nickel.)

As with many of the breakthroughs converging on the eve of the sixties, the space race and the arms race—the twin prospects of infinite expansion and instant annihilation—spurred America and the world into a lightning-flash new era.

• • •

Just over six months after Texas Instruments introduced the microchip, Thomas J. Watson Jr., the president of International Business Machines, held the world's largest closed-circuit television broadcast, beamed from IBM's headquarters in White Plains, New York, to nearly fifty thousand corporate executives at offices and hotel rooms in ninety-two cities across the nation. The purpose was to announce the IBM 1401, the first small, low-cost, high-speed data-processing system—the first modern computer.

The computer was still an exotic device. At the start of the decade, only twenty computers existed in the entire United States, most of them for military purposes. In 1954, General Electric became the first private company to take delivery of a computer—the UNIVAC, or Universal American Computer, built by the Eckert-Mauchly Computer Corporation. The UNIVAC was a beast of a machine. Powered by eight thousand vacuum tubes, it stood eight feet tall, took up 220 square feet of floor space, and weighed five tons. Even by the end of the decade, few companies could afford one.

By contrast, the IBM 1401 took up just thirty-four square feet of floor space and weighed one and a half tons. In the course of a

single minute, it could perform 193,000 additions of eight-digit numbers and read 800 punch cards of encoded information. Magnetic
tape reels processed data at a speed of 15,000 characters per second.
The 1403 printer, which was sold alongside the 1401, could print
600 lines—or 232 two-line documents, such as payroll checks—each
minute. The system cost $78,800 (the equivalent of nearly a half mil-
lion dollars today) or $1,450 a month to rent.

By the standards of a few decades later, these numbers seem gargantuan, but for a medium-sized company of the late fifties through
mid-sixties, the 1401—which could handle payroll, retail accounting,
freight accounting, and railway reservations—was a marvel of efficiency.

The biggest customer, as expected, was the federal government,
especially the Social Security Administration and the military. The
Peace Corps would use a 1401 to match volunteers with the needs
of undeveloped countries. By 1965, the final year of production for
the 1401, IBM had built and sold ten thousand units—more than
half the number of computers, of all sizes, brands, and models, in the
entire United States.

When the computer was combined with the microchip, IBM and
other fledgling companies could make machines that were dramatically
smaller, lighter, and cheaper. Those trends spurred a spike in demand,
which created economies of scale in production and spawned competition among companies, which together made models smaller, lighter,
and cheaper still—and on and on the spiral swirled, to the point where
a wafer-thin laptop now processes millions of times more data, millions
of times faster, than a room-sized bank of computers could have managed fifty years ago, and for a microscopic fraction of the cost.

•   •   •

Between the launching of Texas Instruments' chip and IBM's
1401—on June 8, 1959, to be precise, at 9:10 A.M.—the submarine USS *Barbero* surfaced nearly a hundred miles off the coast of
Florida and fired a Regulus I guided cruise missile toward the shore.
Fitted with retractable landing gear, so that it could be recovered
and reused for testing, the missile touched down at the Mayport
Naval Auxiliary Air Station, near Jacksonville. Flight time: twenty-
one minutes.

Packed into the missile's nose cone were two small metal boxes containing three thousand envelopes, each stamped with a logo that read: "First Official Missile Mail."

The experiment was the brainchild of Arthur Summerfield, the U.S. postmaster general. Summerfield had gained notoriety in recent months for confiscating copies of *Lady Chatterley's Lover* after declaring the book "obscene." As the Regulus took flight, Barney Rosset—the owner of Grove Press, which had published the book— was suing Summerfield in a Manhattan federal court.

But, like most people, Summerfield was also enchanted by the "space age" and dreamed up the idea of "missile mail" as his chance to join in the adventure. The Defense Department agreed to coop- erate for its own reasons. First, the experiment would serve as a nice gambit in the Cold War, a high-profile demonstration of a new American missile's pinpoint accuracy. Second, it might boost domes- tic political support for the Regulus, as a missile that could serve civil- ian as well as military ends.

In the letter folded inside each of those three thousand enve- lopes, which were addressed to officials from President Eisenhower on down, Summerfield hailed the achievement as "an historic mile- stone" in speeding "communications between the peoples of the earth." Speaking to reporters after the Regulus flight, he predicted that guided missiles "may ultimately provide a solution to problems of swifter mail delivery for international mails, for isolated areas where other transportation is infrequent, as well as supplementary high priority service to big population centers." He added, "I believe we will see missile mail developed to a significant degree before man has reached the moon."

The dream turned out to be no more than that. There were no more missile-mail flights after this one. The Navy wasn't interested in the project as anything more than a onetime gimmick. The costs were too high, the benefits too meager.

However, it typified the era's yearning for instantaneity, for the obliteration of time and space. And it foreshadowed the impulse that—decades later, when fused with the computer and the microchip— inspired the creation of the Internet.

11

The Assault on the Chord

On March 2, 1959, at two-thirty in the afternoon, the trumpeter Miles Davis and his five bandmates stepped up to the microphones at Columbia Records' Thirtieth Street Studio—a former Greek Orthodox church on the east side of Manhattan, harboring a cavernous room one hundred feet square with high ceilings and acoustically warm wood—to lay down the first tracks of an album called *Kind of Blue*. It turned out to be a perfect jazz album: at once swinging, bluesy, intellectually intense, and melodically lyrical, completely spontaneous yet not a step out of place. There has been nothing in jazz, and little in any other creative realm, like it—a huge popular success (the best-selling jazz album of all time) and also the spearhead of an artistic revolution.

When Miles Davis recorded the album, Charlie Parker, the chief architect of modern jazz, the greatest alto saxophonist ever, had been dead for four years—almost exactly to the day—ravaged by heroin and booze at the age of thirty-four. And the denizens of jazz were still waiting, longing, for a successor, "the next Charlie Parker," to remake the music anew.

Along with his trumpeter and sidekick Dizzy Gillespie, Parker had launched the jazz revolution known as bebop. Their concept was to take a standard blues or ballad and to devise a whole new melody on the basis of its chord changes. In itself, this was nothing new. Jazz musicians had long been improvising variations on popular songs that hardly referred to the original melody. Coleman Hawkins, the husky tenor saxophonist of the swing era, had developed this art most prominently in the late thirties with his sinuous improvisation on the show tune "Body and Soul." But Parker and Gillespie—Bird and Diz, they were called—took the concept to a new level, extending the chords to more intricate patterns, building new chords on top of those patterns, and improvising new melodies on top of those chords. They would play these melodies in darting, syncopated phrases, and at breakneck tempo, in a flurry of sixteenth notes (not four steady counts in a bar, as with most jazz solos, but sixteen fast ones), bar after bar after bar, no two phrases sounding the same, all the while never losing their instinctive swing or their grip on the blues.

Listening to the two at their peak was a drenching experience. Many young musicians came away dreading the choice to be made. They could play the way Bird and Diz played; they could consign themselves to the ranks of "moldy figs," the squares of the day; or, as many did, they could put away their instruments and find another line of work.

In the forties, bebop provided a way out of the swing music that had calcified during the war years. By the mid-fifties, bebop was calcifying, too. There were only so many chords that you could lay down in a twelve-bar blues or thirty-two-bar song and only so many variations that you could play on those chords. Shortly before his death, even Parker wondered out loud if there might be something beyond chord-based ballads and blues.

Miles Davis started playing professional jazz trumpet in 1945, at the age of nineteen, as a sideman in Parker's quintet. The son of a middle-class black dentist in East St. Louis, Illinois, Davis went to New York to attend the Juilliard School of Music, but dropped out in his first year, studying instead at the jazz clubs on West Fifty-second Street. He'd come to the city to look for Parker, whom he'd met a few years earlier when the Billy Eckstine Orchestra, which then featured Parker and Gillespie, played in his hometown. By the time Davis arrived, the two had parted ways. Gillespie had started a bebop big band. Parker needed a new trumpeter for his quintet; in Davis, who couldn't play as high or as fast as Diz, he found one who served as more a contrast than a complement to his style.

Like most young musicians on Fifty-second Street, Davis fell under Parker's shadow—including, for a while, his addiction to heroin—but he was always on the lookout for new ideas. Soon after arriving in New York, he met George Russell, a jazz drummer and aspiring composer just in from Cincinnati, who shared his enthusiasm for modern classical music. They would get together and study piano scores by Bartok, Berg, and Stravinsky. Davis once told Russell that he wanted to learn "all the chord changes" and wondered how to go about doing that. At first, Russell didn't understand the remark; clearly, Miles knew how to play all the chords and how to progress from one chord to another. After a while, though, he realized that what Miles was seeking was a new approach to chords, a new way to arrange them and align them with melodies.

Soon after they met, Russell contracted tuberculosis, which forced him to spend the next fourteen months at St. Joseph's Hospital in the Bronx. A nun showed him a piano in the hospital's library, which was almost always empty. He went there nearly every day to play. Once, as Davis was leaving after a visit, he said, "Find me some new notes, George."

With endless time on his hands, Russell embarked on an obsessive study of chords and scales. Digging into music books that friends brought him, he delved into all kinds of scales, including scales—or "modes"—from church music that composers hadn't drawn on for two hundred years. At first he experimented with ways to link certain chords with certain scales. Gradually, he realized that harmonies could consist of scales *instead of* chords.

This approach required a new way not only of playing, but of thinking about how to play. When a bebop musician improvised, the chord changes served as a compass; they pointed the direction to the next bar or the next phrase. Chords followed a particular pattern; you knew what the next chord would be; you knew that the notes you'd play would consist of the notes that comprised that chord, or some variation on them. Playing blues, you also knew that this sequence of chord changes would be finished in twelve bars, and then you'd either end your solo or start the sequence again. You could take flighty excursions on your solo—Parker and Gillespie took some of the flightiest on record—but the structure of the chords determined, or at least strictly limited, which notes you could play, for how long, and how far you could take them.

Improvising on scales seemed, at first glance, easier. You didn't have to hurdle all those chords, didn't have to hone your art to such tight demands. But in another sense it was more challenging. The compass was thrown out the window, or rather its needle was spinning in multiple directions. You could play all the notes of the scale, not just those that made up a chord. You had to find your own way, carve your own path, on the spot. Or, as Russell put it, *"you are free to do anything"* (the italics were his), "as long as you know where home is"—as long as you knew where you were going to wind up. The trick was to fuse the freedom and the discipline, so that what you played sounded neither chaotic nor too controlled, and you still wound up where you started.

Over a period of several years, Russell elaborated his ideas into a full-blown theory, which he spelled out in a book called *The Lydian Chromatic Concept of Tonal Organization for Improvisation.* "The concept," he wrote, "provides the possibilities. It is for the musician to sing his own song really, without having to meet the deadline of a particular chord."

Russell published a brief statement of the idea in 1953, then a more elaborate text, crammed with dozens of musical charts and tables, in 1959. The larger edition was filled with space-age metaphors. (An album that Russell recorded around this time was called *Jazz in the Space Age.*) He wrote of "tonal gravity" and the connections between the law of music and the law of the cosmos. Mastering his theory, he wrote, "will liberate the student's melodic inhibitions and help him to intelligently penetrate and understand the entire chromatic universe."

Miles Davis was well primed to be the ideal student. He fully grasped the theory's implications at once, and used it in the way Russell intended: not as an alternate rulebook but as a vehicle for exploring his own sound. As far back as 1948, after leaving Parker's band to become a leader himself, Davis had fallen in with a circle of innovative composers—John Lewis, Gerry Mulligan, and especially Gil Evans—who met regularly, usually in Evans's one-room basement apartment on West Fifty-fifth Street, to sketch out a new orchestral approach to jazz. (Russell, just out of the hospital, was part of this group, too.) These meetings culminated in the formation of a nine-piece band—which included such unconventional instruments as French horn, tuba, and baritone saxophone along with the usual alto sax, trumpet, trombone, piano, bass, and drums. Davis was the leader; Evans, Lewis, and Mulligan were the arrangers. The music was still based primarily on chords, but it placed a greater premium on tonal colors and lush harmonies than on blues patterns or speed. The band recorded twelve compositions. It wasn't until a few years later, in 1953, that these tracks were combined into a ten-inch LP called *The Birth of the Cool*, which sparked the fifties' "cool jazz" movement, especially on the West Coast. But by then, the ensemble had disbanded; it had played only two gigs, lasting a few weeks, during its single year of existence.

After the band broke up, Davis went back to playing variations on bebop—at first a more soulful version with a backbeat that some called "hard bop," then a softer, more romantic approach, in which he played popular show tunes like "Love for Sale" and "My Funny Valentine," often with a Harmon mute in the bell of his horn, which coated his sound with a burnished glow.

This return to balladry coincided with two major changes in Davis's life. First, in 1954, he kicked his heroin addiction, thus escaping Parker's most baleful influence. Second, in March 1955, Parker himself died; the music's driving force, the man that all modern jazz musicians turned to for a sign of where to turn next, was gone. Like everybody else, Davis was definitively out on his own. That summer, he appeared at the Newport Jazz Festival as a last-minute add-on, and he played the hell out of Thelonious Monk's "'Round About Midnight." The crowd cheered wildly, recognizing the performance as Miles's comeback. George Avakian, the head of Columbia Records' jazz and popular music division, was in the audience. Davis went up to him and said, "Sign me up, George." Avakian offered him a contract on the spot.

Davis had been recording for Prestige, a small label known for hiring all the best junkie jazzmen, who were attracted by the quick sessions and the immediate, though meager, pay. Columbia, by contrast, was where the jazz stars sparkled, and in the pre-Beatles era, these stars—Dave Brubeck, Louis Armstrong, and Duke Ellington—were *pop* stars. They were rich and famous, and now Miles Davis was joining their ranks.

But there was still the post-Parker question: What was the new direction in jazz?

John Lewis, one of the composers on *The Birth of the Cool*, had since formed a chamber-jazz group called the Modern Jazz Quartet, which had grown out of—and itself marked a dramatic departure from—Dizzy Gillespie's bebop big band. In the late fifties, Lewis and Gunther Schuller, a fellow composer and musician, jump-started a new movement that they called "Third Stream," which combined the cadences and improvisation of jazz with the complex structures and harmonies of twentieth-century classical music. Davis was intrigued and took part in some of their recording sessions. But ultimately he found the synthesis dissatisfying; it was too dry, it didn't swing. He said that listening to it was like "looking at a naked woman that you *don't like.*"

In 1958, George Russell was well along in developing his theory; the latest, much-expanded edition of *The Lydian Chromatic Concept* was nearly completed. One night, he sat down with Miles at a piano and showed him the possibilities that the concept allowed. It answered Miles's puzzle of a decade earlier—how to link chords with scales, in almost unlimited ways. Miles was bowled over. Maybe this was the way out of bebop's cul de sac. "Man," he told Russell, "if Bird was alive, this would kill him."

That summer, with the resources of Columbia behind him, Davis recorded an ambitious project with Gil Evans—a jazz orchestration of Gershwin's *Porgy and Bess*, which harkened back to their *Birth of the Cool* sessions but featured a much bigger ensemble, airier harmonies, and more propulsive melodies. There was something else new about Evans's sound—George Russell's influence. Evans's arrangement of "I Love You, Porgy" was built around just two chords. On "Summertime," there was a long passage where the chord didn't change at all.

His meeting with Russell and his recording with Gil Evans marked a new phase for Davis. In an interview that year with the jazz critic Nat Hentoff, he extolled the virtues of playing off scales instead of chords. "When you go this way," Davis explained, "you can go on forever. You don't have to worry about changes, and you can do more with time.

It becomes a challenge to see how melodically inventive you are. When you're based on chords, you know at the end of thirty-two bars that the chords have run out and there's nothing to do but repeat what you've done, with variations.

"I think," he went on, "a movement in jazz is beginning, away from the conventional string of chords and a return to emphasis on melodic rather than harmonic variations. There will be fewer chords but infinite possibilities as to what to do with them."

Davis needed one more element before he could go the full distance with this approach—a pianist who knew how to accompany without playing chords. This was a challenge. Laying down the chords—supplying the frontline horn players with the chords that cued the twists and turns of their melodies, the compass that kept their improvisations from going too far astray—was what jazz pianists *did*; it was the modern jazz piano's main function. Davis needed a new pianist anyway; Red Garland, who'd been playing with him for the past few years, had a serious heroin addiction and was frequently late to club dates. Russell recommended someone he'd hired for a few sessions recently—an intense young white man with close-cropped hair and glasses named Bill Evans.

Bill Evans (no relation to Gil) was trained in classical piano at Southeastern Louisiana University's conservatory and at the Mannes College of Music. He had a particular penchant for the French impressionist composers, like Ravel and Debussy, whose harmonies floated airily above the melody line. When Evans first started playing jazz, he tended not to play the "root" of a chord; for instance, when playing a C chord, he would avoid playing the C note. Instead, he would play some other note in or hovering around the chord, *suggesting* the chord without locking himself to its restraints. This tendency is what attracted him to Russell, who at the time was mounting, as he put it, "an assault on the chord." Russell took Davis to see Evans play at a jazz club in Brooklyn. During a break between sets, Davis asked him to join his band.

There was another force pushing Davis to join Russell's assault on the chord—a growing consciousness, as a black American, of his African roots and a desire to explore that culture, especially its music. Davis and his girlfriend at the time, Frances Taylor, had recently gone to a concert by Ballet Africaine, a dance troupe from Guinea,

and he was entranced by the accompanying musicians—their unconventional, shifting rhythms and the presence of a kalimba player, who
played melodies built on distinctively African scales. Davis wanted
to capture that loose sound, a sound that, as he put it later, was
"freer, more modal, more African or Eastern and less Western." He
was aiming for a sound with the *feel* of blues but not necessarily the
strict form of blues, with its rigid sequence of chords. In other words,
he wanted to create music that was—hence the album's title—*kind
of* blue.

He figured that maybe he could do it with a pianist like Bill Evans.

The recording was spread out over two sessions, the first on
March 2, the second on April 22. At each session, when he arrived at
the Thirtieth Street Studio, Davis passed around sheet music that was
sketchier than usual. It didn't contain finished compositions or even
"heads"—the first twelve or so bars of a tune, with the chords notated
above—but instead just the notes of some scales, on which the players were expected to improvise. For one song, "Flamenco Sketches,"
Bill Evans (who composed at least two of the album's tracks, without credit) had jotted down the notes of five scales, each of which
expressed a slightly different mood. At the top of the sheet, he wrote,
"Play in the sound of these scales."

It was an oddly vague instruction—nothing about how long to
improvise on one of the scales or how to segue into the next one—
and it seemed especially bizarre to the two saxophone players on
the date, John Coltrane on tenor and Julian "Cannonball" Adderley
on alto. The two had been playing with Miles for the past year.
(Coltrane had also played with him a few years earlier; he quit to join
Thelonious Monk's quintet, then came back.) Their last album with
Davis, called *Milestones*, recorded in the spring of 1958, had veered
toward a modal approach—it was the first time he'd adopted some of
Russell's ideas—but this session was leaping several steps beyond.

Coltrane was thirty-two, the same age as Davis, and much more
intense, restlessly seeking the right sound, the right note, as if he were
on a spiritual quest and his life hung in the balance. But like most
other jazz players of the day, he mapped his voyage on charts of
chords, piling and inverting chords on top of chords, expanding
each note of a chord into its own chord, not knowing which combinations might work and therefore trying them all. His specialty was

the blues—his most successful album as a leader up until then was called *Blue Trane*, recorded two years earlier—but it was blues like no other ever heard, frantically fast and preternaturally precise. If Parker commonly split a bar into sixteen notes, Coltrane sometimes crammed it with thirty-two. The critic Ira Gitler described Coltrane's style as "sheets of sound." George Russell, in *The Lydian Chromatic Concept*, likened his sound to "a rocket ship" that "soars into the chromatic universe."

Yet rather than disorient him, as might have been expected, this session's shift from chords to scales sent Coltrane on a new, more sweeping trajectory. He still unfurled his sheets of sound, but since he no longer had to meet what Russell called "the deadline of a particular chord," he could vary his pace, focus more on rhythm, mood, and melody; his solos, while as virtuosic as ever, were more lyrical and lithe.

Adderley was still less suited to this music. He played very much in the bebop style; his tone, a controlled wail, was similar to Parker's but with a rhythm-and-blues cadence and a gospel-laced vibrato. He was two years younger than Davis and Coltrane, agile but less adventurous, ill at ease without a pianist laying down the chords. Evans didn't play the chords; at most, he suggested them; more often, he coaxed tone clusters and chromatic colors from the keyboard, like a jazz-trained Ravel. Yet, Adderley found himself, like Coltrane, settling into this groove, stretching out, expressing more freely the *feeling* of the blues.

And Miles—freed from the final traces of Parker's grip—uncoiled his most limber, graceful, fully realized lines in fourteen years of making music. By the standards of bebop, or of his own previous excursions, Miles played soft, slow, and almost entirely in the middle octaves, where his strength as a trumpeter shone. Yet from a handful of sketches and scales, he improvised complete melodies that were at once simple and complex—haunting, gorgeous, melancholic, soothing, yet riveting. And, set against the probing turbulence of the saxophone solos, the tension had a gleaming knife-sharp edge.

Kind of Blue turned out to be a singularity, an expression of purity and a convergence of sensibilities that would never be replicated. Soon after, Coltrane went his own way and evolved into the most daring jazz improviser of the next decade. Evans left to form one of the most influential piano trios. Adderley started his own band, as well, retreating to his earlier style of soulful bop, though he took away some modal inspiration, occasionally hiring Evans to play as a sideman. Miles himself, after a few years of looking around for the ideal new bandmates, finally found them—in saxophonist Wayne Shorter, pianist Herbie Hancock, bassist Ron Carter, and drummer Tony Williams—and ripped ahead through the next frontier. Other pathbreakers showed up along the way, challenging his primacy and mounting more radical assaults on traditional structures. But the *Kind of Blue* sessions in the spring of 1959 were the ones that broke down the barriers and opened the gates for the chaos and revelations that followed.

12

Revolutionary Euphoria

On the evening of April 15, 1959, Fidel Castro, the new leader of Cuba, landed at National Airport in Washington, D.C., and for the next two weeks—on a whirlwind tour that covered the capital, New York City, Boston, and Houston—he enthralled millions of Americans with a spectacle unseen in their lifetimes. Here, it seemed, was something new under the sun: an independent revolutionary—claiming to be neither Communist nor capitalist—who rose to power without the help of Washington or Moscow and who, therefore, might be the one to carve a new path, a breakout, from the Cold War's grinding duel.

Castro's guerrilla army, commanded by Ernesto "Che" Guevara and Camilo Cienfuegos, had marched into Havana on New Year's Day, just hours after Cuba's dictator, Fulgencio Batista, fled under siege. Starting as a small band of radical nationalists in the Sierra Maestra mountains, Castro and his men had built a genuinely populist movement and army, which gained steam as they marched up the island toward the capital, defeating Batista's troops in battles and skirmishes, rallying support among the poor and middle-class alike, and taking over towns and villages along the way.

For years, Batista had willingly turned Cuba into an American annex, granting favorable terms to U.S. corporations and allowing Mafia chieftains to operate casinos and nightclubs. Castro's ultimate aims were unclear. Many in his entourage were Communists, some openly sympathetic to Moscow, but Fidel himself seemed to be his own man. The U.S. ambassador to Cuba, Philip Bonsal, urged Washington to give Castro a chance. The CIA station chief agreed. And so, on January 7, the United States became the second country, after Venezuela, to recognize the revolutionary regime. Two months later, in a cordial conversation with Bonsal, Castro expressed interest in visiting the States in the spring.

Castro's trip took its cues from Anastasas Mikoyan's visit from Moscow three months earlier. Certainly Castro was conscious of the precedent. At one point during the trip, he looked around at the two hundred uniformed policemen guarding him, and marveled, "I'm getting more cops than Mikoyan!"

He was a far more engaging, charismatic figure than the elderly, dapper Mikoyan. Just thirty-one years old, sporting green army fatigues and a scruffy beard, Castro strolled along the Washington Mall, paying respects to the Lincoln Monument and the Jefferson Memorial, eating ice cream cones, kissing babies, signing autographs, waving to students on buses (many of whom shouted, "Hi, Fidel!") and chatting—in heavily accented but fluent English—with anyone who approached him. In New York, he lunched with Wall Street bankers, fed a Bengal tiger at the Bronx Zoo, and spoke before thirty thousand people at a nighttime rally in Central Park. Later, in Houston, he accepted a blue-blooded quarter horse as a gift and granted oilman Frank Water permission to make a movie about the revolution. (Water wanted to cast Marlon Brando as Castro and Frank Sinatra as his brother, Raul. The project never got off the ground.)

Just as Mikoyan wanted to reassure the Americans after Khrushchev's bellicose threats against Berlin, Castro wanted to convince the same Americans that he wasn't a Soviet agent and that, therefore, they shouldn't invade his fledgling nation.

During a conversation with a group of teenagers in a downtown park, one of them asked, "What do you call your government—'socialism' or what?" Castro replied, "Cubanism!" In a meeting at the Capitol with eighteen members of the Senate Foreign Relations Committee, he exclaimed, "We have no interest in expropriating U.S. property." When anyone would ask about the Communists in his government, he would wave his hand and say, "Their influence is nothing." Pressed about his cabinet's firing squads, which had executed 521 people so far, he would insist that the men shot were "war criminals" and that this phase of his rule would soon be over. He promised that Cuba would soon have a free press and, within four years, free elections.

Castro had been invited to the States by the American Society of Newspaper Editors, which asked him to speak at its annual luncheon. His appearance sparked the group's highest demand for tickets since General Douglas MacArthur spoke after returning from Korea. The editors received Castro with tentative applause as he walked to the podium—and enthusiastic cheers when he walked away after finishing his speech two hours later.

To a far greater degree than Mikoyan, who for all his charms was still the enemy, Castro—in part because the book was still open on precisely who, or what, he was—sparked dreamlike reverie from much of the American press corps.

A *New York Times* editorial exclaimed, "This young man is larger than life." Another called his revolution "one of the most remarkable phenomena in the history of Latin America." The *Times* reporter who covered his visit to Washington wrote that even skeptics were "dazed." Castro, he explained, had swept into the capital "not only out of another world, the world of fierce Latin passion, but also out of another century—the century of Sam Adams and Patrick Henry and Tom Paine and Thomas Jefferson. Perhaps," the reporter went on, "because he stirred memories, long dimmed, of a revolutionary past, and recalled a new order once deeply felt ('Bliss was it in that dawn to be alive, but to be young was very heaven'), Fidel Castro succeeded in achieving a suspension of disbelief—at least partial and temporary."

The suspension did not last long. Even while Castro was drawing huge crowds in New York, the *Times*'s Havana correspondent was reporting that Communists were organizing in every Cuban town and infiltrating every trade union. The report reflected a dispatch that the U.S. embassy had sent the day before Castro embarked on his trip. Even so, Ambassador Bonsal believed there were still "many opportunities" for "discreetly influencing Castro," and suggested giving the Cubans as much time as possible to straighten our their problems "before unlimbering our artillery."

Christian Herter, who was the acting secretary of state while John Foster Dulles lay in a hospital dying of cancer, agreed. Herter hosted a champagne-and-steak lunch for Castro and his entourage—most of them security guards decked out, like their boss, in green fatigues and long beards.

President Eisenhower, perhaps remembering Mikoyan's blindsiding, arranged to be away, playing golf in Augusta, Georgia, for all five days that Castro was in Washington. Herter told the president afterward that it was a shame the two didn't meet. Castro, he said, was a "most interesting individual," adding that he spoke in English with restraint and personal appeal but that, when reverting to his native Spanish, he turned voluble, even "wild." Eisenhower laughed and recalled that Jawaharlal Nehru, the prime minister of India, had once said that when Arab leaders speak in public, the crowds get worked up in a frenzy, which excites the speaker to a greater frenzy still. It was an odd remark: wild Cubans, wild Arabs—did Eisenhower think they were, for all practical purposes, the same?

Vice President Richard Nixon did meet with Castro, for two and a half hours on a Sunday afternoon at his office inside the all-but-deserted Capitol building. He was impressed with Castro's charisma but little else. In a summary of his conversation afterward, he wrote that Castro was "either incredibly naïve about Communism or under Communist discipline—my guess is the former"—and that his ideas on how to run an economy or a government were "less developed than those of almost any world figure I have met in fifty countries." Still, Nixon concluded, "he has the power to lead," and so "we have no choice but to try to orient him in the right direction."

However, Nixon's notion of "the right direction"—which coincided with that of every other U.S. official—was exactly where Castro did not want to go: aligning firmly with the West in the Cold War struggle against Communism; keeping doors wide open to foreign investors; and taking loans from the International Monetary Fund in exchange for maintaining a free market economy and strict fiscal discipline.

The very hope that Castro inspired—that a country in the Caribbean might stay unaligned to either superpower—was itself a source of deep concern in Washington. Even Ambassador Bonsal worried about Castro's "benevolent tolerance" toward Communism. The State Department's top regional specialist warned of Castro's tendency toward "nationalistic neutralism, which the Communist will exploit to the fullest."

As far back as his days in the Sierra Maestra mountains, all of Castro's closest comrades—his brother Raul, Che Guevara, Camilo Cienfuegos, and others—were Marxists or Communist Party members. Fidel was probably not in their camp as yet. But his economic policies were bound to alienate the United States. When he took power, Cuba had only a few months' worth of reserves in hard currency and gold. He would need economic assistance, and military protection, from somebody. At first, he sent Guevara to Asia and Africa, in search of assistance from the "nonaligned" nations. When their pockets proved empty, the Soviet Union seemed a logical source, if the Kremlin was willing to take the gamble.

Back in March 1959, a month before Castro flew to Washington, he seized the Cuba Telephone Company, which had been owned by the American corporation ITT. In May, two weeks after returning from his trip, he signed the Agrarian Reform Law, which expropriated foreign-owned property and barred foreign businesses unless they turned over their shares to Cubans. None of this should have been surprising; nor did it necessarily imply a connection to Moscow. Land reform was Castro's rallying cry on his path to power. The United States had held dominion over Cuba since 1898. The revolution was, at least in part, about independence from the empire to the north.

Still, in a telegram to the State Department, Ambassador Bonsal wrote that the law had been pushed by Cuba's most radical faction, which included Che Guevara, and that Son Marin, the relatively moderate minister of agriculture, had opposed it. An official at the State Department replied to Bonsal with a telegram, noting that Castro's law was causing "great consternation" among U.S. officials and sugar-company executives.

The Sugar Act was coming up for renewal in the U.S. Congress. This was the law, passed during Batista's time, guaranteeing that 70 percent of American sugar imports would come from Cuba. On June 1, an interagency group of officials discussed the issue and agreed that Eisenhower should not ask Congress to renew the bill. All told, U.S. companies had $9 billion invested in Latin America. Every country in the hemisphere was waiting to see how Washington reacted to Cuba's expropriation. Tolerance might endanger corporate holdings in those other countries, as well. The president should at least wait to see what Castro did next.

It didn't take much waiting. The same month that Fidel flew to Washington, his brother Raul sent an assistant to Moscow to ask for help in creating a Marxist-Leninist cadre within the new Cuban army. The Kremlin dispatched a regiment of former officers who'd fought in the Spanish Civil War. Several months later, in October 1959, Aleksandr Alekseyev, a senior KGB agent, visited Cuba to discuss supplying the island with economic assistance and weapons. Soon after, Fidel put Raul in charge of a new Ministry of Revolutionary Armed Forces, which prompted a spate of Cuban defections to the United States, and the defectors confirmed intelligence about Havana's new relationship with the Soviet Union.

Finally, in November 1959, the Eisenhower administration secretly decided to overthrow the Cuban government. A State Department memo to the president noted that it was now futile to "hope that Castro will voluntarily adopt policies and attitudes consistent with minimum United States security requirements and policy interests." Eisenhower agreed. Allen Dulles, Foster's brother and the director of the Central Intelligence Agency, ordered plans for Castro's assassination on the grounds that no successor enjoyed "the same mesmeric appeal" and that, therefore, Fidel's disappearance "would greatly accelerate" the regime's collapse.

The lock between Moscow and Havana was sealed three months later, when Anastas Mikoyan, Khrushchev's emissary—and, more pertinent, the last of the Old Bolsheviks, the Party members who had fought alongside Lenin in 1917—visited Cuba to open a Soviet exhibition and came back ecstatic. "I felt as though I had returned to my childhood!" he reported to the Presidium. Fidel, he proclaimed, "is a genuine revolutionary—completely like us."

On August 7, 1960, Castro seized $750 million worth of American-owned properties in a single day, justifying the move as retaliation for U.S. "economic aggression," and declared that he would accept assistance from the Soviet Union and all other Communist nations "with gratitude."

The following month, he visited New York once more, for a session at the United Nations, and the atmosphere had chilled considerably. There were no casual strolls, no rhapsodic editorials, no rallies or speeches to the masses or the elites. At first, Castro and his entourage of fifty officials and bodyguards couldn't find any hotel rooms. UN officials pressured one Midtown hotel to offer quarters, but Castro stormed off after the manager demanded a $10,000 bond and accepted instead an invitation to stay at the Theresa Hotel up in Harlem, on 125th Street and Seventh Avenue, where the neighborhood's population of blacks and Latinos welcomed the Cubans with enthusiasm. And instead of holding one-on-one sessions with State Department officials and the mainstream press, Castro met with the radical Black Muslim leader Malcolm X and gave interviews to reporters from black newspapers, praising them for being less "brainwashed" by Washington propaganda than their white counterparts. Cubans, Africans, and American Negroes, he told them, were all in the same boat.

Khrushchev also dropped by the Theresa to visit Castro, calling him a "heroic man." The next morning, at the UN, Castro rose and cheered vigorously when the Soviet premier entered the General Assembly. Khrushchev in turn greeted Castro with a bear hug. Castro's boasts of an alliance with Moscow, which he'd made at rallies back home the previous month, were palpably confirmed.

And so began the cycle that, over the next few years, would culminate in some of the decade's most dangerous crises—the failed U.S. invasion at the Bay of Pigs and the U.S.-Soviet standoff over nuclear missiles that nearly triggered World War III.

Much of this was probably inevitable, and in this sense it's beside the point to speculate whether Castro was always a Communist, or exactly when he became one, or whether things might have gone differently if Eisenhower had met with him during the historic visit of April 1959, instead of fleeing to play golf. Given the nature of his revolution, Castro could not have caved to U.S. corporate interests or followed the IMF rulebook. Given the nature of mid-century American capitalism and foreign policy, no president would have tolerated such a revolution so close to home, especially once Che Guevara started trying to export it throughout the hemisphere. Given Cuba's scarce resources and its inability to survive on its own, Castro would have had to align with some larger power. And given the hardening of the world into two hostile blocs, the Soviet Union was bound to be that power. Whatever Castro's initial motives, he inescapably found himself boxed in a global game beyond any small nation's control.

• • •

Yet for several years more, despite these clear realities, Castro's Cuba was still seen by many as a beacon for the breakthroughs that might be possible. The most eloquent and influential of these boosters—hardheaded in some ways, romantic to the point of delusional in others—was a renegade sociologist named C. Wright Mills.

A boisterous Texan, six feet tall and broad-chested, Mills taught at Columbia University, a favorite professor among students but not so much among the faculty. He was provocative and ill-mannered when he wanted to be, and unabashedly radical, seeing sociology as a tool not just for social analysis but for political change.

Mills lived in Rockland County, just north of New York City, in a house that he built himself, and he would roar to campus on a BMW motorcycle, dressed in plaid shirts and jeans, looking more like a Beat poet than an Ivy League professor. His best-known books of the early to mid-fifties—*White Collar* and *The Power Elite*—were not only serious studies of America's class structure but also critiques of that structure. They were highly regarded, though controversial, in his field. And, most unusual for sociology books, they also sold well—in the case of *The Power Elite*, very well.

In March 1959, Mills published an essay called "Culture and Politics: The Fourth Epoch," in which he saw humanity moving into "a post-modern period." The previous era's major intellectual constructs—liberalism and socialism—no longer explained the world, Mills argued. The basic premise of the Enlightenment itself—that the rise of rationality goes hand in hand with the rise of freedom—was also in doubt. Rational organizations had grown remarkably complex; science and technology held a central place in society and culture. Yet people behaved no more reasonably, nor were they any less beholden to myth and superstition. In fact, Mills wrote, the instruments of rationality often served as "a means of tyranny and manipulation." They produced the Nazi death camps and the atomic bombs that leveled Hiroshima and Nagasaki. And the "brisk generals and gentle scientists" who were now "rationally—and absurdly—planning the weapons and the strategy of the Third World War" were also indisputably "efficient, rational, technically clean-cut." Thanks to modern science and technology, "men *can* now make history," but, by those same forces, the means of making history were becoming more and more centralized.

Mills meant his analysis to apply to both superpowers, which, for all their differences, were growing increasingly similar in that respect. The "very terms of their world antagonism"—the technological competition and the "military metaphysic" of atomic-war plans—were reinforcing this dehumanizing trend.

It was a deeply pessimistic view of the future—uncharacteristically so for Mills, who, though not at all rosy-eyed, was no cynic either.

And so, when Castro charged down from the mountains and took power through a popular revolution, completely apart from the epochal pattern, with no outside backing or allegiance, Mills saw a flicker of hope, a redemptive hero whose path might be the way out for humanity.

In the summer of 1960, Mills went down to Cuba with a portable tape recorder, interviewed many of Castro's officials and top supporters, and banged out a short paperback—more a political pamphlet, really—called *Listen, Yankee!* In his introduction, Mills described the Cuban revolutionary as "a new and distinct type of left-wing thinker and actor" who "is neither capitalist nor Communist." While Mills raised an eyebrow over Castro's tendency toward "absolute power," he regarded it as a brief phase. "I believe," he wrote, "that Cubans have a good chance to keep the society they are building practical and humane," if the United States left them alone.

The book sold 400,000 copies worldwide, but even his admiring biographer would later detect "a touch of mysticism" in Mills's view of Castro. A "willing victim" to "revolutionary euphoria," Mills had fallen prey to the "great illusion" that Cuba "could be a third way," some force that by determination alone could evade the Cold War's confines.

However, at the end of 1959, several months before his trip to Cuba, Mills began to write a more sober and nuanced—though still impassioned—essay that explored the broader, global implications of Castro's revolution. Titled "Letter to the New Left," it called for a clean break from the ideology that many of his intended readers—young intellectuals in the United States and England—still embraced. In an elaboration of his ideas in "Culture and Politics: The Fourth Epoch," he cautioned against viewing the Soviet Union as any sort of model. He'd recently been in Moscow, interviewing apparatchiks for a prospective book about the international power elite; the Kremlin, he noted, was at least as bureaucratized and stuffy as any capitalist power center.

More than that, Mills called for a break from Marxism itself. The working class, he wrote, was no longer an agent of change. Marx's idea of a proletarian vanguard was the residue of a social order, rooted in Victorian England, that no longer existed. The agents of change today, Mills proclaimed, somewhat self-servingly, were the intellectuals. "Who is it that is getting disgusted with what Marx called 'all the old crap'?" he asked. "All over the world—in the bloc, outside the bloc, and in between—the answer's the same: the young intelligentsia."

In Turkey, South Korea, Okinawa, and Tokyo, students were rioting in the streets against corruption, U.S. military bases, and atomic-weapons depots. In England, students were rallying for nuclear disarmament. Even in the American South, white students were joining with black men and women to protest segregation. And there was Cuba, where, as Mills put it, "a genuinely left-wing revolution begins full-scale economic reorganization—without the domination of U.S. corporations. Average age of its leaders: about 30"—and none of them were industrial workers.

When he wrote this article, Mills recognized that there was no New Left in the United States. There were only young cynics disaffected from politics, like the Beats, and former Old Leftists who interpreted the death of Marxist socialism as "the end of ideology." Mills saw that phrase—the title of a much-touted new book by another Columbia sociologist, Daniel Bell—as "a slogan of complacency" embraced by "the middle-aged" in "rich countries." Anyone who claimed the end of ideology in Africa, Asia, or Latin America would be laughed out of the room. By writing his essay, Mills hoped to jump-start an American New Left—a movement that would engage in direct, nonviolent action. "The Age of Complacency is ending," he wrote in his conclusion, banking more on hope than on data. "Let the old women complain wisely about 'the end of ideology.' We are beginning to move again."

And, as Norman Mailer was also grasping around this time, something *was* happening. Halfway across the country, Tom Hayden, the editor of the student newspaper at the University of Michigan in Ann Arbor, was among those creating an organization called the Students for a Democratic Society. Hayden read "Letter to the New Left" and felt that Mills was speaking to him directly. Hayden found Mills a compelling icon who seemed to combine, as he later put it, "the rebel life of James Dean and the moral position of Albert Camus" while also laying out "the comprehensive portrayal of the American condition" that he and his comrades were trying to capture themselves.

The SDS was formed as a splinter group from the student wing of the League for Industrial Democracy, an Old Left group led by former Communists who were disillusioned by Stalin but still caught up in party feuds—just the sort of group that Mills had dismissed as irrelevant to the era.

In March 1962, Mills died of a heart attack at the age of forty-five. When the news came, Hayden was writing *The Port Huron Statement*, the SDS manifesto, which would become the rallying cry for an American New Left movement. And its principles came straight out of C. Wright Mills's later writings—not his celebration of Cuba but, more broadly, his search for a way out of the Cold War nightmare.

Later in the sixties, as American cities erupted in flames and social structures crumbled, the New Left would collapse into violence and nihilism. But the movement's initial impulse was humanistic. *The Port Huron Statement* was an assault on "depersonalization," the "human degradation" of bigotry, "the enclosing fact of the Cold War" and the "common peril" of the A-bomb," which forced people to live with the fact that they "might die at any time" (an echo of Norman Mailer's "The White Negro" but infused with a youthful search for a political solution). The "estrangement" of modern life, Hayden wrote, "cannot be overcome by better personnel management, nor by improved gadgets" (pure Mills!), but only by a "participatory democracy," in which individuals could find "meaning in life that is personally authentic." The apparent contentment of many Americans, he continued, was really "a glaze" that covered over "deeply felt anxieties about their role in the world" and "a yearning to believe that there *is* an alternative to the present." The student movements that Mills enumerated, though still small and scattered, had the best chance of "breaking the crust of apathy" and organizing a real New Left to "start controversy across the land."

That controversy would grip the land, as would a New Left, as the Cold War hardened and a hot war in Southeast Asia began, both in the summer of 1959.

13

Breaking the Logjam,
Hitting the Wall

On July 7, 1959, the Soviet premier Nikita Khrushchev met in the
Kremlin with a group of American governors and told them that
he would like to visit the United States and meet face-to-face with
President Eisenhower. The next day, the *Washington Post* reported
Khrushchev's remark in a front-page story. Eisenhower was asked
about it at a press conference that morning. The question came as
a surprise—the president hadn't read the article—but afterward, he
called Christian Herter, his secretary of state, and told him to send
the premier an invitation. A talk, Eisenhower said, might be just the
thing to "break the logjam."

The logjam, of course, was the Cold War, with its spiraling arms
race, its crushing defense budgets, its militarization of the economy—
all of which Eisenhower, the old Army commander, found wasteful
and degenerative. He was angry at the current crop of generals for
spreading rumors of a "missile gap"—the idea that the Soviets were
ahead of the United States in intercontinental ballistic missiles—and
he was angry at Democratic senators for making political hay of
it all. Eisenhower knew that the top-secret intelligence didn't support the claim. He regarded the claim's very premise as absurd. To
his mind, there was no such thing as missile superiority. Once a great

power had enough nuclear weapons to make its adversaries behave prudently—enough to persuade them that if they launched a first strike, they would be hit back with a devastating counterblow—the contest was meaningless; there was no point in building any more.

Eisenhower had resisted Khrushchev's earlier requests for face-to-face talks, mainly on the stern advice of John Foster Dulles, who opposed negotiating with Communists as a matter of moral principle and who further argued that such a meeting would enhance Khrushchev's standing and undermine the solidarity of NATO.

But Dulles had died of cancer a month and a half earlier. Herter, who was more pragmatic, had no problem with the idea of talking with Khrushchev, and neither—the more he thought about it—did Eisenhower. Why not give it a chance? He sent the premier an invitation on July 10. Khrushchev accepted on July 21.

It would be the first time that any Soviet leader had ever visited the United States.

The agenda would be similar to Mikoyan's and Castro's. Khrushchev would meet briefly with American officials, tour the country for twelve days (at Mikoyan's urging, for humanizing purposes, he would bring his wife and children, who had always been kept out of public view in Moscow), and finish up with a serious talk—in Khrushchev's case, two days of talks at the Camp David retreat in the woods of Maryland—with the president.

Vice President Richard Nixon had already made his own ten-day trip to the Soviet Union in mid-July, to attend an exhibition of American consumer technology at Moscow's Skolniki Park. As a high point of that trip, Nixon gave Khrushchev a tour of the show, with special focus on the modern kitchen as a showcase of American capitalism. Khrushchev refused to be impressed, dismissing the Western wonders as either commonplace ("We have such things. . . . We are up with you on this, too. . . . We have steel workers and we have peasants who also can afford to spend fourteen thousand dollars for a house") or contemptible ("Don't you have a machine that puts food into the mouth and pushes it down? Many things you've shown us are interesting, but they are not needed in life. . . . They are merely gadgets").

The Nixon-Khrushchev encounter, which became known as "The Kitchen Debate," was a comic disaster. Nixon didn't know how to do this sort of thing; he came off like a nervous real-estate agent, trying to close a big sale. Khrushchev was a master of the game: boisterous, bellicose, brimming with energy, and funny.

In one sense, though, the debate had an effect. It revealed, in case anyone had doubts, that Russia was far behind America in technology and in living standards—and Khrushchev was so outrageously defensive, he must have known this, too.

Khrushchev and his entourage—sixty Russians in all, most of them officials and high party members—arrived at Andrews Air Force Base, outside Washington, on September 15. All three American television networks covered the landing live. The Russians had flown nonstop from Moscow in a Tupolev-114, an enormous four-engine turboprop plane, one-third larger than the Boeing 707. The plane was still in the experimental phase; its designers protested that it wasn't ready for such an important flight. But Khrushchev insisted; he wanted to show the Americans that the Soviets had built the world's biggest airplane. (The Soviet merchant marines stationed trawlers and cargo ships along the plane's flight path, with instructions to perform search-and-rescue missions if the plane crashed into the ocean.)

The day before his voyage, the Soviets launched the Lunik 2 space vehicle. Like the Lunik 1, which was launched right before Mikoyan's trip to America the previous January, it was meant to crash into the moon. The Lunik 1 had missed, though it went on to achieve something greater. This time, the Lunik hit the target; in fact, it scored a direct hit on the crater that it was aimed at.

The space flight was timed to coincide with Khrushchev's trip—as the Lunik 1 had been with Mikoyan's—and the premier made the most of it. "Mankind lives in a wonderful time today," he wrote in a message sent out on the official Tass wire service. "It is a time of the flourishing of science and technology . . . when fairy tales are becoming reality." Noting that his trip to America coincided with the Soviet Union's successful targeting of the moon, Khrushchev concluded, "Only people who deliberately shut their eyes and do not want to see the reality can have any doubts about the unlimited prospects that Communism opens up for the progress of mankind."

Yet, for all his bluster, Khrushchev knew that his country was in trouble. Since Mikoyan's trip eight months earlier, conditions had only worsened. Labor productivity was down. Agriculture production was off by 4 percent over the previous year. Khrushchev boasted about his missiles—he'd recently claimed that one plant was churning them out like sausages—but, in fact, his first two R-7 ICBMs were just coming off the production line, and the missile had been successfully tested only once. He confided to his son, Sergei, that if the Soviet Union were forced into an arms race with the United States, "we'll lose our pants."

And there was the crisis over Berlin. Mikoyan had come to Washington back in January to soften Khrushchev's bellicose demand the previous fall to end West Berlin's status as a Western enclave. Khrushchev had given the West six months to accept this new reality— or face war. Now the premier himself was coming to tell Eisenhower that he was suspending the ultimatum—as part of a wider plan to extract the Soviet Union from the Cold War's terrible trap.

The visit began testily. Security was so tight, Khrushchev wasn't allowed to go out and shake hands with the American people. He was constantly on the go, but he felt imprisoned. When his motorcade passed through the streets of Washington and New York, hundreds of people lined the sidewalks, but they neither cheered nor booed; they just stared, in curiosity. Khrushchev found the reaction strange, but he told one of his escorts that he understood it. Many people in the Soviet Union had never seen a camel; if you paraded a camel in front of them, they'd come out and see it, maybe pull its tail. He was a Communist camel in the citadel of capitalism; people will come out and gaze at him, maybe pull his tail.

And Khrushchev, of course, was more than a camel, more than just an unusual spectacle. He was *the* enemy, the stubby, scowling Communist who, just two years earlier, had bellowed to a gathering of Western diplomats, "We will bury you!" Even if the phrase was mistranslated—"We will outlive you" would have been more accurate—the implication was only somewhat less alarming. His ideology was wrapped up with the collapse of the Western way of life, and, given the widespread impression that the Soviets were outgunning the West in every area of competition—especially in space and in missiles—that seemed to be the way things were heading. There was hope surrounding Khrushchev's visit, but also apprehension.

On the West Coast, the trip turned outright sour. Khrushchev wanted to visit Disneyland, but American security officials wouldn't let him. "Is there an epidemic of cholera or something?" he asked them, fuming. "Or have gangsters taken hold of the place?" Still angry, he moved on to a tour of Twentieth Century-Fox Studios in Hollywood, only to get into a fierce argument with Spyros Skouras, the studio's president, over the merits of capitalism versus Communism.

Finally, on the train from Los Angeles to San Francisco, Henry Cabot Lodge, the U.S. ambassador to the United Nations, who had been assigned to escort Khrushchev across the country, suggested to the security detail that they treat the trip more like a political campaign—hold some whistle-stops on the way, let him get out and meet the people, have a drink or two with the reporters on the back cars of the train, get a taste of America. Lodge said he would take personal responsibility for the premier's safety.

Suddenly the trip turned pleasant. Khrushchev got out at Santa Barbara, talked with smiling people on the streets, shook their hands. In San Francisco, he went all over, unimpeded, to similar greetings. "I have seen some real live Americans," Khrushchev beamed to reporters afterward. "It seems they are just as real and as good as our kind Soviet people."

Before going back to Washington, he flew to Des Moines, Iowa, then drove to the small town of Coon Rapids, to visit a farmer named Roswell "Bob" Garst. Khrushchev and Garst had been corresponding for years. During the Depression, Garst led the movement to boost food production by using nitrogen as a fertilizer. In the mid-fifties, he traveled to the Soviet Union, promoting the idea of improving East-West relations through agricultural exchanges. In 1958, Khrushchev sent top food officials to spend three months at Garst's farm, learning his techniques. Now he wanted to meet the great man himself.

Khrushchev came away from the meeting elated—full of ideas to pass on to collective farm managers back home—but also disheartened by just how far behind the Soviet Union really was. Even back in San Francisco, he told Lodge that he admired and envied Americans' high standard of living; this trait, he said, was capitalism at its best. Before the trip, Khrushchev had boasted that the Soviet economy would catch up with America's by 1970. Now, he told Lodge, he saw that this dream would take much longer.

Finally, on September 26 and 27, he met with Eisenhower in the isolated woods of Camp David. At meals, they chatted amiably, reminiscing about World War II, especially the mistakes that Hitler and

Stalin had made. Khrushchev, who had fought in the war as a foot soldier, told Eisenhower that the Russian people always admired him as the Supreme Allied Commander. But, he added, it was strange now to see him, a former general, talking about peace.

Eisenhower replied frankly that he was afraid of nuclear war and that everyone should be. During World War II, there may have been moments of exhilaration in commanding a huge army, but war today, with atomic weapons, would be nothing more than a brutal struggle for survival.

During their formal talks, which went on for two or three hours at a time, Khrushchev admitted that he'd acted brashly in putting forth an ultimatum on Berlin, but he said that he'd been exasperated and saw no way out diplomatically. Eisenhower acknowledged that the status of West Berlin—a free capitalist city in the middle of communist East Germany—was "abnormal." But, he went on, the American people would never allow Khrushchev to grab the city unilaterally. Berlin wasn't just a symbol of freedom. Two million people lived there, and the United States was obligated to protect their security. Khrushchev asked if Eisenhower could at least assure him that the United States did not intend to occupy West Berlin permanently. Eisenhower gave him that assurance, adding that he would be very surprised if Western troops stayed there for another twenty-five years.

At the end of the meeting, Eisenhower agreed to a summit sometime the next year involving the United States, the USSR, Britain, and France—the four powers occupying Berlin since the end of World War II—and that they would discuss not just Berlin but disarmament.

Khrushchev was slightly disappointed. He'd hoped for a substantive agreement on the spot at Camp David. He came to understand that Eisenhower faced pressures from Congress and elsewhere. He also knew about the American president's heart attack and stroke. Eisenhower was only four years older than Khrushchev, but he seemed much older; he seemed tired.

Still, Khrushchev did get the firm promise of a summit to discuss Berlin and disarmament. That's what he'd wanted, at a minimum; and in that sense, the trip was a triumph. Arriving back at Vnukovo Airport in Moscow, he told his Kremlin colleagues, who came to greet and cheer him, that he felt Eisenhower "sincerely wishes to see the end of the Cold War." And he finished his speech with words that no Soviet leader had spoken or probably felt since the war, and that none would speak or feel again for another thirty years: "Long live Soviet-American friendship!"

A few months later, at a Communist Party plenary session, Khrushchev went further. He said that during his trip to America, he had spoken with many businessmen and captains of industry. The "most sensible of them," he said, were confident that the American economy could cope with a shift to production of peaceful goods. This notion marked a drastic break from Leninist doctrine, which held that capitalist economies required military production and imperial expansion and that, therefore, war between capitalism and Communism was inevitable. Now Khrushchev was saying—as Mikoyan had been telling him for a year—that this wasn't so.

Once that point was accepted—and given the firm grip that he still held over the party, it was accepted right away—he further argued that the Soviet Union could afford to let down its guard.

Khrushchev wanted to bargain away as much as possible to get a settlement on Berlin at the upcoming Paris summit. And so he laid out to his comrades a radical plan for disarmament. He would withdraw one million troops—one-third of the entire Soviet army—from Eastern Europe, unilaterally and unconditionally, and invite the United States and NATO to respond in kind. He would also offer to destroy all Soviet missiles, and even discuss some form of on-site inspection to verify the dismantlement, if the Americans agreed to do the same.

In January 1960, Khrushchev spelled out the details of this plan at a *public* session of the Supreme Soviet. The CIA's Soviet analysts regarded the speech as serious and significant. Even the CIA's director, Allen Dulles, who had been skeptical of Moscow's peace feelers in the past, said at a National Security Council meeting that the speech might herald a sea change in the Cold War.

The Democrats and a band of Air Force generals nonetheless kept up the drumbeat about a "missile gap." The intelligence still didn't support their claims, but it didn't conclusively refute them, either. Allen Dulles told the president that one more U-2 flight might settle the matter. For the past few years, the CIA had secretly flown U-2 spy planes over Soviet territory. The Soviets had denounced such flights as intrusions on Soviet sovereignty, as tantamount to an act of war. In response, Eisenhower had canceled further flights, as a goodwill measure and to avoid further risks. But Dulles's recommendation was too tempting. If one more overflight could produce the proof that he thought it might—the proof that there was no missile gap—the cause of peace in the long term would be advanced. So Eisenhower approved one more flight.

The four-power summit—the one that Eisenhower had promised at Camp David—was scheduled to begin in Paris on May 15, 1960. The U-2 took off on May Day, with orders to enter Soviet airspace from Greenland, fly over Murmansk, and take pictures along a railroad line north of the new ICBM facility near Plesetsk.

Near the village of Sverdlovsk, in the Ural Mountains, Soviet air-defense batteries shot the U-2 down. U-2 pilots were trained to chew a cyanide pill under such circumstances, to keep the mission secret and deniable in the event of capture and interrogation. The pilot of this U-2, Francis Gary Powers, did not chew the pill. Instead, he parachuted out of the plane. Villagers retrieved him and, seeing that he wasn't a Russian, turned him over to authorities.

The Soviets announced that they had shot down a U-2, but for several days, they kept Powers's capture a secret. Believing that Powers was dead, Eisenhower went into standard denial mode, saying that he knew nothing about a spy mission, that the United States didn't do that sort of thing; if a plane was captured, the pilot must have drifted off course. Then the Soviets produced Powers, who'd confessed his mission. Eisenhower was forced to acknowledge that he had lied.

Khrushchev was livid. He'd taken great political risks in proposing his disarmament plan. Some hawks within the Kremlin were skeptical of its wisdom. More ominous, the Chinese Communist Party, ruled by Mao Zedong, had issued fierce protests, accusing Khrushchev of ideological heresy. Though Western intelligence hadn't yet picked up on it, there was a widening rift between the Soviet and the Chinese Communist parties. Mao was hoping that his ideological purity would lure Communists in third-world countries into his camp and away from Moscow's. Such an open split could seriously weaken the Kremlin's grip on power—both its leadership of the international vanguard and its monopoly rule over domestic politics throughout the USSR.

To these skeptics, the U-2 flight and Eisenhower's deception seemed to confirm the Chinese doubts about Khrushchev's new approach. Angered and embarrassed, Khrushchev stalked out of the Paris peace talks. The prospects of an East-West détente, much less an end to the Cold War, were kaput.

After this rupture came the United Nations session where Khrushchev banged his shoe on the podium and embraced Fidel Castro. In 1961, when a young new president, John F. Kennedy, took charge of the White House, Khrushchev renewed his threats to take over West Berlin.

On August 13, a few minutes past midnight, East German troops occupied the border separating East from West Berlin and laid the first layers of brick and barbed wire for what would soon become the Berlin Wall. In retrospect, the Wall represented a cruel solution to the crisis, especially to the exodus of East German students. But the move surprised the West, and it was seen as an act of aggression. Kennedy began to take countermeasures—building up conventional forces in Europe, even briefly considering a disarming nuclear strike against the Soviet Union's missile sites and air bases. By October, the Soviets had closed off all but one border crossing into West Berlin. On October 27, Soviet and American tanks faced one another along that checkpoint at short range for sixteen hours, at which point negotiations were held, the Soviet tanks backed off, and the crisis faded away.

The next year, Khrushchev took a still bolder move—secretly shipping medium-range nuclear missiles to Cuba. He was motivated in part by a desire to defend his new Caribbean ally from the threat of an American invasion. But he also felt a need to compensate for the weakness that he'd revealed in the showdown over Berlin.

The Americans' new Discoverer photoreconnaissance satellite— which orbited too high to be shot down—revealed that the Soviets had only four ICBMs. The Americans knew at last that there was no "missile gap"—or rather, that there was a gap, but the United States, not Russia, held the lead. By sending missiles to Cuba, just ninety miles off the American coast, Khrushchev could close the gap; he would now have the ability to strike American territory, just as Kennedy had the ability to strike Soviet territory.

The Cuban missile crisis didn't end well for Khrushchev, either. The CIA spotted the missiles in transit. Kennedy called Khrushchev's bluff. But as the crisis progressed through its thirteen days, Kennedy came to a realization. Mounting air strikes against the missiles in Cuba, as the Joint Chiefs of Staff were advising, would only prompt Khrushchev to grab Berlin in retaliation, which might trigger a U.S.-Soviet nuclear war. It would be better to offer Khrushchev a face-saving way out of the crisis before it escalated. So he secretly made a deal: if the Soviets removed their missiles from Cuba, the United States would remove its fifteen medium-range missiles from Turkey. That's how the crisis was settled.

Afterward, realizing how close the world came to catastrophe, Kennedy proposed nuclear arms reductions, limits on nuclear testing, a superpower hotline, and several other measures to reduce tensions. Khrushchev was interested, but it was too late. Kennedy was assassinated in November 1963. Meanwhile, the missile crisis and his capitulation destroyed Khrushchev's power base inside the Kremlin. Within a few months, some of his underlings started whispering about a takeover. By October 1964, they had enough strength to force his ouster at a Party Congress, denouncing his "hare-brained schemes." The new leader, Leonid Brezhnev, was a hard-liner. He quickly ordered the military to catch up with and surpass America in nuclear weaponry. Four years later, he also crushed Alexander Dubček's government in Czechoslovakia, which was trying to create "socialism with a human face," and moved in five armored divisions to solidify Moscow's dominance.

The Cold War was back at full roar. And despite a period of détente in the 1970s, when tensions were reduced and the arms race was regulated (though not reversed), the Cold War continued to dominate global politics until the late 1980s, when the Soviet Union faced another economic crisis, and another reformer, Mikhail Gorbachev, rose to power, this time setting a path toward disarmament and explicit Westernization, which resulted in the unraveling of the entire Communist apparatus and, finally, the Soviet Union itself.

If Francis Gary Powers hadn't been shot down, or if he'd swallowed that cyanide pill, would the Cold War's logjam have been broken thirty years earlier? Might decades of arms races, crises, and proxy wars have been averted? It's doubtful. Khrushchev was willing to slash his military and dismantle his missiles only if the West surrendered West Berlin. And, as Eisenhower said repeatedly, that wasn't going to happen. No American president or European prime minister would have done that in exchange for a Soviet premier's promises.

The Cold War wasn't *only*, as Allen Ginsberg bemoaned, "the imposition of a vast mental barrier." It was also the *existence* of a vast *physical and political* barrier that blocked and shaped the course of human activity. Certain kinds of breakthroughs were simply not going to happen until that bigger wall came tumbling down.

14

The Frontier's Dark Side

On July 8, 1959, one day after Nikita Khrushchev announced that he would like to visit America, six of the eight U.S. military advisers in Hoa Binh—a tree-lined provincial center twenty miles northeast of Saigon—were shot in their mess hall after dinner. They had been watching a movie, a steamy courtroom drama called *The Tattered Dress*. When one of the men turned on the lights to change reels, a squad of Viet Cong guerrillas stuck their automatic rifles through the windows and sprayed the room with gunfire. Major Dale Buis and Master Sergeant Chester Ovnand were killed in the attack. They were the first of 58,217 Americans who would die over the next sixteen years in the war in Vietnam.

Nobody knew it at the time—least of all the Americans—but 1959 marked the start of what came to be called the Second Indochina War. French colonialists fought the First Indochina War, which began in the aftermath of World War II and ended with their crushing defeat in 1954, when ten thousand of their soldiers were surrounded in their garrison at Dien Bien Phu by five times as many guerrillas of the Vietnam Independence League, also known as the Viet Minh. To the guerrillas and much of the Vietnamese population, the Second Indochina War was simply a continuation of the First, with Americans replacing the French.

The leader of the nationalists was a charismatic Marxist named Ho Chi Minh, and the irony was that toward the end of World War II, he had cooperated with U.S. intelligence agents from the Office of Strategic Services, the antecedent to the CIA. Japan was occupying much of Vietnam, having ousted the French colonialists, and the OSS recruited Ho to harass Japanese troops and to help rescue American pilots who had been shot down.

As part of this campaign, the Allies divided Vietnam in two, sending Chinese nationalists to fight the Japanese in the northern half of the country and British troops to do so in the south.

After Japan surrendered, the guerrillas took back Hanoi, and Ho Chi Minh proclaimed himself president of the newly formed Democratic Republic of Vietnam. His OSS handlers had given Ho a copy of the Declaration of Independence during their days of alliance, and he now publicly recited key passages ("We hold these truths to be self-evident . . .") in an effort to win U.S. recognition.

However, in 1946, the British handed the southern half of Vietnam back to the French, who tried to recapture the whole country, going on a rampage against the Viet Minh, bombing Haiphong Harbor in the north, and forcing Ho Chi Minh out of Hanoi and into the jungle. There, Ho organized the resistance and built the guerrilla army that, eight years later, forced the French to surrender and withdraw after losing a total of ninety thousand colonial soldiers.

Initially, the United States stayed out of the French-Indochina War, but in 1949, Mao Zedong and his Communist rebels took over China, expelling Chiang Kai-shek and the Nationalist Army. Suddenly there loomed the specter of a Soviet-Chinese alliance—a Red bloc stretching all across Eurasia. Ignoring the specific context of the Vietnam conflict, or more likely not bothering to learn it, President Harry Truman and his advisers viewed Ho Chi Minh as a mere puppet of Beijing and Moscow. So, in 1950, the United States set up a Military Assistance Advisory Group in Saigon and, over the next four years, sent the French over $3 billion worth of heavy armaments, at one point supplying three-quarters of the French troops' war materiel.

When Dwight Eisenhower was elected president in 1953, he affirmed America's support of the French and coined the "domino theory"—the idea, which presidents would recite for the next twenty years, that if the Communists won in Vietnam, all the countries of Asia would fall, one by one, like a "row of dominoes."

A year later, during the siege at Dien Bien Phu, the French pleaded for direct assistance. Secretary of State John Foster Dulles proposed offering the French two tactical atomic weapons, but Eisenhower demurred. Vietnam may have been important, but it wasn't *that* important. Nor did Eisenhower believe that conventional bombing would be effective. And, having just signed a stalemate of an armistice that let him withdraw American soldiers from a brutal three-year war in Korea, he had no appetite for sending ground troops to fight another war in Asia. He seemed to agree with Admiral Arthur Radford, the chairman of the Joint Chiefs of Staff, who wrote in a memo, "Indochina is devoid of decisive military objectives, and the allocation of more than token U.S. armed forces in Indochina would be a serious diversion of limited U.S. capabilities."

So, having no choice, on May 7, 1954, the French surrendered. The next day, delegates from the major powers—the United States, Britain, China, and the Soviet Union, as well as France, the Viet Minh, and even Bao Dai, Japan's puppet emperor during its occupation of South Vietnam—met in Geneva to negotiate the country's future.

On July 21, an agreement was struck: Vietnam would be divided at the 17th Parallel. Ho Chi Minh would control the north; Bao Dai—or actually the prime minister that he would soon install, Ngo Dien Diem—would rule the south. This was explicitly a temporary formula. The agreement further mandated that within two years, there would be countrywide elections.

But Diem refused to sign the accord, saying that elections wouldn't be fair under the north's Communist rule (and perhaps fearing that Ho might win the elections in the north and the south). Dulles sided with Diem and also declined to sign the accord.

In July 1956, as the deadline for elections approached, North Vietnamese officials beseeched the Geneva signatories to enforce their agreement. But they did nothing, realizing that as long as the South Vietnamese prime minister and the American president opposed it, any gesture would be futile. The temporary partition was hardening into a permanent border. Even the Soviet Union, Hanoi's main ally, proposed admitting North and South Vietnam into the United Nations as two separate nations. Eisenhower rejected that idea as well, refusing to recognize North Vietnam as a legitimate government.

Ho Chi Minh's regime was exceedingly harsh. He imposed land reform along Maoist lines, executing as many as fifty thousand "land-lords" who wouldn't submit to his regimen. Thousands more escaped to the south and told nightmare tales of the north's regimented life.

But Diem was no democrat, either. He placed fifty thousand people in "political reeducation centers"—which even the Pentagon's official history of the war would later describe as "little more than concentration camps for potential foes of the government." Diem also made it a capital crime to join the Communist party or to assist a Communist, and he enforced the law through military tribunals that allowed no appeal. He shut down newspapers that criticized him, replaced almost all the provincial chiefs with loyal military officers, abolished elections for once-autonomous village councils, stacked them with his cronies, and handed over large parcels of land to his friends and relatives.

In 1957, organized rebellions against Diem's government broke out. They sprang not from Communists but from oppressed and frustrated peasants, most of whom until recently had no interest in politics. However, the Viet Minh—whom the south's leaders called Viet Cong, meaning Communist Vietnamese—did exploit the tensions. When the partition was imposed, ninety thousand Viet Cong who had been living in the south moved north, but a trained cadre of five to ten thousand—estimates would differ—stayed behind. They were instructed not to engage in direct action against Diem's regime, but to recruit and organize new members, quietly and gradually. As Diem's regime triggered violent protests from its own people, the Viet Cong easily recruited members by appealing not to ideology but to social justice and nationalism.

No Americans, not even officials on the ground, knew anything about this covert organizing—and little about the historical context that enabled it—until the mid-sixties, when Viet Cong prisoners were interrogated. Many of these prisoners said that if Diem's regime hadn't been so unpopular, their recruitment efforts would not have been nearly so successful.

It could also be argued that if Eisenhower had signed and observed the Geneva Accords, there might have been no war at all.

At the time, though, nearly every American who thought about Vietnam assumed that the rebel attacks were directed by Ho Chi Minh, who in turn was following orders from Moscow or Beijing.

Certainly Diem believed this—he sincerely promoted the notion to his American allies—and so he responded to the attacks not by reforming his policies or by softening his repression but rather by cracking down even harder. The peasants retaliated with still more daring acts of violence, and the spiral escalated.

Meanwhile, the American military advisory teams, which Truman had sent to South Vietnam in 1950 to help the French, were still inside the country and increasingly active, though now they were assisting and training Diem's South Vietnamese army.

As a result, the North Vietnamese viewed Diem and the Americans as synonymous. The Viet Cong came up with a catchword for the enemy, to make the association explicit: *My-Diem*, meaning America-Diem. Rather than back down, the guerrillas stepped up their attacks, killing South Vietnamese officers and sabotaging American equipment.

In response to this, in May 1959, President Eisenhower authorized the American military advisory teams to accompany South Vietnamese battalions in the field and to give them "on-the-spot advice" about combat tactics. The advisers were still forbidden to participate in the fight, but before this point, their activities had been restricted to training and supplying the local troops on their bases. Eisenhower's decision marked a significant step toward American intervention.

At this point, Ho Chi Minh realized that a purely political strategy of organizing and recruiting would no longer be effective. He also calculated that the balance of forces in the south had shifted, that opinion in the countryside now weighed heavily against Diem. And so, he concluded, the time was ripe to escalate the conflict, to launch a full-scale war on the south.

The same month that the American advisers stepped up their role, the Central Committee of the Lao Dong (North Vietnam's Communist party) passed a resolution at its annual plenum, articulating new aims—the overthrow of Diem's government, the ejection of the Americans, and the unification of all of Vietnam under the North's rule—to be achieved through military force. The resolution also explicitly identified the United States as the main obstacle to these goals.

The July 8 attack in Hoa Binh that killed Major Buis and Sergeant Ovnand marked not just the first time that Vietnamese Communists had deliberately killed American soldiers but also the opening shot of a new chapter in the Indochina War—a chapter in which the United States would be the last colonial occupier.

• • •

As this new war began, in fact through the entirety of the Cold War up till then, the idea that the United States was a colonial or imperial power would have struck nearly all Americans—including politicians of both parties and foreign-policy experts of all suasion—as preposterous. After all, despite the enormous power that it had amassed in the victory of World War II, America did not seek to conquer foreign territory.

However, in 1959, at the University of Wisconsin in Madison, a thirty-eight-year-old professor of American History named William Appleman Williams published a book titled *The Tragedy of American Diplomacy*, which put forth a revisionist view—that, since the beginning of the twentieth century, U.S. foreign policy had been built on a doctrine of "Open Door imperialism," which aimed to achieve imperial goals not through the conquest of foreign lands but through the control of foreign markets.

The term was a nod to John Hay, the secretary of state under Presidents William McKinley and Theodore Roosevelt, who at the turn of the century promulgated an "Open Door" policy toward China. Concerned that Japan and the European powers were about to carve up China, Hay convinced them to allow free and open trade with the kingdom—purportedly for China's sake but in fact to protect U.S. commercial interests, which were only beginning to expand into Asia.

In his research of government archives, Williams found repeated and surprisingly explicit statements by top policymakers in many administrations—well after Teddy Roosevelt's—to the effect that the American economy would collapse without the constant expansion of markets. Presidents and their advisers had devised moral imperatives (spreading Western civilization) and strategic doctrines (the balance of power) to justify—and persuade themselves of—the righteousness and necessity of their policies. Williams allowed that these rationales had some objective basis and that American leaders sincerely believed them. But the main underlying motive, he concluded, was economic.

President Woodrow Wilson, for instance, famously championed "self-determination" for other nations in the wake of World War I. However, his concerns weren't as purely moral as most historians made them out to be. Williams noted that at one point, Wilson, revealing his true intentions, said, "*When properly directed*, there is no people not fitted for self-development"—properly directed, that is, by American business interests. Wilson had also once remarked, "It is always well to have a frontier on which to turn loose the colts of *our race.*"

Wilson, McKinley, and John Hay had all been inspired by Frederick Jackson Turner's 1893 essay "The Frontier in American History," which argued that the "fluidity of American life"—its "restless, nervous energy" and "dominant individualism"—was a product of the frontier's vast emptiness, which allowed a continuous "expansion westward," each step creating "new opportunities" and "perennial rebirth." Many years later, John F. Kennedy, who began campaigning for president in the year of Williams's book, would similarly invoke the promise of a "New Frontier."

Williams, too, was influenced by Turner, though as a scholar focusing on the causes and consequences of expanding and contracting frontiers. Even in Turner's day, America was running out of open space to conquer and settle on its continent. Turner wrote his essay not only to explain "the American character," but also to pose a dark question: How would that character change after the frontier's spaces filled up?

It was a formative coincidence that Williams chose to do his research at the University of Wisconsin. Turner had graduated from Wisconsin, then a land-grant college, in the 1880s and, after earning a Ph.D. at Johns Hopkins, returned there to teach. When he wrote his famous frontier essay, he was a professor on the Madison campus. When Williams arrived there a half century later, in the 1940s, as a war veteran and a graduate student in the History Department, Turner's legacy was still strongly felt. It had been kept alive by Professor Fred Harvey Harrington, a transplanted New Yorker who started teaching at Wisconsin in the late 1930s, concentrating on the domestic sources of U.S. foreign policy. Harrington reveled in standing apart from the East Coast universities' "court historians" who, he felt, attached their ideas and ambitions to the State Department's line.

Harrington became a mentor to Williams and arranged for him to deliver a paper at the 1950 meeting of the American Historical Association. Williams's paper amounted to an early expression of his ideas about Open Door imperialism—and it was not well received.

The orthodox view among American diplomatic historians of the day was that U.S. foreign policy was entirely virtuous, motivated solely by the need to defend the free world against the Soviet Union, whose motives were entirely nefarious. At the same convention where Williams read his critical paper, Samuel Eliot Morison—the association's president and the author of several highly regarded textbooks on American history—delivered an address that called on his fellow historians to write "from a sanely conservative point of view," emphasizing America's accomplishments, honoring its leaders, and paying tribute to its financiers and industrialists.

By the end of the fifties, some other critical voices had emerged—not least that of C. Wright Mills at Columbia—but there weren't many, and even they were regarded by most colleagues as outsiders, or worse.

It was no coincidence that Mills, too, had spent his graduate-school years at the University of Wisconsin, which, throughout the century, was a breeding ground for critical thinking—and a magnet for students who didn't fit in elsewhere. In 1959, the year that Williams published *The Tragedy of American Diplomacy*, a group of rebellious students planned an "Anti-Military Ball"—as an alternative to the annual military ball sponsored by ROTC, the Reserve Officers' Training Corps. The Anti-Mil Ball, as it was called, attracted not just a livelier crowd of students but a larger one as well.

Williams was a charismatic lecturer, and his teachings inspired a "Wisconsin School" of American history—just as, at the University of Chicago, Milton Friedman's libertarian teachings inspired a "Chicago School" of economics. In both cases, many of their students would spread their ideas—their unorthodox approaches to their subjects—in books and at universities elsewhere. By 1971, a poll of the Organization of American Historians cited *The Tragedy of American Diplomacy* as one of the most influential books ever published.

In 1959, some of Williams's students—most of them members of the Socialist Club—started a magazine called *Studies on the Left* and distributed it to left-liberal campuses across the country. One of its readers, Tom Hayden at the University of Michigan, joined the board. In the months leading up to the formation of the SDS and the writing of the *Port Huron Statement*, the journal fostered the network for the intellectual wing of the American New Left.

When the Vietnam War began to escalate, Williams's acolytes were among the first to foresee the impending disaster. His ideas served as the basis for a critique of the war—questioning not so much the way the politicians and generals were fighting the war but, more radically, the underlying motives for intervening in the first place.

Williams's thinking had its flaws. He overstated the economic roots of foreign policy. And, in part because of this tendency, he understated the Soviet Union's role in aggravating Cold War tensions. (If capitalism was the driving force in aggression, how could the leader of world Communism be aggressive?)

But he was the first serious American historian of the Cold War era to recognize that the U.S.-Soviet conflict was not entirely a struggle between good and evil—that, as he put it in a column in the *Nation* in 1957, when many regarded such sentiments as treasonous, America was "neither the last best hope of the world nor the agent of civilization destined to destroy the barbarians," adding, "We have much to offer, but also much to learn."

15

The New Language of Diplomacy

For a country beginning to flex its global muscle, the United States—its people, its politicians, even its diplomatic envoys—knew stunningly little about the rest of the world.

An official survey, taken in the spring of 1958, revealed that fewer than half of the State Department's foreign service officers had the ability to speak a foreign language.

In response, the Foreign Service Institute launched a crash program in language instruction. As a result, by the fall of 1959, only 15 percent of U.S. diplomats still lacked any linguistic skills. Even so, Harold Hoskins, the institute's director, admitted that much work was needed in the languages of the Middle East, Africa, and Asia—areas that now affected the balance of power in the Cold War competition. (Only six diplomats, for instance, could speak Vietnamese, despite the escalation of U.S. involvement there.)

If the goal was simply to remake the world in America's image—or if it was assumed that the rest of the world wanted to be just like America, and would be if only its people were set free—sensitivity to foreign politics and cultures might not have been so important. But many officials were now realizing that the world was more complex. A central aim of U.S. foreign policy was still to lure other nations away from Communism and into the camp of the Free World; there was almost no dissent on this point. However, officials now began to realize that this task was a major challenge, that they would have to make an active case for the Western way—that the rest of the world would have to be won over.

This was why officials were nervous about the rise of the "non-aligned" movement—charismatic nationalists and revolutionaries who wanted to tread a path independent of Washington or Moscow. Many of these leaders were in the Middle East, Africa, and Asia, those areas where Americans' language skills were still weak. The worry was that the Russians were more adept at attracting these leaders and their people—that, especially in the poorer countries, the ideas, or at least the slogans, of Communism had more visceral appeal than those of capitalism.

In 1954, when President Eisenhower and Secretary of State John Foster Dulles took their first steps toward replacing the French occupiers in Vietnam, they set up an organization that they hoped would do in that region what NATO had done in Western Europe—provide a tool of collective security and a patina of multinational legitimacy for American control. They called it the Southeast Asia Treaty Organization, SEATO, and pressured all the region's countries to join.

Several governments resisted—most notably those of India, Burma, Indonesia, and Ceylon (later called Sri Lanka). One year later, they invited the leaders of twenty-five other Asian and African nations—together representing over half the world's population—to attend a conference in Bandung, Indonesia, where the nonaligned movement was first formed.

Most of these nations had won their independence from colonial domination only in the previous decade, shortly after the end of World War II, and they wanted to stay free of both superpowers' spheres as the Cold War began to heat up.

At the opening of the Bandung Conference, John Kotelawa, the premier of Ceylon, declared, "Moscow and Washington must realize that there are others, too, in the world" and that "the main concern of these others is peace." The conference's concluding document condemned "colonialism in all of its manifestations"—which was taken as a critique of the Soviet Union *and* the United States.

But the fact that stood out most visibly among those who gathered at this conference was that almost none of them—neither the participants nor the observers—were white. A black American news-paper that covered the conference made the point explicitly, noting that the event marked "a turning point in world history"—a "clear challenge to white supremacy" by "the world's yellow, brown, and black people."

Race was America's shame. Segregation, brutal oppression, lynch-ings, and blatant inequality all threw stinging doubt on the nation's claims of freedom and democracy. And Communist propaganda sheets highlighted every dreadful incident to drive the point home further. If the nonaligned nations at Bandung were going to make race a Cold War issue, the United States would have a hard time winning.

And so, alarm bells went off when Adam Clayton Powell Jr., the black U.S. congressman from Harlem, announced that he was going to Bandung as an observer. Eisenhower and Dulles had decided not to send a delegate, preferring to pretend that the conference had no significance. Dulles's staff tried to talk Powell out of going, but he insisted. Powell was dashing, young, and elegant. In the late thirties, he'd been sympathetic to Communist causes, until the Hitler-Stalin Pact at the start of World War II, which crushed the illusions of many Western leftists. Still, he was regarded as a bit of a radical, a loose cannon, and Powell liked the image.

But Powell turned out to be a surprise. At Bandung, he frankly crit-icized the Eisenhower administration for ignoring the proceedings and acknowledged that America had to "clean up" its race problems. But he also mounted a rousing defense of the United States and challenged Communist delegates on their own records whenever they brought up "the color question." Powell came home a hero among Democrats and Republicans alike; Eisenhower met with him personally.

Having amassed some credibility, if only for the moment, Powell proposed a plan for boosting the nation's image around the world. Stop sending symphony orchestras and ballet companies on interna-tional tours, he told his contacts in the State Department. The Soviets were doing that with the Bolshoi, and we couldn't compete with that. Instead, he said, give the world's people a taste of some "real Americana." Let them see and hear our jazz bands. Not only would jazz tours refute the Soviet line that America lacked a native culture; they would also soften the image of American racism, as many jazz bands featured black and white musicians playing together.

The Voice of America had recently started broadcasting a program, hosted by Willis Conover, called *Music USA*, which highlighted jazz, and it was attracting huge audiences, especially behind the Iron Curtain. Conover had told his bosses that people love jazz "because they love freedom." The black novelist Ralph Ellison had recently written an essay that described jazz as an artistic parallel to the American political system. Soloists can play anything they want as long as they stay within the key and the tempo—just as, in a democracy, individuals can say anything they want as long as they respect their neighbors and follow the law.

The State Department approved Powell's idea. Powell convinced his good friend Dizzy Gillespie to make the first goodwill tour, leading an eighteen-piece big band. The band headed out in March 1956 for a ten-week trip, starting in Iran and proceeding to Pakistan, Lebanon, Turkey, Yugoslavia, and Greece. In most of these countries, audiences that had never heard jazz before started tapping their feet, and by the concert's end, they were dancing. A Pakistani newspaper editorialized that the language of diplomacy "ought to be translated into the score for a bop trumpet." The American ambassador in Lebanon cabled back to Washington, "This music makes our job so much easier." Another wrote, "Maybe we could have built a new tank for the cost of this tour, but you can't get as much good-will out of a tank as you can out of Dizzy Gillespie's band."

Gillespie's last stop, in Athens, was particularly tense. Students had recently stoned the local headquarters of the United States Information Service in protest of Washington's support for Greece's right-wing dictatorship. Yet many of those same students now greeted Gillespie with cheers, lifting him on their shoulders, throwing their jackets in the air, and shouting, over and over, "Dizzy! Dizzy!"

The trips were like that everywhere. A few years later, when Louis Armstrong arrived in the Congo as part of a tour through Africa, drummers and dancers paraded him through the streets on a throne. When he played in Katanga Province, a truce was called in a long-standing civil war, so combatants on both sides could go see him play. When Benny Goodman took out his clarinet for an impromptu recital in Red Square, hundreds of Muscovites crowded around him in a rare act of spontaneity. Dave Brubeck's quartet traveled all across the Middle East in 1958, landing in Baghdad as a coup d'état was under way. Duke Ellington and his big band went on several tours, in the Middle East, South Asia, and Eastern Europe. (Much later, in 1971, when Ellington traveled to Moscow, an American diplomat wrote in his report that crowds greeted Duke as something akin to "a Second Coming," with one young Russian yelling, "We've been waiting for you for centuries!")

Musicians like Gillespie, Armstrong, Goodman, Ellington, and Brubeck were superstars, and their tours became sensations. A cartoon in the *New Yorker* around this time depicted some pin-striped officials in Washington sitting around a table, with one of them saying, "This is a diplomatic mission of the utmost delicacy. The question is, who's the best man for it—John Foster Dulles or Satchmo."

The jazzmen were happy to play their part in this Cold War pageant for hearts and minds. After his first tour, Gillespie said with pride that he had dealt a "powerfully effective" blow "against Red propaganda." But he also refused to be a puppet. When the State Department tried to brief him on how to answer questions about American race relations, he said, "I've got 300 years of briefing. I know what they've done to us"—meaning what whites had done to blacks—"and I'm not going to make any excuses."

Armstrong canceled a 1957 trip to Moscow after Eisenhower refused to send federal troops to Little Rock, Arkansas, to enforce a court order to integrate the schools. "The way they are treating my people in the south, the government can go to hell," Armstrong said. "It's getting so bad, a colored man hasn't got any country."

His anger startled many younger black musicians, especially the beboppers, who'd always detested his stage antics—the broad smiling and clownish bowing. The boppers created a very different persona—serious faces, little or no chitchat, just playing complex music that demanded close listening, that wasn't meant to be simply entertaining. They'd devised that persona in part as a rebuke to Armstrong's Uncle Tomming, as a declaration that a new generation of black men had taken to the stage. (Gillespie liked to clown, but he did it with a hip, intellectual demeanor, the goatee, and the horn-rimmed glasses that made him so alluring to the Beats and that no one could confuse for a moment with Satchmo's broad beaming.) But Armstrong's tongue-lashing at Eisenhower—still a few years before civil rights was a popular cause—gave many young black skeptics encouragement and hope.

In the broader political world, administration officials feared that this harangue, especially coming from the genial "Ambassador Satchmo"—as he liked to be called—might trigger a diplomatic disaster. Already, Dulles had told Attorney General Herbert Brownell that the situation in Little Rock was "ruining our foreign policy" and that its effect in Asia and Africa "will be worse for us than Hungary was for the Russians."

Two weeks later, facing pressure from many quarters, Eisenhower finally sent the National Guard to Arkansas. Armstrong pronounced the news "just wonderful" and agreed to go on a goodwill tour of South America later in the year.

It was never clear whether the Jazz Ambassadors—whose tours continued through the early seventies—affected world opinion of American foreign policy; probably not. But in many countries, they did have a substantial impact on the broader image of America, its vitality and its culture.

The influence worked both ways. On their tours, the jazzmen didn't just play; they also listened to local musicians. And just as they brought a taste of America to the rest of the world, they also brought a taste of the world back home. Dave Brubeck and his quartet were sent on an exhaustive tour in 1958, encompassing East Germany, Poland, Turkey, Afghanistan, Pakistan, India, Ceylon, Iran, and Iraq—a "circle of Russia," as Brubeck's wife, Iola, would later call it.

Walking around Istanbul one morning, Brubeck heard a group of street musicians playing an exotic rhythm, fast and syncopated. It was in 9/8 time—nine eighth notes per measure—a very unusual meter in Western music, and the players phrased the notes in a still more jarring way: not 1-2-3, 1-2-3, 1-2-3, as might be expected, but *1*-2, *1*-2, *1*-2, *1-2-3*.

Later that day, Brubeck had an interview scheduled at a local radio station. Like many broadcasters at the time, the station had its own symphony orchestra. When Brubeck arrived, the musicians were taking a break from a rehearsal. He told some of them about the rhythm that he'd heard on the streets and asked if anyone knew what it was. He hummed the tune, and several of the musicians started playing it, adding flourishes and counterpoint, even improvising on it. It was a traditional Turkish folk song, widely known—at least in Turkey.

Odd meters weren't entirely new to Brubeck. He'd studied music at Mills College with Darius Milhaud, a classical composer whose works stressed multiple rhythms and dissonant tonalities. When Brubeck was still uncertain whether he should pursue a career in classical music or in jazz, he came to Milhaud for advice. Milhaud told him, "Travel the world, and keep your ears open." And here he was, doing precisely that.

All during the 1958 tour, Brubeck heard odd meters and raga rhythms from local musicians, and when his quartet played with them, they were all astonished that his drummer, Joe Morello, could match these rhythms precisely.

When Brubeck got back to the United States, he was inspired to make an album that would break out of the standard 4/4 time that marked almost all jazz tunes, no matter how adventurous they might otherwise be. And he especially wanted to write something based on that 9/8 folk tune he'd heard in Istanbul.

Brubeck was one of the most famous jazz musicians in the country. In the early fifties, he hit on the idea of booking concerts on college campuses. He played a cool style of jazz—swinging but sophisticated, even cerebral. His alto saxophone player, Paul Desmond, had a similarly cool sound, which he himself likened to a "dry martini." The college concerts were wildly popular and led to a contract with Columbia Records. In November 1954, Brubeck made the cover of *Time* magazine. (The fact embarrassed him; he later said that one of the worst days of his life was when Duke Ellington showed him the cover. Brubeck knew that Ellington was more deserving of the recognition, except that he was black while Brubeck was white.)

In short, as much as any jazz musician alive, Brubeck could do pretty much whatever he wanted. Yet even so, Columbia's executives were loath to underwrite an album that consisted entirely of original music composed in weird meters. They finally agreed, but only if Brubeck first recorded an album of traditional songs from the South, including "Ol' Man River," "Swanee River," "Camptown Races," "Georgia on My Mind," and—the album's title tune—"Gone with the Wind." The concept was conventional to the point of jejune, but everyone figured that the album would sell big. He started recording it in Columbia's Hollywood studio on April 22, 1959—the same day that Miles Davis was in New York's Thirtieth Street Studio, wrapping up *Kind of Blue*.

Two months later, having fulfilled his side of the bargain, Brubeck and the quartet flew to New York and—over three sessions, on June 25, July 1, and August 18—made the album that he'd wanted to make. It was called *Time Out*, and it would become, after *Kind of Blue*, one of the biggest-selling jazz albums ever. After they realized that they had a hit on their hands, Columbia Records executives also released a 45-rpm single—consisting of two songs from the album—and it sold a million more copies. On one side of the single was "Take Five," a Paul Desmond composition in 5/4 time (five quarter notes per measure instead of the usual four). On the other side was "Blue Rondo à la Turk," based on the staccato 9/8 rhythm of the Istanbul street song.

The record's huge success signaled that American audiences, on the eve of the sixties, were ready, even yearning, for at least a taste of the exotic.

16

Sparking the Powder Keg

On the night of August 25, 1959, Miles Davis was nearing the end of a two-week engagement at Birdland, a swank, 400-seat jazz club on Broadway and Fifty-second Street that was named after his old mentor, Charlie Parker. Davis's new album, *Kind of Blue*, had been released the week before, and it was selling very well. A half-hour television special, *The Sound of Miles Davis*, was scheduled to air in primetime nationwide on CBS. The sets at Birdland, for which John Coltrane had briefly returned to the band, were a success, as well, attracting celebrities like Marlon Brando, Elizabeth Taylor, and Ava Gardner night after night, eager to soak up the cool.

Between sets, Miles escorted a young white woman to a taxi and paused on the sidewalk to take in the air and light a cigarette. A policeman named Gerald Kidduff told him to move along. Davis replied, in his hoarse voice, "I work here," adding, "That's my name up there," pointing to the club's marquee. The two exchanged a few more words. A plainclothes cop named Donald Rolker, sensing the worst, dashed over and beat Davis over the head with his blackjack— "like a tom-tom," as Miles later put it.

The two policemen then placed Davis under arrest, charged him with assault and disorderly conduct, and led him not to a hospital but to the station house around the corner. He was released only after paying a $1,000 bail. Doctors had to sew five stitches in his head to close the wound.

A few dozen bystanders witnessed the beating outside Birdland. A photo appeared in newspapers the next day, showing the celebrated trumpeter in handcuffs with dark bloodstains on his white jacket. A panel of three New York judges in a Special Sessions court eventually cleared him of all charges, but the incident left him bitter for years.

That summer, Miles Davis was rich and famous, a celebrity among celebrities. But to a couple of white policemen—not in the Deep South, but in the heart of midtown Manhattan, outside the fashionable jazz club where he'd been bringing in tens of thousands of dollars' worth of business—he was just another uppity Negro.

• • •

Two weeks later, on September 9, the U.S. Civil Rights Commission, which had been created only two years earlier, released its first document, a 668-page tome crammed with charts and tables and anecdotes, based on a year of field reports and inquests. The commission concluded that the nation's treatment of its 18 million Negro citizens—many of them denied the right to vote, attend public schools, or gain access to good housing—was "an affront to human dignity" and a violation of "American principles and historic purposes."

The report marked the first time the federal government had explored the topic of racial discrimination in any systematic detail, and even then its findings were far from universally accepted. The commission's three southern members issued a dissenting statement at the beginning of the report, taking exception to the idea that the original Constitution—as distinct from its amendments—guaranteed equal protection under the law.

A few days after the report's release, a group of southern senators tried to block a bill to renew the commission's term for an additional two years. In a colloquy on the floor, Senator James Eastland of Mississippi, said, "Isn't a segregated life the proper life? Isn't it the law of nature?" His colleague, Strom Thurmond of South Carolina, who'd run for president a decade earlier as an explicitly segregationist candidate, replied, "That's the way God made the races."

When Senator Jacob Javits of New York tried to push for the bill's passage, Eastland replied that, in the South, there were no "gangs roaming the streets, juvenile delinquency, knifings, cuttings, rape, murder, filth," like Javits had in New York City, yet southern senators weren't making a fuss about his problems. "Let the poor South alone," Thurmond chimed in.

The bill passed, mainly because the Soviet premier Nikita Khrushchev was arriving in Washington the next day, and enough senators—even some of the southern ones—knew that America's standing in the Cold War would be damaged if Congress was arguing about racial equality while the leader of world Communism was in town.

The South was hardly alone in its institutionalized racism. The commission's report concluded that the problems were "not limited to one region"—that housing discrimination was "particularly critical in the great metropolitan centers of the North and West" and that school segregation was a problem that "the whole country is now sharing."*

Five years earlier, in the case of *Brown v. Board of Education*, the U.S. Supreme Court had ruled unanimously that "separate educational facilities are inherently unequal" and ordered schools nationwide to integrate with "deliberate speed." Ten years before that, in 1944, the Court had banned the exclusion of blacks from voting in primaries, a practice that had been common and even legal throughout the South. Yet, it was obvious that schools were still segregated and that, in many states, black citizens still couldn't vote.

So, after much pressure and compromise, wrangled mainly by the Senate majority leader Lyndon Johnson, Congress passed, and President Eisenhower signed, the Civil Rights Act of 1957. It was a watered-down bill, but it did create a federal Civil Rights Commission, empowered to investigate charges of racial discrimination in schools, housing, and voter-registration boards and to make recommendations for remedial action.

---

*Even the editors of the *Village Voice*, the liberal New York weekly newspaper cofounded by Norman Mailer, were less open-minded than they may have thought. As late as May 27, 1959, in an editorial calling for an end to segregation in housing, they wrote, "A great myth of the 20th century is about to be laid to rest. . . . There is no longer any real belief in the notion that segregation is in the nature of things." The astonishing thing here is that it took until this late for even the *Voice* to comment that the belief in segregation "no longer" had basis.

The commission received its first sworn complaint on August 14, 1958, alleging—as the official docket put it—"that through threats of bodily harm and losing of jobs, and other means, Negro residents of Gadsden County, Florida, are being deprived of their right to vote."

The commission sent out field agents to look into the charges and to hold public hearings. The hearings marked the first time in nearly a hundred years that the U.S. government had taken a formal interest in these issues. As a result, more black Americans—not many, but still *some*—came forward, filed complaints, and told their stories. Over the next twelve months, the commission received petitions about the denial of voting rights from twenty-nine counties in eight states, and it held hearings in all of them.

The response was sufficiently encouraging that the Southern Christian Leadership Council, the civil-rights organization headed by Martin Luther King Jr., launched a "Crusade for Citizenship Campaign," shifting tactics, for the moment, from nonviolent protest—such as the boycott two years earlier that desegregated the public buses in Montgomery, Alabama—to voter-registration drives. Ella Baker, the SCLC staff secretary, coordinated the new campaign, holding meetings in over twenty southern cities, using the Civil Rights Commission as an instrument to mobilize black citizens, first as witnesses, then as activists.

In Alabama, ninety-one black men and women in six counties came forward to testify that they'd been denied the right to vote. In Montgomery alone, thirty-three black citizens made the charge; ten of them were college graduates, six held Ph.D.s, all of them were literate, most owned property, and two were World War II veterans who'd received Bronze Stars for valor in combat.

In Mississippi, twenty-four witnesses from three counties testified before the commission. In Forrest County, where 7,406 voting-age black citizens lived but only 16 were registered to vote, one black man said that he had unsuccessfully tried to register twice a year for each of the last eight years. The most recent time, he'd asked if there was a reason for the denials. The registrar replied, "No." Another man said that the registrar gave him a quiz, asking him to define "due process of law" and "the class assessment of land." Dissatisfied with the answers, the official refused to let him register.

The petitions prodded some action, but more often they incited obstruction. In Bullock County, Alabama, the Third Circuit Court

Judge, George C. Wallace—a fierce segregationist who, four years later, would be elected governor and, in 1968, run for president on an openly racist "independent" ticket—simply impounded the voter-registration records, rather than open them for federal inspection, and threatened to lock up any Civil Rights Commission agent who came down to challenge his action. As a further barrier to federal prying, the Alabama legislature passed a bill permitting the destruction of voter-registration records every thirty days.

When the commission investigated a violation of school-desegregation laws—or when the Justice Department tried to enforce them—the evasions turned particularly creative. The legislatures of Mississippi and South Carolina repealed their statutes requiring school attendance, in order to preempt desegregation orders. North Carolina and Texas allowed parents to release their children from mandatory schooling if they found integration unseemly.

Arkansas went one step further, allowing schools to close if the local board of education deemed it in the public interest to do so. Little Rock, Arkansas, was where, two years earlier, after much hesitation and pressure, President Eisenhower had sent the National Guard to enforce desegregation laws. Now the black citizens themselves put up a fight.

On April 29, 1959, the Arkansas Supreme Court, by a 4–3 margin, upheld the state's school-closing law as a valid exercise of state rights. Six days later, in protest, the moderates on Little Rock's school board resigned. The remaining members escalated the clash by dismissing, without cause, forty-four teachers who were known to be sympathetic to integration. The board president, Ed I. McKinley Jr., declared that teachers who believed that a U.S. Supreme Court ruling was the law of the land "have no place in our school system, however qualified professionally."

Arkansas citizens, mainly black but some white, organized a group called Stop This Outrageous Purge, or STOP. Segregationists fought back with the Committee to Retain Our Segregated Schools, or CROSS. The STOP activists moved for a recall election of the school board on May 25. The three leading segregationists on the board were voted out, and members of STOP were elected to replace them. On June 18, a federal appeals court overruled the Arkansas court's pro-segregation decision. The following September, the high schools were reopened under federal supervision.

This wasn't the only judicial victory that year. In Atlanta, a federal judge ruled that the laws segregating the city's bus and trolley system were unconstitutional. (The lawsuit against the city had been brought by two black ministers, the reverends Sam Williams and John Porter.) A Virginia appeals court overruled state laws mandating segregation in the schools, as a result of which black students were allowed in formerly all-white schools for the first time ever. In Seattle, a Coast Guard commander who had put his house up for sale refused to sell it to a black postal worker who'd offered to pay for it in cash; the black man sued, and a state housing board ordered the commander to make the sale. These were unprecedented triumphs, but each inch gained only highlighted the miles left to go.

On April 24, 1959, in the small town of Poplarville, Mississippi, a twenty-three-year-old black truck driver named Mack Charles Parker was about to go on trial for allegedly raping a white woman. The victim hadn't firmly identified Parker in the police lineup. The state branch of the National Association for the Advancement of Colored People had found Parker a good lawyer. There was a chance that the charge might not stick. So a mob of twenty white men broke into the sheriff's office, dragged Parker out of his cell, hauled him away in a convoy of cars, brutally beat him, and finally shot him to death, leaving his corpse in the Pearl River, where it was discovered nine days later, mutilated and pocked with two bullet holes.

The NAACP's field officer, Medgar Evers, hired a photographer to take pictures of the corpse, then petitioned the U.S. Justice Department to investigate. FBI agents swarmed the county. The sheriff later complained that they'd interrogated him "as though I were a nigger or a dog."

Through his involvement in the Parker case, Medgar Evers attained national prominence. He embarked on a two-week speaking tour, mainly before NAACP conferences around the nation, often shaming his listeners into taking more action.

At a conference in Los Angeles on May 31, he opened his talk by noting the remarkable achievements and discoveries of this "century of wonders—the United Nations, Sputnik, explorers, space, atoms." Such progress made it all the more remarkable, he continued, that Negro teachers in Mississippi were browbeaten into signing pledges not to join or give money to the NAACP. Evers mentioned not only

Mack Parker, whose name was in the news, but also the Reverend G. W. Lee, who was murdered for refusing to take his name off a voter-registration list, and Lamar Smith, who was beaten and shot to death on his way to pick up absentee ballots to distribute to his neighbors. He outlined what he called the "Gestapo-like actions" that white racists employed to keep African Americans from voting. He noted that in Lumberton, the town where Mack Parker had lived, no black citizens were registered to vote. Across the entire state, nearly a half-million Negroes were of voting age, he said, but fewer than thirty thousand were registered.

"When we think in terms of the people in Los Angeles, with the great opportunity that you have here to register and to vote without any obstacles," Evers said, "it is really amazing to us . . . that you, in many instances, fail to take advantage of your situation out here. Because to take advantage of it out here would help us in Mississippi." He particularly chastised the "Uncle Toms" who were given prestigious jobs, especially in the schools, for the sole purpose of suppressing "the more militant Negro people" and "any semblance of a fight for justice and equality." Negroes in Los Angeles, San Francisco, and New York might think they were free, but they should look at the pictures of Mack Parker, Evers said, calling the images "the most atrocious thing that I'd ever seen"—he'd brought the pictures along with him, he'd show them to anyone who asked. "Any sensible Negro" who looks at these pictures, he added, will "know that until every Negro in Pearl River County is free, we have no freedom in this country."

Medgar Evers was thirty-three. When he was in the Army, during World War II, he'd read about Jomo Kenyatta's Mau Mau reign of terror and its armed uprising against British colonialism in Africa. For a while, he dreamed of organizing his own blackshirts to extract vengeance against racist despots back in America. But Evers was a Christian, too, and his religious principles—"two wrongs don't make a right"—overwhelmed his other impulses.

He did, however, take action. He'd seen the world while fighting for freedom as a soldier—Normandy, Le Havre, Liege, Antwerp, and Cherbourg. After the war, back home in Decatur, Mississippi, he led his brother and four of their friends down to the county courthouse, to register to vote. When they strolled into the registrar's office, more than a dozen white men, all carrying arms, blocked their way. That night, some of these men paid a visit to Evers's parents, threatening them with violence if their boys did that again.

In 1954, the year of *Brown v. Board of Education*, Evers started a local branch of the NAACP and drove all over the state, logging seventy-eight thousand miles in the next two years, looking into reports and rumors of civil-rights abuses and brutality. By the time the Civil Rights Commission was set up, Evers had more than laid its groundwork in Mississippi, just as Martin Luther King and Ella Baker had done in Alabama. By 1959, when he started publicizing the Mack Parker case, Evers found his name on the death lists of several chapters of the White Citizens' Council.

Martin Luther King also took a new direction that year. He'd gained much fame and admiration for the Montgomery bus boycott and his stirring oratory. He wrote a best-selling book and appeared on the cover of *Time* magazine. But he felt that the SCLC, his organization, was floundering. It needed focus, an impassioning idea.

Back in February 1959, barely thirty years old, King traveled to India. He had been reading about Mohandas Gandhi's "nonviolent army," thought it might provide a model for the American civil-rights movement's next step, and wanted to learn more. He dined with India's prime minister, Jawaharlal Nehru. He flew to the remote ashram where, in 1930, Gandhi had embarked on the "Salt March"—the nonviolent protest against Britain's monopoly tax on India's salt, sparking the first wave of civil disobedience in the drive for Indian independence. Finally, he met Vinoba Bhave, the Gandhian mystic, joined him on one of his daily walks, and spoke, both of them passionately, about race, colonialism, nonviolence, and nuclear disarmament.

Back home that spring, King's head was clear: nonviolent protest would be the watchword of the civil-rights movement, the strategy for integrating America and healing the nation's wounds.

But an alternative model of protest was taking shape in a few cities up north. During the week of July 13, 1959, the TV newsman Mike Wallace hosted a two-and-a-half-hour documentary—split into half-hour episodes, one aired each night, and syndicated nationwide—called *The Hate That Hate Produced*.

The program was about, as Wallace put it in his opening remarks, "a call for black supremacy among a small but growing segment in the Negro community," led by Elijah Muhammad's Nation of Islam and especially the minister of its New York chapter, Malcolm X.

The Black Muslims, as Elijah's followers were often called, thought that integration was a sham. The "white man" was the devil. Christianity was a religion of black enslavement. The American government had reneged on every promise. Why integrate with liars and betrayers? Black people needed to build their own institutions, totally apart from the white power structure.

Wallace meant for the program to shock, and it did. In one scene, at a rally in Washington, D.C., ten thousand black people—the men dressed in black bowties, the women in white burkas—were seen cheering wildly when Elijah Muhammad railed against "the white man" as "the greatest liar in history . . . the greatest murderer in history." In an interview afterward, the preacher said that sometime in the next decade there would be a war between the forces of God and the Devil—the black man and the white man—and that, in this war, "there will be plenty bloodshed."

Malcolm X was, as Wallace said, "a remarkable man"—a former pimp and drug dealer, born as Malcolm Little, who converted to Islam in prison, and cleaned up his bad habits, after reading Elijah Muhammad's works and realizing that he shouldn't be ashamed to be a black man. He, too, was interviewed on Wallace's program; he spoke in a calmer tone than Elijah; he seemed more urbane and sophisticated. But his message was the same: "The black man, by nature, is divine," he said, while the white man, by nature, is "evil." The serpent that drove Adam and Eve out of the Garden of Eden was a biblical metaphor for the white man. The Nation of Islam had set up schools in Chicago and Detroit. They were like ordinary schools except that they left out stories like "Little Black Sambo," which bred a sense of inferiority, and they taught that the Devil and Hell are not mythical abstractions. The Muslim child who goes to these schools, Malcolm said, "will tell you that Hell is right where he has been catching it."

Mike Wallace was an intrepid, well-known television journalist. At forty-one, he had just been lured away from ABC, one of the big three networks, by National Telefilm Associates, an upstart syndicate that offered him his own nightly, half-hour show and let him do pretty much what he wanted. Wallace hired as his assistant a black journalist named Louis Lomax, who had two master's degrees, from

American University and Yale—an extremely unusual accomplish-
ment at the time—and who, as a reporter for the American Negro
Press (the black counterpart to the National Press Club), had sold
some stories to the *Nation* and other magazines, which Wallace had
read and admired.

Lomax was an advocate for racial integration, but he found
Malcolm X fascinating, even appealing. Lomax had come up with the
idea for the program about racial hatred. He approached Malcolm
for an interview, simply taking the subway up to the Nation of Islam's
restaurant in Harlem, where Malcolm could frequently be found.
Lomax also supervised the filming of the Nation of Islam rallies and
conducted all the interviews. Wallace, who was white, could not have
come anywhere near the subjects; they wouldn't have agreed to speak
with him, certainly not on camera.

Wallace appeared on the show between the pretaped interviews
and the documentary footage, standing in the studio and reading
his script to the camera. It was a balanced script, filled with shock-
laden descriptions of Elijah and Malcolm—"a gospel of hate," "a fla-
grant doctrine of black supremacy," "organized hate"—but also with
an understanding of the movement's origins. "The burden of being
a black man in America has proved to be more than some of them
can bear," Wallace told his viewers. The Black Muslims' hate was a
response to "the hate that most American Negroes have received
for the last 300 years." Hence the show's title: *The Hate That Hate
Produced.*

In one part of the show, five random black people on the streets
of Harlem were asked what they thought about the Nation of Islam;
all of them had good things to say. One black man said he supported
the Nation's idea of "self-determination" and added, "If this is what
is classified as hate, then I suppose I am guilty of preaching such an
ideology." A young woman said, "I don't feel the NAACP's views are
the way out. . . . Together with our own people, more can be accomplished. . . . We've always been expecting too many crumbs from this
man," meaning the white man.

The show caused a sensation, so much so that, the following week,
it aired again, on July 22, this time all in a single two-hour program.

Malcolm was out of the country during all the broadcasts. Two
years earlier, Elijah Muhammad had sent a congratulatory telegram

to Egypt's president, Gamal Abdel Nasser, for hosting the Afro-Asian Solidarity Conference in Cairo—a follow-up to the Bandar conference of nonaligned nations. Nasser wrote back, a correspondence ensued, and finally he invited Elijah to visit him. Elijah asked Malcolm to go on his behalf. So, in July 1959, he embarked on a three-week trip to Egypt, Saudi Arabia, Lebanon, and Sudan.

When he returned to New York, the phone at his temple's restaurant was ringing all day long. Reporters who'd never heard of Malcolm X or the Nation of Islam before Mike Wallace's show now wanted him to elaborate on his alarming views. He was suddenly a national figure, and he started speaking out in public around the country.

Wallace's show might have puzzled or terrified white people, but it prodded black people to sign up. Membership in Malcolm's New York branch doubled, from 1,125 before the show to 2,369 after. Nationwide, numbers more than tripled, from about twenty-one thousand to seventy-five thousand. (They peaked at about one hundred thousand, in 1963, as Malcolm spoke more actively around the country.)

The show had other effects. Elijah Muhammad didn't like the way he came off. Neither he nor Malcolm liked it when Mike Wallace called their religion "hate gospel." Now that they were nationally known, they decided never again to lay themselves open to white editors. So, in November 1959, they started their own newspaper, *Muhammad Speaks*. Each issue included an insert of news about the Nation of Islam, but otherwise it looked like a regular newspaper—the editors even hired experienced journalists to write the stories—covering national and world news. By the late sixties, it was America's most widely read black newspaper, with over a half million readers.

Finally, just as traveling to India altered Martin Luther King's thinking about civil rights, so traveling to the Middle East opened a new line of thinking for Malcolm X. Malcolm didn't go to Mecca in July 1959—that would happen during a later trip—but he did meet Arab Muslims for the first time, on their native soil, and he realized that his own mentor, Elijah Muhammad, had wildly departed from orthodoxy. For instance, Elijah claimed to be the prophet of Allah. But, according to the ancient texts that the Arab scholars studied, the Prophet Mohammad, who lived in the sixth and seventh centuries, was His only true messenger. Elijah also taught an oddball history, in which blacks once ruled Earth until a scientist named Yakub invented the evil white race, which conquered civilization. The Tribe of Shabazz escaped to Africa, this tale continued, but the white man captured them again and took them to America as slaves. Sometime in the near future, this chronicle concluded, a Mother Ship will come down to Earth, lift the black people up, and destroy the white devils. This was the spiritual rationale for opposing integration—to remain racially separate and pure in preparation for the Rapture.

Malcolm now realized that this fable, like Elijah's self-declared status as Allah's prophet, had no basis in real Islam. Though he wouldn't articulate them publicly for another few years, the trip stirred Malcolm's first doubts about the Nation of Islam generally. From Muslims who had attended the conferences of nonaligned nations, he also began to realize—as did King around this time—that segregation was damaging America's image in the Cold War and that black leaders could use this fact as leverage in political struggles domestically. By the end of the year, in some of his speeches, Malcolm began to invoke the language of the civil-rights movement—using words like "freedom," "justice," and "equality"—though he continued to champion black self-reliance and to deride integrationist campaigns as self-deceptive.

• • •

On November 2, a grand jury assembled in Pearl River County, Mississippi, to hear evidence on the murder of Mack Parker. In response to Medgar Evers's pressure campaign, the Justice Department had sent down sixty FBI agents, who conducted a month-long investigation, culminating in a 378-page report that charged a dozen prominent local white men with taking part in the abduction and murder; some of these men had even confessed their guilt to the agents. However, the judge, Sebe Dale, a member of the White Citizens' Council, urged the jurors to ignore the FBI's evidence, and they did. On November 5, they returned their verdict, declining to indict any of the accused. They all went free; the case was closed.

The day before the grand jury met in Mississippi, a white man named John Howard Griffin boarded a plane from Dallas to New Orleans. His plan was to darken his skin with chemicals, so that he would look like a black man, then to roam the Deep South and write about the experience.

John Howard Griffin was born in Dallas in 1920 and grew up amid segregation in a household so paternalistic toward its black servants that he didn't recognize it as racist. A precocious boy, he sailed to France at age fifteen to study at a *lycée* in Tours. There were black Africans in his class, and he congratulated himself for tolerating their presence. But one day, while having lunch with a French friend, he expressed indignation that blacks were allowed to *eat* right next to white people. His friend calmly asked, "Why not?" Suddenly Griffin realized, "with a sick feeling," as he put it later, that he'd never heard anyone ask that simple question and, even more, he'd never asked it himself.

Griffin remained in France to study medicine and became an assistant to the director of an asylum. When the Germans invaded in 1940, most Americans in France fled, but Griffin stayed and joined the Resistance, using the asylum's ambulances to smuggle Jewish children out of Tours. The next year, he returned to Dallas and joined the Army Air Forces. He was shipped to the Pacific and, on the basis of his linguistic skills, assigned to a remote island in the Solomon chain to learn everything about the natives' culture and then to persuade them to join the Allied cause against the Japanese.

He became friendly with the natives, including the tribal chief. Then he had an epiphany. He had regarded the natives as inferior; and yet *he* was the one who could barely speak *their* language and who needed a five-year-old child to guide him through the jungle. From the islanders' point of view, *he* was inferior, "the other"; *they* were superior; and he realized that, under the circumstances, they were right.

Toward the end of the war, Griffin was working in a radar tent at the edge of an airstrip. One day, the site came under attack; an explosion knocked him unconscious. When he awoke, he could barely see. A doctor declared him legally blind. His vision was 20/200, and within a year, it deteriorated further; he couldn't see at all. He sailed back to France, went into retreat at the Abbey of Saint Pierre of Solesmes, studied Gregorian chants, and immersed himself in Catholicism. He now realized that color was irrelevant, and he was angered that people with vision treated him as inferior.

He moved back to Mansfield, Texas, gave lectures on blindness and on the history of music, and wrote a modestly successful novel.

He got married in 1953 and became involved in a prolonged but ultimately unsuccessful legal battle for school desegregation. In 1957, all of a sudden, Griffin regained some vision. A doctor prescribed medication to restore blood circulation in his eyes, and over time he recovered completely.

In October 1959, Griffin called the publisher of *Sepia*, a black magazine in Fort Worth, to propose the idea of going to the Deep South disguised as a black man. He got the assignment. On November 1, he flew to New Orleans, where a dermatologist with whom he'd spoken gave him an accelerated dose of Oxsoralen, a drug that heightened the skin's sensitivity to light. For the next week, he lay under an ultraviolet lamp for as long as fifteen hours each day. Finally he shaved and stained his head. Looking in a mirror, he saw, as he later wrote, "the face and shoulders of a stranger—a fierce, bald, very dark Negro."

On November 8, he ventured into the streets in his new guise for the first time, and found that he could easily "pass" as black to both races. Within five days, he lived in black rooming houses, ate and talked with black men, and, as he put it, realized emotionally what he had long known intellectually—"that the *Other* was not other at all," that within the context of home and family, everyone's problems were pretty much the same.

Looking for work, he called employers on the phone; they sounded interested, but when he came in for the interview, they awkwardly turned him away. The only possible reason for their sudden coolness was his color.

On November 14, he went to the bus station to buy a ticket to Mississippi. The white woman in the ticket booth glared at him "with such loathing"—he called it "the hate stare." Walking to a bench, he got another "hate stare" from a white man sitting nearby. "Nothing can describe the withering horror of this," Griffin wrote. "You feel lost, sick at heart before such unmasked hatred, not so much because it threatens you as because it shows humans in such an inhuman light. You see a kind of insanity, something so obscene the very obscenity of it (rather than the threat) terrifies you."

A few hours earlier, Griffin had gone to see Sterling Williams, the black proprietor of a shoeshine stand just off Jackson Square. Griffin had befriended Williams before the ultraviolet treatments, then came

No one diagnosed and personified the era's restlessness more intensely than Norman Mailer, who, after penning the Great American Novel in the wake of World War II, switched tracks, plunged into jazz and marijuana, and emerged with a key insight about the nuclear age—its dual prospects of infinite expansion and instant annihilation—and a new pathbreaking style of writing, which combined literature, journalism, and personal confession.

Mailer took some of his cues from the Beats, especially Allen Ginsberg (far right) and Jack Kerouac (left side, full face), who broke through arbitrary forms to write in meters that matched their own natural cadence and who set the stage for the coming decade's "generation gap."

William Burroughs introduced the Beats to the Romantic poets and wrote his own novel, *Naked Lunch*, a mad collage of hallucinogenic sensations set down in hyper-vivid prose, which he hoped would tap "some excess of feeling or behavior that will shatter the human pattern."

Barney Rosset, the owner of the Grove Press, published the uncensored text of D. H. Lawrence's *Lady Chatterley's Lover*, successfully sued the federal government when it banned the book's distribution, and so dealt a crucial blow against the nation's obscenity laws, paving the way for a new era of free speech.

Lenny Bruce transformed nightclub comedy with jazz rhythms, urban-Yiddish lingo, wicked social satire, and profanity, which led to multiple arrests and plunged him into martyr's self-destructiveness—but would influence generations of comics to come.

Herman Kahn, a mordant physicist and nuclear strategist from the RAND Corporation, delivered marathon public lectures on how to fight, survive, and win a nuclear war, riveting thousands at the peak of obsession with the bomb.

Anastas Mikoyan, the deputy premier of the U.S.S.R., began the year with a spontaneous visit to the United States (the first ever by a high-ranking Soviet official), which expanded into a much-touted countrywide tour and a one-on-one meeting with President Eisenhower, touching off a new era in personal superpower diplomacy.

Fidel Castro, the new revolutionary leader of Cuba (seen here eating ice cream at the Bronx Zoo), set out on his own American tour in the spring, spurring wild excitement and hopes of a new brand of third-world leader who might go his own way, independent of both superpowers and thus breaking the Cold War's mold, though this dream would soon shatter.

C. Wright Mills, a popular renegade sociologist, fell too hard for Castro's illusions but in the process wrote an essay that planted the roots, and directly inspired the student leaders, of the sixties' New Left.

The alto saxophonist Ornette Coleman (with the trumpeter Don Cherry at the Five Spot nightclub) emerged out of nowhere with a new "free jazz," which broke through standard rhythms and chord changes.

George Russell, one of several composers looking for an escape from be-bop's maze of standard chord changes, found the key in ancient church scales (or "modes") and unleashed a different, more lyrical sort of playing free.

The trumpeter Miles Davis took Russell's discovery to its grandest heights with the album *Kind of Blue*, which became a huge hit and made Miles a star—but not enough to break through the racism that led a white cop to beat him over the head one night while he was standing on the sidewalk outside the Manhattan jazz club where he'd been attracting full-house crowds.

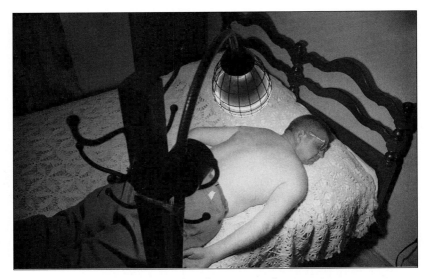

John Howard Griffin, wanting not merely to report on but to experience racism, chemically dyed his skin black and traveled around the Deep South, then wrote a book, *Black Like Me*, which shocked many white northerners and predicted the rage to come.

The photographer Robert Frank, a Swiss Jewish immigrant, took a road trip across America, exposing a lonely country that had been invisible to many natives and pioneering an improvisational, and influential, style of photography inspired by Beat poets and abstract expressionist painters.

The actor John Cassavetes broke out of the Hollywood studio system to direct the first indie film, *Shadows*, shooting on the streets of New York and using little-known actors who largely improvised their dialogue.

Robert Rauschenberg created a new type of art, which combined abstract painting and sculpture made from objects found on the street, liberating modern art from the flat canvas. *Photography by Kay Harris, courtesy of the Estate of Robert Rauschenberg; Art © Estate of Robert Rauschenberg/Licensed by VAGA, New York, NY*

Allan Kaprow went further, merging reality and art with the first Happenings, which joined artist and audience in one grand playful spectacle.

Frank Drake (left) set up the first experiments in radio-astronomy to search for extra-terrestrial intelligence.

Jack St. Clair Kilby, a tinkerer-engineer, invented the integrated circuit (also known as the microchip), which spawned the digital revolution and transformed human existence.

Margaret Sanger, a dainty firebrand who'd been a feminist pioneer for decades, sought out and sponsored scientists to invent the birth-control pill, which liberated women from traditional roles and overhauled social customs.

back to see him right after. Williams was one of the few people that Griffin let in on his secret, and he'd given Griffin useful tips on how to dress and how to behave.

Williams was normally good-natured, but on this day, Griffin's final day in New Orleans, he seemed "glum and angry." It turned out that Williams had just learned about what happened nine days earlier in Mississippi—the grand jury's refusal to indict anyone for the murder of Mack Parker. He'd read about it in the *Louisiana Weekly*, a local black newspaper. "This is what we can expect from the white man's justice," Williams read aloud from the paper's editorial. "What hope is there when a white jury won't even look at the evidence against a lynch mob?"

Griffin would write, presciently, at the end of his book: "If some spark does set the keg afire, it will be a senseless tragedy of ignorant against ignorant, injustice answering injustice—a holocaust that will drag down the innocent and right-thinking masses of human beings. Then we will pay for not having cried for justice long ago."

Back in Texas, he spent much of December 1959 writing his articles for *Sepia*. They ran in installments from April to September 1960, under the title "Journey into Shame." He expanded the articles into a book, which was published in the fall of 1961, under the title *Black Like Me*.

By then, Griffin was already famous, the result of dozens of radio and TV interviews. The book sold a hundred thousand copies in hardcover and, over the next few years, 5 million in paperback. Critics hailed it as "a scathing indictment of our society," "a basic text for study of this contemporary social problem," a book that captured "the feel, sight, sound and sweat of what the abstractly titled 'Negro problem' is all about." Griffin spent three weeks of every month on the road, recounting his book's stories and pressing home its lessons, mainly to white audiences, who believed him more than they would have believed a real black man.

The tinderbox of race wouldn't explode until a few years later. But it was in 1959 that the kindling was sorted, the fuses prepared, and the matches lined up.

Just one month into the new decade, on February 1, 1960, four black college students in Greensboro, North Carolina—inspired by the previous year's buildup of protests, hopes, and horrors—held the first "sit-in," deciding to sit down at an all-white lunch counter, even though it meant they would be thrown in jail. Their action was spontaneous; it took the civil-rights leaders by surprise. But the simplicity of the gesture, the clarity of its appeal to justice, and its resonance with the principles of nonviolent protest, were overpowering. By the end of April 1960, over sixty thousand young people, black and white, most of them students, had taken part in sit-ins; well over ten thousand had been arrested. That month, Ella Baker, the SCLC's staff secretary, organized a youth wing called the Student Nonviolent Coordinating Committee, or SNCC (pronounced "snick"), which over the next few years would play a leading role in campaigns to test civil-rights laws all over the South.

Medgar Evers didn't think sit-ins would work just yet in Mississippi, so instead, he organized a black boycott of all the merchants in Jackson who hired only white employees. The campaign slashed business at those stores by 75 percent and inspired similar demonstrations in the supposedly nonracist North and West. In Las Vegas, the NAACP threatened to lead a boycott of the casinos—and they started hiring black people on the spot. In Kansas City, pressure from the National Urban League forced the city's buses to start hiring black drivers.

Over the next few years—as a cumulative result of the protests, the Civil Rights Commission, the examples of Evers, King, and Malcolm, and, finally, the signing of the Civil Rights Act in July 1964—the foundations of institutionalized racism would begin to collapse.

But the segregationists refused to surrender just yet. On June 28, 1963, Medgar Evers was shot to death outside his home after returning from an NAACP meeting. On February 21, 1965, Malcolm X was murdered while speaking at the Audubon Ballroom in New York City, almost certainly by members of the Nation of Islam, from which he had broken a year earlier. On April 4, 1968, Martin Luther King was assassinated while standing on a motel balcony in Memphis.

All over America, the streets of the cities went up in flames, and many white people wondered why the rioters were so angry. But the answers, the warning signs, were clear in 1959. This was the keg set afire that John Howard Griffin warned about. It was the culmination of what Mike Wallace had diagnosed on nationwide television as "the hate that hate produced."

17

Civilizations in the Stars

On September 19, 1959, scientists around the country opened the new issue of *Nature* magazine with a shock. There, along-side the usual assortment of reports and lab findings—about transistor electronics, the heterogeneity of human hemoglobin, a new way to predict patterns of bee swarming, and recent discoveries in developmental biology—was an article titled "Searching for Interstellar Communication."

Outer-space creatures had been a suspect topic for scientific inquiry since the turn of the century, when Percival Lowell, an eminent astronomer of the day, claimed to detect canals on Mars and argued that an intelligent race had dug them in order to tap water from the planet's polar ice caps for the irrigation of crops—only to be thoroughly discredited a few years later, when sharper telescopes revealed that the canals had been optical illusions. More recently, dubious sightings of flying saucers and far-fetched science-fiction stories about outer-space travel only stiffened the topic's taboo.

Nature was a highly reputable science magazine, in its ninetieth year of publication. Its articles were aimed at a broad audience, but they were peer-reviewed. And the authors of this article, Philip Morrison and Giuseppe Cocconi, were physicists of unimpeachable reputation. If the editors of *Nature* were giving ink to this idea, then it had to be taken as something other than the stuff of juveniles and madmen. Science and technology *had* made huge strides since the war. Readers wondered: were we now on the verge of the ultimate breakthrough—the discovery of intelligent life on other planets?

The previous summer, the National Academy of Sciences had established a Space Science Board to study "scientific-research opportunities opened up by the advent of modern rocket and satellite tools," and asked Phil Morrison to be a member.

Morrison was a nuclear physicist at Cornell University. During the war, he served on the Manhattan Project, which designed and built the atom bomb. He participated on the team that sparked the first nuclear chain reaction. He was the one who calculated how much plutonium would be needed to trigger an implosion (about six kilograms). He installed the core of the test bomb at Alamogordo, near Los Alamos, and witnessed the explosion's fireball and mushroom cloud. He assembled the actual A-bomb that was dropped on Nagasaki, piecing it together inside the plane as the pilots hurtled toward their target.

After the war, Morrison emerged as one of several atomic scientists who feared a nuclear arms race and spoke out against the bomb. He had been a Communist in his youth and still held socialist views, which got him into trouble at Cornell during Senator Joseph McCarthy's Red hunts. In 1953, he decided to lower his public profile. Realizing that most research projects in his field would be linked in some way to nuclear weapons and in any case funded by the federal government, Morrison shifted his focus from particle physics to astronomy.

Morrison was thoroughly hardheaded when it came to the scientific method and rules of evidence. He scoffed at the prospects of interstellar travel. He made a hobby of debunking reports about flying saucers and the Bermuda Triangle.

However, when the National Academy appointed him to the Space Science Board, the question of extraterrestrial life—and how to detect it if it exists—unavoidably came up.

The Space Science Board was a by-product of the International Geophysical Year, a project involving forty-six nations, lasting from July 1957 to December 1958, with the aim of fostering international harmony through science.

One ironic result of the IGY was the triggering of the space race. Two years before the project began, President Eisenhower announced that, as part of its contribution to the project, the United States would build a "small Earth-circling satellite" called the Explorer. The Soviet premier Nikita Khrushchev, who had taken no interest in IGY until then, perked up and responded that the Soviet Union would beat the United States to the punch with a bigger satellite. The Explorer flopped. But the Soviets successfully launched Sputnik, followed by Lunik, spurring the fears of a missile gap and deepening an overall crisis of confidence in the West.

But the IGY did widen the sphere of knowledge in other ways. Experiments conducted in its name led to the discovery of the mid-ocean submarine ridge and the Van Allen Belt. Expert panels were set up to study cosmic rays, the ionosphere, gravity, geomagnetism, meteorology, oceanography, the upper atmosphere, among other phenomena.

In December 1958, the Space Science Board met twice in the office of its chairman, Professor Bruno Rossi, at the Massachusetts Institute of Technology. Rossi had worked with Morrison on the Manhattan Project and had since become a leading figure in X-ray astronomy. They talked about space probes—the relative merits of landing them on a planet or taking measurements from a distance, what kinds of measurements to take, how to take them, and what kinds of signs to look for as indications of some form of life, past or present.

When Morrison got back to Cornell, he discussed the problem with Giuseppe Cocconi, a close friend and colleague in the physics department. Morrison had just completed a paper on gamma rays. Cocconi wondered: if there are people out there on other planets, wouldn't they use gamma rays to communicate with possible civilizations orbiting other stars?

Morrison was intrigued by the notion but thought they should examine other possibilities, not just gamma rays. At some point, they hit upon radio signals, and that struck them as more plausible. Celestial bodies emitted lots of radio frequencies. The bourgeoning specialty of radio astronomy was based on the discovery that much could be inferred about a star or a planet from the traits of these emissions. As a teenager, Morrison had fiddled with a crystal radio kit; he earned a radio operator's license and thought about studying radio engineering before he was captivated by the allure of physics. Years later, he would acknowledge that this adolescent obsession probably drew him to all his later interests.

After limiting their inquiry to radio frequencies, Morrison and Cocconi addressed a specific problem: What frequency would an alien civilization use to broadcast these signals? One of the most common elements in the universe was hydrogen. Anyone familiar with radio astronomy knew hydrogen atoms emitted electromagnetic waves fluttering at frequencies around 1420 megahertz. If alien civilizations were trying to communicate, they would have some familiarity with radio astronomy. They would want to send a signal that someone out there might be trying to pick up. Therefore, that was the frequency they would likely use. More to the point, that should be the frequency that our own scientists should focus on while pointing their radio telescopes to the nearest stars.

This was the argument that Morrison and Cocconi laid out in their article for *Nature*. They stopped short of claiming that intelligent aliens were definitely out there, beaming signals. However, they wrote, it "seems unwarranted to deny . . . that near some star rather like the Sun, there are civilizations with scientific interests." If so, they've probably been eyeing our own sun as a likely source of a similarly evolved species. We should therefore assume these extraterrestrials "long ago established a channel of communication that would one day become known to us, and that they look forward patiently to the answering signal from the Sun which would make known to them that a new society has entered the community of intelligence."

Morrison and Cocconi acknowledged that their argument must seem like science fiction. However, they countered, "the presence of interstellar signals is entirely consistent with all we know," and "if signals are present, the means of detecting them is now at hand." Finding intelligent life in the universe would be a profound discovery. "The probability of success is difficult to estimate," they granted, "but if we never seek, the chance of success is zero."

Neither author knew it at the time, but in the mountains of Green Bank, West Virginia, someone was already seeking.

Six months before the *Nature* article appeared, a twenty-nine-year-old astronomer named Frank Drake was setting up the equipment to *do* what Morrison and Cocconi were only proposing.

When Drake was a precocious eight-year-old in Chicago, tinkering with tools and building model airplanes, his father told him about the existence of other planets like Earth. Frank took the statement literally, envisioning planets *exactly* like Earth, with people, houses, cars, and the rest. He was soon disabused of this notion, but the image stuck with him, excited his curiosity.

Later, as a graduate student in astronomy at Harvard, Drake spent some of his time observing the Pleiades cluster, the bright array of stars within the constellation Taurus, through a twenty-five-foot radio telescope. One night he detected a strong signal that hadn't been there before. It was very close to the frequency of a hydrogen wave, the same frequency that Morrison and Cocconi would calculate that aliens might use to communicate—an inference that Drake now drew on his own. He wondered if someone or something was sending a signal from Pleiades.

He soon realized that nothing of the sort was happening. To test the hypothesis, he steered the telescope away from Pleiades but continued to hear the pulse, meaning that what he'd detected was terrestrial interference—a stray electromagnetic signal from some-where on Earth or in the atmosphere. Still, for those few minutes, when he thought that he might have stumbled onto the greatest dis-covery in human history, the thrill was intense—he'd never experi-enced any sensation quite like it.

At the start of 1959, Drake got a job helping to set up what was designed to be the best radio observatory in the world, built around a new eighty-five-foot telescope, in Green Bank, West Virginia. The site was cold, snowy, and isolated. Only a few scientists were lured to work in its earliest stage. One day over lunch, Drake told his col-leagues about the Pleiades experience and speculated that if aliens were sending out radio signals, the observatory's new, much more powerful telescope might be able to pick them up.

Drake's boss, Lloyd Berkner, a pioneer in studying the ionosphere and also a risk taker, liked the idea of conducting an experiment to see if anyone was out there, but he wanted to keep it quiet. The observatory was funded by tax dollars, through the National Science Foundation, and the whole project could be jeopardized if Congress found out that they were looking for little green men. Berkner limited Drake's budget to $20,000. Drake dubbed the experiment "Project Ozma," after the princess who ruled the Land of Oz in Frank Baum's novels.

In March 1959, Drake started assembling the necessary equip-ment. He acquired a narrow-band radio receiver, to home in on the right frequencies; a high-powered amplifier, to boost what would be a very weak signal sent from so far away; and a tape recorder, so that he could later analyze whatever signals might be detected.

When the Morrison-Cocconi article appeared in *Nature* six months later, Drake felt that his instincts were vindicated. As a student, he had known Morrison slightly and had heard some of his celebrated lectures. If a physicist of Morrison's stature was thinking along these lines, Drake figured that he must be on the right track.

But Otto Struve, who had since replaced Berkner as the observatory's director, was livid. Struve, a Russian émigré in his early sixties, was widely regarded as the greatest astronomer alive. He was also one of the very few serious scientists who had long argued the case for intelligent life in other solar systems. For that reason, when he first came to Green Bank, he gave his full backing to Drake's experiment. Struve was also a shrewd veteran of academic politics; he knew the importance of getting credit for having an idea first. The upside of the *Nature* article was that Project Ozma no longer had to be kept in the closet; such research was now legitimized. So Struve went up to MIT to give a lecture about Drake's project, its vast scientific and philosophical importance, and, above all, the fact that it had gotten underway well before the *Nature* article was published.

As a result of Struve's lecture, the word of Project Ozma spread quickly. An electronics company donated more sophisticated equipment. Newspaper and magazine reporters started visiting Green Bank to write stories about the work.

On the morning of April 8, 1960, the search was ready to begin. Drake aimed the telescope at the first target, Tau Ceti, a star much like the sun, just twelve light-years away, and turned on the recorders. Nothing happened. In the afternoon, he steered the telescope to another nearby star, Epsilon Eridani—and, suddenly, as Drake later put it, "Wham!" Bursts of noise came through the loudspeaker at eight times a second. "Could it be this easy?" he wondered. The signal soon disappeared. Rumors spread that Drake and his team had heard from creatures on another planet. Reporters called, wondering if it was true. Drake replied that he couldn't comment, which only heightened the suspicions. Finally, after ten days, the signals returned—only this time they were coming not only from the telescope but from a small horn that Drake had stuck out his window.

The signal had to be atmospheric interference. He soon realized that it was coming from an airplane flying by.

Drake and his team kept checking on the two stars for another month, altering the frequencies slightly. They rested for a month, then tried for still another month. In all, the system operated for two hundred hours. They heard nothing. Project Ozma shut down.

But the subject was now respectable, so much so that in November 1960, the National Academy of Sciences sponsored a conference at Green Bank, inviting a group of scientists and business leaders to discuss how to turn the search into a systematic inquiry. The members of the group called themselves the Order of the Dolphin, in honor of John Lilly, one of the participants, who had recently conducted studies concluding that dolphins were an intelligent species. Also at the conference were Frank Drake, Phil Morrison, Otto Struve, and a young astronomer from Cornell named Carl Sagan—who, a decade later, when radio probes resumed in earnest, would become the public face of the "search for extraterrestrial intelligence," or SETI, as the discipline came to be called.

The tragedy was that, even if the SETI teams were to detect a real signal, there probably wasn't much they could do with it. If it came from a solar system as near as ten light-years away, that would mean the signal had been transmitted ten years earlier—and a reply wouldn't reach the distant planet for another ten years still, assuming the original senders were still listening. If the two civilizations could somehow find a common language (Drake thought that they might be able to communicate in a binary code of 0s and 1s), the most basic exchanges could drag on for a century or longer.

As for visiting one another, Drake never put much stock in that prospect. In the early sixties, he investigated several UFO sightings, and, unlike Morrison, kept an open mind about them. But he found that all of them were either natural phenomena—such as airplanes, helicopters, and meteorites—or hoaxes, some of them impressively elaborate.

More than that, the math just didn't add up. Light travels at 186,000 miles per second, or 670,616,629 miles per hour. Ten light-years—the distance that a beam of light travels in the course of ten years—amounts to more than 58 trillion miles. If mankind could build a spacecraft that could fly that far at merely one-tenth the speed of light—that is, at 67 million miles per hour—it would take a hundred years, more than an astronaut's lifetime, to get there. And, Drake calculated, providing the power for such a trip would be an insuperable task, requiring all of the energy produced on Earth over a period of two hundred years.

If space was the next frontier, it was wondrous for exploration, but less so for expansion, much less for conquest. We could watch and listen, but the possibilities for true breakthroughs in the cosmos were limited; we were ultimately marooned on Earth.

To Drake's mind, though, this didn't matter. He was certain that other advanced civilizations were out there. Given the billions of stars in the galaxy, it seemed extremely unlikely that there weren't. Finding one of these civilizations would be an event of such momentousness, it was worth a lot to keep searching, even if the effort took decades. The process of discovery and the potential breakthrough in knowledge were enough for Drake. In this sense, he was still that eight-year-old boy in Chicago.

Phil Morrison shared this outsize curiosity and wonderment. But underlying Morrison's quest was also a political passion—specifically a horror of nuclear weapons, which he had seen close up, had helped to create, and now wanted to see wiped out before they wiped out humanity. And in this context, space exploration might have very practical consequences.

In 1979, Morrison wrote an article called "Twenty Years After," in which he reminisced about the essay that he and Cocconi had written for *Nature* and the first SETI experiments at Green Bank. Morrison ended the piece with a passage from Arthur C. Clarke's science-fiction story "When the Aliens Come." Clarke wrote that the "most important result" of extraterrestrial contacts "might be the simple proof that other intelligent races do exist," that these races "had safely passed their nuclear crises," and that, therefore, we might pass our crisis as well. The ultimate purpose of these searches, the story concluded, was to "give us renewed hope for our own future."

18

A Great Upward Swoop of Movement

On Wednesday, October 21, 1959, the doors swung open at the Solomon R. Guggenheim Museum, perched on Fifth Avenue at Eighty-ninth Street, across from Central Park, and looking like nothing else around it—nothing else in New York City, maybe in the world. Its designer, Frank Lloyd Wright, the world's most famous architect, modeled it after the ancient ziggurats of Mesopotamia. Various critics likened it to an upside-down cupcake, a beehive, a hot cross bun, a giant Jell-O mold, a ball of mud. *Time* magazine called it "a mighty tower and Babel of discord." An editor of the *New York Mirror* wrote that the building itself should be put in a museum, "to show how mad the 20th century is."

Certainly it was the nation's oddest art museum. It was the first major American museum dedicated exclusively to nonrepresentational art. And Wright designed it to be a celebration more of architecture—of Frank Lloyd Wright himself—than of the art inside. The Guggenheim, then, stood as a double-edged artifact of the orbit-breaking age—architecture transcending its function, art unfettered by the tangible world.

And yet, because it was so strange and so blatantly new, people flocked to it as they had to no other museum of art, much less a museum of abstract twentieth-century art. On the first Sunday after its opening, ten thousand people showed up, lines stretching around the corner all the way to Madison Avenue, many waiting over an hour to get in, a few thousand turned away. One million people visited the museum in its first year, three-quarters of a million in each of the few years that followed.

Solomon Guggenheim had died ten years earlier, at the age of eighty-eight, but he had taken a very hands-on role in the museum— its vision, its design, and the nature of the art that it would hold. He was one of eight sons of Meyer Guggenheim, a Swiss Jew who immigrated to America in the 1840s and made a fortune in railroad investments and metals. Solomon made millions more in gold mining, retired in 1919, and devoted most of his time to collecting art. He and his wife traveled extensively in Europe, buying an impressive array of paintings by the Old Masters, until, in 1927, he met the Baroness Hildegard Rebay von Ehrenwiesen—Hilla Rebay, as she liked to be called—an eccentric German artist who was hired to paint Guggenheim's portrait. Almost twice her age (he was sixty-six, she was thirty-seven), Guggenheim fell under the baroness's spell, embarking on a love affair—and a radically new direction in art collecting—that lasted the rest of his life.

Rebay persuaded him to abandon the Old Masters in favor of "non-objective art"—which she defined as "painting that represents no object or subject known to us on earth" but rather exists as "simply a beautiful organization of colors and forms to be enjoyed for beauty's sake." Just as some wealthy suitors plied their mistresses with jewelry and fine dresses, Guggenheim treated the baroness to paintings by the leading non-objective artists—Wassily Kandinsky, Marc Chagall, Paul Klee, Fernand Léger, most of whom were her friends. She particularly lobbied Guggenheim to buy the works of Rudolf Bauer—a third-rate artist, a pale imitation of Kandinsky, but also one of Rebay's former lovers. None of Bauer's paintings had ever sold for more than $500; Guggenheim paid $10,000 for each of the first two that Rebay persuaded him to purchase.

By the late 1930s, Guggenheim owned more than seven hundred paintings, including over a hundred Kandinskys and two hundred Bauers. He hung dozens of them on the walls of his suite at the Plaza Hotel and stored the rest in Rebay's apartment above Carnegie Hall.

Ever since he started buying art, Guggenheim had planned eventually to donate his collection to the Metropolitan Museum. But Rebay planted the idea of building his own museum, as a "monument" to his—now, their—collection.

Originally the idea of non-objective painting stemmed from the insight that photography freed artists from an obligation to reproduce nature. Instead, they could paint colors, forms, and lines for their own sake. But some of these artists—very much including Rebay—imbued this idea with a mystical flavor. They focused on Platonic forms, such as triangles and circles, which lay outside anything in reality but reflected a higher order. To Rebay, these sorts of paintings were "alive with spiritual rhythm and organic with the cosmic order which rules the universe." A museum devoted to this art could serve as a "temple to the spirit," in which humanity might find an inner serenity, a social utopia, perhaps a path to world peace.

In 1939, Guggenheim set up the Museum of Non-Objective Painting in a townhouse on East Fifty-fourth Street, with the baroness as its artistic director. But they considered this a temporary installation. A few years later, Rebay began to search for an architect who could build the larger temple of her dreams. And in that quest, she found Frank Lloyd Wright.

Rebay had interviewed several leading architects and wasn't pleased with any of them. When a friend suggested that she try Wright, she was surprised that he was still alive. (He was in his late seventies.) She read a few of his books and realized that he might be the one. Wright shared her streak of romantic idealism; he wrote frequently, and sweepingly, about "organic architecture" and its unity of forms with sculpture, art, and music.

Wright was born in 1867 on the plains of Wisconsin, and reached adulthood during an era of romantic revolt against eighteenth-century rationalism. His hero from childhood was Ralph Waldo Emerson, and as an architect, he sought to design structures in line with what he saw as the universal laws of nature. He also possessed enormous self-confidence; his mother's forebears had led a breakaway Unitarian sect whose motto was "Truth against the world," and Wright lived by that belief, regarding himself as the personification of Truth.

Rebay wrote to Wright in June 1943, asking him to build her temple. Non-objective paintings, she explained, are about "order

creating order and are sensitive (and corrective even) to space," adding, "I need a fighter, a lover of space, an originator, a tester, and a
wise man."

In July, Wright wrote back to Guggenheim directly, in language
designed to appeal, expressing great interest in building "a new type
of Treasury for works of art . . . a true refreshment of the spirit . . .
a genuine relief from the cinder heap old New York is bound to
become." Guggenheim gave him the commission.

By the beginning of 1944, Wright had an idea of what this art
temple would look like. "A museum," he wrote to Rebay, "should be
one extended, expansive, well-proportioned floor space from bottom
to top—a wheel-chair going around and up and down, throughout.
No steps anywhere."

It was a remarkably concise description of the museum that
would finally open fifteen years later.

In late 1945, he presented a blueprint and a plexiglass model
of the building, first to Guggenheim and Rebay, then to a group of
newspaper and magazine editors. "The building is built like a spring,"
he boasted at their press conference. "When the first atomic bomb
lands on New York, it will not be destroyed. It may be blown a few
miles into the air, but when it comes down *it will bounce!*"

By 1946, Guggenheim was growing worried about his architect's
well-known egotism. He wrote a letter to Wright, stressing that, while
the building "must, and should, enhance the paintings," those paintings must in no way be "overwhelmed by the building." The museum
was going to exhibit paintings, not the other way around.

Guggenheim had cause for worry. Rebay had shown him a letter
in which Wright referred to architecture as "the Mother-art of which
Painting is but a daughter." Wright had also told her that he didn't
care for art generally, didn't own any art—except for Japanese prints,
of which he had an impressive collection—and that he regarded the
works of Kandinsky and particularly of Bauer as nearly worthless.

Wright tried to calm Guggenheim's concerns, explaining that he
hadn't hung art in any of his earlier structures because "the old representational picture does not enhance the interiors." However, he went
on, non-objective paintings "harmonize" with his concept of space, and,
if they'd been available, "we would have them constantly on view in
the houses I build." Far from overwhelming these paintings, he went

on, the museum's interior would bathe them in a surrounding that unified the architecture, the art, and the beholder. One plan that he had for ensuring this unity was to place the paintings not flush against the wall—which would be impossible, given that the walls were curved—but rather recessed within the wall or tilted on an easel, so the observer could see a painting as the artist had seen it.

Guggenheim liked this idea in the abstract, but remained puzzled by the particulars. "For some time, I have been trying to visualize how our paintings are going to look in the new museum," he wrote to Wright in another letter in 1946. In the three years that followed, until Guggenheim died, Wright never did answer the question. Instead, Wright would wax lyrical on the general concept. "In a great upward sweep of movement," he wrote, referring to the museum's ramps and spirals, "the picture is seen framed as a feature of Architecture. The character of the building itself as Architecture amounts to 'framing' . . . much as jade or a jewel is set as a signet in a ring." This arrangement would mark the "liberation of Painting by Architecture," as paintings would no longer be "compelled by the 'straight-jacket' of the tyrannical rectilinear." By comparison, the Metropolitan Museum, a quarter-mile south on Fifth Avenue, was a "Protestant barn," a "coffin for the spirit," a "morgue."

But these flowery passages didn't amount to a description, either.

After Guggenheim's death in 1949, his nephew Harry Guggenheim, a thoroughbred horse owner who had made his own fortune in copper mining, took over as chairman of the board. Wright struck up a friendly, if sometimes annoyingly avuncular, relationship with his new boss, who kept him on as the project's celebrity architect and defended his design to all doubters.

The baroness, however, was fired. Everyone in the Guggenheim family had long despised her—for her autocratic personality, her manipulation of Sol, and her doctrinaire taste in art. (The cutoff was total, and mutual. She wasn't invited to the opening of the museum that she'd conceived. She died in 1967, without ever once setting foot inside. Not until 2005 did the museum acknowledge her by holding an exhibition devoted to her influence and her art.)

For much of the decade leading up to its completion, the museum faced one obstacle after another. A suitable plot of land was found in 1951, but it took another four years to get a construction

permit from the New York City Buildings Department, whose officials were always leery of unconventional designs. The project would
probably have been rejected out of hand, were it not for the intervention of Robert Moses, the city's master builder and destroyer. For two
decades, Moses controlled every bridge, park, thruway, and major
construction project in New York. He also happened to be a distant
cousin of Wright's. Moses hated modern art and didn't like Cousin
Frank's design either, but entirely out of friendship, he rammed
through his application, telling the building commissioner, "Damn
it, get a permit for Frank, I don't care how many laws you have to
break."

By this time, frustrated by the delays, Wright had moved to New
York City, setting up shop and residency in a deluxe suite at the Plaza
Hotel in August 1954. Once construction began two years later, he
frequently walked the mile and a half up Fifth Avenue to the site, to
oversee the work.

He also carried on a ferocious feud with Hilla Rebay's replacement as director, a former curator at the Museum of Modern Art
named James Sweeney, who proposed solving Sol Guggenheim's
puzzle—how to display paintings on a spiral—by hanging them on
spikes that would jut out horizontally from the walls. Wright hated
the idea and complained that Sweeney was out to destroy his whole
concept. In letters to Harry Guggenheim, he denounced Sweeney
as "an ambitious exemplar of 'the old square,'" a man entrusted with
"our precious violin" who "can only play the piano." He even told
Sweeney personally that Solomon Guggenheim "would have hated in
his guts" the kinds of changes he was making and that he would have
donated "not a cent" to build "the kind of museum you want or to pay
your salary."

In July 1958, after more than a year of this bickering, Harry
Guggenheim told Wright to calm down. He had reviewed Wright's correspondence with his uncle and found "not one shred of evidence" to
support his claims about the benefactor's wishes. Sol had asked Wright
many times how the art would be presented, Harry reminded him.
"You never did let him know," he noted, and, in any case, presenting
art is the job of a museum's director, not its architect. "Now, Querido
Francisco," Harry continued, addressing Wright by the nickname that
he often invoked in letters, "cease your diabolical maneuvers because

your building is for the angels. Stop causing everyone, including your-self, quite unnecessary bile and labor. Let us finish this job that your cussedness would have killed aborning without our help, and help us dedicate in harmony your beautiful and ingenious pile to an eager world."

Wright died on April 9, 1959, six months before the building was complete. For all the bitter arguments with Wright and the wide-spread loathing of Hilla Rebay, the Guggenheim Museum turned out to be remarkably faithful to their original visions. The building was Wright's inverted Ziggurat, with its gently sloping, seamless spiral—wrapping a path nearly a quarter-mile long from top to bottom—and its feel of "a curving wave that never breaks," as he once put it. More remarkable, the artworks were—almost all of them—a reflection of Rebay's taste. Out of the 128 works on display at the opening exhibi-tion, 23—far more than any other single artist—were by Kandinsky, and there were a fair number of paintings by Klee, Mondrian, Miro, Léger, Delaunay, and the other non-objectivists, too (though, signifi-cantly, *no* works by Bauer).

And yet the fears of the museum's namesake were well borne out. Wright had once said that the building would reveal "20th century art and architecture in their true relation"—and, to his mind, that meant architecture would triumph. In this sense, he succeeded. The *New York Times*'s architecture critic, Ada Louise Huxtable, wrote in her review of its opening that the Guggenheim "is less a museum than it is a monument to Frank Lloyd Wright." And the *Times*'s art critic, John Canady, called its layout "a war between architecture and paint-ing in which both come out badly maimed."

Almost no critics commented on the paintings—remarkable, given that this was the most sweeping array ever presented of Solomon Guggenheim's collection. But that may have been because, by the time the museum opened, a different kind of abstract art had come into prominence, and its emergence stemmed in good part from the spon-sorship of another Guggenheim, Solomon's niece and Harry's cousin, Marguerite or, as she called herself, Peggy.

Peggy's father, Benjamin, was the least successful of the Guggenheim brothers. He squandered most of his inheritance on dismal investments and, in 1912, went down on the *Titanic*—as a gentleman, sitting calmly in his evening clothes—leaving Peggy with a sum of money that, though minuscule compared with the rest of the family's fortune, was substantial by any other standard. She moved to Paris in 1920, befriended many avant-garde artists, had affairs with most of them, and, in 1938, opened a gallery in London to commission and sell their paintings.

She was keenly aware of Uncle Sol's dalliances with Hilla Rebay—whom she despised, referring to her as "the Nazi baroness" or "the B" (for bitch as well as baroness)—and their plans to create a Museum of Non-Objective Art in New York. Peggy's gallery promoted some of the same artists that Rebay patronized, especially Kandinsky. But she had much broader tastes than Rebay, thanks in part to Marcel Duchamp, the flamboyant artist and pioneer of the Dada movement, whom she'd met shortly after arriving in Paris and who introduced her to much of the city's art world, especially the surrealists.

When the war broke out in 1939, she went on an art-buying spree—buying dozens of works by Max Ernst (whom she would soon marry briefly), René Magritte, Man Ray, Paul Klee, Marc Chagall, and Pablo Picasso—with an eye toward starting her own modern art museum, in either London or Paris. But as the war spread, her plans were derailed.

In July 1941, she gathered her collection and steamed back to New York. Many of her surrealist friends, fleeing fascism and war, came with her. She set herself up in an apartment overlooking the East River—some called it "the headquarters of surrealism"—and, in October 1942, opened not a museum but a gallery, on West Fifty-seventh Street, called Art of This Century. Initially, she exhibited only the art of her exiled entourage. Neither she nor they consorted much with the natives.

By the following spring, she'd fallen out with most of her European friends. Ernst left her for a young American surrealist artist named Dorothea Tanning, and she had personal and business feuds with several of the others. Her few American art friends urged her to look at some of the young New York artists. (One of these friends was James Sweeney, who was about to become the director of the Museum of Modern Art's painting and sculpture department and who, many years later, would get into ferocious quarrels with Frank Lloyd Wright after replacing Hilla Rebay as director of the Guggenheim Museum—quarrels that may have had their roots in internecine family feuds.)

So, in April 1943, Peggy Guggenheim announced a "Spring Salon for Young Artists" and called on artists under the age of thirty-five to submit works for consideration. Duchamp and Piet Mondrian helped her judge the entries. The resulting exhibition, which opened at her gallery in May, turned out to be a seminal event. Because of Peggy Guggenheim's renown, all the major critics came to review the show. It marked the first public showing for a group of New York artists who, over the next several years, would come to be called abstract expressionists, especially Jackson Pollock.

The show featured other unknown artists who soon became famous—most notably Mark Rothko and Robert Motherwell—but Pollock was clearly the star, "a real discovery," as the *New Yorker*'s art critic, declared. Pollock was just thirty-one and the personification of the struggling young artist. To make money, he was working as a janitor at Solomon Guggenheim and Hilla Rebay's Museum of Non-Objective Painting. (The coincidence no doubt enhanced his appeal to Peggy—to unearth a great new artist, a creator of tomorrow's master-pieces, toiling at menial labor right under the dread baroness's nose!)

Pollock was also an ideal exemplar to those yearning in the war years for a distinctly American artist, free of Europe's influence. He was born in Cody, Wyoming, and received his formal training from Thomas Hart Benton, the landscape painter of the American West. At the time of the show, he wasn't yet painting his massive "drip" can-vases. His works were rife with surrealist symbols—the painting that got him into the Spring Salon show, *Stenographic Figure*, was almost cartoonish—but they displayed a fierce energy and a flair for compo-sitional balance.

Pollock was an unlikely object of Peggy Guggenheim's patronage. Personally crude and frequently drunk, he once threw up at a lunch-eon that she held in his honor for a group of rich collectors, and at one of her parties, he urinated in her fireplace. (Pollock would die in 1956, smashing his car into a tree while driving drunk.) But she put him on retainer, paying him $150 a month against royalties, so that he could give up his janitorial job and paint full-time. She commis-sioned several works, including a famously large mural for the foyer of her apartment, and she lent him $2,000 so that he could marry his fiancée, the artist Lee Krasner, and buy a cottage and studio in the Hamptons.

In 1947, she suddenly moved back to Europe, to create, finally, her own museum—the Peggy Guggenheim Collection—on the Grand Canal in Venice, where she remained until she died in 1979. (The collection, which she willed to the foundation set up by her Uncle Sol, is widely regarded to this day as the finest array of cubist, surrealist, and abstract expressionist paintings on the Continent.)

When she left New York, she closed her gallery on West Fifty-seventh Street and couldn't find anyone to assume her monthly retainer for Pollock, who suffered financially as a result. (Not until years after his death would his canvases sell for millions of dollars.)

But her legacy was considerable. Her Spring Salon of 1943 aroused excitement about not only Pollock but New York's other abstract artists as well. Their paintings started to be shown at exclusive galleries. A few were purchased by museums. Some of them even became household names. In 1948, *Life* magazine featured a roundtable discussion about the new art. In 1949, it published a huge photo spread of Pollock's new drip paintings, with a headline blaring, "Jackson Pollock: Is He the Greatest Living Painter in the United States?" It was a question, not a proclamation (and *Life*'s editors clearly had their doubts), but still, the story elevated his importance—and that of the entire group of abstract painters. There could be no doubt that as a result of their prominence, New York had eclipsed Paris, and all of Europe, as the center of modern art.

In 1952, the art critic Harold Rosenberg published an essay called "The American Action Painter," which articulated a philosophy for this new art. "At a certain moment," he wrote, "the canvas began to appear to one American painter after another as an arena in which to act—rather than as a space in which to reproduce, re-design, analyze or 'express' an object. . . . What was to go on the canvas was not a picture but an event. The painter no longer approached his easel with an image in his mind; he went up to it with material in his hand to do something to that other piece of material in front of him. The image would be the result of this encounter." It was a heroic image of the artist, who reveled in his "liberation" from the world around him and who "took to the white expanse of the canvas as Melville's Ishmael took to the sea."

Rosenberg especially championed Willem de Kooning, a Dutch artist who immigrated to New York in 1926 and painted with bold colors and ferocious brushstrokes. Another critic, Rosenberg's main rival, Clement Greenberg, was spellbound more by Pollock. After Peggy Guggenheim's 1943 salon, he called Pollock "the strongest painter of his generation and perhaps the greatest one to appear since Miro." And in 1955 he wrote an essay, called "American-Type Painting," which argued that the unique character of modern art lay in its open celebration of the flatness of the canvas and that, therefore, artists who emphasized this flatness, who refused to indulge in the illusions of depth or perspective, were the purest modern artists.

Both concepts—which had more in common than either critic cared to admit—went way beyond the Platonism of Hilla Rebay and her coterie of non-objective painters, who abandoned representation to worship the geometry of universal forms. The action, or American-type, painter broke through the confines of *all* forms simply to attack an empty canvas with the vitality of self-expression.

After Rebay was fired from the Guggenheim Museum, her replacement, James Sweeney, Peggy Guggenheim's erstwhile gallery adviser, persuaded the board to broaden its collection. By the time it opened, the museum had purchased over a hundred additional paintings, by turn-of-the-century impressionists as well as postwar abstract expressionists. The inaugural exhibition, in October 1959, included a smattering of these works: one each by Pollock, de Kooning, Kline, Sam Francis, and Adolph Gottlieb, as well as—from an earlier era of modernism—a Cézanne, a Seurat, two Braques, and a Picasso still life.

But the non-objective paintings—the Kandinskys, Klees, and so forth—took up most of the wall space; they were, after all, the centerpieces of Solomon Guggenheim's collection and therefore the reason for the museum's existence. Yet they may have made Frank Lloyd Wright's design seem more out of whack than it was; the building may have overwhelmed the art, because the art was so easy to overwhelm. In the fifteen years that had passed since Wright first drew up the blueprints, a new American art had emerged that made Hilla Rebay's once-radical entourage seem static and quaint by comparison. Wright's Ziggurat, with its vast open space, its ramps and spirals and domes, was fresh and dynamic; it just needed fresh and dynamic art to come into its own—as, in fact, it later did, when its curators devoted whole shows to the likes of Pollock, de Kooning, and more adventurous artists still.

In the decade after the Guggenheim opened, a number of spiraling buildings began to go up. Philip Johnson, who once poked fun at Wright as "the greatest architect of the 19th century," put stacked balconies in the lobby of his New York State Theater at Lincoln Center. Spheres figured prominently in Marcel Breuer's Whitney Museum of American Art on Madison Avenue, I. M. Pei's National Gallery on the Capitol Mall, and Mies van der Rohe's Neue National Gallerie in Berlin. Wright's ideas also inspired such superstar architects as Rem Koolhaas, Renzo Piano, and especially Frank Gehry, whose Guggenheim Museum in Bilbao, Spain, resembles something like Wright's Fifth Avenue original, blown out to the sixth dimension. Perhaps Wright's greatest legacy was the notion that there could *be* such a thing as a "superstar architect"—the idea that architecture could stand out as an art form, as a work of abstract expressionism all its own, quite apart from its function.

19

Blurring Art and Life

At the same time that the Guggenheim was opening its spiraled ramps to an enchanted if mystified public, the Museum of Modern Art—the Rockefeller family's thirty-year-old Midtown temple to the titans of high modernism—was taking delivery of some new artworks that were as strange and jarring as anything about Frank Lloyd Wright's structure.

The works were for a new show, about to open, called *Sixteen Americans*. The Guggenheim was purporting to be an aesthetic step ahead of MoMA, but *Sixteen Americans* would jump the charts of where "new art" was supposed to go or what it was supposed to look like. Most of the show's artists were in their twenties or thirties; none were well known. Their works were scrambled together not as a unified movement or school but rather, in the words of the show's catalogue, "simply as individuals and Americans." And the brashest of the bunch, the most individual and, in a sense, the most American, were two artists who were just coming into their own in the cliquish coterie of Manhattan galleries and who'd never had their works shown in any museum, much less in the world's standard-bearer of modern art—Robert Rauschenberg and Jasper Johns.

Rauschenberg's contributions to the show were the most collar-grabbing: seven large pieces—combinations of painting and sculpture that he called "combines"—some as large as twelve feet wide and seven feet high. The canvases were covered with splashings of color and furious brushstrokes, reminiscent of de Kooning, but Rauschenberg had also slapped objects onto the surface—scraps of fabric, strips of wood, a necktie, a pants leg, newspaper clippings, a Coke bottle, a metal zipper, electric lightbulbs. One of his combines was topped with a paint-smeared stuffed pheasant. Earlier that spring, the highlight of his one-man show at the Leo Castelli Gallery, on East Seventy-ninth Street, was a stuffed goat standing on an abstractly painted wooden platform with a tire stuck around its neck.

Jasper Johns's paintings—he also had seven in the show—were as circumspect as Rauschenberg's were exuberant, but no less at odds with the spirit of the art world around him. The subjects of his works—and most vanguard paintings of the era didn't have subjects at all—were objects from life: target circles, numbers, an American flag, painted all white or all green or in lots of colors, often layered with encaustic, a hot wax that dries quickly and leaves a thick veneer. They were mundane but somehow beautiful, simple but perplexing: objects that were commonly seen, even overlooked, mysteriously transmogrified into textured, sensual art.

In the show's catalogue, Johns wrote that he created art in which "the boundary of a body is neither a part of the enclosed body nor a part of the surrounding atmosphere." Rauschenberg's statement said much the same thing: "Painting relates to both art and life. Neither can be made. (I try to act in that gap between the two.)"

After a decade of the abstract expressionists, who deliberately avoided real life in their art, Rauschenberg and Johns were trying to meld the two, but in some new form, on their own terms, which would be at once a restoration and a breakthrough.

Milton Robert Rauschenberg was born in 1925 to a fundamentalist Christian family in the poor farm village of Port Arthur, Texas. As a child, he loved to draw and became very good at it, but it never occurred to him that someone could do this for a living until he joined the Navy and, on his way to Camp Pendleton, dropped in at an art gallery in San Marino and, for the first time in his life, saw original oil paintings. After the war, he studied at the Kansas City Art Institute on the GI Bill, then—having read someplace that all real artists go to Paris—enrolled at the Academie Julian, where Matisse, Bonnard, Vuillard, and Léger had studied. He soon realized that times had changed, and he sailed back to America.

In the fall of 1948, he attended Black Mountain College, in Asheville, North Carolina, the experimental college where William Carlos Williams taught poets to write about ordinary objects in the natural rhythms of their own breath. The school's art department was chaired by Josef Albers, a former leader of the Bauhaus movement in Berlin who'd fled the Nazis in 1933, and whose philosophy was similar to that of the poets, emphasizing the nature of art materials—not just paint, watercolor, pastels, and pencils but also straw, leaves, sticks, newspaper. Learning about color was more important than painting a good picture. Drawing what you saw, with efficient lines, was more important than developing a personal style. Albers was also obsessed with order. After he left Black Mountain for Yale, he became famous for painting squares—nothing but squares, for thirty years—changing only the colors, experimenting with the relationships between one color and another. Rauschenberg had no interest in his notion of order (for that reason, Albers hated the work that Rauschenberg produced in his classes), but it was from Albers that he learned the rudiments of the sort of art he wound up doing.

Rauschenberg moved to New York in the spring of 1949, just as the abstract expressionists began to emerge. Most of them had apartments in Greenwich Village, on or near East Tenth Street, and they hung out almost every night in the neighborhood bars, especially the Cedar Tavern on University Place, where they talked and quarreled for hours on end and got ferociously drunk. Rauschenberg, very amiable and a good drinker, joined the festivities. In the spring of 1951, Leo Castelli held the first show of abstract expressionists in a gallery on Ninth Street, involving sixty-one artists—including Pollock, de Kooning, Franz Kline, Mark Rothko, Robert Motherwell, and Clyfford Still—and they invited Rauschenberg, just twenty-six, to contribute a painting.

It was at this show that Rauschenberg met John Cage, a composer thirteen years his senior. Cage had studied with Arnold Schoenberg, the pioneer of twelve-tone classical music, but then moved in a different direction after immersing himself in Zen Buddhism and the *I Ching*. His new music emphasized chance and playfulness. He had just written a piece called *Imaginary Landscapes No. 4*, in which two performers turned the dials on two radios. One would adjust only the volume knob, the other just the frequency knob. Cage wrote very precise instructions on how much to move the dials, and in what direction, up or down, but he had no control over what music the station would be playing. Cage also invented the "prepared piano," which involved putting objects like bells or slabs of metal inside a piano in order to create strange but again very specific percussive sounds.

After they talked at the gallery, Rauschenberg gave Cage one of his canvases, a pink-and-tan collage. Later, he went to Cage's apartment, let himself in while Cage was out, and painted over the canvas with black enamel. At first Cage was furious, but then he grew to love it—both the painting and the audacity of the act.

To Cage, art was "an affirmation of life—not an attempt to bring order out of chaos nor to suggest improvements in creation, but simply to wake up to the very life we're living."

Cage had taught at Black Mountain College the summer before Rauschenberg arrived, writing scores for Merce Cunningham's dance classes. (Cage and Cunningham were lovers as well as collaborators.) Cage was planning to return to Black Mountain the coming summer, and Rauschenberg, now an artist with a résumé, went back as well. Josef Albers had moved on to Yale by then, so Rauschenberg felt free to explore.

That summer, Rauschenberg made *The White Paintings*, four large canvases on which he applied white enamel paint, using rollers to make the paint as smooth as possible—so smooth that it reflected a viewer's shadow and took on a different shade, depending on the time of day and the quality of light.

Some of Rauschenberg's fellow artists were puzzled, others mesmerized. Cage was among the latter, calling the paintings "airports for lights, shadows and particles." *The White Paintings* inspired him to write *4'33"*, his most notorious composition, which called for a performer to open the lid of the keyboard, sit still for four minutes and thirty-three seconds, then shut the lid and leave. The "music"—which, by nature, changed with every performance—consisted of all the sounds off the stage: people coughing or ruffling their programs, horns honking outside the hall.

The idea of both works was to break down the barrier between art and raw reality. "There is no such thing as an empty space or an empty time," Cage would later write. "There is always something to see, something to hear." Rauschenberg would express the same notion: "There is no poor subject. . . . A canvas is never empty."

Back in New York, Rauschenberg started making what he called the *Black Paintings*—thickly textured not just with dense slabs of black paint but with newspapers stuffed between the paint and the canvas. One day at an art store, he bought several unmarked paint cans that were on sale. They turned out to be various shades of red, so he turned out a series of *Red Paintings*, some of them adorned with comic strips, pieces of fabric, or shards of mirrored glass.

By this time, the abstract expressionists, whom he'd befriended two years earlier, were dominating the New York art scene to the point where a young artist wasn't taken seriously if he didn't paint in their style.

Rauschenberg was as dazzled by them as anyone—by the free motion of their brushstrokes, their dynamic use of color—especially by de Kooning, who was clearly the king of the crowd. Yet he also found himself uncomfortable with their sensibility. They were too grim, talked too much about art as struggle and pain. Rauschenberg was poor, but he thought the whole idea of art was to have fun. Nor did he understand when they talked about, say, red expressing "passion." To Rauschenberg, red was just *red*.

In 1953, he went with John Cage to a show of Dadaist art at the Sidney Janis Gallery and was exposed for the first time to the work of Marcel Duchamp, who for forty years had caused scandals by turning ordinary objects—"ready-mades," he called them—into objects of art: a bicycle wheel turned upside down on a stool, a toilet seat inscribed with his signature, a reproduction of the *Mona Lisa* marked with a moustache.

Duchamp and Cage were friends; they'd arrived in New York in the same year, 1942, and met at Peggy Guggenheim's apartment. Cage derived much of his sensibility from Duchamp. Since Duchamp didn't consort much with the New York artists, it was largely through Cage that his influence spread. And Rauschenberg was especially ripe for his influence.

Around the time that he saw the Duchamp show, Rauschenberg realized that he had to make a clean break from the abstract expressionists. One afternoon, he knocked on de Kooning's apartment door and asked him for one of his drawings, but for a bizarre purpose. Rauschenberg wanted one of the master's drawings so that he could erase it.

De Kooning was generous with younger artists. He let Rauschenberg in, told him that he understood his request. DeKooning slowly went through several folders of his drawings, rejecting some because they meant too much to him, some because they meant too little, others because they'd be too easy to erase. Finally, he found one that struck just the right balance. Rauschenberg took it home and spent the next month rubbing the paper as clean as he could, using up forty erasers in the process, leaving only a wispy glow. He framed the result, attached a plaque that read "Robert Rauschenberg—*Erased de Kooning Drawing—1953*," and hung it in his next gallery show. It caused a scandal—literally wiping out a work of art! And though he never let on publicly, it infuriated de Kooning, who accepted the Oedipal nature of Rauschenberg's act—every artist has to break away from his master—but assumed that the transaction would be kept private.

In the winter of 1954, Rauschenberg was introduced to Jasper Johns, an aspiring artist who had just moved to New York and was working at a midtown bookstore. The two had much in common; like Rauschenberg, Johns had grown up poor in the South—born in Georgia, raised by uncles and aunts in South Carolina—and was still a bit dazed by the big city. To make money, they started working together on elaborate window displays for Tiffany's and Bonwit Teller, under a pseudonym. Through a friend, they found loft apartments—Rauschenberg's a floor above Johns's—in a building on Pearl Street in Lower Manhattan. Soon they fell into an intense relationship, personally and professionally.

Rauschenberg would later recall that he and Johns started each day of work, self-consciously determined to "move out" from the abstract expressionists' influence. In 1955, Rauschenberg created the first of more than sixty combines that he would make over the next five years. He would walk around the block, picking up stray objects, even street trash, that he found interesting. If nothing caught his eye, he would walk over to the next block and circle it. He brought back buttons, zippers, cardboard cutouts, shreds of fabric, pieces of mattress foam, old radios, bicycle wheels (an homage to Duchamp), occasional exotica like the stuffed pheasant and the Angora goat, and he used them all in his art. He also pasted newspaper headlines, comic strips, and magazine ads across his canvas, along with swaths and lines of paint.

If vanguard art was supposed to look flat and stand apart from reality, as Clement Greenberg and Harold Rosenberg had declared, then Rauschenberg's art was an act of total rebellion—three-dimensional and physically enmeshed with the world's detritus, found on the streets outside his window and in the pop culture all around him. If the abstract expressionists liberated the canvas from the prison of representation, Rauschenberg sought to liberate art from the prison of the canvas.

Johns started from the same impulse. Soon after he and Rauschenberg met, they went to see a show of over forty Dada works at the Philadelphia Museum and came back enthralled. But Johns's temperament was less frantic. He was more inclined to focus on the fine details of discrete objects: "things," as he put it, "which are seen and not looked at"—like flags, numbers, letters, targets. At one of his gallery shows, he overheard an abstract expressionist painter grumbling that Johns might as well put up two beer cans and call them "art." Johns thought this was an excellent idea, and soon began work on a sculpture of two beer cans.

When *Sixteen Americans* opened at MoMA near the end of 1959, it set off a huge controversy. Many viewers were repelled, many were delighted; either way, most didn't quite know what to make of it. It marked a departure for the museum. Alfred Barr, the chief curator, regretted that he'd been slow to pick up on the abstract expressionists—except for Pollock, whose works he began to acquire at Peggy Guggenheim's first show—and he was now on the lookout for the next revolution, whatever it might be. The show marked MoMA's first bold step into the post-Pollock art world—and thus the modern art establishment's as well.

The *New York Times*'s art critic, Stuart Preston, came away from the show puzzled but receptive. "Say what you will," he wrote in his review, "these sixteen are 'making it new.' The old forms are no longer capable of containing their ideas." Four days later, Preston wrote a follow-up essay, mulling over the implications of those ideas. The show, he wrote, in no way marked a return to realism or to representation in art. "Nevertheless," he noted, "the most rewarding works on view here do strive to come to terms with things outside themselves."

For precisely that reason, the abstract expressionists didn't much like these new artists' work and resented their emerging success. But many slightly younger artists were deeply influenced by the idea that ordinary objects and pop-culture artifacts could be suitable subjects for art. Andy Warhol's paintings and screen prints of Campbell's soup cans, Coke bottles, and Marilyn Monroe head shots; Roy Lichtenstein's riffs on comic-strip panels; Claes Oldenburg's transmogrifications of humdrum objects into luscious soft sculptures—the whole movement of Pop Art that enlivened the sixties and widened the vocabulary of modern art—stemmed directly and explicitly from the works, and the attitudes, of Rauschenberg and Johns.

· · ·

On October 4, 1959, at the Reuben Gallery, a narrow third-floor loft on Fourth Avenue near Ninth Street—in the heart of the New York art scene—a thirty-two-year-old bearded artist-philosopher named Allan Kaprow staged a work called *18 Happenings in 6 Parts*, which took the influence of Pollock, Cage, and Rauschenberg to a self-consciously extreme level.

It was the first of many "Happenings," which Kaprow defined as "events that, put simply, happen." They may have "a decided impact— that is, we feel, 'Here is something important,'" he wrote, but "they appear to go nowhere," make no "particular literary point," and involve the audience not merely as observers but as fellow artists in the spectacle. If Rauschenberg worked in the spaces between art and life, Kaprow aimed to obliterate all boundaries and distinctions.

Kaprow, just two years younger than Rauschenberg, was born in 1927 in Atlantic City, New Jersey. His family moved to Tucson, mainly to relieve his childhood asthma, but he came back east to New York to attend the High School of Music and Art. He majored in philosophy at New York University but also studied painting with Hans Hofmann— whose Eighth Street studio was a gathering spot for the abstract expressionists—and, in 1952, he wound up receiving a master's degree in art history at Columbia, where he studied with Meyer Schapiro. The next year Kaprow took a teaching job at Rutgers University but kept current with the Manhattan art scene. In 1957, he took a night class on "experimental music," taught by John Cage, at the New School for Social Research. Kaprow started to see art, music, and life in a new light that blurred all three—and everything—together. (Many years later, he titled a collection of his writings *Essays on the Blurring of Art and Life*.)

Kaprow had been painting "action collages," as he called them, very much inspired by de Kooning's "action paintings" and Rauschenberg's combines (though they lacked either artist's fleet touch or compositional balance). He kept making the collages bigger and bigger, until finally he just filled an entire gallery with collage materials—paint, photos, newspapers, tin foil, mirrors, straw, a hodgepodge of stuff— so that viewers walking into the room would feel as though they were *entering into* an abstract painting.

He saw these collages as an extension of the large all-over paintings of Jackson Pollock. In an essay for *Art News*, published in June 1958, two years after Pollock's death in a car accident, Kaprow came up with a novel twist on his legacy. Pollock, it was well known, painted his larger works by laying the canvas on the floor and splashing paint over it. He was unable to see the whole thing at any one time, certainly not its outer edges. Therefore, it could be said that Pollock was "in" his paintings. Similarly, we the viewers can enter his paintings by looking at them up close: the canvas ceases to exist as a reference point; the paintings cease to be mere paintings and become "environments," extending across the entire range of our vision and out into the room. Pollock's art, in this sense, formed a sharp break with a tradition of painting dating back to the Greeks, and instead conjured an ancient, even preliterate age, when "art was more actively involved in rituals, magic and life."

So where, Kaprow asked, do we go now? One route would be simply to continue in Pollock's vein. However, Kaprow proposed an alternative course: "to give up the making of paintings entirely— I mean the single flat rectangle or oval as we know it"—and to follow Pollock's extension farther and farther out into the room, and not just through our visual senses, but through our hearing, touch, smell, and motion. "Action painting" takes on a whole new meaning, by expanding not so much the "painting" as the "action."

"Pollock, as I see him," Kaprow wrote, "left us at the point where we must become preoccupied with and even dazzled by the space and objects of our everyday life, either our bodies, clothes, rooms, or, if need be, the vastness of Forty-second Street. . . . Objects of every sort are material for the new art: paint, chairs, food, electric and neon lights, smoke, water, old socks, a dog, movies, a thousand other things." This bold new art will "disclose entirely unheard-of happenings and events"—this was his first use of the word "happening"—"found in garbage cans, police files, hotel lobbies; seen in store windows and on the streets; and sensed in dreams and horrible accidents." (Kaprow would later tell an interviewer that this list was inspired by some of the things he'd seen during a recent visit to Robert Rauschenberg's studio.)

Working from this insight, Kaprow took his room-size collages— his "Environments"—one step, then another step, further. First, he gave spectators roles to play in these environments: flicking on a light switch, turning on a radio, making funny noises. After a while, the people and their roles became what the artwork was about. An Environment became a Happening.

18 Happenings in 6 Parts was just that. "The performance," he wrote in the program, "is divided into six parts. Each part contains three happenings, which occur at once. The beginning and end of each will be signaled by a bell. At the end of the performance, two strokes of the bell will be heard." The parts were tightly scripted, even choreographed, scored in the much the way that he had scored oddball sound collages in John Cage's classes at the New School. In one room, a performer was supposed to say "Hmmmm!" for two seconds, pause for four seconds, say "But" for one second, then pause for three seconds. In another room, when a buzzer sounded, the performer was to follow this instruction: "Walk to opposite mirror. Stop and look at self. Raise hand thus. Smile maniacally, wait, count to 4. Turn around, keep smiling, count to 3, neutral." At one point, two people standing on either side of a glass wall were given paint brushes; one was told to paint lines, the other to paint a circle. On one night, the painters were Rauschenberg and Johns.

For a brief spell, Happenings were fashionable, and a few of the new Pop artists—Claes Oldenburg, Jim Dine, and Red Grooms— held their own Happenings, some of them far more raucous than Kaprow's. Grooms staged one called *The Burning Building*, in which people dressed in firemen's costumes and ran around with cardboard axes, or dived out of prop windows, all of them screaming and hollering and chasing one another into the audience.

After a while, most of these artists exhausted the limits of the medium and went back to painting or sculpting. Only Kaprow stuck with Happenings, and they became progressively wilder—moving out of the galleries, into the streets and the countryside, involving stunts on subways, or piling up hundreds of car tires, or setting a whole car on fire, or doing a lot of things that required people, usually attractive young women, to take off their clothes.

The Happenings became fun and erotic, but they had less and less to do with any notion of art. Years later, Kaprow would write that in formulating the early Happenings, he'd "half-accepted a sophistry floating around the studios that art was anything! But 'anything' was too easy," he admitted. "If anything was art, nothing was art." The Happenings that he continued to stage, he now labeled "un-art," which, he wrote, "was accomplished by taking the art out of art." In other words, he rationalized, "Leaving art *is* the art."

Many years earlier, Robert Rauschenberg, responding to the French gallery owner Iris Clert's request for a portrait, replied with a telegram that read, "This is a portrait of Iris Clert if I say so—Robert Rauschenberg." That was a witty bit of Dada. By comparison, Kaprow's leaving-art-as-art was mere wordplay, and lame at that.

In the broader culture, in others' hands, the Happening evolved into the love-in, the be-in, the collective acid trip, the riot—the caricatures of the sixties in the decade's frothiest and darkest incarnations.

Yet at the turn of the twenty-first century, the spread of cell phones and the Internet sparked a revival of the spirit of the original Happenings, under the rubric of "pranks," "flash mobs," and "smart mobs"—hundreds or thousands of strangers, contacted by chain e-mails or text messages, who merrily assemble in a public place at an arranged time, do something bizarre, then disperse.

In London, four thousand people came together at Victoria Station one rush hour in April 2007 and started dancing. In New York, in 2003, a few hundred people stood on the stone fences in Central Park and made bird noises. In Berlin, one evening in August of that year, precisely at 6:01 P.M., forty people stopped in the middle of the street, took out their mobile phones, shouted, "Yes, yes!" and applauded. On a rainy night in May 2008, seven hundred people formed a line on the walkway of the Brooklyn Bridge and set off flash cameras over and over, creating an undulating wave of light.

Were these assemblages art? Certainly not in any conventional sense—except for the Brooklyn Bridge flash show, which, though transient, was as authentically a work of public art as the weightiest plaza sculpture. But they asserted a new form of expression, at once communal and individual, meticulously planned and gleefully spontaneous—a new type of community in an age, and with a technology, that otherwise tends to obliterate community—a Happening for the cyber-century, a new twist on John Cage's concept of art as "an affirmation of life—not an attempt to bring order out of chaos nor to suggest improvements in creation, but simply to wake up to the very life we're living."

20

Seeing the Invisible

In the fall of 1959, after winning his lawsuit to lift the ban on *Lady Chatterley's Lover*, Barney Rosset, the owner of Grove Press, was putting the final touches on an odd book called *The Americans* by a thirty-five-year-old Swiss-born Jewish photographer named Robert Frank. A French edition of the book, which had been on sale for much of the year at the Museum of Modern Art's bookshop, was already circulating among New York artists and writers. But Rosset's edition would include a bonus that Frank's Paris publisher had bafflingly rejected—a swooning introduction by the Beat novelist Jack Kerouac.

The Americans was like no other photo book ever published. It consisted of eighty-three black-and-white photographs, which Frank selected from over twenty-seven thousand exposures that he'd shot with a handheld Leica camera during a yearlong journey to eight cities and lots of towns in between, crisscrossing ten thousand miles of American roads beginning in the summer of 1955 and continuing into 1956. What he came up with was a portrait of the country that few had seen and that no one had displayed so starkly.

The book's first photo is labeled "Parade—Hoboken, New Jersey," but it doesn't show a parade. Instead, it's a close-up of a building that presumably overlooks a parade. There's a window on the left side of the frame, another window (though seen incompletely) on the right, a section of brick wall between them, and above an American flag (though it's cut off at the top) waving in the breeze. People are looking out from each window, but we barely see their faces; one is partly covered by a shade, the other by the bottom of the flag.

In another picture, which Rosset put on the book cover, a New Orleans trolleycar zips by, looking like a prison, its passengers cut off from one another by the vertical bars between each open window. To the left, sitting toward the front of the trolley, a white woman glares with suspicion at Frank's camera—at us. Just to the right, in the seats behind her, two small children stare back at the camera with open curiosity. Behind them, a black man looks out with a desperate expression, as if beseeching us to help or at least to pay attention—though behind him, a black woman smiles at something off to the side. Underneath these faces, the trolley's chassis—dark but shiny—reflects blobs of light and shadow, like a metallic abstract painting. Along the top of the picture, five mirrored windows—one above each row of passengers—reflect blurred images of people and objects on the sidewalk, like an action collage.

Frank takes pictures of rodeos, funerals, movie premieres, candy stores, gas stations, jukeboxes, hotel elevators—but rarely does he show the main attraction, or any action at all. More often, he shoots along the periphery, often from behind the subjects' backs, sometimes looking at people looking, all of them evoking isolation, loneliness, but also intensity, grief, or an inner ecstasy.

Kerouac wrote in his introduction, "Robert Frank, Swiss, unobtrusive, nice, with that little camera that he raises and snaps with one hand, he sucked a sad poem right out of America onto film, taking rank among the tragic poets of the world."

In January 1955, six months before Frank set off on his road trip, a photo exhibition called *The Family of Man* opened at the Museum of Modern Art, a massive show, consisting of 503 pictures taken by 273 photographers in sixty-eight countries—an upbeat visual saga of birth, life, love, labor, and death, intended, in the words of its curator, Edward Steichen, to serve as "a mirror of the essential oneness of mankind throughout the world." Steichen was seventy-six, a celebrated photographer of wars, movie stars, and fashion models, who believed that photography had the power to change the world and that this show might dissolve the distrust among nations, melt the Cold War, and pave the path to peace on Earth.

By the end of the decade, when *The Americans* was published, *The Family of Man* had traveled to forty countries, had been seen by 9 million people, and had come to be widely regarded as the model of how photographic art should look and how it should make its viewers feel. In his social outlook and in his aesthetic style, Robert Frank was rubbing raw against this model, against the spirit of the time—and very deliberately so.

Frank immigrated to the United States in 1947, at the age of twenty-two. He found an apartment in Greenwich Village and was instantly enthralled with New York's tempo, vitality, and constant crowded motion—such a contrast with his native Switzerland's innate cautiousness.

Already an experienced photographer, he found work at the fashion magazine *Harper's Bazaar*, but soon quit to take pictures on his own terms. In 1949, he met a sixteen-year-old dancer and art student named Mary Lockspeiser, who was taking painting classes with Hans Hofmann at his Eighth Street Studio and who introduced Frank to the New York school of artists. Frank became friends with Franz Kline and Willem de Kooning, whose studio was behind his own apartment on Third Avenue. He admired their bohemian lifestyle and their concept of art as a spontaneous creation, a confrontation with the canvas. Inspired, he started taking pictures that put less emphasis on compositional beauty, and more on improvisational discovery.

In 1951, Edward Steichen bought four of Frank's pictures for a show of young American photographers that he was putting together at MoMA. Steichen was also beginning to organize his *Family of Man* exhibition, and he bought seven of Frank's photos for that. But Frank, who had once courted Steichen's approval and sponsorship, was moving out of his orbit, regarding the show's philosophical premise and aesthetic style as repugnantly sentimental.

Frank was encouraged in this direction by his budding friendship with Walker Evans. Evans was fifty when Frank met him in 1953. During the Depression, Evans had taken a series of photos of impoverished farm families, which he turned into a book in 1941 called *Let Us Now Praise Famous Men*, with essays by the poet-critic James Agee. Three years before that, Evans published a book of his own called *American Photographs*, which influenced Frank deeply. It featured photos of factories, gas stations, roadside fruit stands, people in subways—stark pictures of everyday life, full of empathy for his subjects, neither harsh nor treacly. When Frank took his own trip around the country—which was financed by a Guggenheim grant that Evans helped him win—he brought *American Photography* with him, as a guide for where to go and as a reminder that mundane scenes were permissible subjects for art.

But Frank parted from Evans in one respect. Evans would compose his shots with fastidious care, waiting sometimes for hours to catch just the right light. The resulting photos were gorgeous, even when the subject was miserable; the composition's beauty could overwhelm the content's emotional wallop. Frank chose to take pictures in a way that style matched substance.

The same year that Frank met Evans, he also befriended Allen Ginsberg. *Howl* hadn't yet been written, but the Beats were already a phenomenon—Clellan Holmes's *New York Times Magazine* article "This Is the Beat Generation" had appeared the previous fall—and Ginsberg was its public avatar. Frank talked with Ginsberg about poetry. He wanted people looking at his photos "to feel the way they do when they want to read a line of a poem twice." Ginsberg would talk about the virtues of spontaneity ("first thought, best thought" was a Ginsberg Zen-line that Frank repeated often) and of expressing ideas in one's own voice with one's own feelings up front ("writing down what you're really thinking, actually").

What Ginsberg was doing with words and the abstract expressionists were doing with lines and colors, Frank felt he could do with photographed images—as a sort of visual poetry, or representational expressionism.

These were the influences—a mix of Evans, de Kooning, and Ginsberg—that Frank had internalized when he hit the road in June 1955, driving a used 1950 Ford Business Coupe, first to Detroit and Savannah, then to Miami, Houston, Los Angeles, San Francisco, Chicago, and places in between, "to see," as he put it, "what is invisible to others."

Frank could see these things, in large part, because he was an outsider. Even while growing up in Zurich, during the years when the Nazis came to power in neighboring Germany, he had to deal with widespread anti-Semitism. He loved the vitality of America—he'd applied for citizenship, which would take several more years to come through—but he knew little of the country beyond a few square miles of Manhattan.

So he noticed things that lifelong Americans took for granted. He saw the way people sat side by side at lunch counters without exchanging a word or even looking at one another. He grasped the sheer oddity of the drive-in theater, where people watched movies— by nature a communal experience—in the isolation of their cars. He took a close look at the massive auto factories, where workers were just another set of cogs in the machinery. And he gazed in horror at segregation in the South and the strange hypocrisies it produced. (In his book, he places a picture of a black nurse in Charleston, South Carolina, holding—being entrusted with—someone's ivory white baby, just a few pages before his shot of the segregated New Orleans trolleycar.) But Frank also saw, and captured, moments of private tenderness in public parks, open sorrow at funerals, mesmeric holiness in prayer, and the pervasive obsession with the car and the road, both of which intensified the nation's appealing vitality and speed but also its appalling loneliness.

Frank snapped his pictures fast, with little if any preparation, sometimes because he was in a dicey situation. (Several times along his tour, he was told to get out of town; once, in McGhee, Arkansas, he was arrested for looking like a Communist and interrogated for four hours after the police learned that he was Jewish.) But even when there was no danger, his aim was to capture the "humanity of the moment." Many art photographers waited for "the moment of equilibrium," but Frank thought that certain truths—there was, to his mind, no single truth—revealed themselves at "the in-between moments." As he later put it, "I like a certain disorder; then I can find something in it."

His act of finding something was hardly random. Frank may have taken pictures quickly, and relied on chance, like his abstract expressionist friends. But, also like them, and like Ginsberg with his poetry, he reordered and retouched his work afterward; revision, after all, was part of the creative act.

When Frank got back to New York in the summer of 1956, he developed over 660 rolls of film, amounting to 27,000 frames. He printed one thousand of them, arranged them by theme, tacked them up on boards, laid them out, and reshuffled them on the floor. It took him

until the following spring to whittle his choices down to one
hundred prints, and he cropped many of those—cutting off tops, bot-
toms, edges, turning horizontal shots into vertical or vice versa—in
order to highlight certain objects, people, relationships, or angles, to
make the images more compelling, in some cases to make them look
more spontaneous than they really had been.

In the end, *The Americans* consisted of a mere eighty-three photos.
He laid them out so that when the book was open, a single picture was
framed on the right-hand page while the left-hand page was blank
except for the picture's caption in small letters. He wanted people to
look at each shot closely. He also spent months figuring out the order
in which the pictures would appear—to imply connections and contrasts,
but not too obviously. And he wanted the feel of this sequence "to
create a kind of rhythm."

Walker Evans wrote an introduction to the book, but Frank
reluctantly rejected it; it was too much about Evans's own feuds with
Edward Steichen, not enough about the subject of Frank's work.
On September 5, 1957, along with many other New Yorkers, Frank
read Gilbert Millstein's ecstatic *New York Times* review of Kerouac's
On the Road. Frank had never met Kerouac, but judging from the
review, they seemed to share a sensibility; both of their books were
about restless, questing road trips. A few days later, he met Kerouac
at a mutual friend's party, showed him some of his pictures, and asked
if he would write an introduction to his book. Kerouac agreed.

The French publisher, Robert Delpire, didn't like Kerouac's
essay. He also didn't like the idea of leaving every other page blank.
So he cluttered the left-hand side of the book with quotations from
the works of John Dos Passos, Walt Whitman, Richard Wright, and
Alexis de Tocqueville, all of the words critical of America and thus
blunting the ambiguity of many of Frank's photos. The French edition, *Les americaines*, came out in the spring of 1958. When Barney
Rosset printed the American edition, he restored the introduction by
Kerouac—whose articles and poems he had often printed in his literary magazine, the *Evergreen Review*—and honored Frank's vision of
leaving the left-hand pages nearly blank.

The book caused much displeasure. Millstein praised it in
the *New York Times*, but he was in the minority. The editors of

Popular Photography were so outraged, they printed three reviews, all unfavorable, slamming the book as "an attack on the United States," an "intense personal vision marred by spite, bitterness, and narrow prejudices," full of "meaningless blur, grain, muddy exposures, drunken horizons and general sloppiness." Only 1,100 copies were sold. After one year, the book was out of print.

Frank abandoned still photography and started making short films, including, later in 1959, a thirty-minute frolic called *Pull My Daisy* with Allen Ginsberg, his fellow Beat poets Peter Orlovsky and Gregory Corso, and the painter Larry Rivers, all playing themselves, and narration written and read by Kerouac.

But *The Americans* didn't disappear. The Art Institute of Chicago exhibited Frank's work in the spring of 1961. A 1962 show at MoMA traveled to a smattering of cities across the nation for a couple of years. Finally, in 1968, the year of rebellion on campuses and rioting in the streets, Aperture published a new edition of Frank's book, and it was finally acclaimed as a revelation, its portraits of alienation, hypocrisy, and racial prejudice hailed as startlingly prescient. Its visual style, its rejection of prettification for its own sake, had found its era. The *Village Voice* called it "a quietly ticking time bomb which has yet to be defused."

In the seventies, Frank started taking pictures again. More than that, every significant photographer who came up during this time, and a number of painters as well—Lee Friedlander, Garry Winogrand, Joel Meyerowitz, Cindy Sherman, Ed Ruscha, among others—took many of their cues from Frank's critical attitude and visual vocabulary. In 2008, to honor the book's impending fiftieth anniversary, the National Gallery of Art in Washington, D.C., published a pristine new edition. In 2009, it released a collection of scholarly essays about the book, and mounted an exhibition of its original photos, which afterward traveled to several other museums, including the Metropolitan in New York.

Edward Steichen's *Family of Man* wound up inspiring mawkish advertisements about human harmony and togetherness for AT&T, Kodak, and Hallmark greeting cards. Robert Frank's *The Americans* inspired a new way of looking at the restless diversity and tensions of a widening, splintering world.

21

The Off-Hollywood Movie

On the night of November 11, 1959, at the Fashion Industries Auditorium on West Twenty-fourth Street in Manhattan, Amos Vogel's adventurous Cinema 16 club screened the first two films of a series called "The Cinema of Improvisation." The opening film was *Pull My Daisy*, Robert Frank's half-hour whimsy starring his Beat friends. The main attraction was a full-length feature, directed by John Cassavetes, called *Shadows*.

Cassavetes, a few weeks shy of thirty, was a successful actor with a long string of credits in theater and television drama who was trying to break into movies but hadn't yet hit it big. A year before, he'd written a jeremiad in the journal *Film Culture*, titled "What's Wrong with Hollywood?" Its first two sentences: "Hollywood is not failing. It has failed." Cassavetes complained that he could find a fair amount of serious acting work on television, where sponsors ruled upfront, but not so much in the movies, where commercial considerations dominated more subtly.

"Without individual creative expression," Cassavetes wrote, "we are left with a medium of irrelevant fantasies that can add nothing but slim diversion to an already diversified world. The answer cannot be left in the hands of the money men. . . . The answer must come from the artist himself."

A few years earlier, he and a friend named Burt Lane had started an actors' workshop in the Variety Arts Building on West

Forty-sixth Street, in the heart of the Broadway theater district. In January 1957, during one of those workshops, Cassavetes sketched out some characters, based on a few of the students in his class, and asked them to improvise on a storyline about a young black woman trying to pass for white. He quickly realized that it might make for a good film.

Cassavetes had been spending a lot of time at the Thalia, a cinema on the Upper West Side that often showed foreign films, which had just started getting serious distribution in the United States. He was especially moved by the Italian neorealists—Vittorio de Sica, Roberto Rossellini, and the early works of Federico Fellini and Michelangelo Antonioni—whose powerful films were shot in the streets for little money. He began to think that maybe he could make a neorealist film in New York City.

A shrewd publicity hound, Cassavetes went on a live radio talk show called *Night People*, hosted by Jean Shepherd. The show aired on WOR-AM after midnight, but it attracted a devoted following, mainly young misfits who lionized Shepherd as a rare voice of sane outrage. Shepherd was a sick comic, a merry prankster who staged Happenings before Allan Kaprow invented the term. He would tell his listeners, "Tonight at midnight, open your window and shout as loud as you can, 'Screw New York!'" And his listeners would do it. He would tell them to go into a bookstore the next day and ask for a copy of *I, Libertine* by Frederick R. Ewing, and suddenly it became a hotly discussed item in literary circles, even though neither the book nor the author existed.

Shepherd had said nice things about *The Edge of the City*, a TV show in which Cassavetes had starred, so Cassavetes asked if he could use *Night People* to stage his own publicity stunt, and Shepherd happily complied.

Cassavetes went on the show on a Sunday night in early February of 1957. A few minutes into the conversation, he began his pitch. "If there can be off-Broadway plays, why can't there be off-Hollywood movies?" Cassavetes said. "Wouldn't it be terrific if *people* could make movies instead of all these Hollywood big-wigs who are only interested in business?"

Taking his cue, Shepherd asked, "Do you think you could raise money to make something like that?"

"You bet," Cassavetes replied. "If people really want to see a movie about people, they should contribute money. Just a dollar each would do it, if enough of them contributed."

"Well, there you have it," Shepherd said, wrapping up the interview. He read aloud the address of Cassavetes' workshop and urged his listeners to drop by and contribute to the project.

The next morning, Shepherd fans were lined up outside the Variety Arts Building to donate money. By the end of the week, they mailed or brought in $2,500, almost all of it in one- and five-dollar bills. It was a decent start, enough to encourage Cassavetes that he might really be able to make this movie. (One of the credits at the beginning of *Shadows* would read, as a wink and nudge to the fans, "Presented by Jean Shepherd's Night People.")

From friends in the industry, Cassavetes was able to round up more money and supplies. Erich Kollmar, a documentary filmmaker, offered his services as cinematographer and brought along his own 16mm Arriflex camera. Shirley Clarke, a leading underground film-maker, lent her equipment. Hollywood figures, from the director William Wyler to the gossip columnist Hedda Hopper, also chipped in a few hundred dollars here and there.

Cassavetes began filming at the end of the month and continued for ten weeks. He shot in the streets of Times Square, the caverns of Penn Station, the paths of Central Park, the sculpture garden at the Museum of Modern Art. He hadn't applied for permits from the mayor's office to film on location—that would have cost money and taken time—so he shot mainly at night. One of his actors, a part-time cab driver, sometimes parked nearby, so that in case a curious policeman approached, Cassavetes could shove the camera in the taxi and flee.

The movie wasn't entirely free-form. Cassavetes knew exactly where the plotline was going. He and his assistant, Maurice McEndree, who would get a producer's credit, went over each day's scenes with the actors ahead of time, dictating how they should move, what they should do. Robert Rossen, a friend of Cassavetes' and a formerly blacklisted film director who'd made *All the King's Men* and other Hollywood movies in the forties and fifties, supplied advice on lighting and camera angles.

But the actors were given great latitude with the dialogue, none of which had been scripted. Largely for that reason, Cassavetes shot a staggering amount of footage—thirty hours' worth for what turned out to be a seventy-eight-minute movie. There wasn't much of a plot. The initial premise was still there—a young black woman has an affair with a young man who thinks she's white—and it branched out to involve her brothers, one of whom is an aspiring jazz singer. Like a Beat riff on Fellini's *I Vitteloni*, it was basically about a small group of young men who talk in jazz lingo and carouse around the city, looking for women and music and anything to do.

The movie had a crude, unfinished look, but also a raw energy that few studio productions even tried to achieve. (The Academy Award winners, and thus the industry's models of excellence, in 1958 and 1959, were *Gigi*, a grandiose musical, and *Ben Hur*, a grandiose Roman epic.) Cassavetes stopped filming in May 1957, mainly because he'd committed to act in two Hollywood movies, and he needed the money, having spent $25,000 of his own savings to make *Shadows*. He was away on the West Coast until the fall. After he returned, he took another year to finish the editing.

Meanwhile, Jean Shepherd, who had been keeping his listeners posted on Cassavetes' progress, asked them to call in with suggestions on which jazz musician should do the soundtrack. Their top choice was Charles Mingus. Shepherd passed along the suggestion to Cassavetes, who in turn brought Mingus and his octet into the Variety Arts workshop and asked them to improvise a score on the spot. Mingus, who was an agile improviser but also a meticulous composer, refused; music like this, he insisted, should be *written*. (He did end up composing a couple of themes, which he called "Nostalgia in Times Square" and "Alice's Wonderland," but brought them in too late to be included in the film. He recorded them on one of his albums instead and played them often in clubs.)

Near the end of 1958, Cassavetes arranged to show *Shadows* at three midnight screenings at the Paris Theater, across from the Plaza Hotel in midtown Manhattan. Jean Shepherd helped to promote the event by giving away tickets. Two thousand people showed up in all. Many of them walked out before the film was over. After the show, Cassavetes spoke with some of those who remained and came away agreeing that the film needed at least a bit of structure and more focus on the characters. He decided to do some refilming.

First, he got together with Robert Alan Arthur, who had written the TV and film versions of *Edge of the City*, to draft several expanded scenes—with dialogue. In the spring of 1959, Cassavetes spent ten days shooting the new scenes, some of them in his own apartment. That summer, he went back to Hollywood to star in a new TV show called *Johnny Staccato*, about a crime-solving jazz pianist. The gig didn't last long, but at least it made him solvent again. While he was gone, Maurice McEndree put together a rough cut of a revised *Shadows*. The final version, which cost Cassavetes another $15,000, was a roughly fifty-fifty mix of old, improvised scenes and new, scripted ones. But it all possessed the *feel* of improvisation.

In the fall, Cassavetes enlarged the 16 mm film to a 35 mm print and showed it to Amos Vogel. In the 1930s, as a teenager, Vogel had escaped Austria with his family when Hitler came to power. After the war, he moved to New York, and in 1947—around the same time that the city was blossoming as a serious center of new art forms—he started Cinema 16, one of the nation's first programs to show foreign and underground films. He set it up as a members-only film society—the first of those as well—in order to get around censorship laws, which applied only to public venues. Within a few years, more than five thousand people had signed up as members. (In 1963, Vogel and Richard Roud would start the New York Film Festival, which marked America's first step toward being a capital of international art films.) Vogel loved the revised *Shadows*, gave Cassavetes $250 as a rental fee, the most he'd ever paid for a single film, and scheduled it as the headliner in his "Cinema of Improvisation" series on November 11.

Vogel's announcement stirred excitement, for an ironic reason. When Cassavetes screened the first cut of *Shadows* at the Paris Theater nearly a year earlier, a small number of cineastes had liked it a lot. One of them was Jonas Mekas, the film critic for the *Village Voice* and the publisher of *Film Culture* magazine. Mekas was an enthusiast for everything avant-garde. He was born in Lithuania in 1923, edited an underground Resistance newspaper during the Nazi occupation, and spent the last year of the war in a concentration camp. He came to New York in 1949, learned English by watching movies, and became a regular at Vogel's Cinema 16 screenings. Mekas was struck by the absence of any serious American film journal, like *Sight & Sound* in England or *Cahiers du Cinema* in France. So, in 1954, he started *Film Culture*.

When Mekas saw the original version of *Shadows* at one of the Paris Theater's midnight screenings, he raved about it in his *Village Voice* column and wrote a more elaborate appreciation for *Sight & Sound*. In the January 1959 issue of *Film Culture*, he announced the establishment of an "Independent Film Award" and declared *Shadows* to be its first winner. Cassavetes, he wrote, "was able to break out of conventional molds and traps," creating a film of "improvisation, spontaneity and free inspiration"—traits distinctly lacking in most American movies, with their "excess of professionalism." In the same issue, Mekas wrote an essay titled "A Call for a New Generation of Film Makers," which urged aspiring young directors to follow Cassavetes' example.

As further celebration, and to take advantage of the hoopla he was building, Mekas booked the ballroom at the Waldorf-Astoria Hotel for a fund-raising banquet, at which Cassavetes had agreed to receive his award. Mekas started to sell tickets. But then Cassavetes broke the bad news. First, he couldn't make it to the banquet because he had to be in L.A., shooting *Johnny Staccato*. Second, he'd decided to reshoot large chunks of *Shadows*, so he was reluctant to draw more attention to the present version.

At the end of its Cinema 16 screening in November 1959, the full-house audience—which included Allen Ginsberg, Paddy Chayevsky, Kenneth Tynan, Meyer Schapiro, and other writers and critics—gave the revised *Shadows* a loud, long ovation.

But, once more, Jonas Mekas was in the minority. He didn't like the revision at all and wrote a column in the *Voice*, slamming Cassavetes for selling out, for betraying his original vision.

Meanwhile, as a result of Mekas's rave review in *Sight & Sound*, Cassavetes was invited to show *Shadows* at a "Beat, Square and Cool" film festival in London the following July.

Cassavetes took the print to London, where he also sat for a string of press interviews, hoping to stir interest in a distribution deal. By this time, the distinction between the first and second cuts of *Shadows* had been blurred; few in England were aware that there had been two versions. A title card at the end of the original version had read: "The film you have just seen was an improvisation."

Cassavetes kept it in the revised version, even though it was no longer true. Viewers gasped when they read it, and Cassavetes did nothing to correct matters. In interviews, he even embellished the claim, boasting that he'd shot the film over a period of just a few weeks and making up stories, including one about a New York policeman who thought a fight scene was for real and broke it up by firing a pistol into the air.

Shadows not only found a British distributor, it played to sold-out crowds for months at the Academy Cinema on Oxford Street. The London critics praised it as "a landmark in the American cinema," a stark portrait of "the fringe society of beatniks and insecure intellectuals drinking, necking and talking the night through to a shifty dawn." The *Observer*'s critic, echoing some of Mekas's language, wrote: "To an art half-strangled by professionalism, it brings a breath of spontaneity. It's as though we were offered, instead of a column of glossy print, a smudgy penciled note telling us something we've been wanting to hear."

Despite its success in Britain, *Shadows* could find no distributor in the United States. It played briefly in two theaters, one in New York, the other in Los Angeles, and even then not until the spring and summer of 1961. Cassavetes went back to acting in TV dramas and Hollywood movies. By the mid-sixties, he'd accumulated enough money to resume directing small independent films—*Faces, Husbands, Minnie and Moskowitz, A Woman under the Influence.* They were longer, more artful in their mix of the scripted and the improvisational, more emotionally satisfying, yet none were hits at the box office.

However, over the next two decades, *Shadows* would take on a mythic quality.

Martin Scorsese saw *Shadows* when he was a film student at New York University, and it made him realize, "all of a sudden," he would later recall, that "cinema could be made anywhere." If Cassavetes, an actor with no experience behind the camera, could simply start shooting in 16 mm on the streets of New York, then maybe Scorsese could do that, too—"it was a breakthrough in the way of thinking."

When Scorsese directed his first feature, *Boxcar Bertha*, an exploitation movie produced by Roger Corman, he screened it for Cassavetes, whom he'd since befriended. "Nice work," Cassavetes told him afterward, "but don't fucking ever do something like this again. Why don't you make a movie about something you really care about?" And so Scorsese made *Mean Streets*, inspired in part by his own youth in Little Italy but even more by the high-energy improvisation—whether real or contrived—of *Shadows*. When he later composed the nocturnal street scenes in *Taxi Driver*, Cassavetes' furtive shots in Times Square served as the template.

In its style and its attitude, *Shadows* was the forerunner and inspiration of the American independent film movement, which was launched in the seventies by a group of directors—especially Scorsese and Robert Altman, but also, to some degree, Francis Coppola, Steven Spielberg, George Lucas, and Peter Bogdanovich—who, at least for a while, emulated Cassavetes' improvisational method and his precedent of making films outside the Hollywood system.

• • •

At the same time that Cassavetes was shooting *Shadows*, a group of French directors—most of them film critics who had been writing in *Cahiers du Cinema*—started making their own movies under the banner of a movement that they called *la nouvelle vague*, the New Wave. In May 1959, François Truffaut's first feature, *The 400 Blows*, caused a sensation at the Cannes Film Festival. The same year, Jean-Luc Godard filmed *Breathless*, while Claude Chabrol, Jacques Rivette, and Agnes Varda also started to make their marks behind the camera.

Like Cassavetes, most of them were in their late twenties. They turned to directing at a time when technological breakthroughs allowed them to realize the films that they'd been running in their heads. In Cassavetes' case, it was Kodak's Tri-X film stock, invented just before he started *Shadows*, that permitted shooting at night. For the French New Wave, it was the Nagra III tape recorder, introduced in 1958, weighing just twelve pounds and sporting an electronic speed control that could be synchronized with any camera's shutter speed. (The Nagra III was, for a while, available only in Europe; Cassavetes had to post-dub the dialogue in most of his street scenes.)

More than anything, these filmmakers were driven by the same impulse—to break free of the stiff formats and stale formulas of the established studios: to make films about real people and authentic stories with plausibly loose ends, in real apartments and especially on real city streets.

Ironically, just as Cassavetes was inspired by the Italian neorealists, the French New Wave *auteurs* were heavily influenced by American movies—not the blockbusters against which Cassavetes was rebelling, but genre pictures, which most American critics had dismissed as mere entertainments: Westerns by John Ford and Howard Hawks, gangster movies by Raoul Walsh, and thrillers by Alfred Hitchcock. (Truffaut would publish a famous book of extended interviews with Hitchcock that treated his movies as an *oeuvre* of artworks.) To the French, these movies exuded a vitality that, with few exceptions (most notably, the films of Jean Renoir), their own country's cinema sorely lacked.

Godard, who would turn out to be the New Wave's most radical director (by the late sixties rejecting all structure, like a free-jazz musician), was also drawn to the American Beat writers and abstract expressionist painters. He regarded *Breathless*—a film that he scripted day to day, shot almost randomly, and edited by excising anything that didn't move things forward—as an "action film" in the same sense that the New York artists made "action paintings": a film whose nature was shaped as much by how it was made as by its actors or the storyline.

At the time, neither Cassavetes nor many other Americans knew about these French films. When *Shadows* was being shot, these films hadn't yet been distributed in the United States. But they soon would be. *The 400 Blows* opened in New York on November 16, 1959, the week after *Shadows* played at Amos Vogel's festival. The Swedish master Ingmar Bergman was also introduced to American audiences that year, with *Wild Strawberries*, *The Seventh Seal*, and *The Magician*. Godard's *Breathless* would arrive the following year, setting off a near flood of innovative imports, including Truffaut's second film, *Shoot the Piano Player*, Michelangelo Antonioni's *L'Avventura* from Italy, Roman Polanski's *Knife in the Water* from Poland, and Milos Forman's *Loves of a Blond* from Czechoslovakia, among many others. These were films with serious themes—love, loss, alienation, death—that Hollywood movies of the fifties tended to trivialize or ignore. And while many of these European directors were influenced by American genre pictures, they added their own cultural touches: an insouciant wit, a fatalistic irony, and especially—something forbidden in American films—sex and nudity.

Through the sixties, as art houses proliferated in the major cities and as film societies—modeled after Amos Vogel's Cinema 16—sprang up on college campuses, the next generation of American filmmakers watched, studied, and absorbed all of these works as modern classics of European cinema. And when they started making their own films, they played off these European styles, themes, and taboos, stamping them with their own signatures.

And so a global cinema began to take hold, with national and regional styles bouncing back and forth across oceans, from one continent to the next, setting down old traces and picking up new ones with each reverberation. In 1959, John Cassavetes offered a new slant on what an American film could be. But the year's larger story was that in film, as in other realms of culture and society and politics, America was opening itself up to the world.

22

The Shape of Jazz to Come

On the night of November 17, 1959, hundreds of New Yorkers—not just musicians and critics but artists, poets, beatniks, gossip columnists, and a handful of slumming socialites—lined up in the cold, outside the Five Spot, a small, dank jazz club in the Bowery, to hear an alto saxophonist who had been hyped for months as the harbinger of a new wave in jazz, the next Charlie Parker, a twenty-nine-year-old from out of nowhere with the mysterious name of Ornette Coleman.

Coleman looked strange, too, a thin man with a bristly beard, playing a white alto saxophone made of plastic. His sideman, Don Cherry, was slighter still, wore dark shades, and blew a Pakistani pocket trumpet that looked like a toy. The bassist, Charlie Haden, the quartet's only white player (a rarity in itself, integration in a small jazz band), was twenty-two but looked sixteen and hunched his back over the bass at a nearly ninety-degree angle. The drummer, Billy Higgins, was less exotic in appearance, but he beat and stroked his trapset with astonishing finesse and dexterity.

There was no pianist in the band, nobody to lay down the chords, because there were no chords. The previous spring, Miles Davis had recorded an album of music built on scales instead of chord changes. But Ornette Coleman's music eschewed scales, too. It had no apparent structure, yet somehow it held together. His tone was like a yelp or a moan, but it was exhilarating, emotionally intense. The music—all of it composed by Coleman—wasn't quite atonal; it shifted in and out of tonality, and when he did play a melody, it went in unexpected directions, shifting in tempo, rhythm, and mood. And yet it was completely coherent. Each player seemed to go his own way, but they all shifted together on a dime. How was this happening? What was going on? At first, nobody quite knew.

The opening night crowd—"the largest collection of VIPs the jazz world had seen in many a year," *downbeat* magazine's reporter would write—was mixed. "Some," the reporter continued, "walked in and out before they could finish a drink, some sat mesmerized by the sound. . . . 'He'll change the entire course of jazz.' 'He's a fake.' 'He's a genius.' 'I can't say; I'll have to hear him a lot more times.' . . . 'I like him, but I don't have any idea what he is doing.'"

The controversy spread beyond the jazz world. Coleman was written up in society columns. Dorothy Kilgallen of the *New York Journal-American* wrote several times about the celebrities who came down to the Five Spot during his run, and asked him to write a guest column while she was on vacation. (It was ghostwritten by Mildred Fields, the Five Spot's press agent.) He was reviewed not just in *downbeat* and *Jazz Review*, but also in *Time*, *Newsweek*, and *Harper's Bazaar*, magazines that rarely covered jazz.

Leonard Bernstein, the iconic conductor of the New York Philharmonic, leapt up from his front-row seat in the middle of the set and declared to the audience, "This is the greatest thing ever to happen to jazz!" The next day, he took Coleman backstage at Carnegie Hall and introduced him to the symphony musicians as the most important jazz innovator since Charlie Parker.

Others just shook their heads. Dizzy Gillespie, the trumpeter who revolutionized jazz with Parker in the forties, muttered, "I don't know what he's playing, but it isn't jazz." How could it be? There weren't chords! After one set, Max Roach, who'd played drums with Parker and Gillespie and remained active on the music's forward-leaning edges, tried to slug Coleman in the mouth. A few hours later, at four o'clock in the morning, he stood outside the apartment where Coleman was staying and screamed, "I know you're up there, motherfucker! Come on down here, and I'll kick your ass!"

The old revolutionaries had no tolerance for the new one.

At first, some musicians and critics suspected Coleman simply didn't know how to play. But then they heard him warming up backstage, playing Charlie Parker tunes—"Donna Lee" and "Klack-to-vee-sedstene"—super-fast and note-perfect. The message was clear: he was *choosing* to play onstage by different rules. Once his skeptics realized that his music contained no signposts, no chord changes or other harmonic cues pointing where his music was going—once they learned to take in the music on its own terms, to *listen* with no preconceptions (and, for many, this took a while)—they began to hear the melodies, the patterns, and an emerging strange beauty.

Ornette Coleman was born in Fort Worth, Texas, in 1930. When he was fourteen, he began to teach himself the saxophone. The next year, during a trip to New York, where he stayed with an aunt who was married to the jazz trumpeter Doc Cheatham, he heard Dizzy Gillespie's big band playing in a club. Ornette couldn't read music well, but even then, he had an extraordinary ear, and he came back to Fort Worth suddenly playing bebop solos. He started playing with professional bands for decent money.

One night in 1948, playing tenor saxophone at a dance, Ornette took a solo on "Stardust" and found himself slipping beyond the chord changes, just playing what he felt and what he heard inside his head. The dancers stopped dancing and stared at him. He was fired that night. Over the next few years, he was fired by several bands. At one gig, a group of customers disliked his playing so intensely that they beat him up and broke his horn outside the club afterward.

In 1954, after traveling around the South with rhythm-and-blues bands, he moved to Los Angeles and got a job as an elevator operator in Bullock's department store, where he spent most of his time reading books on music theory that he brought with him to work. At night, he went around to the city's jazz clubs, trying to sit in on jam sessions. The West Coast jazz scene had only recently absorbed Charlie Parker's innovations; nobody was ready for a sound more radical still. Coleman got kicked off bandstands all over town. After a while, musicians, who'd heard about his crazy style, would play tricks on him; they promised him a slot, made him wait until one or two o'clock in the morning, then packed up as soon as he brought his horn to the stage.

He was briefly married to Jayne Cortez, a poet who was active in the Los Angeles arts scene. In the summer of 1956, she told him about a teenaged trumpeter named Don Cherry. The two arranged to meet in a music store. When Cherry walked in, Coleman was trying out some reeds—the thickest on the market—and blowing his sax with such power that people heard him a block away. He wore long hair, a beard, and, although it was ninety degrees outside, an overcoat. Cherry was a bit frightened by him, but he liked what he heard, and they started practicing together regularly.

Cherry was playing around town in a bebop band called the Jazz Messiahs with Billy Higgins, a classmate who'd been playing drums since he was five. Ornette started luring them to his style of playing—a different way of following the melody and expressing oneself without getting locked into what he called the "definite maze" of standard chord changes and meter.

During one rehearsal, when the band got to the end of thirty-two bars, normally the end of a phrase in a song, Ed Blackwell, another drummer who often sat in at these sessions, played a drumroll on the snare, as a "turnaround" before starting the next thirty-two bars. Ornette stopped the music and asked Blackwell, "Why did you end the phrase?" The phrase wasn't finished. The standard song-form says a phrase ends after thirty-two bars, but that doesn't mean it *has* to be so. Listen to the other players; let the phrase run on, if that seems natural.

Coleman hadn't read William Carlos Williams, Allen Ginsberg, or Jack Kerouac. But he shared their impulse—to break free from the confinement of conventional forms and to speak, or write, or blow in his own voice, in phrases and rhythms that matched the rhythms of his own breath. This was also why Coleman sometimes stretched a note to make it sound just a little sharper or flatter than normal. He was trying to express a specific emotion, and the twelve notes of the Western scale didn't always hit the target. In practice sessions, he would sometimes blow a note over and over, adjusting his mouthpiece or embouchure ever so slightly, to get exactly the pitch he wanted. There was nothing random or merely experimental in Coleman's microtonal playing; it was drenched in human feelings and the blues.

His idea that music should sound natural was also why he stayed away from chord changes. He hadn't read George Russell's theories on the Lydian mode; he wasn't consciously trying to revolutionize jazz. He was just playing what he heard in his head. And he realized that if he let himself get locked into a conventional chord or rhythm when he played a certain note, he'd limit his choices of what notes to play next. Some would call this "free jazz," but the tag was misleading; his music wasn't anarchic. His improvisations may not have followed chord changes, but they did follow something—variations on the rhythm or the melody or the mood—and, although he gave the band members lots of latitude, they had to follow along, which meant they had to listen carefully. Cherry would later say that playing Coleman's music was harder than playing most kinds of jazz, because it required "developing your ear along with your technical proficiency. . . . We have to know the chord structure perfectly, all the possible intervals, and then play *around* it."

One night, Coleman sat in with Cherry's band at an L.A. club called The Haig. Red Mitchell, a prominent jazz bassist, was in the audience, and they impressed him. Mitchell had recorded some albums on Contemporary Records, a local jazz label, and suggested that Coleman try to sell some of his songs to its proprietor, Lester Koenig.

Coleman went to see Koenig, who took him over to a piano in the studio. Coleman said he didn't know how to play piano. Instead he took out his plastic alto sax and began to blow the tunes. Koenig liked the songs, but he also liked Coleman's playing and asked him to bring in his group to audition for a recording session. He assembled the musicians he'd been practicing with—Cherry, Higgins, and a bass player they knew named Don Payne—and added a pianist named Walter Norris. The tryout went well. Koenig signed them up to make an album and set a date: February 10, 1958.

The timing was fortuitous. Coleman had given up on a life in music; he'd planned to go back to Fort Worth and get a normal job. The day he first met with Koenig, his mother sent him money for a bus ticket home. Now he decided to give jazz another chance.

Koenig, a music scholar and a jazz fan, started Contemporary Records in 1951 and wound up recording most of the major West Coast players—Art Pepper, Hampton Hawes, Chet Baker, Benny Carter, and Shorty Rogers. Around the time he signed up Coleman, he was also recording albums by Sonny Rollins, one of the top two tenor saxophonists from New York, and Cecil Taylor, a pianist whose music was at least as far-out as Ornette's. But he had eclectic tastes and also recorded Dixieland musicians like Kid Ory, Turk Murphy, and Bob Scobey.

Coleman's album, which Koenig titled *Something Else!!!!*, was a good first effort. It was released in January 1959, at which point he signed a contract to make a second album. Only this time, Koenig brought in some of his label's better-known musicians—Shelley Manne on drums and Red Mitchell, Ornette's discoverer, on bass—to back Coleman and Cherry on their horns.

The first session, on January 16, was disastrous. Manne was a swing drummer; he gave it a game try but had no idea how to play behind Ornette's off-center meters. Mitchell stayed glued to what he heard as chord changes, which weighed the music down. They recorded only one song. The second session, on February 23, was no better, though they managed to record two tunes.

Before the next date, set for two weeks later, Coleman and Cherry drove up to San Francisco to persuade Percy Heath, the bassist for the Modern Jazz Quartet, to replace Mitchell. The previous summer, the three had played together at an after-hours jam session, and Heath was knocked out—so much so that he brought the MJQ's pianist and leader, John Lewis, to see them the next night, and he was knocked out, too. Heath agreed to make the recording date. When he came down, the band recorded six songs in the course of one late night.

The album, which would be released just a couple of weeks before the Five Spot debut the following November, was called *Tomorrow Is the Question!* It was better than the first album, but Manne was still miscast, and even with the agile Percy Heath, there was something stiff about the bass line.

Coleman had heard what that bass line could be the previous fall, when by chance he met Charlie Haden.

It was another one of those nights when Coleman tried to sit in on a jam session at The Haig. He played only a few bars before the other players kicked him off the bandstand, but that was enough to startle Haden, who happened to be sitting in the audience. Since moving to Los Angeles from Shenandoah, Iowa, where his parents and siblings were country and western musicians who performed on a syndicated radio show ("Cowboy Charlie" sang with them from the time he was two until fifteen, when a bout of polio damaged his vocal cords), Haden had played bass with most of the city's jazz musicians. Often he would try to break out of the chord changes—to improvise on the tune's mood, or pluck a counterpoint or a color tone that he heard in his head and thought would sound right—but the other players would rein him in. And now here was a saxophonist who was playing the way that Haden wanted to play. He found out Coleman's name, tracked him down and, one Sunday, met him at a jam session and afterward drove to Coleman's house, where they improvised duets all afternoon. Haden joined Coleman's circle of musicians right after.

Haden's main job at the time was at the Hillcrest Club, playing with the house band led by a pianist named Paul Bley. Haden brought Coleman, Cherry, and Higgins to sit in. Bley was twenty-six, from Montreal by way of New York. He'd played with Charlie Parker, Charles Mingus, Bud Powell, most of the East Coast greats. He was also classically trained, with grounding in avant-garde music, and he was waiting for jazz to catch up. In New York, he'd known Gil Evans and George Russell and other composers who wrote music that roamed outside traditional chord changes—until it hit the bandstand, when the saxophonist would take his solo in the manner of Charlie Parker, and it wound up sounding like just another bebop blowing session. Ornette Coleman was *playing* the way Russell and the others had been trying to *write*, plus some.

In October 1958, Bley fired his vibes player and hired Ornette Coleman and Don Cherry. Coleman was now playing six nights a week with a band that understood his music, and he caught fire. He would write six tunes in a day, then another six the next day, none of them the same. The players learned one another's moves, too; they became almost clairvoyant in anticipating the shifts and feints.

The problem was, not many other people liked what they heard. Bley would later say that you could tell when the band was playing because the sidewalk outside would be crowded with people, and you could tell when the band was on break because that's when everybody would go back inside the club. Surely he was exaggerating, but not by much; after about six weeks, the Hillcrest Club's owner reluctantly fired the band. That seemed to be the end.

But fortunes soon changed. In March 1959, Percy Heath told John Lewis about his guest spot on Coleman's recording date. That rekindled Lewis's memories of watching Coleman and Cherry play the previous summer. In an interview with an Italian jazz magazine, Lewis was asked about new developments in music, and he started talking about the way the two played together. "I've never heard anything like them before," Lewis said. "I can't figure out what it's all about yet. It is, in a sense, an extension of Charlie Parker and the first I've heard."

Lewis and the Modern Jazz Quartet were under contract at Atlantic Records. He told Atlantic's owners, Ahmet and Nesuhi Eretegun, the sons of a Turkish diplomat, about Coleman and Cherry. Nesuhi Ertegun was a longtime friend of Lester Koenig; they regularly exchanged records with each other. Nesuhi had heard the first Ornette record, found it promising. On Lewis's recommendation, he signed Coleman away from Contemporary and asked him to record a new album, on his own terms, as soon as possible.

Coleman called Cherry, Haden, and Higgins. (Though Bley would have been the most suitable pianist around, Coleman didn't really want a pianist, preferring to play without a harmonic net.) This was the quartet that would set the jazz world on fire six months later.

On May 22, 1959, the four musicians went into Radio Recorders studio in West Hollywood—where Elvis Presley and Louis Armstrong had made some of their hit records—and, all in one day, laid down six Ornette Coleman songs, all of which they knew very well, having played them many times at the Hillcrest. It was an extraordinary mix of gentle blues, up-tempo frenzy, and a ballad called "Lonely Woman" that was unlike anything ever heard and that, over the years, would become Coleman's anthem.

"Lonely Woman" begins with Haden playing a slow bass dirge. Higgins follows with a fast drum riff (a pairing of slow bass and fast drums was unusual enough). Then Coleman and Cherry, in unison, blow a sorrowful melody, both of them bending notes, wailing, so naked with emotion that it still raises shivers a half century later. After reciting the theme a couple times, Coleman takes his solo, which wanders off in a different direction; if you were expecting to hear an improvisation on harmony, it might seem like a different song. But he's improvising on other aspects of the song, especially its emotion. The other players do the same. Somehow it all hangs together, and toward the end, they come back to the theme, come back down to Earth, with aplomb.

It was, and still is, a musical miracle.

Ertegun was thrilled with the day's work and decided to turn the album into an Event. He and John Lewis were on the board of the Lenox School of Jazz, an intensive three-week summer program at the Music Inn, in the Berkshires, where aspiring musicians were tutored by such jazz masters as Dizzy Gillespie, Bill Evans, Oscar Peterson, Ray Brown, J. J. Johnson, Kenny Dorham, Jim Hall, Gunther Schuller, and George Russell. Ertegun and Lewis arranged for Coleman and Cherry to be enrolled as students in the school's upcoming August session, with Atlantic Records paying their bills. The idea was to expose the two to the big names in the New York jazz community who would, in turn, build up some buzz about the upcoming album.

Coleman wanted to call the album *Focus on Sanity*, which was the title of one of its faster songs. Ertegun wrote him a letter, proposing a different title: *The Shape of Jazz to Come*. That title, he explained, would give record buyers "an idea about the uniqueness of the LP." Coleman didn't like it, but he gave in.

There was another problem with Coleman: he was growing weary. Half a year had passed since the release of *Something Else!!!!* Only a couple of paying gigs had come out of it. He began to wonder if his prospects were hopeless. In late June, he wrote Ertegun that he was thinking of giving up music and going off someplace to study religion. Ertegun wrote back, "I know you've had some very tough experiences and disappointments in your musical career up to now. However, in my view, your career is just beginning." He also assured Ornette that the Lenox School session was "still on."

In August, Coleman and Cherry went up to the Berkshires, as planned. They hadn't dealt much with East Coast jazz musicians, so they were surprised when their playing set off the same heat and hostility that it had sparked in Los Angeles. Bob Brookmeyer, the trombonist and composer, who was on the faculty that summer, became so angry at the two—at one point, he screamed, "Damn it, tune up!"—that he stormed off and quit the school in protest. (Within a year, Brookmeyer became one of Ornette's most ardent advocates, regretting his initial failure to grasp what he and Cherry were doing.) Most of the musicians at Lenox didn't know what to make of the pair. But others were enthralled. Gunther Schuller had been exploring new directions in jazz as the leader of what he called the "third stream" movement, which sought to combine elements of jazz and twentieth-century classical music; he saw in Ornette someone who'd discovered an entirely new stream on his own. George Russell, who had persuaded Miles Davis to wage a war on chords, heard in Ornette the embodiment—and a radical extension—of the ideas that he'd been formulating for the previous six years.

Perhaps the most crucial enthusiast was a jazz critic named Martin Williams. Only twenty-five, Williams was already regarded as one of the most astute reviewers around, able to write clear journalism about a jam session, evocative liner notes for record albums, and scholarly analyses of, say, a Louis Armstrong solo with the same rigorous detail that a classical musicologist might apply to Beethoven sonatas. Williams, too, was on the lookout for the next Charlie Parker—some genius who might plow a new path out of the harmonic rut—and, on August 10, the first day of the Lenox School's session that summer, he was convinced that he found him. Ornette Coleman stood up to take a solo at a rehearsal session of a big band led by Herb Pomeroy, and as Williams wrote later in *The Jazz Review*, a magazine that he coedited with Nat Hentoff, "It was as if he opened up something in one's soul and opened up the way for jazz to grow." Three days later, after hearing Coleman play some more, Williams phoned Nesuhi Ertegun and left a message with his secretary: "Just wanted to tell you Ornette Coleman is *greatest* ever."

Back in New York, Williams wrote the liner notes for *The Shape of Jazz to Come*, proclaiming, "I believe that what Ornette Coleman is playing will affect the whole character of jazz music most profoundly and pervasively." Too many players were changing chords, or running up and down scales, "like a rat in a harmonic maze," Williams went on. "Someone had to break through the walls that those harmonies have built and restore melody—but, again, we realize this only after an Ornette Coleman has begun to do it."

Williams also phoned the Termini brothers, Joe and Iggy, proprietors of the Five Spot jazz club, and urged them to book the Ornette Coleman Quartet as soon as possible. The jazz scene on Fifty-second Street had been over for a couple of years; Birdland was one of its few holdovers. The gravity had shifted downtown, to the Village Vanguard, the Village Gate, Café Bohemia, the Half Note, but, above all, the Five Spot.

The Five Spot was a tiny, dark room (*Time* magazine would describe it as "a shabby cave"), with chairs and tables crammed together, customers sitting shoulder to shoulder on a packed night. It was located on Third Avenue between Fourth and Fifth Streets—a skid row littered with winos and the occasional bottle fight—only a few blocks from where many of the New York artists had their lofts and studios. The club started out as just another one of their neighborhood bars, attracting Willem de Kooning, Franz Kline, Mark Rothko, and the rest. There was a piano in the corner, and, in 1956, Larry Rivers—a painter who also played the alto saxophone—urged the Terminis to bring in jazz musicians. One of the first they booked was Cecil Taylor, a pianist who attacked the keyboard much like the abstract expressionists went at the canvas. One night, Taylor banged the piano so hard that he broke it. The Terminis threatened to fire him, but the artists liked him—he was, in a sense, one of them—so the piano was fixed, and Taylor stayed on for eleven weeks. When Coleman came to play three years later, the abstract expressionists felt an affinity for his music, too—its free energy and its obliteration of distinctions between the lead and the accompaniment, a sort of sonic equivalent to an "all-over" canvas. (The following year, in the liner notes of his second Atlantic album, *Change of the Century*, Coleman would describe his music as "something like the paintings of Jackson Pollock." His third album, *Free Jazz*, would display a reproduction of Pollock's painting *White Light* on the cover.)

On Monday nights, when the musicians were off, Rivers organized poetry readings, which he sometimes accompanied on saxophone. Jack Kerouac and Allen Ginsberg read at several of these events. One Monday, for a lark, the poet Kenneth Koch declaimed from the phone book while Rivers blew the sax behind him. Afterward, the singer Billie Holiday, who often came to the club, walked up to Koch and said, "Man, your poems are weird."

The Five Spot gained a wider audience in 1957, when Thelonious Monk started playing there. If Cecil Taylor was the jazz piano's Pollock or de Kooning, Monk was its Picasso, splitting chords into angular shards, combining notes that weren't supposed to be played together, yet making them sound strangely right. Monk hadn't played in a New York jazz club since the early part of the decade, when he was arrested for drug possession—the drugs belonged to a friend, but Monk took the rap—and, as a result, lost his "cabaret card," the police department's permit that all musicians needed to perform in the city's nightclubs. Monk and his band, which included John Coltrane on tenor sax, packed the club almost every night; they became the house band, staying for the better part of two years.

Norman Mailer was among those who came to see Monk and Coltrane at the Five Spot nearly every weekend, sitting as far up front as he could get, soaking in the virtuosity and the high-energy tension. Monk was prancing on a much higher tightrope that any other jazz musician Mailer had heard, and it inspired him to take more chances in his writing.

Allen Ginsberg was another regular. He'd moved back to New York in the summer of 1958 and found an apartment right around the corner from the club. He frequently struck up conversations with Monk—a brilliantly mathematical mind but very eccentric, probably a bit bipolar—and, one day, gave him a copy of *Howl*. A week passed; Monk didn't say anything. Finally, Ginsberg asked if he'd read the book. Monk said, "Yeah, I'm almost through." "Well?" Ginsberg asked, a bit nervous. Monk replied, casually, "It makes sense."

By the fall of 1959, the Five Spot was known in hip circles as the place to go hear the most cutting-edge jazz. Those who went down to listen were primed for something dramatically new—whether because they were yearning for "the next Charlie Parker" or simply because so much was changing in the world all around them that changes in the culture seemed more palatable.

Meanwhile, as Nesuhi Ertegun had predicted, the musicians who came back from the Lenox School that summer were buzzing about Ornette Coleman, telling everyone they knew that maybe he was *the one*. Paul Bley, who'd recently moved back to New York, found himself approached on the street by musicians who knew that he'd played with Ornette in L.A. and who wanted the scoop on exactly what this guy with the strange name and the white plastic horn was doing.

When Coleman and his quartet finally made their debut, the Termini brothers put them on a double bill with the Jazztet, a hard-bop quintet fronted by Art Farmer on flugelhorn, Benny Golson on tenor sax, and Curtis Fuller on trombone. Just in case Ornette proved too far-out, the Jazztet would calm things down. The players in that band were all modern but established and highly proficient. After Coleman's first set, one of them looked over to a friend and said, "I guess I'm out-of-date now."

In the next few years, a lot of once-skeptical jazz musicians adopted some of Ornette Coleman's techniques. Miles Davis—who initially said of Coleman, "Hell, just listen to what he writes and how he plays . . . the man is all screwed up inside"—started playing a lot more "free" after he formed a new band of young musicians enthralled with the possibilities that Ornette opened up.

John Coltrane went further. Coltrane had been obsessed with chords. A few weeks after finishing the *Kind of Blue* dates with Miles, he led his own recording date, for an album called *Giant Steps*, which featured him in hair-raising form, piling chords on top of chords within chords, pushing the harmonic complexity beyond their limit. It was a thrilling album, but he had no idea where to go next; the road—his particular frontier—seemed to hit a dead end. When he heard Ornette at the Five Spot, Coltrane said, "Well, that must be the answer." After sets, he went off with Ornette and they talked, sometimes for hours. Ornette gave him informal lessons in nonchordal improvisation. (Much later, Coltrane sent him a check amounting to $30 a lesson). In the summer of 1960, he led a recording session with Coleman's rhythm section (the mesh didn't quite work, and the album wouldn't be released for another six years). For the next seven years, until he died of liver disease, Coltrane played increasingly free and turbulent music—on albums like *A Love Supreme, Ascension*, and *Interstellar Space*—which, though different in many ways from Ornette's music, took off from its premises.

As the Black Power movement took off in the sixties, several jazz musicians took the examples of Coleman, Coltrane, or both as license to play free as a *political* statement—breaking down chords and rhythms as a symbol for breaking down white authority and power, some of them making their horns sound deliberately ugly as a rebellion against white, bourgeois notions of beauty.

Finally, there was the back-and-forth case of Sonny Rollins, who was the same age as Coleman but more seasoned; he played in his youth with Bird, Monk, Miles, and Coltrane, and recorded several albums as a leader since. In 1959, at the peak of his career, Rollins dropped out of the jazz scene. In part, the move stemmed from his intense self-criticism; he thought he just wasn't playing well and needed to bone up on the fundamentals. (He started practicing his horn at night on the Williamsburg Bridge, near his Lower East

Side apartment.) In part, though, he was shaken by the innovations of Coltrane and Coleman and felt he needed to find a new sound of his own.

When Ornette debuted at the Five Spot, Rollins knew what was coming. He'd gotten to know Coleman the year before, when he spent time in Los Angeles, making some albums for Contemporary Records. The two sometimes drove to the beach north of Santa Monica, took out their horns, and played music together in the open air, with the ocean waves as their orchestra.

Rollins returned to the jazz scene in 1962 with great fanfare, and, after a brief spell of playing ballads in much the same way as he had three years earlier, he put together a band that included Don Cherry and Billy Higgins—Coleman's trumpeter and drummer—and played free jazz. After that, he formed another band with some members of Coltrane's rhythm section and played freer still. By 1966, Rollins returned to innovating within song forms; he realized that "free" had its limits, too, and that he wasn't going to reach his full potential— wasn't going to find his own natural sound—in that realm.

Ornette Coleman changed the shape of jazz, but not in his own image; nor was that his intention. To the extent he had a gospel, it was that music was communication and that musicians should express their individuality. After Ornette, many jazz musicians continued to play standards and follow chord changes—just as, after Norman Mailer and William Burroughs, many novelists still wrote conventional plotlines and, after Mort Sahl and Lenny Bruce, many comics still told jokes about their mothers-in-law. What Coleman, and those other innovators, did was to expand the possibilities of the medium and, in the process, redefine what was traditional and what was new. Charles Mingus, the brilliant, turbulent jazz bassist and composer who ran hot and cold on Ornette for the last twenty years of his life, came away from hearing him at the Five Spot that night in 1959 with the key insight: "I'm not saying that everybody's going to have to play like Coleman," he declared, "but they're going to have to stop copying Bird."

23

Dancing in the Streets

On November 19, 1959, in the industrial heartland of Detroit, Ford Motor Company, one of the Big Three car manufacturers, announced that it was shutting down production of the Edsel.

The Edsel had rolled out two years earlier with unprecedented fanfare. A lavish ad campaign, covering television, radio, magazines, and billboards, touted the Edsel as a new kind of car. It was called the "E-car"—Experimental car—during its development phase, in which Ford had invested $400 million. The company added fifteen hundred dealerships to its existing network of ten thousand, to accommodate the expected demand.

On "E-Day," September 4, 1957, the day when the Edsel made its grand debut, three million Americans lined up outside Ford showrooms to get a look. But very few stuck around to buy one or even to take a test drive. For all the hype, the Edsel looked like any other car, but uglier. Its vertical oval grill was compared to a "horse-collar." *Time* magazine said it looked like "an Oldsmobile sucking a lemon." The automatic transmission was operated by push buttons, which were awkwardly placed on the steering wheel, where the horn was on most cars. As the months went by, quality-control reports were riotous: doors didn't close, trunks couldn't open, vital parts were missing, and the push-button transmission sometimes froze. The joke went that Edsel stood for "Every Day Something Else Leaks."

Ford had expected to sell 200,000 Edsels the first year; in fact, it sold 63,100. The second year's figures fell to 45,000. By the time the plug was pulled, sales of the coming year's models totaled just 2,846. In its two-year lifespan, the Edsel line—which was named after Henry Ford's son—lost the company $250 million.

The Edsel had been developed, in flush times, as a higher-priced car to keep Ford customers from trading up to an Olds or a Buick. But by the time it hit showrooms, the economy was in a recession. The Edsel was suddenly too expensive, too big. The Big Three— General Motors, Chrysler, and even Ford—were starting to build compacts. Foreign cars were also entering the market in a significant way. Sales of a squat German car called the Volkswagen were skyrocketing, thanks in part to an ad campaign that ironically made fun of its dowdiness. The International Auto Show, at New York's Coliseum in April, took up one-third more floor space than the previous year's show and featured cars made by sixty-five companies in nine foreign countries, nearly three hundred models of cars in all, many of them sporting—as the *New York Times* reported—"sleeker styling and more powerful engines." For the first time, Japanese cars were on display, including the new brands Toyota and Datsun.

In the wake of these trends, the Edsel's demise marked the first sign of many to come that Detroit could no longer dominate its market, any more than Washington could dictate to the world.

But just at this moment of incipient decline, a different sort of factory was rising up in the city, a musical assembly line called Motown—a wordplay on "Motor City"—that would transform the culture of the nation and the world.

The Motown factory was an eight-room house at 2648 West Grand Boulevard, which its owner, Berry Gordy, called "Hitsville, U.S.A.," because, as he told a local club owner soon after buying the place, in early 1959, it was "a hip name for a factory where hits are going to be built."

It would become the first successful black-owned record company and eventually the nation's largest black-owned enterprise of any sort.

Without Detroit, there could have been no Motown. The company was an outgrowth of the car industry, specifically of the black migration spurred by the industry's swift rise and seemingly endless demand for labor. Industrial migration swelled the black population of most northern cities, but none more quickly than Detroit. Between 1910 and 1930, the number of African Americans nearly tripled in Philadelphia and New York, and quintupled in Chicago. But in Detroit it went up by more than twenty times, from just under 6,000 to over 120,000.

The main draw was Henry Ford's factory, which, in 1914, put out the word that it was paying assembly-line workers five dollars a day. In response, blacks moved from the South to Detroit at the rate of 1,000 per month; by 1922, the figure rose to 3,500 per month. If Ford's lines were full, a strong worker could find a job at some other factory. By 1925, there were three thousand major manufacturing plants in Detroit; thirty-seven of them were building cars. At the start of World War II, Detroit became the arsenal of America's military machine, and the demand for workers soared further. A half million more migrated to Detroit in the war's first two years.

There was little assimilation of the black families that poured into Detroit in the early waves of this migration; most of them were crammed into dilapidated tenements on the city's south side. During the even larger influx brought on by World War II, things got ugly. Most of these new migrants were black, as before, but there were also many Polish immigrants and white Appalachians, all competing for the same jobs. A quarter of the city's 185 war plants refused to hire blacks. Many car factories, even after all these years, would not mix black and white workers on the same assembly line. In 1943, the NAACP and the United Auto Workers staged an "equal opportunity" rally, with over ten thousand black men attending. When, as a result, three black workers were promoted to skilled slots at a Packard plant, twenty-six thousand white workers walked out.

That summer, race riots erupted. President Franklin D. Roosevelt had to send in six thousand federal troops to quell the violence, which left thirty-four people dead (twenty-five of them black), hundreds injured, and $2 million worth of property damage. The city planners responded with the Detroit Plan, which demolished hundreds of buildings and displaced thousands of black families, inspiring the observation that "urban renewal" was a euphemism for "Negro removal."

Amid this de facto segregation, the African Americans in Detroit created their own culture and institutions—and, because of the decent-paying jobs at Ford and other factories, they had enough money to sustain the effort. Detroit produced the Broadside Press, one of the nation's first black-owned publishing houses; the Booker T. Washington Trade Association, one of the largest chapters of black businessmen; the Concept East Theater, the first northern black theater company; and WCHB, the first black-owned and black-operated radio station. It was no coincidence that Detroit was the first headquarters for the Nation of Islam or that two U.S. legislators from Detroit, Charles Diggs Jr. and John Conyers, would help start the Congressional Black Caucus.

And there was music. The blues were ingrained in Detroit culture. The first news of Ford's five-dollar daily pay scale was spread through songs like Blind Blake's "Detroit Bound Blues" ("I'm goin' to Detroit, get myself a good job / Tried to stay around here with the starvation mob / I'm goin' to get me a job, up there in Mr. Ford's place / Stop these eatless days from starin' me in the face"). And, as the workload grew weary, solace, too, came from the blues, like Joe L. Carter's "Please, Mr. Foreman" ("Please, Mr. Foreman, slow down your assembly line / No, I don't mind workin', but I do mind dyin'").

During the economic boom of the war years and after, Detroit's south side was flush with nightclubs, where local and visiting musicians played jazz and the blues. The city offered excellent music programs at the main black high school, Northeastern, which turned out dozens of top-notch jazz players. Most of them moved to New York at the first chance, but many stayed behind, got jobs at the clubs, and mentored young musicians coming up.

When Berry Gordy set up Motown and started looking for a stable of studio musicians, he knew where to find them.

Gordy came from an entrepreneurial family. His grandfather, the son of a slave who was freed after the Civil War, bought up land in rural Georgia, 168 acres in all, and had nine children. One of those children, Gordy's father, moved to Detroit in the 1920s, not to assemble cars but to start his own business, and after much scraping and saving, he bought a grocery store.

Berry was born in 1929. When he was a boy, he lionized Joe Louis and trained to be a boxer, but he also loved jazz, and in 1953, when he got back from the war in Korea, he started a record store called 3D Record Mart—House of Jazz. The problem was, blues was a lot more popular than jazz; it took Gordy too long to realize this; and, within two years, he went out of business. He took a job on the Lincoln-Mercury assembly line, fastening upholstery and chrome strips to the frames pulled down on conveyor belts. But he wanted to be a songwriter. He spent evenings at the jazz and blues clubs on John R Street, especially the Flame Show Bar, where he saw Dinah Washington, Sarah Vaughan, and Billie Holiday sing—and where his sisters, Anna and Gwen, worked the photo and cigarette concessions.

In the fall of 1957, Gordy heard that Al Green, a local talent manager, was looking for someone to write songs for a singer named Jackie Wilson. The most popular musician in Detroit at the time was the blues singer John Lee Hooker. Gordy learned from listening to Hooker that a song should tell a story. So he wrote a song for Green called "Reet Petite" ("the finest girl you'd ever want to meet"). Green bought it, Wilson recorded it, and it became a hit on the R&B charts.

Al Green soon died, and his assistant, Nat Tarnopol, took over the agency. One day Gordy was sitting in Tarnopol's office when a singing group called the Matadors walked in and auditioned. Tarnopol didn't like their song, but Gordy did. He chased the group down the hall and introduced himself to the lead singer, whose name was Bill "Smoky" Robinson. Gordy struck up a writing partnership with Robinson, took over his management, and suggested that the group change its name from the Matadors to the Miracles.

Toward the end of the year, Gordy took Smoky Robinson and the Miracles into a local studio and recorded a song that the two of them had written called "Got a Job." That would be the record's A side; an old standard, "My Mama Done Told Me," which they also recorded, would be the flip side. Gordy signed with a small New York label called End Records to manufacture and distribute the 45-rpm single. It was released on February 19, 1958, Robinson's eighteenth birthday.

Several months later, Gordy got his producer's royalty check in the mail. It was in the amount of $3.19. Robinson told him that he should start his own label. Gordy agreed. In January 1959, he started Tamla Records.

That same month, he borrowed $800 from his family—signing formal loan papers that pegged the sum to future royalties—and found a house on West Grand Boulevard, putting the business offices on the main floor, his home (for himself and his wife and children) upstairs, and the recording studio in what used to be the garage.

The next month, Gordy was walking down the corridor, a lot of troubles on his mind. His receptionist, Janie Bradford, came up and playfully pinched him on the butt, something she did to him nearly every day. He jumped and said he was trying to write some lyrics. She asked what the song was about. He said it was about money. Two things people needed were love and money. There were already a lot of songs about love, so he was writing one about money.

They'd arrived at the studio by this point. He went over to the piano, pounded out some chords, and started singing a song about a man who knows the best things in life are free but he needs money! She laughed and, off the top of her head, made up a second verse, singing that love is a thrill, but it can't pay her bills, give her some money, baby.

A singer named Barrett Strong was in the next room. Hearing the commotion, he came in the studio and sang with them. His voice, soulful with the hint of a moan, was ideal. Gordy assembled some musicians and, over the course of a few days and a couple dozen takes—it was his studio, so there were no constraints on time— they laid down "Money (That's What I Want)." It was the first song recorded at Hitsville.

In August 1959, Gordy put out the single as Tamla 54027. It was only the eighth single he'd released on his Tamla record label, but he slapped on a larger number to give the impression that the label was more established. He sent copies to record stores and radio stations in Detroit, Cleveland, Cincinnati, Washington, D.C., and Baltimore—the extent of his distribution. It did very well, under the circumstances. His sister Anna had her own record label, named after herself (which she later folded into Motown). She'd struck a national distribution deal with Chess, a white-owned company in Chicago that distributed or owned the rights to music by several black artists, including Chuck Berry, Bo Diddley, Muddy Waters, and Howlin' Wolf. So in early 1960, Gordy licensed the recording to Anna. It rock- eted to number two on the R&B charts and number twenty-six on the pop charts. Gordy realized, at that point, that he had to form his own national distribution network—that, to make it in this business, he'd have to control everything.

One of the musicians on the "Money" session was a drummer named William "Benny" Benjamin. In Motown's first year, a corps of musicians settled in—eventually they'd play backup on two or three recording sessions a day, six days a week—including James Jamerson on bass, Earl Van Dyke or Johnny Griffith on piano, Mike Terry on tenor sax, Hank Crosby or Robert White on guitar, and Benny Benjamin or sometimes Richard "Pistol" Allen on drums. They called themselves the Funk Brothers, a name coined by Benjamin. Most of them had moved to Detroit with their parents in one of the great black migrations. Many had studied music at Northeastern High. At the time they started playing at Hitsville, all of them were active jazz musicians on Detroit's nightclub scene. Van Dyke had sat in with Charlie Parker and Sonny Stitt, Benjamin with Dizzy Gillespie, Jamerson with Grant Green and Yusef Lateef.

They spent their days playing at Hitsville, for increasingly good money, but they continued to jam at after-hours sessions in the jazz clubs. It was there that they came to learn each other's moves, how to play off one another—a useful thing back at Hitsville, since Gordy or whoever else was producing a session rarely gave them much more guidance than a few chords scribbled on a piece of sheet music. The riffs, rhythms, and especially the bass lines were all improvised on the spot—and often came from licks they'd played at some jam session a few nights earlier.

Most pop or R&B backup bands played predictable patterns. The pianist pounded out the usual chords; the drummer hit his snare or cymbal in straight four-four time; the bassist plucked two notes per bar, usually the chord's tonic (for instance, a C note to thicken a C chord).

But the Funk Brothers put spins on the music. Van Dyke would lace the chords with some blue notes or ever-so-slightly off-centered variations. Benjamin or Allen would ride the hi-hat cymbal and alter the accent on the snare, to goose the rhythm. Jamerson would delay or stagger the downbeat, and devise his own bass melody in syncopated eighth notes, to add a layer of tension.

As New York jazz evolved more into an art music that drifted away from popular taste, Motown injected pop music with a dash of jazz complexity on top of its spiky backbeat. It was a hip, urban twist on the rural blues that formed the core of black R&B (and its Elvis imitators). And it offered an alluring alternative—dripping with dance rhythms, a soul groove, and a simmering sexuality—to the saccharine doo-wop and surf hymns that dominated the white pop charts.

Buddy Holly, the king of white rock 'n' roll, had died in a plane crash in February 1959. Motown filled the gap. Across the Atlantic, in Liverpool, England, a rock band called the Silver Beetles gradually abandoned Holly's influence and adopted Motown's, especially in John Lennon's wailing vocals and Paul McCartney's looser bass lines. Four years later, when they changed their name to the Beatles and started making records, some of their first covers were Motown songs—"Please Mr. Postman," "You Really Got a Hold on Me," and "Money (That's What I Want)."

But at least as important as this crossover was the appeal and influence of the Motown songs and singers themselves. Beginning with the Marvelettes' "Please Mr. Postman," released in early 1961, Motown records regularly soared to number one not just on the R&B charts but on the pop charts as well. The phrase "R&B"—and, even more, "race music," as it was widely called right up to the end of the fifties—receded into irrelevance. In Motown's first few years, Smoky Robinson, Mary Wells, Marvin Gaye, Stevie Wonder, Diana Ross and the Supremes, Gladys Knight and the Pips, the Temptations, the Four Tops, and the Jackson Five towered as *pop stars*, plain and simple, beyond the category of race. In the widening civil-rights movement, Motown would serve not only as a showcase for black pride and independence but also as a lubricant for social integration. It was hard to be a racist while slow-dancing to Smoky Robinson.

The birth of Motown coincided with the rise of a truly national musical culture. The first portable transistor radio—the Regency TR-1, manufactured by Texas Instruments, the company that would invent the microchip—hit the market in time for Christmas of 1954. It cost $49.95, beyond the typical teenager's budget, but it still sold 150,000 units. Three years later, Sony made its debut in the American marketplace with the smaller, somewhat cheaper TR-63. Soon, prices for pocket radios plunged below the twenty-dollar mark and began to sell in massive quantities—12 million units a year by 1960, when Motown went national. By this time, transistor radios were also installed in 50 million cars nationwide. And television sets, which had penetrated only two-thirds of American households in 1955, were owned by 90 percent at the end of the decade.

The new pop songs were not only more appealing than the hits of a few years earlier—they were also omnipresent and more acutely attuned to a rising new, urban, youthful culture. And the Motown sound that fueled this music would furnish the soundtrack for the steamy turbulence ahead. Norman Mailer's *Advertisements for Myself* was published on October 30, 1959, and it was already, in one sense, dated. Mailer had looked forward to the sixties as an era of revolt turbo-fueled by sex, drugs, and jazz. He hadn't anticipated the jolt and sizzle of Motown rock 'n' roll.

24

Andromeda Freed from Her Chains

Toward the end of December 1959, Dr. Irwin Winter, the director of medical research at G. D. Searle Pharmaceuticals in Chicago, and Dr. John Rock, a professor of medicine at Harvard and the nation's most renowned fertility specialist, met in an office at the U.S. Food and Drug Administration in Washington, D.C., to seek approval for a new drug called Enovid—also known as the birth-control pill.

The FDA's approval would mark the crowning achievement of two women in their eighties—Margaret Sanger, a crusader for women's rights and birth control since the turn of the century, and Katharine McCormick, who at Sanger's urging had financed the development of the Pill with her own family fortune.

Sanger, born Maggie Louise Higgins in Corning, New York, first grew passionate about the subject of birth control in 1898, when she was nineteen years old and her mother died of tuberculosis, at the age of forty-nine, after years of nearly nonstop pregnancies—ten childbirths and seven miscarriages in all. At the funeral, standing over the coffin, Maggie turned to her father and fumed, "You caused this. Mother is dead from having so many children."

In 1902, she married a liberal-minded architect and artist named William Sanger and, assured of financial security, joined the women's committee of the Socialist Party. Though barely five feet tall, she was a firebrand, picketing with the Wobblies at workers' strikes in Paterson, New Jersey, and Lawrence, Massachusetts.

Margaret Sanger had trained as a nurse, with a particular interest in obstetrics, so she took a job with a New York welfare agency on the Lower East Side, where over a half million Jewish and Italian immigrants were crammed in filthy tenement buildings covering an area less than a half square mile.

In 1912, she wrote a series of articles on feminine hygiene for *The Call*, the leading Socialist newspaper, as well as a pamphlet on contraceptives called "What Every Girl Should Know." The U.S. Post Office declared the pamphlets "indecent" and confiscated them under the same Comstock Laws that, for the next forty-seven years, would ban the sale of "obscene" literature.

Diaphragms and condoms had been around for decades, but they were illegal unless prescribed by doctors, most of whom were too embarrassed to discuss such matters with their patients, and vice versa. One of Sanger's patients, Sadie Sachs, a twenty-eight-year-old Jewish mother of three small children, had collapsed while trying to induce an abortion on her kitchen floor after learning that she was pregnant again. Sachs had gone to her doctor and asked what she could do to stop having babies. The doctor suggested that she tell her husband to sleep on the roof. Three months later, Sachs died at the hands of a five-dollar abortionist. There were a hundred thousand illegal abortions a year in New York City. Sanger resolved to do something about it.

In 1914, she started a newspaper called *Woman Rebel*, in which she urged women "to look the whole world in the face with a go-to-hell look in the eyes." The paper's main mission, she wrote, was "to advocate the prevention of conception" and "to impart such knowledge in the columns of this paper." In one such column in the June issue, she coined the phrase "birth control," which had never appeared in print before.

Again, the postmaster general banned *Woman Rebel* from the mail. More than that, two federal agents served Sanger with an indictment for nine violations of the Comstock Laws. If a judge found her guilty, she could serve up to forty-five years in prison. So she fled to England, leaving behind her husband and two children, and stayed with her sister in Liverpool.

Word of Sanger's presence spread through Liverpool's socialist community, and she was invited to tea by Charles Drysdale, a leader of Britain's Neo-Malthusian League, which regarded overpopulation as the root cause of war and all the rest of the world's miseries. Drysdale urged Sanger to narrow her rebelliousness and focus on birth control. He introduced her to Havelock Ellis, author of the seven-volume *Studies in the Psychology of Sex*. She and Ellis met daily in the British Museum, where he gave her reading lists, not just on Malthus and contraception, but also on eugenics—the theory of improving the species through selective breeding. She and Ellis embarked on a passionate love affair, the first of dozens—some estimate as many as a hundred—that Sanger would enjoy in her lifetime.

One day, while Sanger was still in exile, an undercover federal agent came to her house back in New York and, without identifying himself, asked her husband for a copy of his wife's pamphlet. He handed one over. The next day, Anthony Comstock himself showed up and arrested William Sanger for distributing literature that was "obscene, lewd, lascivious, filthy, indecent and disgusting." The judge declared the defendant a "menace to society" and sentenced him to jail for thirty days.

It was all a ploy to lure Margaret home. If she didn't come back, she knew, the state would consign her children to an orphanage. The plot worked. However, several prominent friends whom she'd met through Havelock Ellis, including the novelist (and free-love advocate) H. G. Wells, wrote President Woodrow Wilson a letter, urging him to intervene in her case. Suddenly, the prosecutors dropped the case with no explanation.

The experience only further radicalized Sanger. She became the leader of the National Birth Control League, which had been formed during her exile, and started a magazine called *Birth Control Review*. On October 16, 1916, in Brooklyn, she opened the nation's first birth-control clinic. Ten days later, the vice squad shut it down.

She embarked on a nationwide speaking tour to raise funds for the movement. Everywhere she went, she drew huge crowds—often a mix of avid supporters and Catholic protesters. At those events where she was permitted to take the stage at all, she was usually arrested as she started to speak.

In 1920, Sanger and her husband divorced. Two years later, she married J. Noah H. Slee, an oil-company president who was twenty years her senior and smitten with her cause. He gave over $50,000 to the Birth Control League, keeping it afloat and allowing her to sail to Europe to organize a scientific conference on overpopulation. The involvement of scientists, who linked population control to the cause of world peace, gave contraception a sheen of social responsibility—it wasn't just about sex and poor immigrants—and by the middle of the decade, the league boasted nearly forty thousand paid members.

A turning point came in 1936, when Sanger ordered a new Japanese diaphragm through the mail. U.S. Customs officers confiscated the package and arrested her on charges of indecency. The federal judge, Grover Moscowitz, dismissed the suit and ordered Customs to release the package. President Franklin D. Roosevelt's attorney general decided not to appeal the verdict. From that moment on, contraceptives could legally be sent through the mail. The same year, the American Medical Association declared that birth control was a legitimate topic for doctors to discuss with their patients.

By 1950, Sanger's Birth Control League—or, as it was now called, the Planned Parenthood Foundation—operated two hundred clinics nationwide.

That year, two crucial events took place. First, in October, Margaret Sanger received a letter from Katharine Dexter McCormick. The two had met back in 1917, when Sanger gave a speech on birth control in Boston. Ever since, McCormick had contributed small sums to her organizations, and before the 1936 court decision, she often smuggled contraceptives into the country from her many trips abroad. But now she wanted to do something big.

McCormick came from a wealthy old family. Her great-great-grandfather was President John Adams's secretary of war. Her father was a prominent Chicago lawyer who helped rebuild the city after the Great Fire. She herself was the second woman ever to graduate from the Massachusetts Institute of Technology, with a degree in biology. In 1904, at the relatively mature age of twenty-nine, she married an artist named Stanley McCormick, who was wealthier still; his father, Cyrus McCormick, had invented the reaper and founded the International Harvester Company.

Two years into their marriage, Stanley was diagnosed with schizophrenia. Katharine decided never to have children, for fear of passing along his disease. She went into seclusion, emerging occasionally to play an active role in the suffrage movement, which was how she met Sanger.

In 1947, Stanley died. Katharine spent the next three years in a legal struggle with the McCormick family over her inheritance. She won the battle, emerged with more money than she could ever spend on herself, and so, in 1950, wrote the letter to Sanger, asking what areas of contraceptive research were most promising and in greatest need of financial support.

Around this time, at a dinner party in New York, Sanger was introduced to Dr. Gregory Pincus, a pioneer in the fledgling field of hormone research. In the mid-thirties, Pincus had set off a huge controversy by fertilizing rabbit embryos in a test tube and then announcing the achievement with much fanfare. His Harvard colleagues were either scandalized or jealous, and in 1939 the department denied him tenure and ordered him to leave. (Anti-Semitism no doubt played a role as well; the Harvard faculty sported very few Jews.) So, along with Hudson Hoagland, who had left Harvard a few years earlier to chair the biology department at Clark University in nearby Worcester, he formed his own research lab, the Worcester Foundation for Experimental Biology.

At the dinner party, Sanger told Pincus that, since 1912, she'd been dreaming of a "magic pill" that women could swallow to keep from getting pregnant. Pincus replied that such a pill might be feasible. Barely a decade had passed since scientists parsed the molecular breakdown of reproductive hormones. Maybe one of these hormones could be synthesized in pill form.

In the spring of 1951, Sanger started funneling small grants from Planned Parenthood to Pincus's lab. More important, she wrote a letter to McCormick, telling her about her conversation with Pincus.

McCormick was nearly eighty. She lived in California and didn't like to travel. But on June 8, 1953, she came east and, along with Sanger, visited Pincus at his lab. McCormick, who still remembered her biology coursework, asked him detailed questions, including how much money he would need to get started. Pincus guessed around $125,000. She wrote him a check for $40,000 on the spot and said she'd send him more soon. (By the end of the decade, McCormick's donations would total more than $1 million.)

Pincus soon learned that G. D. Searle Pharmaceuticals, for whom he'd once done some consulting, had recently synthesized a lot of progesterone—the hormone that blocked ovulation—but didn't quite know what to do with it. (Pharmaceutical companies were in a race to develop synthetic hormones for various ailments, but none of them were openly contemplating birth control.)

At his request, Searle sent some samples of the drug to Pincus, who had his chief staff researcher, a young Chinese scientist named Min-Chueh Chang, give the hormone to female rabbits, pair them with males, and see what happened. None of the rabbits got pregnant. He repeated the same experiment with rats, whose reproductive systems more closely resembled that of humans, and achieved the same results.

Now they needed to move on to human trials, which by law could be conducted only by physicians. Pincus asked John Rock to join the team. Rock was an ideal choice. He was an eminent obstetrician and gynecologist at Harvard Medical School, tall, urbane, with a white mane of hair. He had been working with synthetic hormones for the opposite goal—to make infertile women pregnant. But he was also a longtime advocate of birth control. In the forties, he lectured his students on the subject, even though it was a felony in Massachusetts to "exhibit, sell, prescribe, provide, or give out information" about any device to prevent conception. (This law wouldn't formally be taken off the books until 1972.)

More appealing still, for purposes of legitimizing the research, Rock was a devout Catholic. The papal council had declared artificial birth control to be a sin, but Rock believed that the edict was based on a misunderstanding. The Church opposed *blocking* human conception—for instance, placing a barrier, such as a diaphragm or condom, between the sperm and the egg. However, the Church did endorse the "rhythm method" of birth control, by which a married couple deferred sex until the time of the month when the wife wasn't ovulating. Rock argued that a birth-control hormone would merely stretch that period through the rest of the month; it was an extension, not a violation, of nature.

Sanger, who had been persecuted by Catholics for all of her adult life, was suspicious when Pincus told her that Rock had agreed to be the project's new chairman. But McCormick persuaded her that it was a shrewd move. "Being a good R.C."—Roman Catholic—"and as handsome as a god, he can just get away with anything," McCormick wrote her.

In the winter of 1954–1955, Rock, indifferent to the action's illegality, gave the hormone to fifty volunteers among his patients at the Free Hospital for Women. To gauge the pill's possible side effects, he gave regular doses to twelve psychotic women at the Worcester State Hospital, with the permission of their relatives. In the spring of 1956, he and Pincus traveled to Puerto Rico and recruited hundreds of volunteers in the island's housing projects, almost all of them poor and uneducated. (Ethical standards in medical research were rather loose.)

In all the tests, the pill proved nearly 100 percent effective. The only women who got pregnant hadn't taken the dosages as directed. Side effects were considered relatively minor. In November 1956, Pincus and Chang published the results in *Science*, the most widely read journal in the field.

Impressed by the results, Searle, which had supplied the synthetic hormone to begin with, invested in Pincus's project and prepared to manufacture the pill under the brand name Enovid.

In 1957, Searle applied to the FDA for approval to market Enovid as a prescription drug—not for birth control but as a treatment for "menstrual disorders." The FDA granted permission almost routinely, though only for its stated purpose.

Neither Searle nor any other drug company was willing to advocate birth control publicly. One-quarter of Americans were Catholics, and the Catholic Church was politically active, especially on this issue. Selling, distributing, or advertising contraceptive devices was also illegal in seventeen states.

However, Searle did send a wink-and-nudge letter to every licensed obstetrician, gynecologist, and medical clinic in the country, noting that the data suggested that Enovid "will inhibit ovulation . . . and that it is safe for this purpose in short-term medication." In short, word got around—Searle sent it around—as to what this drug was really about. Katharine McCormick endorsed the tactic, writing to Sanger, "Of course, this use of the oral contraceptive for menstrual disorders is leading inevitably to its use against pregnancy—and to me, this stepping stone of gradual approach . . . is a very happy and fortunate course of procedure."

Over the next two years, across the country, doctors suddenly diagnosed a half million women as having menstrual disorders and wrote them prescriptions for Enovid.

As a result, executives at Searle began to contemplate dropping all pretense and applying to the FDA for permission to market the drug explicitly as a birth-control pill. The prospect of enormous profits was too enticing to pass up. And judging from the surge in its demand, even when its real purpose was half-disguised, birth control as a concept might be less offensive to the public than church edicts and state laws suggested.

On July 23, 1959, Searle sent an application to the FDA. On October 29, at the agency's request, it supplied detailed clinical data on field trials involving 897 women who had been on the Pill for a total of 10,427 menstrual cycles. The data filled twenty volumes, the largest file ever submitted in support of a new drug.

Two months later, Dr. Rock and Dr. Winter went to Washington for a hearing. The FDA was a shockingly ramshackle agency, housed along the Washington Mall in wooden barracks that had been built as temporary offices more than forty years earlier, during World War I. Through the 1950s, as a result of breakthroughs in biological lab work, the FDA had received over four thousand applications for the approval of new drugs. Yet, the agency employed only three full-time physicians to assess the applications, supplemented by four part-time consultants who were still in their medical residencies.

Rock and Winter were kept waiting an hour and a half for their appointment. Their harried case reviewer was one of the part-time residents, a young gynecologist named Pasquale DeFelice, who wasn't yet board-certified to practice medicine. Rock was appalled that this "nondescript thirty-year-old," as he later described him, would be passing judgment on *his* work. DeFelice, well aware of Rock's reputation, was nervous. The hearing didn't last long. DeFelice asked Rock and Winter about some of their data, then noted the moral objections that would probably be raised, especially by the Catholic Church. Rock stared him down and snapped, "Young man, don't you sell *my* church short!"

As the interview was ending, DeFelice gathered his notes and said, "I'll go over it all again and you'll hear from me." Rock grabbed him by the lapels and said, "No, you'll decide right now." Rock would later tell interviewers that the official backed down and did what he was told. In fact, the FDA took an additional five months to review the data, canvassing several outside specialists for comment, before finally approving the Pill on May 11, 1960.

The Catholic Church formally condemned its use. In that respect, DeFelice, who was also Catholic, was correct to sell his Church short, as Rock put it. The papal council never bought Rock's theological argument that the Pill merely extended the duration of the Church-approved "rhythm method."

However, American women greeted the Pill as a godsend. One year after the FDA's approval, over 2 million women were taking it regularly. By the start of 1964, the figure doubled to 4 million. By 1966, it reached nearly 6 million and, by 1969, 8.5 million. By 1990, 80 percent of American women born since the end of World War II had been on the Pill at some point in their lives.

Before the Pill, a majority of married couples used some form of contraception—sponges, diaphragms, condoms. But those methods were neither reliable nor pleasant. (To get a diaphragm, a woman had to be fitted and thus awkwardly touched by a doctor, who was almost always male.) In any case, these devices robbed sex of its spontaneity and passion; they made it seem dutiful and were therefore frequently bypassed, with predictable results.

Taking the Pill, on the other hand, was easy and completely separate from having sex. In the sixties, the birth rate in America declined dramatically, and the Pill almost certainly played a major role in this trend.

But the Pill's impact was much more than demographic.

Searle's first advertisement for the Pill, appearing in medical journals, featured a drawing of the mythic princess Andromeda, chained naked to a rock on the coast of Jaffa. The ad copy began, in large, italic letters, *"unfettered."* The copy proceeded to recount how, throughout history, "woman has been a vassal" to the cyclical demands of her reproductive system. But now, with Enovid, "she is permitted normalization, enhancement or suspension of cyclic function and procreative potential. This new physiologic control is symbolized in an illustration borrowed from ancient Greek mythology—*Andromeda freed from her chains.*"

These "chains" and this "normalization" were, clearly, not only menstrual in nature.

The following year, Gloria Steinem, a twenty-eight-year-old free-lance writer—who, a decade later, would spearhead the modern feminist movement—published an article in *Esquire* titled "The Moral Disarmament of Betty Coed," in which she predicted that the Pill would sire a new breed of "autonomous girls" who, like men, would be "free to take sex, education, work, and even marriage when and how they like."

Precisely for this reason, the Pill set off a wave of panic in some quarters. *U.S. News & World Report* asked, "Is the pill regarded as a license for promiscuity? Can its availability to all women of childbearing age lead to sexual anarchy?"

Well, yes, in the sense that young women, if they wanted, could now be as promiscuous as young men had always been—that women no longer had to pay the sole and ultimate price for sexual spontaneity. This release alone would free both sexes from the psycho-skirmishes that had kept young men infantilized and young women's desires suppressed for so many years. Sexual desire pervaded the air in the decade of relative peace and prosperity following World War II. This desire was reflected, and reinforced, in movies, magazine ads, beauty products, and padded bras—all marketed predominantly to teenagers, a demographic group only recently recognized as a market niche, and all designed to scream "Sex appeal!"

During the obscenity trial over *Lady Chatterley's Lover*, Charles Rembar, the lawyer for Grove Press, argued that the whole notion of "community standards"—which a book's "prurient interest" had to violate in order to be deemed "obscene"—was preposterous in the modern media era. "A novel, no matter how much devoted to the act of sex," Rembar said, "can hardly add to the constant sexual prodding with which our environment assails us. . . . Our advertising, our motion pictures, our television and our journalism are in large measure calculated to produce sexual thoughts and reactions. We live in a sea of sexual provocation."

Yet, in this sea, before the Pill, the teenage boys were stamped as predators and the girls as prey. The anthropologist Margaret Mead described the tacit rules of this game. "The first rule of petting," she wrote in a book about men and women in 1949, "is the need for keeping complete control of just how far the physical behavior is to go; one sweeping impulse, one acted out desire for complete possession or complete surrender, and the game is lost. The boy is expected to ask for as much as possible, the girl to yield as little as possible."

With the Pill, impulses could now be—as the Searle ad put it—"unfettered." Relations between women and men could at least potentially achieve—another word in the ad—"normalization."

The upheaval was not only sexual. In the mid-fifties, a team of sociologists asked two thousand teenage girls and a thousand teenage boys about their plans for the future. The boys had very specific plans about what they wanted to do for a living. The girls tended to have only vague notions, if any, and showed little interest in jobs that required long-term commitment. The reason was clear: the girls figured that, even if they went to college, they would get married and have children soon after.

The Pill liberated them from that sure fate and opened other avenues. In the mid-sixties, the director of a national study on fertility concluded that postponing early childbearing—a choice that the Pill facilitated—exposed women to interests besides motherhood, "such as working."

As more women took jobs in the professions, the Pill eased the path to advancement. It became harder for medical schools to deny a woman admission—or for law firms to deny her promotion—on the argument that one spontaneous night of unprotected passion might get her pregnant and thus disrupt her career.

It would take another decade, into the seventies, for the feminist revolution to take hold. The image of woman as little more than housewife, secretary, waitress—as Other, and a supine, subordinate Other at that—was embedded too deeply, in myriad social relations, to fade swiftly or entirely. The fact that the cultural revolts of the sixties were negligent on this score—the Beats, the hippies, and the New Leftists treated women no better than did the squares and reactionaries—further set back the cause of equal rights for women. But the revolution would come; as one of its chief bomb-throwers, Gloria Steinem, understood early on, the Pill made that almost inevitable.

Margaret Sanger, Katharine McCormick, and Gregory Pincus all died within the space of a year during 1966–1967, at the ages of eighty-six, ninety-two, and sixty-four, respectively. (John Rock, who lived on as birth control's respectable face, died in 1984 at the age of ninety-four.) All of them lived to see their creation—the foundation of the revolution—take root in daily life. Sanger had long wished for a "magic pill" so that women could control their own contraception. The Pill freed women to control not only when to have children, and how many, but also what to do with their lives.

25

New Frontiers

By the end of 1959, all the elements were in place for the upheavals of the subsequent decades.

Above all, there was suddenly a palpable sense—brought on by jet travel, space exploration, and the shift from nuclear domination to a competitive arms race—that the world was shrinking and that America was part of that world, locked into it, no longer merely affecting events but also affected by them, with consequences that expanded the nation's horizons but also heightened its vulnerability.

At home, there were the sensations of chains unlocked, belts loosened, a weighty torpor lifted, as forbidden books were permitted, taboo topics unveiled, the actual exercise of "free speech"—of free citizens reading and thinking and hearing and saying whatever they wanted—hurtling much closer to the concept's ideal.

These breakthroughs sired a feeling that change was in the air, that a new era was about to unfold, and so accelerated a breakdown of barriers of all sorts. More adventurous art forms, a more urban and sensual pop music, a more youthful and iconoclastic approach to life—all had a cyclical effect, broadening the audience for these critical diversions and inspiring a mass culture more receptive to exotica generally.

In social relations, civil rights for black Americans may yet have seemed a distant dream in 1959; but the reality of systematic, widespread racism was finally officially recognized that year, catalogued in detail—and strategies for combating it, for achieving those rights, began to be charted and pursued.

Women's liberation was a still more fanciful notion, not even a plank on any mainstream agendas; but the technological prerequisite for liberation was rolled out that year—a pill that allowed a woman to control her reproductive cycles and thus everything else about her prospects in life.

Finally, though its full import would take a while to be appreciated, 1959 was the year when the computer revolution began, with the debuts of the practical business machine and the microchip, which in turn sparked inventions from pocket calculators and pushbutton telephones to multipurpose satellites, the Internet, cellular networks, high-definition televisions, modern weaponry—everything involving digital technology, high-speed circuits, and instantaneous communication: in short, the central artifacts of modern civilization.

Still missing was some coalescing force, some figure who could wrap the array of changes around a theme and stamp it with his signature. On New Year's Day of 1960, this lacuna was filled, when John Fitzgerald Kennedy announced that he was running for president.

It seemed an unlikely, an almost preposterous, quest. Kennedy was young—he'd be just forty-three when he took the oath of office, the youngest man ever elected president of the United States—at a time of crisis and uncertainty when age and experience were widely regarded as essential. His critics, opponents, and several seasoned news reporters all thought he was too young. But Kennedy's strategy was to tout his youth, not disguise it. Dwight Eisenhower would be leaving the White House as the *oldest* president in history, and the tenor of the times—sluggish, shapeless, and anxious—heightened the yearning for a leader who embodied the fresh new era that loomed ahead. "The torch has been passed," Kennedy would declare in his inaugural address, "to a new generation of Americans, born in this century, tempered by war, disciplined by a hard and bitter peace." (Richard Nixon, his Republican opponent, was also born in the twentieth century—he was only four years older than Kennedy— but he looked and acted so old and stiff, and as Eisenhower's vice president, he was seen, no less than Ike, as a remnant of the past.)

Kennedy was also Catholic and from Irish stock, up against a political culture dominated by native Protestants. No Catholic had ever been president; only one, Al Smith, had run for the White House, in 1928, and he lost to Herbert Hoover in a landslide. Kennedy had his patriotic bona fides: he'd been a war hero as a PT boat commander in the Pacific; he'd served three terms in the U.S. House of Representatives and was in his second term as senator. Still, his ethnicity made him an outsider—to many, by dint of his ambitions, a haughty arriviste.

Yet by the end of the decade, being an outsider had at least the lilt of an upside. His father, Joseph Kennedy—who had made millions as a commodities speculator and, during Prohibition, a bootlegger—recognized this new reality. Urging Jack to make the run—as he would push all his sons into politics, with monomaniacal determination—he argued that America was no longer "a private preserve for Protestants," that there was "a whole new generation out there," filled with "sons and daughters of immigrants," who would be "mighty proud that one of their own was running for president."

Finally, Jack Kennedy was handsome and cool. His opponents dismissed him as a "pretty boy," a "celebrity," and those tags might have derailed his chances five or six years earlier. But in an age of movie magazines and TVs in almost every household, his glamour helped him more than it hurt.

Kennedy had been thinking about running for president as far back as Thanksgiving 1956—after Adlai Stevenson, the quintessential milquetoast liberal, lost his second election against Eisenhower, the war hero—and it didn't take much effort to raise his profile. In 1957, Kennedy received over 2,500 speaking invitations, and he accepted 144 of them, spread out across forty-seven states. The following year, he maintained the same schedule, while the number of invitations doubled. In 1959, in October and November alone, as the election year approached, he made speeches in Illinois, Indiana, West Virginia, New York, Nebraska, Louisiana, Wisconsin, Oregon, California, Delaware, Kansas, and Colorado—visiting some states two or three times.

Only twelve states held competitive Democratic primaries; most candidates ignored them, appealing instead to the party bosses, who would handpick most of the convention's delegates. But Kennedy campaigned in the primaries with full force and won ten of them—enough to persuade the bosses that they'd be foolish to dismiss his popular appeal.

He secured the nomination that July at the Democratic Convention in Los Angeles and decided—in another novel move—to deliver his acceptance speech not in a hotel ballroom but outdoors, at the L.A. Coliseum, as the sun set, before a crowd of eighty thousand people and a television audience in the millions. In the speech, he mentioned the word "new" twenty-eight times, "the future" nine times. And he articulated, and seemed to embody, the spirit of change that was wafting through every corridor of American life.

"We stand today," he proclaimed that night, "on the edge of a New Frontier—the frontier of the 1960s—a frontier of unknown opportunities and perils—a frontier of unfulfilled hopes and threats."

Years later, Kennedy's speechwriter, Ted Sorensen, would say he couldn't remember where the phrase "New Frontier" came from, but that may have been because the expression was so pervasive. In January 1959, New York's Hayden Planetarium held a much-publicized show about space exploration, called "The Sky Is the New Frontier." Several *New York Times* stories about the space race cited the same metaphor. And it was applied not just to space. The *Times* printed an editorial called "The Oceans—a New Frontier." The secretary of labor said the New Frontier consisted not of "roads to the west" but of "the minds and souls of men." A report by a New York state commission called for "a bold New Frontier in housing."

The "frontier thesis" that Frederick Jackson Turner had expounded sixty years earlier—that the "American character" had developed from the frontier, with the "new opportunities" and "perennial rebirth" of each "expansion westward"—was well known and frequently cited in speeches, book reviews, and newspaper stories.

There was an enormous desire to break out of the shackles of the day, to find new ways to explore life's possibilities, whether in politics, the arts, science, or sex: the whole gamut. The closing of the frontier was an inspired metaphor for this sense of confinement—just as the invocation of a New Frontier was a stirring image of the impulse to escape.

Kennedy's twist was to identify the frontier as one of time, specifically of the decade that lay just ahead—"the frontier of the 1960s" (one of his campaign slogans was "A New Leader for the '60s").

In his speech, Kennedy said that some might believe "that all the horizons have been explored . . . that there is no longer an American frontier." (In fact, Turner himself was saying just that, and worrying about its implications, back in 1893.) "But I tell you," Kennedy continued, "the New Frontier is here, whether we seek it or not. Beyond the frontier are the uncharted areas of science and space, unsolved problems of peace and war, unconquered pockets of ignorance and prejudice, unanswered questions of poverty and surplus." Pointing to his fellow Democrats in the stadium and the viewers at home, he declared, "I am asking each of you to be pioneers on that New Frontier."

Among those listening in the L.A. Coliseum that night was Norman Mailer. One night, earlier that spring, Mailer was at the Five Spot to hear some jazz. Clay Felker, the features editor for *Esquire* magazine, walked into the club. The headwaiter knew Felker and sat him at Mailer's table, figuring the two knew each other. In fact, they didn't. Felker sat awkwardly as Mailer and his wife, Adele, had a nasty spat, which ended with her demanding the car keys and storming out. Mailer was in the midst of his revival, having recently published *Advertisements for Myself*, which had been excerpted in *Esquire*. Felker initiated some small talk and, before long, asked Mailer, out of the blue, if he'd like to cover the Democratic Convention for the magazine that summer. Mailer had never written political journalism, but he agreed.

And so was launched the next chapter of Mailer's literary career—arguably his most brilliant, certainly his most stylish and daring—which came to include his books about the antiwar march on the Pentagon, *Armies of the Night*, and the political conventions of 1968, *Miami and the Siege of Chicago*.

Watching Kennedy perform in L.A., Mailer came to see him as a political incarnation of the existential adventurer that he'd celebrated in *Advertisements for Myself*—"The Hipster As Presidential Candidate," Mailer called him in the article he filed for *Esquire*'s November issue, which would hit newsstands a few weeks before the election.

Americans, Mailer wrote in that piece, had long led "a double life." There was the surface history of politics—"concrete, factual, practical, and unbelievably dull." And there was "a subterranean river of untapped, ferocious, lonely and romantic desires" that made up "the dream life of the nation." In the vapid Eisenhower years, the "life of politics and the life of myth had diverged too far." Americans needed "a hero central to his time," a leader who could capture their "secret imagination" and reengage "the myth of the nation" with its "pioneer lust for the unexpected and incalculable." Kennedy was that hero, the "matinee idol" in an age of movie-star heroes, an age when politics would redefine itself as "America's favorite movie."

But Mailer also understood that the country was divided, and almost evenly so. Not everyone wanted this hero. As many people wanted to step back from the New Frontier—even to indulge in a countermyth of a simpler time, small towns, and provincial values, when categories were stark and choices seemed clear: a clash of myths that would define much of American politics in the decades to come, even into the next century. The question that Mailer posed, and that the country has contemplated in a few elections since, was whether the majority would choose the man of glamour and mystery who would intensify the myth of future frontiers—or the odorless company man who would bask complacently in terrain safely occupied.

Mailer titled his essay "Superman Comes to the Supermarket," and, like many of his essays, it was in certain respects an outpouring of his own fantasies. Yet, as was also typical, it captured core truths—about Kennedy and the nation—that eluded more seasoned commentators. Mailer was clearly smitten with Kennedy, as were many others. But the essay was largely *about* this mass romance, and Mailer sagely diagnosed its roots.

Kennedy and his speechwriters were onto the same core truths. The invocation of a New Frontier, and the call for Americans young in spirit to awaken and rise as its new pioneers, appealed to this "secret imagination," this hankering that Mailer sensed.

And yet, the New Frontier was vague enough to encourage a wide range of interpretation, and deliberately so. At bottom, the term implied a man and a nation of action, decision, and—Kennedy's favorite word—vigor (or, as pronounced with his Boston accent, *vig-ah*). In a speech at the National Press Club a week before his inauguration, he said that Americans "may have preferred" Eisenhower's "detached, limited concept of the presidency" in 1952 and 1956, but that they now yearned for "a vigorous proponent of the national interest." They no longer wanted a leader "in the turbulent sixties" who would sit "cringing in the White House, afraid to move."

Here, too, he tapped into a pulse. Arthur Schlesinger Jr., the author of *The Vital Center* and a multivolume biography of Franklin Roosevelt, had supported Adlai Stevenson in those elections of the fifties, and in the 1960 primaries, but now he was a Kennedy enthusiast. "S is a much richer, more thoughtful, more creative person," he wrote in his journal, referring to Stevenson, "but he has been away from power too long; he gives me an odd sense of unreality. . . . In contrast, K"—Kennedy—"gives a sense of cool, measured, intelligent concern with action and power." Stewart Alsop, the influential columnist, agreed, privately describing Kennedy as "Stevenson with balls."

Kennedy took the most literal voyage out on the New Frontier four months into his presidency, on May 25, 1961, when he declared that America would put a man on the moon by the end of the decade. To those who asked "Why the moon?" Kennedy responded that they might as well have asked earlier explorers why climb the highest mountain or fly across the Atlantic. "We choose to go to the moon in this decade, and do the other things," he said, "not because they are easy, but because they are hard, because that challenge is one that we are willing to accept, one we are unwilling to postpone, and one which we intend to win."

That last phrase—"we intend to win"—was the key, and the player to beat was Moscow. In his first few months in office, Kennedy had considered abolishing NASA. As late as March, he'd nearly decided to withhold funds for Project Apollo, the space agency's program for manned flights beyond Project Mercury. Eisenhower had never been thrilled with space; he didn't think the Soviets' launch of Sputnik was such a calamity, and he regarded the idea of landing a man on the moon as a "stunt." Kennedy tended to agree.

But then, in April, a cosmonaut named Yuri Gagarin orbited Earth in a Soviet space capsule. Vice President Lyndon Johnson, a space enthusiast from way back (as president, he'd move NASA to his home state of Texas), wrote in a memo to Kennedy, "Control of outer space would determine which system of society and government"— freedom or Communism—will "dominate the future. . . . In the eyes of the world, first in space means first, period; second in space is second in everything." Werner von Braun, the Army's legendary rocket scientist, affirmed that a manned moon landing within a decade was feasible and that the United States had a "sporting chance" of beating the Russians. The race was on; in Kennedy's mind, there was no choice but to embrace it.

And so, Kennedy's trademark New Frontier initiative was motivated entirely by Cold War politics. But this did nothing to tarnish or temper the excitement of the promise in an era when expansion and destruction were so intricately linked. The connection held a specific logic, as well. Much of NASA was driven and funded by military programs. More to the point, the New Frontier was *about* bold action, daring decisions, and coolly calculated risk.

This vision made no distinction between domestic and foreign policy. In fact, the boldest actions were bound to take place abroad, where a president has always been granted the most leeway.

During his campaign, Kennedy had told advisers that he wanted to "break out of the confines" of the Cold War, so that he could build good relations with third-world nations and divert money from the military to solve domestic problems. However, as president, he soon fell into the trappings of high office. He formed strong relationships with the Army's smarter generals—James Gavin and Maxwell Taylor—and grew fascinated with their theories of counterinsurgency and "limited war." For a brief time, he let himself be persuaded that he could break out of the Cold War by winning it, through sheer will and brain power, just as strategists like Herman Kahn thought they could master the nuclear conundrum. (It was no coincidence that many of Kennedy's second-tier officials, especially in Robert McNamara's Pentagon, had been strategic analysts at the RAND Corporation.)

And so, Kennedy reaffirmed Eisenhower's campaign to overthrow Castro and the CIA's plan to invade the island of Cuba through the Bay of Pigs. Although he learned early on that there was no missile gap, he boosted spending for nuclear weapons as well as conventional forces (though not to the degree that the Joint Chiefs of Staff desired). Most tragically, he stepped up the number of military advisers in South Vietnam.

Arthur Schlesinger, who was in France when the Bay of Pigs operation blew up, expressed disappointment in his journal. The New Frontier, he wrote, was supposed to mean "new policies for the US," not "a continuation of the Eisenhower-Dulles past."

In fact, though, there was no contradiction. In his 1959 book, *The Tragedy of American Diplomacy*, William Appleman Williams traced the long-standing links between Turner's thesis about frontiers and American statesmen's desire for new markets—"Open Door" imperialism, he called it—and Kennedy's moves, both in Cuba and in Vietnam, fit the pattern.

It took Kennedy a couple of years to come to his senses and disentangle the strands of his thinking. The Bay of Pigs taught him that the CIA didn't always know what it was doing. Discussions with the Joint Chiefs about policy toward Communist incursions in Laos—the Army suggested sending in troops, the Air Force urged bombing with B-52s, and the Navy pressed for sending in carrier-based attack planes—showed him that the competing branches of the military could be as narrow and parochial as any other bureaucracy.

Finally, the Cuban missile crisis of 1962—which Kennedy resolved through a mix of forcefulness and diplomacy with Khrushchev, while all his advisers, civilian and military, argued strenuously that he shouldn't make a deal, that he should bomb the Soviet missile sites, even while knowing that the act might spark World War III—made him realize that though he needed others for advice, he could trust only his own judgments.

After the crisis, he exchanged more notes with Khrushchev, pushed for a nuclear test-ban treaty, and seemed on the verge of pulling back from Vietnam. But his assassination on November 22, 1963, put an end to all that. He had never shared his evolved thinking, or much else, with Vice President Johnson—not even the fact that he'd made a secret deal to end the Cuban crisis—and so Johnson sallied forth along every tract of the New Frontier, its glitter and its doom.

Meanwhile, Kennedy didn't accomplish much on the domestic side of the frontier. He may have won the election because of a surge of support from black voters (at least in those areas where they were allowed to vote). The surge came late in the campaign, when Martin Luther King was thrown in jail in Atlanta, and Kennedy phoned King's wife to offer his support and best wishes. Kennedy's native Boston was hardly less segregated than many southern cities; he himself was barely more adept than Nixon at dealing with black Americans. He'd only vaguely heard of King when he called on Harry Belafonte, the popular black singer, for advice on how to attract black voters, and Belafonte urged him to get friendly with King. But at least Kennedy thought to ask Belafonte, and at least he called King's wife, which was more than Nixon did.

Another stroke of luck for Kennedy came at the end of 1959, when the U.S. Civil Rights Commission recommended that federal registrars be sent to areas where local officials were preventing black Americans from registering to vote. This was one of the commission's most high-profile proposals. Civil-rights leaders were making a big deal of it. But President Eisenhower openly rejected it, and Nixon gave no sign that he felt otherwise.

And so, black voters may have put Kennedy over the top in Illinois, Michigan, and New Jersey, more than enough to swing the election.

Yet in office, Kennedy did little to pay them back, reasoning that he lacked the votes in Congress to push civil-rights legislation and that he shouldn't spend precious political capital until after the 1964 election. Here, too, he grew more confident and progressive with time. In June 1963, when the Alabama governor George Wallace tried to block a court order to admit two black students into the state university, Kennedy shrewdly maneuvered Wallace into backing down.

To the surprise of many, after Kennedy was killed, Lyndon Johnson, the southerner, did much more on the race issue, more than any president since Lincoln, ramming through two major civil-rights packages that did everything the original, pre-watered down draft of the 1957 Civil Rights Act would have done, and much more.

But too much time had passed since the government promised justice with deliberate speed. In Norman Mailer's language, the life of politics and the life of myth—which, for black Americans, meant simply the enforcement of the Constitution—had diverged too widely. The political system, as it was composed, could not accommodate the range, or the rage, of demands.

At the same time, Johnson went full-bore on the Vietnam War, sending in a half million combat troops—Kennedy had sent only advisers—and activating the draft to do so, thus alienating a generation of young Americans from seeking a stake in the system.

The ensuing protests and revolts stemmed directly from the appetite and the impulse for free expression and critical inquiry that sprang to life at the end of the fifties.

In the absence of a legitimate authority, which might have responded to the revolts, it was only natural that this impulse would give way to chaos and anarchy. The New Left, which began as a philosophy of participatory democracy but never came up with a strategy for attracting followers, slid into nihilism—as did the Black Power movement, which had grown out of Malcolm X's principles of self-determination (without the religion).

Similarly, the withering of the prudish Comstock laws uncorked gusts of freedom in bookstores, publishing houses, and movie theaters—but it also let in rank pornography, which triggered a backlash in the subsequent "culture wars." Sexual liberty infused millions of lives with relief and excitement—but it also wrecked untold numbers of families.

On an individual level, too, high-wire prancing had its dangers. It wasn't just "Moloch"—Allen Ginsberg's biblical metaphor for society's evils—that destroyed the best minds of his generation. Jack Kerouac drowned himself to death in alcohol. Dozens of jazz musicians damaged or killed themselves with drug addiction. Norman Mailer, self-absorbed in his "White Negro" romanticizing of psychopathic violence, drunkenly stabbed his wife with a penknife at a party one night in late November 1960. He would tell the judge, "My pride is that I can explore areas of experience that other men are afraid of." The judge replied, "Your recent history indicates that you cannot distinguish fiction from reality." (Mailer spent seventeen days at Bellevue; his wife dropped charges; they divorced soon after.)

On a purely artistic level, too many creative minds came to confuse freedom for license. They forgot, if they ever knew, that much of the spontaneous art of the late fifties was more structured than it seemed. Ginsberg may have said, quoting the Zen masters, that "first thought is best thought," but he refined and redrafted those first thoughts to make his poems read better. Ornette Coleman abandoned harmony as the organizing principle of jazz, but he didn't abandon organizing principles; "free jazz" didn't mean simply blowing whatever came into his head or out of his fingers, as some of his aspiring disciples seemed to think. Allan Kaprow's Happenings slammed into the dead-end of self-indulgence when he threw out his instructions and let the participants do their own random thing.

And yet, despite the excess and destruction, for all the added risk and strain and restlessness, the breakaways and breakthroughs of 1959 eased, enriched, and emboldened the conditions and prospects of American life.

Either by themselves or through the dynamics set in motion, they broke down the barriers of space and time, opened the world and the galaxies to more intimate acquaintance, and stretched, loosened, sometimes shattered the hierarchies that once loomed so stiff and inviolable—the boundaries between art and life, which defined what art (or literature or jazz or any other creative genre) could and could not be; between men and women, which dictated who would be on top and bottom, in every sense of that equation; between black and white, which expanded or gravely limited a human being's achievable goals; between old and young, insider and outsider, which prescribed who would hold the reins of power and stand guard at the political and cultural gates.

Yet at the same time, more vital boundaries—between life and death, peace and holocaust, survival and extinction—were also fissuring and seemed perilously thin, in hot crises nearly vaporous, as a result of the hydrogen bomb, long-range missiles, the arms race, and the more diffuse, uncontrollable crises that gripped the world after the Cold War ended and the power centers shriveled.

This dual tension between "unknown opportunities and peril," as Kennedy put it, did much to spark the creative energy of the era. It marked the onset of a new era in modern history, when—for better and for worse—nothing seemed out of the question, no option definitively foreclosed. Life's hairpin curves could be avoided through various means—drugs, therapy, denial, or dropping out. But those who immersed themselves in the voyage experienced the thrill and vertigo that came from streaking across the edge of a tomorrow that might bring miracles or catastrophe in an instant—a tomorrow that still haunts us today.

Acknowledgments

I turned five years old in 1959 and so have no memory of the events chronicled here—except for the space program, which even then thrilled me and everyone around me. I don't recall the Lunik launch, but I do remember the seven American astronauts; I memorized their names, along with those of my favorite baseball players and the order of the nine planets. I also remember getting a picture book that year (I've since purchased a copy on eBay, to confirm my image of it) called *You Will Go to the Moon*, about a boy and his father who routinely take a flight to the Space Station and, from there, to the moon. This was the future that many people were sure was coming, if nuclear war didn't blow everything up first—and I well remember the "duck and cover" school fallout drills, too. This duality—a view of the future at once utopian and nihilistic—always fascinated me and probably influenced my decision, much later, to study and write about nuclear strategy and arms control. And it's what this book has turned out to be about, as well.

But that's not what compelled me to write this book. I've been writing about culture and the arts, especially music and movies, for much of my life—for longer than I've been writing about politics and war—and several years ago, it occurred to me that some of the most important—or at least some of my favorite—books, movies, and record albums were made in 1959. Was this just coincidence, or was there something significant about that year? The more I looked into it, the more it struck me that this truly was a pivotal year—not only in culture, but also in politics, society, race, science, sex: everything. In that sense, this is a revisionist history of previously unnoticed linkages and, in some cases, forgotten events.

I have many people to thank for helping me on this project. For sharing memories, I thank David Amram, Paul Bley, Dave Brubeck, Ornette Coleman, Frank Drake, Daniel Ellsberg, Charlie Haden, Cyrus Harvey, Nat Hentoff, Sy Johnson, Dick Katz, Dan Morgenstern, Sonny Rollins, Barney Rosset, and Gunther Schuller.

I also benefited greatly from conversations or exchanges with Richard Brody, William Burr, Ray Carney, R. C. Davis, Morris Dickstein, Donald Fagen, Gary Giddins, Larissa Goldston, Richard Gott, Sarah Greenough, Suzanne White Junod, John Koenig, J. Michael Lennon, Manning Marable, Astrid Myers, Lance Rembar, Lawrence Schiller, George Schuller, John Snyder, Clive Thompson, Kosta Tsipis, and Penny Von Eschen.

I am grateful to Sharon Ghamori-Tabrizi for sharing files from her book about Herman Kahn; Sarah Greenough of the National Gallery of Art for giving me advance copies of her essays in the NGA's then-forthcoming book on Robert Frank's photography; Manning Marable of Columbia University for letting me read part of his still-forthcoming biography of Malcolm X; Astrid Myers for providing historical materials from Grove Press and *Evergreen Review*; Alice Russell for supplying a hard-to-find copy of the 1959 edition of her husband George Russell's book about his theory of jazz improvisation; George Schuller for letting me watch his as-yet-unreleased documentary about the Music Inn; and Wolfgang Frank of Concord Records/Fantasy Jazz for giving me permission to quote from the albums *"I Am Not a Nut, Elect Me!"* and *The Sick Humor of Lenny Bruce*.

At the Atlantic Records archives, Grayson Dantzic supplied me with some of the papers of Nesuhi Ertegun. At the Guggenheim Museum archives, Rachel Chatalbash led me to the papers from the Frank Lloyd Wright collection and correspondence. At the Harry Ransom Research Center at the University of Texas, Richard Workman, Steve Mielke, Molly Schwartzburg, and Jen Tisdale guided me through the papers of Norman Mailer, Allen Ginsberg, and Gregory Corso. At the Museum of Modern Art archives, MacKenzie Bennett did the same with the Dorothy C. Miller Papers and some Oral History transcripts. Dan Morgenstern led me through the valuable files of the Institute of Jazz Studies at Rutgers University–Newark. I thank all of these invaluable archivists and their staffs.

Dawn Stanford excavated useful documents from IBM's Corporate Archives, as did Jack Cox with the archives of Pfizer (which now owns G. D. Searle). Anne Peterson of the DeGolyer Library at Southern Methodist University fulfilled several requests for items from Jack St. Clair Kilby's then-uncatalogued papers. Brendan Rittenhouse Green assisted in researching the Philip Morrison papers at MIT's Institute Library.

I am grateful to Eric Nelson, my editor at Wiley, for his enthusiasm, encouragement, and trenchant ideas for how to make this book more sensible. I thank the entire team at Wiley, especially John Simko and Ellen Wright.

For the second time in two years—and the third time in twenty-five—I thank my agent, Rafe Sagalyn, for his advice, support, and friendship.

I thank all my friends for acting interested when I told them what I was up to. I also thank Mark Harelik and Spencer Kayden for their hospitality.

To Brooke Gladstone, my wife, best friend, insistent conscience, and ideal reader, I owe everything.

The love and integrity of our daughters, Maxine and Sophie, once again inspired me to no end (and no tuition bills were needed to spur me this time).

Finally, I thank my mother, Ruth Kaplan Pollock, who, back in 1959, stocked our house with books and taught me how to read them.

Notes

Epigraphs

"I mean, man, whither goest thou?" Jack Kerouac, *On the Road* (New York: Viking, 1957), 110 (page number refers to the 1999 Penguin edition).

I tell you, the New Frontier John F. Kennedy, acceptance speech, Democratic National Convention, July 15, 1960.

What we in hindsight call change Morris Dickstein, *Gates of Eden: American Culture in the Sixties* (Cambridge: Harvard Univ. Press, 1977), 54 (page number refers to the 1997 paperback edition).

1. Breaking the Chains

1   *Lunik I space capsule* Max Frankel, "Rocket a Lunik to the Russians," *New York Times*, Jan. 4, 1959; John W. Finney, "Challenge of Lunik Spurs U.S. Effort," *New York Times*, Jan. 11, 1959; "Lunik," *Time*, Jan. 12, 1959; William Shelton, *Soviet Space Exploration: The First Decade* (New York: Washington Square Press, 1968), 74.

1   *"a turning point"* "Push into Space," *Time*, Jan. 19, 1959.

2   *"the jet age"* "The Age of the Jet," *New York Times*, Sept. 6, 1958.

2   *"I christen thee"* "US Jet Airliner on First Trip," *New York Times*, Oct. 17, 1958.

2   *"the possibility of hurdling"* Paul J. C. Friedlander, "Jet-Age Prospect," *New York Times*, Oct. 26, 1958.

2   *"the space age"* "Rendezvous with Destiny," *Time*, Apr. 20, 1959.

2   *"new geography"* See, for instance, "Push into Space"; William L. Laurence, "Science in Review: Principle of Lunik Orbit Was Discovered by Newton in the 17th Century," *New York Times*, Jan. 11, 1959; "To the Planets and Beyond," *New York Times Magazine*, Jan. 11, 1959.

2   *"blast-off," "countdown"*   Sean Topham, *Where's My Space Age? The Rise and Fall of Futuristic Design* (New York: Prestel, 2003), 25.

2   *Madison Avenue picked up*   For instance, in *Time's* issue of Jan. 19, 1959, Lockheed has an ad blaring "The Jet Age"; one for North America Aviation, showing a postal delivery, reads, "Someday this letter home may come from Mars." In July 2, a Chrysler ad likens a ride in its new car to "Space Travel . . . Start your countdown—at Chrysler's unique control center!" A Ford Motors ad in the July 13 issue boasts "Product for the Space Age." Similar ad campaigns can be found in *Time, Life*, and other major magazines throughout the year.

2   *"American character"—its "restless"*   Frederick Jackson Turner, *The Frontier in American History* (New York: Henry Holt, 1920); Turner first presented his "Frontier Thesis" in a paper at a conference in Chicago in 1893.

6   *Today the collapse of power centers*   See Fred Kaplan, *Daydream Believers: How a Few Grand Ideas Wrecked American Power* (Hoboken, NJ: John Wiley & Sons, 2008).

6   *spark revolutions in artificial intelligence*   See, for instance, Ray Kurzweil, *The Singularity Is Near: When Humans Transcend Biology* (New York: Penguin, 2006).

7   *"No one in America"*   Allen Ginsberg, "Poetry, Violence, and the Trembling Lambs," *Village Voice*, Aug. 26, 1959.

2. A Visitor from the East

8   *"a fortnight's holiday"*   Mikoyan made this comment during a stop-over in Denmark. "Ten Hours in Copenhagen," *New York Times*, Jan. 4, 1959.

8   *"sterile"*   Eisenhower said this during his White House meeting with Mikoyan and various U.S. officials, including Dulles. Memorandum of Conversation, "Mikoyan's Call on the President," Jan. 17, 1959. Dwight D. Eisenhower Library, Ann Whitman File, International File, Box 53.

8   *So, on December 17, 1958*   "Mikoyan Coming to US," *New York Times*, Dec. 19, 1958.

8   *a dozen elite organizations*   See, for instance, the Western Union telegram from John J. McCloy, chairman of the Council on Foreign Relations, addressed to "Anastasy Mikoyan, Deputy Premier, The Kremlin, USSR,"

Dec. 24, 1958, in *Records of Meetings*, vol. 21, July 1958–June 1959 (M–Z), Archive of the Council on Foreign Relations, New York.

8 *"aroused more excitement"* "Mission to Moon—and a Visitor from Moscow," *New York Times*, Jan. 14, 1959.

9 *"But," he said, "I will certainly try"* "Dulles to Try to See Him," *New York Times*, Jan. 4, 1959.

9 *Mikoyan hit the road* For instance the following stories from the *New York Times*: "Streetlight Falls Near Him," Jan. 5; "Mikoyan, in US, Inspects Restaurants, Motel, Capitol," Jan. 5; "Moscow Leader Kisses Jerry Lewis in Byplay During Visit to Film Studio," Jan. 13.

9 *Mikoyan delivered speeches* Harrison Salisbury, "Mikoyan's Success," *New York Times*, Jan. 11, 1959.

9 *"We are all tired"* Harrison Salisbury, "Mikoyan Appeals for a 'Hot Peace,'" *New York Times*, Jan. 9, 1959.

9 *"a nyet, nyet, nyet"* Harrison Salisbury, "Mikoyan Asks 'Da' Not 'Nyet' Relations," *New York Times*, Jan. 14, 1959.

9 *"a presidential campaign"* Salisbury, "Mikoyan's Success."

10 *"Old Bolshevik"* "An Old Bolshevik Trader; Anastas Ivanovich Mikoyan," *New York Times*, Jan. 5, 1959.

10 *He had traveled to the United States once before* "Mikoyan Evoked Jeers on '36 Trip," *New York Times*, Jan. 5, 1959; "The Survivor," *Time*, Sept. 16, 1957.

10 *During World War II* "The Survivor."

11 *"my Armenian"* "Mission to Moon—and a Visitor from Moscow."

11 *Berlin was the Cold War's hot spot* See Fred Kaplan, *The Wizards of Armageddon* (New York: Simon & Schuster, 1983), chap. 20.

12 *To Sergei Korolev* Brian Harvey, *Russia in Space: The Failed Frontier?* (Chirchester, UK: Praxis Publishing, 2001), 4.

12 *During the previous fall and winter* "Now 'Lunik': Stepped-Up Cold War," *New York Times*, Jan. 4, 1959. On Oct. 11, 1958, Pioneer 1 fell back to Earth after reaching an altitude of 71,000 miles. On Nov. 8, Pioneer 2 crashed after ascending to 7,500 miles. On Dec. 6, Pioneer 3 went down after reaching 68,000 miles. The moon is 240,000 miles away from Earth.

12 *"unquestionably the greatest"* Ibid. The *Times* story speculated that Lunik was timed to give Mikoyan "the maximum possible political and propaganda advantage" and "a major psychological advantage in any bargaining he might plan to engage in with American officials." See also

"Lunik Adds New Note to Disarmament Talks," *New York Times*, Jan. 11, 1959.

12   *What no American knew*   See Aleksandr Fursenko and Timothy Naftali, *Khrushchev's Cold War: The Inside Story of an American Adversary* (New York: Norton, 2006), chap. 8.

13   *"He brought nothing"*   Salisbury, "Mikoyan's Success."

14   *"deficit of vigor"*   "Johnson Ascribes a 'Deficit of Vigor' to Administration," *New York Times*, Jan. 8, 1959.

3. The Philosopher of Hip

15   *He'd been in a funk*   Letter, Mailer to Mickey Knox, Mar. 20, 1958, Norman Mailer Papers, Box 534, Folder 9, Harry Ransom Research Center, University of Texas, Austin.

15   *Maybe the rush would reenergize him*   Letter, Mailer to Mickey Knox, Jan. 8, 1959, Norman Mailer Papers, Box 535, Folder 26.

15   *"astonishing book"*   Quoted in Mary V. Dearborn, *Mailer* (Boston: Houghton Mifflin, 1999), 62–63.

15   *Since his freshman year*   "For Anyone Who Knows Anything About Writing" [ca. 1950s], Norman Mailer Papers, Box 36, Folder 5.

16   *He had started to write another novel*   Letter, Mailer to Mickey Knox, Mar. 20, 1958.

16   *So he put the novel aside*   He refers to the compilation project in two letters to George (last name unstated), dated June 18 and Oct. 29, 1958, Norman Mailer Papers, Box 534, Folder 2.

16   *advanced him a mere $3,500*   The contract with Putnam is in Norman Mailer Papers, Box 753, Folder 4.

16   *"an underground revolution"*   Norman Mailer, *Advertisements for Myself* (New York: G. P. Putnam, 1959), 278. (All page numbers refer to the 1992 Harvard Univ. Press paperback edition.)

16   *had to be "perfect"*   Dearborn, *Mailer*, 71.

16   *Mailer, in fact, had joined the Army*   He admits this in Mailer, *Advertisements for Myself*, 28; see also Dearborn, *Mailer*, 39.

16   *He and his first wife, Bea, were in Paris*   Dearborn, *Mailer*, ch. 4.

17   *"this evil-smelling novel"*   Mailer quotes from the pans in *Advertisements for Myself*, 105.

17   *His publisher rejected the draft*   Ibid., 231ff.

17   *The second was the purring fuel*   Ibid., 232.

17 *"I was out of fashion"*   Ibid., 234.

17 *After he came back home from Mexico*   Dan Wakefield, *New York in the '50s* (Boston: Houghton Mifflin, 1992), 111–112; Peter Manso, *Mailer: His Life and Times* (New York: Simon & Schuster, 1985), 286; Dearborn, *Mailer*, 108.

17 *All these new sensations*   The journal can be found in Norman Mailer Papers, Box 1014, Folder 1.

18 *"the start of more ideas"*   Mailer, *Advertisements for Myself*, 234.

18 *"What terrifies me"*   Norman Mailer Papers, Box 1014, Folder 1, page 37.

18 *He invested $5,000*   Mailer, *Advertisements for Myself*, 277; Manso, *Mailer*, 222.

19 *As an up-yours gesture*   Mailer quotes from the pans in *Advertisements for Myself*, 245–247.

19 *He was in the mood for war*   Ibid., 277.

19 *"A Column for Slow Readers"*   Ibid., 279.

19 *"This guy Mailer"*   Ibid., 288.

19 *"slightly punch-drunk"*   Ibid., 331.

19 *Most parties thrown by the* Voice   Wakefield, *New York*, 142; Nat Hentoff, interview with author, Aug. 18, 2008.

19 *his good friend, Robert Lindner, died*   Mailer, *Advertisements for Myself*, 303–305.

19 *He was the one who'd urged Mailer to keep*   Mailer refers to Lindner often in the journal; a second copy in the Norman Mailer Papers (Box 1014, Folder 2) is the one that Mailer had sent to him in the mail. Mailer also wrote a letter to Lindner, on Aug. 25, 1955, about his experimentations with LSD (Box 530, Folder 19).

20 *"Hip," he wrote, "is an American existentialism"*   Mailer, *Advertisements for Myself*, 314–315.

20 *"years of intense pessimism"*   Ibid., 325.

20 *Mailer quit the* Voice   Ibid., 318.

20 *"the first lick of fire"*   Ibid., 283–284.

20 *In April 1957*   Mailer's cover letter to Howe, dated Apr. 29, 1957, says he spent all April writing the piece. Norman Mailer Papers, Box 533, Folder 4.

20 *"Wild thought"*   Norman Mailer Papers, Box 1014, Folder 1.

20 *"Probably," the article began, "we will never be able"*   Mailer, "The White Negro," *Dissent* (Summer 1957); reprinted in Mailer, *Advertisements for Myself*, 337–358; see his commentary on the essay, 331–336, 359–375.

21 *Mailer rented a saxophone*   Hillary Mills, *Mailer: A Biography* (New York: Empire Books, 1982), 190.

21 *"really liked Norman"*   James Baldwin, "The Black Boy Looks at the White Boy," *Esquire*, May 1961.

21 *In a notebook that he kept*   Sterling Notebook, Norman Mailer Papers, Box 36, Folder 1.

22 *"I have a fair chance"*   Mailer, *Advertisements for Myself*, 107.

22 *"had any chance"*   Manso, *Mailer*, 254.

22 *"The White Negro" and the other essays*   Mailer, *Advertisements for Myself*, 336, where he writes that in that essay "can be found the real end of this muted autobiography of the near-beat adventurer who was myself."

22 *He wondered whether to write prefaces at all*   Letter, Mailer to "George," Oct. 29, 1958, Norman Mailer Papers, Box 534, Folder 2.

22 *One evening, soon after moving back to the city*   Dearborn, *Mailer*, 138.

22 *"pretentious" and "sentimental"*   Mailer, *Advertisements for Myself*, 466.

22 *"with a sinking heart"*   Wakefield, *New York*, 166–167.

22 *For their part, Ginsberg and Kerouac had some problems*   Marc D. Schleifer, "Allen Ginsberg: Here to Save Us, But Not Sure from What," reprinted in *The Village Voice Reader* (New York: Grove Press, 1963), 36; Manso, *Mailer*, 258–260.

23 *"Unconsciously," Mailer said many years later, "I was trying"*   Manso, *Mailer*, 274.

24 *Mailer wrote Trilling a letter*   Letter, Mailer to Diana Trilling, "Aug. 10 (I think) 1960," Norman Mailer Papers, Box 540, Folder 11.

24 *"When writers who do not feel"*   Reprinted in Philip Roth, *Reading Myself and Others* (New York: Farrar, Straus & Giroux, 1975), 178.

4. Generations Howling

26 *On the night of February 5*   Diana Trilling, "The Other Night at Columbia: A Report from the Academy," *Partisan Review* (Spring 1959); Morris Dickstein, *Gates of Eden: American Culture in the Sixties* (Cambridge: Harvard Univ. Press, 1977), 3–5; Robert Genter, "'I'm Not His Father': Lionel Trilling, Allen Ginsberg, and the Contours of Literary Modernism," *College Literature* (Spring 2004).

26 *On October 7*   John Tytell, *Naked Angels: Kerouac, Ginsberg, Burroughs* (New York: Grove Press, 1976), 103–105; Gregory Corso and Allen Ginsberg, "Lit. Revolution in America" [n.d.], Gregory Corso

Papers, Box 5, Folder 6, Harry Ransom Research Center, University of Texas, Austin.

26 *"I saw the best minds"* Allen Ginsberg, *Howl and Other Poems* (San Francisco: City Lights Books, 1956).

26 *"a strange ecstatic intensity"* Corso and Ginsberg, "Lit. Revolution in America."

27 *"a spontaneous bop prosody"* Ginsberg, *Howl*, dedication page.

27 *"You know, this is a really* beat *generation"* John Clellan Holmes, "This Is the Beat Generation," *New York Times Magazine*, Nov. 16, 1952; the Holmes-Kerouac conversation is reported in Dan Wakefield, *New York in the '50s* (Boston: Houghton Mifflin, 1992), 163. Kerouac would later claim that "Beat" was short for "beatific," but that was a post hoc formulation, inspired by his mid-fifties turn to Buddhism.

27 *"authentic work of art"* Gilbert Millstein, "Books of the Times; The 'Beat' Bear Stigmata Those Who Burn, Burn, Burn," *New York Times*, Sept. 5, 1957.

27 *The review was a fluke* This story is revealed in Wakefield, *New York*, 162–164; he got the tale from Millstein directly.

28 *"You wouldn't want"* Bill Morgan and Nancy J. Peters, eds., *Howl on Trial: The Battle for Free Expression* (San Francisco: City Lights Books, 2006), 2–3. This book contains a comprehensive account of the arrests, trial, and aftermath.

28 *"far out" as Sputnik* Herb Caen, *San Francisco Chronicle*, Apr. 2, 1958.

29 *"This town is Squaresville"* "Squaresville U.S.A. vs. Beatsville," *Life*, Sept. 21, 1959.

29 *"a foul word"* Quoted in James Campbell, *This Is the Beat Generation: New York, San Francisco, Paris* (Berkeley: Univ. of California Press, 1999).

29 *"The general public image"* Letter, Ginsberg to Kerouac, Oct. 6, 1959, Allen Ginsberg Papers, Box 1, Folder 6, Harry Ransom Research Center, University of Texas, Austin.

29 *Kerouac and Ginsberg met* Tytell, *Naked Angels*, sec. 2; James Grauerholz and Ira Silverberg, eds., *Word Virus: The William S. Burroughs Reader* (New York: Grove Press, 1998), introduction, 3–12.

30 *"I'm apparently some kind of agent"* Grauerholz and Silverberg, *Word Virus*, xiv–xvi.

30 *Carr stabbed him repeatedly* Tytell, *Naked Angesls*, 58ff.

31 *Caleb Carr is his son* For a revealing reminiscence of his father, see "The *Salon* Interview: Caleb Carr," *Salon*, Oct. 6, 1997.

31 *As a prankish protest* Tytell, *Naked Angels*, 83.

31 *He was rescued the following summer* Ibid., 53.

31 *One day in the spring of 1948* Ibid., 18–19.

32 *Ginsberg was saved* Ibid., 92ff.; Diana Trilling, "The Other Night."

32 *Williams took a liking to Ginsberg* Tytell, *Naked Angels*, 96ff.

32 *Williams came out of the Black Mountain school of poets* Martin Duberman, *Black Mountain College: An Exploration in Community* (New York: E. P. Dutton, 1972).

32 *You had to* listen Ginsberg makes this point in a cantankerous interview on Jan. 8, 1960, Allen Ginsberg Papers, Box 1, Folder 1.

33 *Gillespie improvised a melody* Donald L. Maggin, *Dizzy: The Life and Times of John Birks Gillespie* (New York: HarperCollins, 2005), 125, 138–139.

33 *"the vigorous space dash"* Jack Kerouac, "The Essentials of Spontaneous Prose," *Evergreen Review* (Summer 1958). He wrote it a few years earlier, just for Ginsberg and Burroughs to read (interview with Kerouac in *Beat Writers at Work: The Paris Review*, ed. George Plimpton [New York: Modern Library, 1999], 116).

33 *"I have been looking"* Allen Ginsberg, letter to Eugene Brooks, Aug. 16, 1955, quoted in Morgan and Peters, *Howl on Trial*, 33.

33 *He later told a critic* This is from a long, angry, justly famous letter that Ginsberg wrote to John Hollander, Sept. 7, 1958, after he and other critics denounced *Howl* as ignorant of form. Excerpted in Morgan and Peters, *Howl on Trial*, 86–92. It is widely regarded as Ginsberg's most eloquent and detailed explanation of his technique. At one point in the letter, he identifies his inspiration as an "old trumpet solo on a JATP 'Can't Get Started' side." "JATP" refers to Jazz at the Philharmonic, a series of live jazz recordings produced by Norman Granz. "I Can't Get Started" was played on a 1946 session that featured Gillespie, Charlie Parker, and Lester Young. It should be noted, though, that in a 1966 interview with the *Paris Review*, Ginsberg says, though uncertainly, the JATP solo might have been by Illinois Jacquet, who played tenor saxophone (Plimpton, ed., *Beat Writers at Work*, 35). The (much) earlier recollection is likely to be the accurate one.

34 *"not expressionistic enough"* Ginsberg, letter to Hollander, ibid.

34 *"I think what is coming"* Quoted in Genter, "'I'm Not His Father.'"

34 *He wrote back, saying that he didn't* Letter, Lionel Trilling to Allen Ginsberg, May 29, 1956, reprinted in Ginsberg, *Howl: Original Draft*

Facsimile, Transcript, and Variant Versions, Fully Annotated by Author, with Contemporaneous Correspondence, Account of First Public Reading . . . (New York: Harper Perennial, 2006), 156.

34   *"a principle of control"*   Lionel Trilling, "William Dean Howells and the Roots of Modern Taste," in Lionel Trilling, *The Moral Obligation to Be Intelligent: Selected Essays*, ed. Leon Wieseltier (New York: Farrar, Straus and Giroux, 2000), 96.

34   *"rejection of the ordinary social values"*   Genter, " 'I'm Not His Father.' "

35   *"have become excited"*   Trilling, "William Dean Howells."

35   *"He's got no orgones"*   William S. Burroughs, *The Letters of William S. Burroughs, 1945–1959*, ed. Oliver Harris (New York: Penguin Books, 1993), 293.

35   *"a crazy letter"*   "From the Notebooks of Lionel Trilling," *Partisan Review—50th Anniversary* (1984), 498.

35   *"a twinge of pain"*   Ibid., 509–510.

35   *"I have only a gift"*   Ibid., 511.

36   *"I predicted that"*   Ibid., 513.

36   *"how deeply he scorned"*   Diana Trilling, *The Beginning of the Journey: The Marriage of Diana and Lionel Trilling* (New York: Harcourt Brace, 1993), 372–373; all of chapter 13 reads, poignantly, along these lines.

36   *When Ginsberg returned to Columbia*   The account of the reading is based mainly on Diana Trilling, "The Other Night at Columbia"; all of the direct quotations are from this essay as well.

37   *"I'm crazy like a daisy"*   "Fried Shoes," *Time*, Feb. 9, 1959. In her essay, Trilling writes of thinking, as the reading began, "Here we go; he'll tell us how he's crazy like a daisy and how his friend Orlovsky is crazy like a butterfly.' I had been reading *Time*; who hadn't?"

5. The Cosmonaut of Inner Space

39   *On March 17, 1959*   Gerald E. Brennan, "Naked Censorship: The True Story of the University of Chicago and William S. Burroughs' *Naked Lunch*," *Chicago Reader*, Sept. 29 and Oct. 6, 1995.

39   *One afternoon in 1951*   James Grauerholz and Ira Silverberg, eds., *Word Virus: The William S. Burroughs Reader* (New York: Grove Press, 1998), 41–42; John Tytell, *Naked Angels: Kerouac, Ginsberg, Burroughs* (New York: Grove Press, 1976), 41–46.

39   Queer *and* Junky   Grauerholz and Silverberg, *Word Virus*, 43–46.

40   *"There is only one thing"*   Ibid., 169.

40   *"This novel is about"*   Ibid., 130, 134, 135.

40   *"a cosmonaut of inner space"*   Ibid., 272.

40   *Paul Bowles, the American writer*   Paul Bowles, "Burroughs in Tangier," *Big Table* (Summer 1959).

41   *"William Seward Burroughs"*   Allen Ginsberg, *Howl and Other Poems* (San Francisco: City Lights Books, 1956), dedication page.

41   *"unpublishable mad routines"*   Letter, Allen Ginsberg to Robert LaVigne, June 8, 1957, Allen Ginsberg Papers, Box 1, Folder 7, Harry Ransom Research Center, University of Texas, Austin.

41   *"horrible nightmares"*   Interview with Jack Kerouac, in *Beat Writers at Work: The Paris Review*, ed. George Plimpton (New York: Modern Library, 1999), 108.

41   *Ginsberg got a letter from Irving Rosenthal*   The story of the *Chicago Review* and *Naked Lunch* is told in Brennan, "Naked Censorship," and Eirik Steinhoff, "The Making of *Chicago Review*: The Meteoric Years," *Chicago Review* 52, nos. 2/3/4 (2006).

41   *"the only one unpublished"*   Reprinted in Steinhoff, "The Making of *Chicago Review*," 301.

42   *"She seized a safety pin"*   Ibid., 305.

42   *"Filthy Writing on the Midway"*   Quoted in ibid., 306.

42   *"a very serious effect upon fundraising"*   Ibid., 307.

43   *"Get a bigger table"*   Brennan, "Naked Censorship."

43   *They were greeted with huge crowds*   "Fried Shoes," *Time*, Feb. 9, 1959.

43   *Even Ferlinghetti had rejected it*   Brennan, "Naked Censorship."

43   *"book burners"*   John Ciardi, "The Book Burners and Sweet Sixteen," *Saturday Review*, June 27, 1959.

43   *$800 advance*   William S. Burroughs, *The Letters of William S. Burroughs, 1945–1959*, ed. Oliver Harris (New York: Penguin Books, 1993), 418.

43   *an English-language series*   Charles Rembar, *The End of Obscenity: The Trials of Lady Chatterley, Tropic of Cancer, and Fanny Hill* (New York: Harper & Row, 1986), 170.

44   *Rosset bought the American rights*   Editors' Note in William Burroughs, *Naked Lunch: The Restored Text*, ed. James Grauerholz and Barry Miles (New York: Grove Press, 2001), 241.

6. The End of Obscenity

45 *In March 1959, shortly before* Charles Rembar, the lawyer, later wrote an account of this and other similar trials in his book *The End of Obscenity: The Trials of Lady Chatterley, Tropic of Cancer, and Fanny Hill* (New York: Random House, 1968); see especially chaps. 1–7 (quoted page numbers come from the 1986 paperback edition by Harper & Row); and interview with Barney Rosset, June 24, 2008.

45 *Lawrence had written three versions* Mark Schorer, "On *Lady Chatterley's Lover*," *Evergreen Review* (Spring 1957). This was the first issue of the magazine, which was published and edited by Rosset; Schorer's article was meant to be the introduction to the Grove Press book; when that was delayed, Rosset published it in the magazine.

45 *Rosset was thirty-seven* Biographical material comes mainly from interview with Rosset; and from *Obscene*, a documentary film directed by Daniel O'Connor and Neil Ortenberg (Arthouse Films, 2008).

47 *Rosset hired a lawyer named Ephraim London* Interview with Rosset; "'Miracle' Decision Hailed As Victory," *New York Times*, June 26, 1952.

47 *Rosset's plan for* Lady Chatterley *was to provoke* Raymond T. Caffrey, "*Lady Chatterley's Lover*: The Grove Press Publication of the Unexpurgated Text," *Syracuse University Library Associates Courier* (Spring 1985); and interview with Rosset. (Thanks to Astrid Myer, Rosset's wife and the editor of *Evergreen Review*'s online edition, for supplying the Caffrey piece.)

48 *So, on March 18* "Lawrence Novel to Be Reissued," *New York Times*, Mar. 19, 1959. The timing of the *Big Table* seizure was coincidental, though Rosset supported the magazine's editors, giving them jobs at Grove Press while they awaited their own court ruling. (Interview with Rosset.)

48 *Rosset knew Rembar from the Hamptons* Interviews with Rosset and with Lance Rembar, Charles Rembar's son, June 25, 2008. (Charles died in 2000.)

48 *Growing up, Mailer worshiped Rembar* Mailer admits this in an introduction that he wrote for a short-lived paperback edition of Rembar's book, published by Simon & Schuster in 1968. The introduction did not appear in any other edition because Rembar considered it overblown. (Interview with Lance Rembar, who supplied me with a copy of the introduction.)

49   *Rembar advised him to spell it "fug"*   Rembar, *The End of Obscenity*, 15n, 17n.

49   *"to deprave and corrupt"*   Ibid., 16ff.

50   *"a valve for pressurized cultural"*   Quoted in the press materials for the film *Obscene*.

50   *"absolute protection for every"*   Quoted in Rembar, *The End of Obscenity*, 48. The *Roth* decision and Rembar's novel interpretation of it are elaborated on pages 45–58, 119, 126, and 129–134.

51   *"The protection given speech"*   Quoted in ibid., 49.

51   *On a sheet of paper, Rembar drew*   Ibid., 126.

52   *"Whether you agree with Lawrence"*   Ibid., 131–132.

52   "unless," *Gillespie emphasized*   Ibid., 129–131.

53   *"theme is the presentation of adultery"*   See U.S. Supreme Court, *Kingsley Pictures Corp. v. Regents*, 360 U.S. 684 (1959); the decision's significance for Rosset's case is discussed in Rembar, *The End of Obscenity*, 145–146.

53   *Three weeks later*   The Post Office appealed Judge Bryant's verdict; a three-judge appellate panel upheld his ruling, without dissent or caveat, in January 1960.

54   *The week after the* Kingsley *ruling*   "Adultery Is an Idea," *Time*, July 13, 1959.

54   *By the fall, the Grove Press edition had sold*   Caffrey, *"Lady Chatterley's Lover."*

54   *"The average man"*   Rembar, *The End of Obscenity*, 120.

54   *Other novels on that summer's top-ten list*   *Time*, July 6, 1959.

7. Sickniks

55   *"Ladies and gentlemen"*   The guest spot can be heard on Lenny Bruce, *Let the Buyer Beware* (Shout! Factory, 6-CD boxed set with booklet, 2004), disc 6, track 1.

55   *"sick comics" or "sickniks"*   "The Sickniks," *Time*, July 13, 1959.

55   *Ralph J. Gleason, a leading jazz critic*   Liner notes to Lenny Bruce, *Live at the Curran Theater* (Fantasy Records, 1971, recorded Nov. 19, 1961); Gleason describes Bruce's jump-cut streams-of-consciousness at this date as "modal improvisations à la Coltrane," as contrasted with his "earlier things," which "were verbal jazz improvisations à la Charlie Parker."

56   *At the start of the year, Fantasy Records*   *The Sick Humor of Lenny Bruce* and *"I Am Not a Nut, Elect Me!"* were the first albums entirely of Bruce material. An earlier album, *Interviews of Our Time*, released in 1958, was a strange hodgepodge of various comics; only a few tracks featured Bruce. Concord Records, which now owns the Fantasy catalogue, has no documents on exactly when *Sick Humor* was released. However, *The Beat Generation*, a CD boxed set by Rhino Records, which includes one track from this album, reports that it was released in January 1959. *Let the Buyer Beware* also contains a Studs Terkel radio interview of Bruce in February 1959, during which he mentions the album, so it had to have been out before then.

56   *In one long bit, called "Religions, Inc."*   The bit is on *The Sick Humor of Lenny Bruce*. Thanks to Wolfgang Frank of Fantasy Jazz for giving me permission to quote from the album. Many of Bruce's monologues are transcribed in *The Essential Lenny Bruce*, ed. John Cohen (New York: Ballantine Books, 1967).

57   *In another bit, Christ and Moses*   This is on *"I Am Not a Nut, Elect Me!"*, though the best version is on Lenny Bruce, *Carnegie Hall, February 4, 1961: The Complete Unabridged Concert* (United Artists, released in 1972), a three-LP set that captures Bruce at his peak.

57   *In a track called "How to Entertain"*   This too is on *"I Am Not . . . ,"* which, though released in 1960, was recorded in 1959.

57   *White people in the audience*   The jazz musician David Amram, who is white, tells me that when this album came out, Percy Heath, the black bassist for the Modern Jazz Quartet, invited him over to listen to the bit. Amram was uncomfortable listening to it, but Heath was laughing out loud. Heath told him afterward that white liberals treated him like the one that Bruce was satirizing all the time.

57   *Lenny Bruce was born*   Bruce wrote an autobiography, *How to Talk Dirty and Influence People* (New York: Playboy Publishing, 1967), though much of it is fictitious. A more reliable source is Gerald Nachman, *Seriously Funny: The Rebel Comedians of the 1950s and 1960s* (New York: Back Stage Books, 2004), 389–436.

57   *he did routine stand-up comedy*   Gilbert Millstein, "Man, It's Like Satire," *New York Times Magazine*, May 3, 1959. This is the same Millstein whose *Times* review of *On the Road* put Jack Kerouac on the literary map (see chap. 4 of this book); he helped legitimize Bruce, too.

57   *San Francisco was a Mecca*   Nachman, *Seriously Funny*, 9.

58   *"Please don't grace us"*   Ibid., 12.

58   *He came there on Christmas night*   Mort Sahl, *Heartland* (New York: Harcourt Brace Jovanovich, 1976), 12. Sahl's autobiography is extremely bitter. See also Nachman, *Seriously Funny*, 49–98.

59   *"What I do"*   Nat Hentoff, "The Iconoclast in the Nightclub," *The Reporter*, Jan. 9, 1958; Sahl, *Heartland*, 18.

59   *"This is a hold-up"*   Sahl, *Heartland*, 14.

59   *"Joe McCarthy doesn't question"*   Nachman, *Seriously Funny*, 61.

59   *"Eisenhower is for integration"*   Robert Rice, "The Fury," *New Yorker*, July 30, 1960.

59   *"Is there any group"*   This was usually the side-closer on his comedy albums of the 1950s, most of them recorded live on the Verve jazz label, including *Mort Sahl at Sunset, The Future Lies Ahead, Look Forward in Anger*, and *A Way of Life*.

59   *"I wish I had a cause"*   Rice, "The Fury."

59   *He was making $5,000 to $7,500*   Ibid.

59   *"an indication that something in our society"*   Quoted in Nachman, *Seriously Funny*, 76–77.

60   *Senator John Kennedy asked*   Sahl, *Heartland*, 80ff.; Nachman, *Seriously Funny*, 80–81.

60   *When Hugh Hefner*   Nachman, *Seriously Funny*, 402–403.

60   *"say something funny"*   Ibid., 72.

60   *"You can't be afraid"*   Hentoff, "The Iconoclast."

61   *"It suggests," he said, "that they don't care"*   Bruce tells this story on *"I Am Not a Nut"* and on *Let the Buyer Beware*, disc 1, track 10.

62   *The shift in attitude Lenny Bruce spawned*   John Kifner, "No Joke! 37 Years After Death Lenny Bruce Receives Pardon," *New York Times*, Dec. 24, 2003.

62   *a "jumpy" nation*   James Thurber's contribution to "State of the Nation's Humor," *New York Times Magazine*, Dec. 7, 1958.

62   *whenever he saw an airplane*   Herbert Mitgang, "Anyway, Onward with Mort Sahl," *New York Times Magazine*, Feb. 8, 1959.

8. Thinking about the Unthinkable

63   *All through the spring of 1959*   Sharon Ghamari-Tabrizi, *The Worlds of Herman Kahn* (Cambridge: Harvard Univ. Press, 2005), 40, 81, 206–207, 245.

63 *Had he taken a different path* This is based on my own observations (I interviewed Kahn twice, at length, in the early 1980s) and that of his many friends and colleagues from RAND days. Daniel Ellsberg, a former RAND analyst who later leaked the Pentagon Papers, recently told me that Kahn was one of the funniest people he ever knew. Ellsberg very much doubts that Kahn was familiar with Sahl or Bruce. Ellsberg saw both comedians many times in those days and owned all their record albums; he also talked frequently with Kahn; if Kahn had seen or heard either comic, Ellsberg is sure the subject would have come up.

63 *Kahn had spent most of the decade* Ghamari-Tabrizi, *The Worlds of Herman Kahn*; and Fred Kaplan, *The Wizards of Armageddon* (New York: Simon & Schuster, 1983), chap. 14.

64 *a 652-page tome* Herman Kahn, *On Thermonuclear War* (Princeton, NJ: Princeton Univ. Press, 1960). (Page numbers here refer to the 1969 paperback edition by Free Press.)

64 *It was the year of the "missile gap"* See Fred Kaplan, *Wizards of Armageddon*, chap. 19.

64 *Albert Wohlstetter, published a widely read* Albert Wohlstetter, "The Delicate Balance of Power," *Foreign Affairs* (Jan. 1959).

64 *"the first look ever taken"* "Valuable Batch of Brains," *Life*, May 11, 1959.

64 *"moderate-sized" nuclear attack* "Facts of Attack," *Time*, July 6, 1959.

64 *Meanwhile, the U.S. Public Health Service* Many *New York Times* articles highlighted these findings, for instance: "8 of 10 Cities Show Rise in Strontium," Jan. 5, 1959; "Faster Fallout Is Now Indicated," Mar. 30, 1959; "Fallout of Strontium-90 Is Found Highest in U.S.," Mar. 22, 1959; and others.

64 *Nelson Rockefeller, the governor* "Civil Defense: Right to Die," *Time*, Aug. 17, 1959.

65 *"Can you live with that?"* Unless otherwise noted, all the quotes or paraphrasings come from Herman Kahn, "Transcript of Lectures on Thermonuclear War in the 1960–1970 Period," Woodrow Wilson Hall, Princeton University, March 13, 14, 1959. (Thanks to Sharon Ghamari-Tabrizi for providing me with a copy of the 293-page document, which was produced by a certified shorthand-reporter at the time.)

65 *"would not preclude normal and happy"* Quoted by Ghamari-Tabrizi, *The Worlds of Herman Kahn*, 16.

65 *Over five thousand people* Kahn, *On Thermonuclear War*, xxvi.

66 *"Kahn does for nuclear arms"* The reviewer was the Columbia sociologist Amitai Etzioni; quoted in Ghamari-Tabrizi, *The Worlds of Herman Kahn*, 10.

66 *"the most fascinating thing"* Quoted in ibid., 237.

66 *RAND had its origins* Kaplan, *Wizards of Armageddon*, chap. 4.

67 *"first came into contact"* Kahn, *On Thermonuclear War*, 484.

67 *The way Kahn saw it, only 2 million* Ibid., 169; and interviews that I conducted with many former RAND analysts in the early 1980s for my book *Wizards of Armageddon*; these included two interviews with Kahn in his Hudson Institute office, on Feb. 6 and Aug. 4, 1981.

67 *The U.S. Strategic Air Command's war plan* Kaplan, *Wizards of Armageddon*, chap. 18.

68 *"Gentlemen, you don't have a war plan"* Ibid., 220–221.

68 *"doomsday machine"* Kahn, *On Thermonuclear War*, 144ff.

68 *Stanley Kubrick would borrow* Fred Kaplan, "Truth Stranger Than 'Strangelove,'" *New York Times* (Arts & Leisure), Oct. 10, 2004.

68 *William Weed Kaufmann, another strategist* Kaplan, *Wizards of Armageddon*, chap. 13.

69 *Counterforce was, at best, a desperation strategy* In 1961, when John F. Kennedy became president, he and his secretary of defense, Robert McNamara, accepted the argument. McNamara created an office of systems analysis in the Pentagon and brought in several RAND analysts to run it. He also hired William Kaufmann as a part-time special assistant. Soon after entering office, McNamara heard a briefing on the nuclear war plan from the commanding general of SAC. Appalled by its horrible destructiveness, he instituted changes along the lines of Kaufmann's counterforce strategy—at least to give the president some "option," should he ever need one, between surrender and holocaust. Kahn never went to work in the Pentagon, nor did he go back to RAND. After his term at Princeton, he set up his own think tank, called the Hudson Institute, in Croton-on-Hudson, New York. He died of a heart attack in 1983, at the age of sixty-one.

70 *"to create a vocabulary"* Kahn, *On Thermonuclear War*, 5, 240.

71 *"Why Go Deep Underground"* Quoted in Ghamari-Tabrizi, *The Worlds of Herman Kahn*, 201–202.

71 *"the imposition of a vast"* "The Art of Poetry, No. 8: Interview with Allen Ginsberg," *Paris Review* (Spring 1966).

9. The Race for Space

72 *On March 3, the Pioneer IV* "Pioneer IV Soars Nearer the Moon, Sends Back Data," *New York Times*, Mar. 4, 1959; "Pioneer IV Passes Moon and Nears Own Solar Orbit," *New York Times*, Mar. 5, 1959.

72 *"very screwball" project* Lloyd S. Swensen, James M. Grimwood, and Charles C. Alexander, *This New Ocean: A History of Project Mercury* (NASA Special Publication-420, NASA History Series, 1959), chap. 6.

73 *On April 9, NASA* "Space Fliers Underwent Rigid Tests Before Selection," *New York Times*, Apr. 10, 1959.

73 *"Do you realize we'll soon"* Letter, Allen Ginsberg to Jack Kerouac, Oct. 16, 1957, Allen Ginsberg Papers, Box 1, Folder 6, Harry Ransom Research Center, University of Texas, Austin.

74 *"Poem Rocket"* In Allen Ginsberg, *Kaddish and Other Poems, 1958–1960* (San Francisco: City Lights Books, 1961), 37–39.

74 *"Air and space comprise"* House Committee on Science and Astronautics, *Hearings on Missile Development and Space Science*, Feb. and Mar. 1959, 76–77.

74 *"Aerospace" was a key device* Lieutenant Colonel Frank W. Jennings, "Doctrinal Conflict over the Word 'Aerospace,'" *Airpower Journal* (Fall 1990); Frank W. Jennings, "Genesis of the Aerospace Concept," *Air Power History* (Spring 2001).

74 *As a result, each of the service chiefs fought* See Fred Kaplan, *The Wizards of Armageddon* (New York: Simon & Schuster, 1983), chap. 15.

74 *"I never heard of that term"* House Committee on Science and Astronautics, *Hearings on Missile Development*, 247.

75 *Pioneer IV put the Air Force back* Jennings, "Doctrinal Conflict."

75 *"should be used wherever"* Ibid., note 41.

10. Toppling the Tyranny of Numbers

76 *On March 24, 1959* Texas Instruments, news release, "Texas Instruments Demonstrates Tiny Semiconductor Solid Circuit," Mar. 24 (for release Mar. 25), 1959, Jack Kilby Papers, Box 1, Folder 29, DeGolyer Library, Southern Methodist University, Dallas, Texas; "No-Hands Driving By Radar Studied," *New York Times*, Mar. 25, 1959.

76 *Jack Kilby grew up* Biographical material comes from T. R. Reid, *The Chip*, rev. ed. (New York: Random House, 2001), esp. 62–70;

Texas Instruments' Web site on Kilby (www.ti.com/corp/docs/kilbyctr/ jackstclair.shtml); and a Web site maintained by the Kilby Monument Foundation, which includes articles from the *Great Bend Tribune* (www.jackkilby.com/articles.html).

76   *In 1938, a ferocious blizzard*   Many sources, including Reid, refer to a blizzard of 1937, but a Great Bend historian, looking through old press files, discovered that in fact the fateful storm took place in 1938. See www.jackkilby.com/article2.html.

76   *He would later say*   Ibid.

77   *Kilby bought spare parts*   Reid, *The Chip*, 68–69.

77   *In 1947, he got a job*   Texas Instruments Web site.

77   *By Christmas 1954*   Reid, *The Chip*, 11; Michael Brian Schiffer, *The Portable Radio in American Life* (Tucson: Univ. of Arizona Press, 1991), 178–179.

77   *"the tyranny of numbers"*   Reid, *The Chip*, 3–6, 14–20.

78   *In July, most employees took their two-week*   Ibid., 3; Texas Instruments Web site.

79   *"The following circuit elements"*   Reid, *The Chip*, 77; see also page 22.

79   *On September 12, 1958*   Texas Instruments Web site.

79   *When the executives displayed*   Texas Instruments, "Texas Instruments Demonstrates Tiny Semiconductor Solid Circuit."

80   *A story in the next day's* New York Times   "No-Hands Driving By Radar Studied."

81   *That wouldn't happen until the beginning*   Reid, *The Chip*, 145–146, 151–152; Texas Instruments Web site.

81   *By 2000, after the consumer market*   It should be noted that the microchip has a coincidental coinventor—Robert Noyce, a physicist and one of the founders of Fairchild, who came up with his own version of the idea in January 1959 but laid it aside. Only when he learned of TI's presentation at the March 1959 trade show did he take another look and push the scheme. A huge legal battle erupted between the two corporations over which should be entitled to the patent. Fairchild won, and in fact Noyce's specific design, involving a printed circuit, is the one that served as the most common prototype. But it was Kilby's insight, and application, that set the technology in motion. Soon after developing the integrated circuit, Kilby also invented its first commercial application—the handheld calculator. Kilby died in 2005 at the age of eighty-one after a brief struggle with cancer. He won the Nobel

Prize for Physics in 2000. Noyce died in 1990. When Kilby received the Nobel, he said that had Noyce lived the two would no doubt have shared the prize. (See Tom Wolfe, "The Tinkerings of Robert Noyce," *Esquire*, Dec. 1983.)

81 *Just over six months after Texas Instruments* The closed-circuit broadcast took place on Oct. 5, 1959. IBM, press release, Oct. 5, 1959, IBM Archives; Angelo M. Donofrio, "For the 1401—Up, Up and (Now) Away," *Think*, April 1971.

81 *At the start of the decade, only twenty computers* R. Moreau, *The Computer Comes of Age: The People, the Hardware, and the Software* (Cambridge: MIT Press, 1986), 48.

81 *In 1954, General Electric became* Robert Sobel, *IBM: Colossus in Transition* (New York: Times Books, 1981), 141.

81 *The UNIVAC was a beast* Moreau, *The Computer Comes of Age*, 54.

81 *By contrast, the IBM 1401 took up* "IBM 1401 Fact Sheet," and IBM Technical Information, "Fact Sheet: 1401 Data Processing System," Oct. 5, 1959, in IBM Archives.

82 *The Peace Corps would use a 1401* Donofrio, "For the 1401."

82 *By 1965, the final year* Sobel, *IBM*, 167.

82 *on June 8, 1959* Russell Baker, "US Missile Delivers the Mail," *New York Times*, June 9, 1959; William Ronson, *United States Navy Missile Mail: First Complete Documentation* (privately published, 1964).

83 *Summerfield had gained notoriety* See chap. 6 of this book.

83 *"an historic milestone"* Reprinted in Ronson, *United States Navy Missile Mail*; see also message from Chief of Naval Operations to Arthur E. Summerfield, June 9, 1959, Dwight D. Eisenhower Library, Arthur Summerfield Papers, Box 36, Missile Mail folder.

83 *"may ultimately provide"* Baker, "US Missile Delivers the Mail"; Ronson, *United States Navy Missile Mail*.

11. The Assault on the Chord

84 *On March 2, 1959* Dates and times come from Ashley Kahn, *Kind of Blue: The Making of the Miles Davis Masterpiece* (New York: DaCapo Press, 2000), 88, 124. Kahn based much of his research on Columbia Records' archives.

84 *Along with his trumpeter and sidekick* For more on bebop, see Scott DeVeaux, *The Birth of Bebop: A Social and Musical History*

(Berkeley: Univ. of California Press, 1999); Ira Gitler, *Swing to Bop: The Oral History of the Transition in Jazz in the 1940s* (New York: Oxford Univ. Press, 1987); Gary Giddins, *Celebrating Bird: The Triumph of Charlie Parker* (New York: Beech Tree Books/ Morrow, 1987).

85 *Miles Davis started playing* For biographical information, see Miles Davis, *Miles: The Autobiography* (New York: Simon & Schuster, 1989); Ian Carr, *Miles Davis: A Critical Biography* (London: Quartet Books, 1982); Jack Chambers, *Milestones 1: The Music and Times of Miles Davis to 1960* (Toronto: Univ. of Toronto Press, 1983).

86 *They would get together and study piano scores* Kahn, *Kind of Blue*, 28.

86 *"all the chord changes"* Pat Wilson, "George Russell's Constant Quest," *downbeat*, Mar. 1972.

86 *A nun showed him a piano* Ibid.

87 *"you are free to do anything"* George Russell, *The Lydian Chromatic Concept of Tonal Organization for Improvisation* (New York: Concept Publishing Co., 1959), 27. (I thank Alice Russell for sending me a copy of this hard-to-find edition.) See also Wilson, "George Russell's Constant Quest"; "George Russell Interview," *Cadence*, Dec. 1977; Eric Nisenson, *The Making of Kind of Blue: Miles Davis and His Masterpiece* (New York: St. Martin's Press, 2000), chap. 4.

87 *"The concept," he wrote, "provides the possibilities"* Russell, *The Lydian Chromatic Concept*, 49.

87 Jazz in the Space Age The album, recorded in late 1959 and released on Decca in March 1960, included Bill Evans and Paul Bley alternating on piano. Russell chose the title and took the outer-space metaphor seriously. Titles of compositions on the album included "Chromatic Universe," "Dimensions," and "Waltz from Outer Space." Just to clarify, though: Unlike Sun Ra, the brilliant but eccentric big-band leader of the era, Russell did not believe that he *came* from outer space.

87 *"will liberate the student's melodic"* Russell, *The Lydian Chromatic Concept*, 1. See also George Russell and Martin Williams, "Ornette Coleman and Tonality," *Jazz Review*, June 1960.

88 *"hard bop"* Classic Miles albums in this vein were *Walkin'* and *Bags' Groove*, both on Prestige, released in 1954.

88 *a softer, more romantic approach* Listen to the ballad tracks on the five "legendary quintet" albums on Prestige, all recorded in three marathon sessions in 1956: *Miles*, *Workin'*, *Steamin'*, *Relaxin'*, and *Cookin'*.

The band included John Coltrane, Red Garland, Paul Chambers, and Philly Joe Jones.

88 *"Sign me up"* John McDonough, "George Avakian Remembers Miles Davis," *Wall Street Journal*, July 7, 2005. A recording of this performance was finally released by Sony in 2004, as part of a three-CD collection of highlights from the Newport Jazz Festival, *Happy Birthday, Newport: 50 Swinging Years*.

89 *"looking at a naked woman"* Nisenson, *The Making of Kind of Blue*, 70.

89 *"Man," he told Russell* Ibid., 72.

89 *"When you go this way"* Nat Hentoff, "An Afternoon with Miles Davis," *Jazz Review*, Dec. 1958.

90 *"an assault on the chord"* Russell and Williams, "Ornette Coleman and Tonality."

90 *Davis and his girlfriend* Kahn, *Kind of Blue*, 111.

91 *"freer, more modal"* Davis, *Miles*, 220.

91 *"Play in the sound of these scales"* A photo of the sheet music on Cannonball Adderley's bandstand, taken by the session's engineer Fred Plaut, appears in Kahn, *Kind of Blue*, 70.

92 *"sheets of sound"* Ira Gitler, "Trane on the Track," *downbeat*, Oct. 16, 1958.

92 *"a rocket ship"* Russell, *The Lydian Chromatic Concept*, Appendix, xviii.

92 *"the deadline of a particular chord"* Russell and Williams, "Ornette Coleman and Tonality."

12. Revolutionary Euphoria

94 *On the evening of April 15* "Crowd Hails Castro As He Reaches US for an 11-Day Visit," *New York Times*, Apr. 16, 1959.

94 *Castro's guerrilla army* For histories, see Tad Szulc, *Fidel: A Critical Portrait* (New York: William Morrow, 1986); Clifford L. Staten, *The History of Cuba* (New York: Palgrave Macmillan, 2005); Richard Gott, *Cuba: A New History* (New Haven: Yale Univ. Press, 2005).

95 *And so, on January 7* Szulc, *Fidel*, 481.

95 *He was a far more engaging* Ibid.; "Castro Maintains a Hectic Pace," *New York Times*, Apr. 18, 1959; "Central Park Rally and Visit to Bronx Zoo Occupy Cuban Premier," *New York Times*, Apr. 25, 1959; "Humanist Abroad," *Time*, May 4, 1959.

95   *Later, in Houston*   "Away from It All," *Time*, May 11, 1959.

95   *"What do you call your government"*   "The Other Face," *Time*, Apr. 27, 1959.

95   *"Their influence is nothing"*   "Castro Rules Out Role As Neutral; Opposes Reds, Says in TV Interview Cuba Will Honor Agreements— Supports the West," *New York Times*, Apr. 20, 1959.

95   *Pressed about his cabinet's firing squads*   "The Other Face."

96   *The editors received Castro*   Ibid.; "The First 100 Days," *Time*, Apr. 20, 1959; "Castro Declares Regime Is Free of Red Influence," *New York Times*, Apr. 17, 1959.

96   *"This young man"*   "Visitor from Cuba," *New York Times*, Apr. 25, 1959.

96   *"one of the most remarkable"*   "Fidel Castro's Visit," *New York Times*, Apr. 15, 1959.

96   *"not only out of another world"*   "Castro Leaves Big Question Mark," *New York Times*, Apr. 19, 1959.

96   *Even while Castro was drawing huge crowds*   "Reds' Alleged Role in Certain Regions Alarming Havana," *New York Times*, Apr. 23, 1959.

96   *The report reflected a dispatch*   Dispatch, Embassy of Cuba to Dept. of State, Apr. 14, 1959, U.S. State Dept., *Foreign Relations of the United States, 1958–1960, Cuba: Vol. 6 (1958–1960)* [hereafter cited as *FRUS Cuba*], 460. (Available online at http://digicoll.library.wisc.edu/ cgi-bin/FRUS/FRUS-idx?type=header&id=FRUS.FRUS195860v06.)

96   *"many opportunities" for "discreetly"*   Telegram, Embassy of Cuba (Bonsal) to Dept. of State, Apr. 14, 1959, *FRUS Cuba*, 456–457.

96   *Christian Herter, who was the acting*   Memo, Asst. Sec. Rubottom to Herter, Apr. 15, 1959, *FRUS Cuba*, 468–469.

96   *Herter hosted a champagne-and-steak lunch*   "The Other Face"; "Castro Is Lunch Guest of Herter on First Day of Visit," *New York Times*, Apr. 17, 1959.

97   *President Eisenhower, perhaps remembering*   Szulc, *Fidel*, 488; "Herter Arranges Lunch for Castro," *New York Times*, Apr. 7, 1959.

97   *"most interesting individual"*   Memorandum of Conversation Between the President and the Acting Secretary of State, Augusta, Ga., Apr. 18, 1959, *FRUS Cuba*, 475–476.

97   *"either incredibly naïve"*   Nixon's summary of his conversation with Castro was attached to a memo he wrote to John Foster Dulles on Apr. 24, 1959. See *FRUS Cuba*, 476.

97   *"benevolent tolerance"*   Dispatch from Embassy, Apr. 14, 1959.

97 *"nationalistic neutralism"* Memo, Asst. Sec. Rubottom to Herter, Apr. 15, 1959.

98 *As far back as his days in the Sierra* Szulc, *Fidel*, 403.

98 *When he took power, Cuba had only a few months'* "Austerity Held Near for Castro," *New York Times*, Apr. 23, 1959.

98 *Back in March 1959* Staten, *History of Cuba*, 92.

98 *Still, in a telegram to the State Department* Telegram, Embassy of Cuba to Dept. of State, May 19, 1959, 5 p.m., *FRUS Cuba*, 509–510.

98 *"great consternation"* Telegram, Dept. of State to Embassy of Cuba, ibid.

98 *On June 1, an interagency group* Memo of Conference, Washington, June 1, 1959, *FRUS Cuba*, 519. See also the memorandum of a June 5 meeting of the Council on Foreign Economic Policy, *FRUS Cuba*, 520.

99 *The same month that Fidel flew to Washington* Aleksandr Fursenko and Timothy Naftali, *Khrushchev's Cold War: The Inside Story of an American Adversary* (New York: W. W. Norton, 2006), 296.

99 *futile to"hope that Castro"* Ibid., 299–300.

99 *"the same mesmeric appeal"* Ibid., 300.

99 *"I felt as though I had returned"* Ibid., 296.

99 *"economic aggression"* "Castro Forces Carry Out Seizure of U.S. Properties," *New York Times*, Aug. 8, 1960.

99 *At first, Castro and his entourage* "Castro Can't Find Lodging Here; One Hotel Cancels Reservation," *New York Times*, Sept. 16, 1960.

100 *Theresa Hotel up in Harlem* "Cuban in Harlem," *New York Times*, Sept. 20, 1960.

100 *And instead of holding one-on-one* Ibid.

100 *"heroic man"* "Russian Goes to Harlem, Then Hugs Cuban at U.N.," *New York Times*, Sept. 21, 1960.

101 *A boisterous Texan* For biographical material, see Irving Louis Horowitz, *C. Wright Mills: An American Utopian* (New York: Free Press, 1983); Dan Wakefield, *New York in the '50s* (Boston: Houghton Mifflin, 1992), 32–36 passim; and Wakefield's introduction to C. Wright Mills, *Letters and Autobiographical Writings*, ed. Kathryn and Pamela Mills (Berkeley: Univ. of California Press, 2001), 1–18.

101 *"a post-modern period"* "Culture and Politics: The Fourth Epoch," *The Listener*, Mar. 12, 1959; reprinted in C. Wright Mills, *Power, Politics & People: The Collected Essays of C. Wright Mills*, ed. Irving Louis Horowitz (New York: Oxford Univ. Press, 1963), 236–246.

102 *And so, when Castro charged down*   Horowitz, *C. Wright Mills*, 292–293.

102 *"a new and distinct type"*   C. Wright Mills, *Listen, Yankee! The Revolution in Cuba* (New York: McGraw Hill, 1960).

102 *"a touch of mysticism"*   Horowitz, op.cit., 293–294, 298.

103 *"Who is it that is getting disgusted"*   C. Wright Mills, "Letter to the New Left," *New Left Review*, Sept.–Oct. 1960; reprinted in Mills, *Power, Politics & People*, 248–259.

103 *When he wrote this article*   Horowitz, *C. Wright Mills*, 314.

103 *"a slogan of complacency"*   Mills, "Letter to the New Left."

104 *"the rebel life of James Dean"*   Tom Hayden, *Reunion: A Memoir* (New York: Random House, 1988), 78, 80, 81.

104 *The SDS was formed*   See ibid.; Kirkpatrick Sale, *SDS* (New York: Random House, 1973); Todd Gitlin, *The Sixties: Years of Hope, Days of Rage*, rev. ed. (New York: Bantam, 1993).

104 The Port Huron Statement   The document, essentially Hayden's draft, was presented as the SDS manifesto at the organization's first convention in Port Huron, Michigan, on June 15, 1962. It is available at many online sites, for instance, www2.iath.virginia.edu/sixties/HTML_docs/Resources/Primary/Manifestos/SDS_Port_Huron.html.

13. Breaking the Logjam, Hitting the Wall

105 *"to break the logjam"*   Memorandum of telephone conversation between President Eisenhower and Secretary of State Herter, July 8, 1959, 11:15 a.m., U.S. State Department, *Foreign Relations of the United States, 1958–1960, Vol. 10: Eastern European Region, Soviet Union, Cyprus, Pt. 1* [hereafter cited as *FRUS Soviet*], 307–308.

105 *"missile gap"*   See Fred Kaplan, *The Wizards of Armageddon* (New York: Simon & Schuster, 1983), chap. 10.

105 *He regarded the claim's very premise as absurd*   Aleksandr Fursenko and Timothy Naftali, *Khrushchev's Cold War: The Inside Story of an American Adversary* (New York: W. W. Norton, 2006), 249–257.

106 *Eisenhower had resisted*   *FRUS Soviet*, 309–310.

106 *He sent the premier an invitation*   Ibid.

106 *at Mikoyan's urging, for humanizing*   Fursenko and Naftali, *Khrushchev's Cold War*, 230.

106 *"We have such things"*   Transcript, "The Nixon-Khrushchev 'Kitchen Debate,'" July 24, 1959; available at several online sites.

107 *The Russians had flown nonstop* Fursenko and Naftali, *Khrushchev's Cold War*, 228.

107 *The day before his voyage, the Soviets launched* John Finney, "Washington Praises Feat; Hopes for Sharing of Data," *New York Times*, Sept. 14, 1959.

107 *"Mankind lives in a wonderful time"* Tass, "Text of Khrushchev's Reply to Messages in Connection with His U.S. Trip," *New York Times*, Sept. 15, 1959.

108 *"we'll lose our pants"* Fursenko and Naftali, *Khrushchev's Cold War*, 242–243.

108 *When his motorcade passed* Gay Talese, "Crowds on Street Curious But Silent," *New York Times*, Sept. 18, 1959.

108 *He was a Communist camel* Harrison Salisbury, "Khrushchev's Visit: Impact in U.S.," *New York Times*, Sept. 20, 1959.

108 *"We will bury you!"* "We Will Bury You!" *Time*, Nov. 26, 1956. Khrushchev's full remark, as rendered by a simultaneous translator, was, "Whether you like it or not, history is on our side. We will bury you." In context, the Russian phrase—*My vas pokhoronim*—would have been more properly translated as "We will outlive you" or "We will be present at your funeral." It did not suggest that Khrushchev, or the Soviet Union or Communism, would *actively* bury America or capitalism; more, that historical forces would bring about capitalism's demise.

108 *"Is there an epidemic of cholera"* "Premier Annoyed By Ban on a Visit to Disneyland," *New York Times*, Sept. 20, 1959.

109 *Still angry, he moved on to a tour* "Film Stars Fete Russian in Studio," *New York Times*, Sept. 20, 1959.

109 *Finally, on the train from Los Angeles* Henry Cabot Lodge, Memorandum of Conversation with the President, *FRUS Soviet*, 454. Lodge sent Eisenhower summaries of his conversations with Khrushchev, some of them very lengthy, throughout the trip; they are all fascinating, a much more sophisticated and relaxed version of what the Kitchen Debate might have been; they are reprinted in *FRUS Soviet*.

109 *"I have seen some real live Americans"* William J. Jordens, "Soviet Chief Sees Ordinary People," *New York Times*, Sept. 21, 1959. See also Harrison Salisbury, "Khrushchev Greeted by Cheers in San Francisco," *New York Times*, Sept. 21, 1959.

109 *Khrushchev and Garst* Fursenko and Naftali, *Khrushchev's Cold War*, 236; "Missionary of Food: Roswell Garst," *New York Times*, Sept. 22, 1959.

109 *Khrushchev came away from the meeting* At a plenary session of the Kremlin on Dec. 14, 1959, Khrushchev told his comrades that his trip to the United States revealed that American workers were closer to the kind of democratic society that he expected communism would produce. See Fursenko and Naftali, op.cit., 244–245.

109 *Even back in San Francisco, he told Lodge* Lodge to Eisenhower, Memorandum of conversation with Khrushchev, San Francisco, Sept. 21, 1959, *FRUS Soviet*, 439.

109 *At meals, they chatted amiably* Memorandum of conversation, Eisenhower and Khrushchev, "Khrushchev's Wartime Experience," Camp David, Sept. 26, 1959, *FRUS Soviet*, 459–464.

110 *Eisenhower replied frankly* Memorandum of conversation, Eisenhower and Khrushchev, "Nuclear Exchange; Communist China," Sept. 27, 1959, *FRUS Soviet*, 477.

110 *Khrushchev admitted that he'd acted brashly* Memorandum of conversation, Eisenhower and Khrushchev, "Berlin and Germany," Camp David, Sept. 26, 1959, U.S. State Department, *Foreign Relations of the United States, 1958–1960, Vol. 9: Berlin Crisis, 1959–1960, Germany, Austria* [hereafter cited as *FRUS Berlin*], 39.

110 *Eisenhower acknowledged that the status* He made this point several times during the Camp David talks. See Ibid., 36–46; also *FRUS Soviet*, 395, 464.

110 *Eisenhower gave him that assurance* President's Report on His Private Meeting with Khrushchev, Sept. 27, 1959, *FRUS Berlin*, 45–46.

110 *At the end of the meeting* Ibid.; see also 36–41.

110 *Khrushchev was slightly disappointed* Fursenko and Naftali, *Khrushchev's Cold War*, 239.

110 *"sincerely wishes to see the end of the Cold War"* Quoted in Paul Marantz, "Prelude to Détente: Doctrinal Change Under Khrushchev," *International Studies Quarterly* (Dec. 1975).

111 *The "most sensible of them"* Ibid.

111 *He would withdraw one million troops* Ibid.; Fursenko and Naftali, *Khrushchev's Cold War*, 247–252.

111 *Even the CIA's director* Fursenko and Naftali, *Khrushchev's Cold War*, 252.

112 *The U-2 took off on May Day* Ibid., 263–291.

113 *In 1961, when a young new president* For the Berlin crisis, see Fred Kaplan, *Wizards of Armageddon*, chap. 20; and Fred Kaplan, "JFK's First-Strike Plan," *Atlantic*, Oct. 2001.

113 *But he also felt a need to compensate*   See Sheldon M. Stern, *Averting "The Final Failure": John F. Kennedy and the Secret Cuban Missile Crisis Meetings* (Stanford: Stanford Univ. Press, 2003).

115 *"the imposition of a vast mental barrier"*   "The Art of Poetry, No. 8: Interview with Allen Ginsberg," *Paris Review* (Spring 1966).

14. The Frontier's Dark Side

116 *On July 8, 1959*   U.S. State Department, *Foreign Relations of the United States, 1958–1960: Vietnam, Vol. 1* (hereafter cited as *FRUS Vietnam*), 220; Stanley Karnow, *Vietnam: A History* (New York: Viking, 1983), 10–11.

116 *The leader of the nationalists*   Dixee R. Bartholomew-Feis, *The OSS and Ho Chi Minh: Unexpected Allies in the War against Japan* (Lawrence: Univ. Press of Kansas), 2006.

117 *"row of dominoes"*   President Dwight Eisenhower, news conference, Apr. 7, 1954.

118 *"Indochina is devoid"*   Memo, Arthur Radford to Secretary of Defense, "Studies with Respect to Possible US Action Regarding Indochina," May 26, 1954, in *The Pentagon Papers: The Defense Department History of United States Decision-making in Vietnam (Senator Gravel Edition), Volume 1* (Boston: Beacon Press, 1971), 511. For Eisenhower's view on fighting in Asia, see Fred Kaplan, *The Wizards of Armageddon* (New York: Simon & Schuster, 1983), 177.

118 *But Diem refused*   *The Pentagon Papers*, 245–247.

118 *Dulles sided with Diem*   In a telegram to the U.S. Embassy in Vietnam on July 7, 1954, Dulles wrote that "elections might eventually mean unification . . . under Ho Chi Minh," which "makes it all more important they should be only held as long after cease-fire agreement as possible and in conditions free from intimidation to give democratic [i.e., anti-Communist] elements best chance." Ibid., 546–547.

119 *Ho Chi Minh's regime was exceedingly harsh*   Ibid., 245.

119 *"little more than concentration camps"*   Ibid., 253, and 254–258.

119 *In 1957, organized rebellions*   Ibid., 242–243, 252, 257–258.

119 *No Americans, not even officials*   Ibid., 328–329.

119 *At the time, though, nearly every American*   A U.S. Government "white paper" on Vietnam in 1961, and another in 1965, attributed the insurgency to Hanoi's aggression, holding that the Viet Cong were merely tools of North Vietnam. Ibid., 251–252; see also 265.

120 *The Viet Cong came up with a catchword*   Ibid., 252.

120 *"on-the-spot advice"*   Telegram, Secretary of State (Herter) to Embassy in Vietnam, July 7, 1959, *FRUS Vietnam*, 217–218; *Pentagon Papers*, 269.

120 *The same month that the American advisers*   *Pentagon Papers*, 264; Karnow, *Vietnam*, 253.

121 *"Open Door imperialism"*   William Appleman Williams, *The Tragedy of American Diplomacy* (Cleveland: World Publishing Co., 1959). The book went through a few revised editions, most recently in 1972, published by W.W. Norton.

122 *"When properly directed"*   Paul M. Buhle and Edward Rice-Maximin, *William Appleman Williams: The Tragedy of Empire* (New York: Routledge, 1995), 182; see also 53.

122 *"It is always well"*   Quoted in John B. Judis, *The Folly of Empire* (New York: Scribner, 2004), 85. (It is worth noting that Judis makes the case that Wilson changed his thinking on empire before his term was up.)

122 *"The Frontier in American History"*   See chap. 1 of this book.

122 *Williams, too, was influenced by Turner*   Buhle and Rice-Maximim, *William Appleman Williams*, 34–35, 86.

122 *Harrington reveled in standing apart*   Ibid., 37, 52.

123 *"from a sanely conservative"*   Quoted in ibid., 71.

123 *It was no coincidence that Mills, too*   Irving Louis Horowitz, *C. Wright Mills: An American Utopian* (New York: Free Press, 1983), esp. 38–54.

123 *"Anti-Military Ball"*   Buhle and Rice-Maximim, *William Appleman Williams*, 103.

124 *"We have much to offer"*   Quoted in ibid., 82.

15. The New Language of Diplomacy

125 *An official survey*   James Reston, "Foreign Service Woes," *New York Times*, Mar. 19, 1958. Not until the previous fall had the State Department even required foreign service officers to know a foreign language. The new policy was set forth in Department of State Circular Airgram 9241 and Circular 267, spelled out in "New Foreign Language Institute Language School Overseas," printed in the department's newsletter of Sept. 15, 1957.

125 *As a result, by the fall of 1959*   James Reston, "U.S. Envoys Gain in Language Skills," *New York Times*, Nov. 19, 1959.

125 *Only six diplomats*   Table in ibid.

126 *"Moscow and Washington must realize"* For more on the Bandung Conference, see Penny M. Von Eschen, *Race Against Empire: Black Americans and Anticolonialism, 1937–1957* (Ithaca, NY: Cornell Univ. Press, 1997), 167–171.

127 *"a turning point in world history"* Quoted in ibid., 170.

127 *"real Americana"* Some of this section first appeared, in a shorter and different form, in Fred Kaplan, "When Ambassadors Had Rhythm," *New York Times* (Arts & Leisure section), June 29, 2008. See also Penny M. Von Eschen, *Satchmo Blows Up the World: Jazz Ambassadors Play the Cold War* (Cambridge: Harvard Univ. Press, 2004); *Jam Session: America's Jazz Ambassadors Embrace the World* (Washington, DC: Meridian International Center, 2008), which is a catalogue for a Spring 2008 photo exhibit about the jazz tours; and Iain Anderson, *This Is Our Music: Free Jazz, the Sixties, and American Culture* (Philadelphia: Univ. of Pennsylvania Press, 2007), chap. 1.

128 *"because they love freedom"* "Who Is Conover? Only We Ask," *New York Times Magazine*, Sept. 13, 1959.

128 *The black novelist Ralph Ellison* Quoted in Anderson, *This Is Our Music*, 72. For a similar view, see Marshall Stearns, "Is Jazz Good Propaganda? The Dizzy Gillespie Tour," *Saturday Review*, July 14, 1956. Stearns, one of the pioneering jazz educators, accompanied Gillespie on the tour and gave lectures to foreign audiences on jazz history.

128 *"ought to be translated"* Quoted in Von Eschen, *Satchmo Blows Up*, 33.

128 *"Maybe we could have built"* Quoted in Anderson, *This Is Our Music*, 20.

129 *"a Second Coming"* Von Eschen, *Satchmo Blows Up*, 206.

129 *"This is a diplomatic mission"* Reprinted in ibid., 13.

129 *"powerfully effective"* Quoted in ibid., 34.

129 *"I've got 300 years"* Dizzy Gillespie (with Al Fraser), *To Be or Not to Bop* (New York: Doubleday, 1979), 414.

129 *"The way they are treating"* Gary Giddins, *Satchmo* (New York: Doubleday, 1988), 160–165.

130 *"ruining our foreign policy"* Von Eschen, *Satchmo Blows Up*, 64.

130 *"circle of Russia"* Iola Brubeck, quoted in ibid., 54.

130 *Walking around Istanbul* Interview with Dave Brubeck. May 9, 2008.

131 *"Travel the world"* Ibid.

131 *All during the 1958 tour* Dave Brubeck remarks on this, especially on Morello, in the liner notes of the 1997 Sony/Legacy CD reissue of *Time Out*.

131 *In November 1954, Brubeck* "The Man on Cloud No. 7," *Time*, Nov. 8, 1954.

131 *They finally agreed, but only if* Darius Brubeck, "1959: The Beginning of Beyond," in *The Cambridge Companion to Jazz*, ed. Mervyn Cook & David Horn (Cambridge, UK: Cambridge Univ. Press, 2002), 199. Darius Brubeck, a musician and musicologist in his own right, is Dave's son.

131 *He started recording it* Ashley Kahn, *Kind of Blue: The Making of the Miles Davis Masterpiece* (New York: Da Capo Press, 2000), 149.

132 *on June 25, July 1, and August 18* Recording dates are cited on the 1997 CD reissue.

16. Sparking the Powder Keg

133 The Sound of Miles Davis Ashley Kahn, *Kind of Blue: The Making of the Miles Davis Masterpiece* (New York: Da Capo Press, 2000), 126– 130. The entire TV show is featured on a bonus DVD disc of Sony's 50th anniversary reissue of Miles Davis's *Kind of Blue*.

133 *The sets at Birdland* Miles Davis, *Miles: The Autobiography* (New York: Simon & Schuster, 1989), 236.

133 *"like a tom-tom"* "Music News," *downbeat*, Oct. 1, 1959; "Miles Exonerated," *downbeat*, Feb. 18, 1960. The *New York Times* published only a brief news item, accepting the policemen's position; see "Miles Davis Seized; Jazz Trumpeter Is Accused in Attack on Patrolman," Aug. 26, and "Jazzman Freed on Bail," Aug. 27, 1959. See also Davis, *Miles*, 238; Jack Chambers, *Milestone 1: The Music and Times of Miles Davis to 1960* (Toronto: Univ. of Toronto Press, 1983), 314–316.

134 *"an affront to human dignity"* Report of the U.S. Commission on Civil Rights, 1959, submitted to the President and the Congress, Sept. 9, 1959 (Washington, DC: Government Printing Office, 1959), 9, 134, 534.

134 *The commission's three southern members* Ibid., 2.

134 *"Isn't a segregated life"* Russell Baker, "Congress Agrees on Rights Plan in Wind-up Rush," *New York Times*, Sept. 15, 1959.

135 *"not limited to one region"* Report of the U.S. Commission on Civil Rights, 15.

135 *"A great myth of the 20th century"* "Death of a Myth," *Village Voice*, May 27, 1959.

135 *So, after much pressure and compromise*   For a detailed description of how Johnson maneuvered the bill through the Senate, see Robert A. Caro, *The Years of Lyndon Johnson: Vol. 3, Master of the Senate* (New York: Alfred A. Knopf, 2002), part 5.

136 *"that through threats of bodily harm"*   *Report of the U.S. Commission on Civil Rights*, 71.

136 *The response was sufficiently encouraging*   The connection is cited in Manning Marable, *Malcolm X: A Life of Reinvention* (New York: Viking, forthcoming); thanks to Professor Marable for letting me read a portion of the draft.

136 *In Alabama, ninety-one black men*   *Report of the U.S. Commission on Civil Rights*, 71, 80.

136 *In Mississippi, twenty-four witnesses*   Myrlie Evers-Williams and Manning Marable, *The Autobiography of Medgar Evers: A Hero's Life and Legacy Revealed through His Writings, Letters, and Speeches* (New York: Basic Civitas Books, 2005), 124.

136 *In Forrest County, where 7,406*   Ibid.; and *Report of the U.S. Commission on Civil Rights*, 61.

136 *In Bullock County, Alabama*   *Report of the U.S. Commission on Civil Rights*, 71, 88, 95.

137 *As a further barrier*   "30-Day Limit Is Set on Alabama Data," *New York Times*, Feb. 19, 1959.

137 *The legislatures of Mississippi and South Carolina*   *Report of the U.S. Commission on Civil Rights*, 237–238.

137 *"have no place in our school system"*   Ibid., 199; for the whole story, see 196–201.

138 *In Atlanta, a federal judge*   "Bus Segregation in Atlanta Upset," *New York Times*, Jan. 10, 1959.

138 *A Virginia appeals court*   Anthony Lewis, "Federal Tribunal Rules Closings Illegal and Hits at 'Evasive Tactics,'" *New York Times*, Jan. 20, 1959.

138 *In Seattle, a Coast Guard commander*   "Seattle Couple Ordered to Sell House to Negro," *New York Times*, May 2, 1959.

138 *On April 24, 1959*   See Evers-Williams and Marable, *Autobiography of Medgar Evers*, 133ff.; and Howard Smead, *Blood Justice: The Lynching of Mack Charles Parker* (New York: Oxford Univ. Press, 1988).

138 *"as though I were a"*   Evers-Williams and Marable, *Autobiography of Medgar Evers*, 150.

138 *"century of wonders"* Ibid., 141; the speech is reprinted on pages 140–150.

139 *Medgar Evers was thirty-three* Biographical information based on ibid., passim; and Medgar Evers, with Francis H. Mitchell, "Why I Live in Mississippi," *Ebony*, Nov. 1958, reprinted in Evers-Williams and Marable, *Autobiography of Medgar Evers*, 111–117.

140 *Back in February 1959, barely thirty years old* Taylor Branch, *Parting the Waters: America in the King Years, 1954–63* (New York: Simon & Schuster, 1988), 250–259.

140 *"a call for black supremacy"* I viewed *The Hate That Hate Produced*, at the Paley Center Museum of Broadcasting in New York. This section also draws on chap. 6 of Marable, *Malcolm X* (forthcoming), and on an interview with Manning Marable, Aug. 5, 2008.

142 *Lomax was an advocate for racial integration* Lomax was a fascinating figure. After earning his two master's degrees, he spent five years in a federal prison for operating a scam that involved renting cars, forging title papers in his name, and selling them. After getting out of prison, he went straight and turned to journalism. After he made a mark with several publications, Mike Wallace hired him to pre-interview guests on his show. After the success of the documentary on black nationalists, Lomax gave speeches and wrote books on race in America. The books included *The Reluctant African* (1960), *The Negro Revolt* (1962), and *When the Word Is Given* (1963), the last of which Marable regards as the single best book on the Nation of Islam. Lomax also became friends with Malcolm X and debated him—on integration vs. separatism—in several public forums. In 1970, after a research trip in California, he was driving late at night, back to New York, where he taught at Hofstra University, when his rented car skidded out of control and flipped over several times, killing him. (This comes from my interview with Manning Marable, and from "Louis Lomax, 47, Dies in Car Crash," *New York Times*, Aug. 1, 1970.)

144 *Malcolm now realized that this fable* Thanks to Manning Marable for insight on this episode.

144 *On November 5, they returned their verdict* Evers-Williams and Marable, *Autobiography of Medgar Evers*, 139n; Smead, *Blood Justice*, chap. 11; Anthony Lewis, "U.S. Jury to Sift Parker Lynching," *New York Times*, Nov. 6, 1959; Anthony Lewis, "Rogers Assails Mississippi Role in Lynching Case," *New York Times*, Nov. 18, 1959.

144 *The day before the grand jury met* See John Howard Griffin, *Black Like Me* (Boston: Houghton Mifflin, 1961); and Robert Bonazzi, *Man in the Mirror: John Howard Griffin and the Story of* Black Like Me (Maryknoll, NY: Orbit Books, 1997). *Black Like Me* is written like a diary, with dates heading each chapter. Page numbers cited here refer to the 2003 paperback edition.

145 *His friend calmly asked, "Why not?"* Bonazzi, *Man in the Mirror*, 8.

145 *From the islanders' point of view* Ibid., 14.

146 *"the face and shoulders"* Griffin, *Black Like Me*, 10.

146 *"that the Other was not other at all"* Bonazzi, *Man in the Mirror*, 48.

146 *"with such loathing"* Griffin, *Black Like Me*, 50–51.

147 *"glum and angry"* Ibid., 46.

147 *"If some spark does set the keg afire"* Ibid., 164.

147 *"a scathing indictment"* Reviews and sales figures are cited in Bonazzi, *Man in the Mirror*, 170–171.

147 *Just one month into the new decade* Evers-Williams and Marable, *Autobiography of Medgar Evers*, 169–171; Branch, *Parting the Waters*, 272ff.

148 *In Las Vegas, the NAACP* Evers-Williams and Marable, *Autobiography of Medgar Evers*, 179–181.

148 *But the segregationists refused to surrender* Medgar Evers's killer, a fertilizer salesman and Ku Klux Klan member named Byron De La Beckwith, was tried the next year but was freed after the all-white jury deadlocked. Forty years later, he was tried again after new evidence materialized, and was found guilty. He died in prison in 2001, at the age of eighty. The December before Malcolm X was gunned down, Louis Farrakhan, aka Louis X, the minister of the Nation of Islam's Boston temple, wrote in *Muhammad Speaks* that Malcolm was "deserving of death." Farrakhan was never formally charged with the murder. Martin Luther King's assassin, James Earl Ray, was arrested while using a false passport at London's Heathrow airport. Extradited to Memphis, he confessed his guilt and was sentenced to ninety-nine years in prison. He later tried to recant his guilty plea, saying that he was part of a murder plot coordinated by a Canadian named "Raoul." Many conspiracy theories have been floated, most of them involving the FBI, but no real evidence of a plot has surfaced over the decades.

17. Civilizations in the Stars

149 *There, alongside the usual assortment*   Listed in the table of contents, *Nature*, Sept. 19, 1959.

150 *"scientific-research opportunities"*   Letter, L. V. Berkner, National Academy of Sciences, to Philip Morrison, Aug. 29, 1958, Philip Morrison Papers (MC 52), Box 2A, Folder 25, Institute Archives, Massachusetts Institute of Technology, Cambridge, MA.

150 *Morrison was a nuclear physicist*   Much of the biographical material draws on Kosta Tsipis, "Philip Morrison: Nov. 17, 1915–Apr. 22, 2005," National Academy of Sciences Biographical Memoirs series (2009); also interview with Kosta Tsipis, Aug. 2008.

151 *"small Earth-circling satellite"*   Paul Dickson, *Sputnik: The Shock of the Century* (New York: Walker & Co., 2007), 10ff. For a glimmer of the exuberance that the International Geophysical Year reflected and attempted to propagate, listen to Donald Fagen's song "I.G.Y." on his album *The Nightfly* (Warner Bros., 1982).

151 *In December 1958*   Minutes of the 2nd meeting, Committee on Space Projects of the Space Science Board, Dec. 11, 1958. (The minutes also refer to a previous meeting on Dec. 1.) Philip Morrison Papers, Box 2A, Folder 25.

151 *When Morrison got back at Cornell*   Morrison recounts this story, differing slightly on the details, in Philip Morrison, "Twenty Years After . . . ," *Cosmic Search*, Jan. 1979; and Philip Morrison Oral History Interview, by Owen Gingerich and David Kaiser, Feb. 22, 2003, Niels Bohr Library, American Institute of Physics, College Park, MD.

151 *As a teenager, Morrison had fiddled*   Philip Morrison, lecture at celebration of his 70th birthday in 1985, Philip Morrison Papers (AC 199), Box 2, Tape 9.

152 *"seems unwarranted to deny"*   "Searching for Interstellar Communications," *Nature*, Sept. 19, 1959.

152 *When Drake was a precocious eight-year-old*   Interview with Frank Drake, Aug. 20, 2008. Unless otherwise indicated, what follows comes from this interview.

153 *One day over lunch*   Frank D. Drake, "A Reminiscence of Project Ozma," *Cosmic Search*, Jan. 1979; and interview with Drake.

155 *The members of the group called themselves*   Amir Alexander, "The Search for Extraterrestrial Intelligence: A Short History," The Planetary Society, 2001 (www.planetary.org/explore/topics/seti/seti_history_06.html).

It was at this conference that Frank Drake drew on the blackboard an equation—which came to be called "the Drake Equation"—for calculating the number of planets in the galaxy that might have the means to transmit radio signals into outer space. That number (N) would be equal to R° (the average rate of star formation) times Fp (the fraction of those stars that have planets orbiting them) times Ne (the average number of planets per star that are capable of sustaining life) times Fl (the fraction of those planets where life has evolved) times Fi (the fraction of *those* planets where *intelligent* life evolves) times Fc (the fraction of those planets that communicate) times L (the lifetime of the communicating civilization). The product of those seven factors should provide an estimate of how many communicating civilizations are in the galaxy. Drake designed the equation strictly as an analytical tool. The answer to the problem depends greatly on the estimate for each factor, which of course was—and remains—highly uncertain. Those who have guessed their way through the Drake Equation come up with numbers ranging from 2 to over 10,000.

155 *As for visiting one another*   Interview with Drake.

156 *Clarke wrote that the "most important result"*   Quoted in Morrison, "Twenty Years After."

18. A Great Upward Swoop of Movement

157 *Its designer, Frank Lloyd Wright, modeled it*   Letter, Frank Lloyd Wright to Hilla Rebay, Jan. 26, 1944, Collection of Frank Lloyd Wright (A0021), Box 691320, Folder 41, Solomon R. Guggenheim Museum Archives, New York (hereafter cited as "Guggenheim Archives").

157 *Various critics likened it to*   Ada Louise Huxtable, "That Museum: Wright or Wrong," *New York Times Magazine*, Oct. 25, 1959; Sarah Knox, "New Art Museum Opens on 5th Avenue," *New York Times*, Oct. 21, 1959; "Last Monument," *Time*, Nov. 2, 1959; *New York Mirror* editorial quoted in Robert Alden, "Art Experts Laud Wright Design," *New York Times*, Oct. 22, 1959.

158 *On the first Sunday*   Lawrence O'Kane, "10,000 Flock to Wright Museum, But Only 6,039 Manage to Get In," *New York Times*, Oct. 26, 1959.

158 *One million people visited*   Jane King Hession and Debra Pickrel, *Frank Lloyd Wright in New York: The Plaza Years, 1954–1959* (Salt Lake City: Gibbs Smith, 2007), 116.

158 *"painting that represents no object"*　Joan Lukach, *Hilla Rebay: In Search of the Spirit in Art* (New York: George Braziller, 1984), 144.

158 *None of Bauer's paintings*　William J. Hennessey, "Frank Lloyd Wright and the Guggenheim Museum: A New Perspective" [n.d.], Collection of Frank Lloyd Wright, Box 100506, Folder 107, Guggenheim Archives.

159 *But Rebay planted the idea*　Lukach, *Hilla Rebay*, 183.

159 *Originally the idea of non-objective*　"History of the Museum of Non-Objective Painting," [n.d.], Collection of Frank Lloyd Wright, Box 691320, Folder 47, Guggenheim Archives; and Ada Louise Huxtable, *Frank Lloyd Wright* (New York: Viking, 2004), 228ff.

159 *"alive with spiritual"*　Quoted in Vivian Barnett, *Art of Tomorrow: Hilla Rebay and Solomon R. Guggenheim* (New York: Guggenheim Foundation, 2005), 5.

159 *"temple to the spirit"*　Letter, Rebay to Wright, June 1, 1943, Collection of Frank Lloyd Wright, Box 691320, Folder 41, Guggenheim Archives.

159 *social utopia, perhaps a path to world peace*　Huxtable, *Frank Lloyd Wright*, 228–229.

159 *In 1939, Guggenheim set up*　"Solomon R. Guggenheim Museum: A Chronology" [n.d.], Collection of Frank Lloyd Wright, Box 100506, Folder 96, Guggenheim Archives.

159 *Wright was born*　Biographical material mainly from Huxtable, *Frank Lloyd Wright*.

159 *"order creating order"*　Letter, Rebay to Wright, June 1, 1943.

160 *"a new type of Treasury"*　Letter, Wright to Solomon R. Guggenheim, July 14, 1943, Frank Lloyd Wright Correspondence (A00006), Box 517, Folder 1, Guggenheim Archives.

160 *"A museum," he wrote to Rebay, "should be"*　Letter, Wright to Rebay, Jan. 20, 1944, Collection of Frank Lloyd Wright, Box 691320, Folder 41, Guggenheim Archives.

160 *"The building is built like a spring"*　"The Modern Gallery: The World's Greatest Architect," *Architectural Forum*, Jan. 1946.

160 *"must, and should, enhance"*　Letter, Solomon Guggenheim to Wright, August 20, 1946, Frank Lloyd Wright Correspondence, Box 517, Folder 1, Guggenheim Archives.

160 *"the Mother-art of which Painting"*　Quoted in Lukach, *Hilla Rebay*, 195.

160 *"the old representational picture"* Letter, Wright to Solomon Guggenheim, Aug. 14, 1946, Frank Lloyd Wright Correspondence, Box 17, Folder 4, Guggenheim Archives.

161 *"For some time, I have been trying"* Letter, Solomon Guggenheim to Wright, Aug. 10, 1946, quoted in letter, Harry Guggenheim to Wright, July 8, 1958, Frank Lloyd Wright Correspondence, Box 518, Folder 24, Guggenheim Archives.

161 *"In a great upward"* Frank Lloyd Wright, "An Experiment in the Third Dimension," 1958, Collection of Frank Lloyd Wright, Box 691320, Folder 37, Guggenheim Archives.

162 *Everyone in the Guggenheim family had long* Huxtable, *Frank Lloyd Wright*, 233; Hession and Pickrel, *Frank Lloyd Wright*, 98.

162 *"Damn it, get a permit for Frank"* Quoted in Hession and Pickrel, *Frank Lloyd Wright*, 102. In a letter to Harry Guggenheim, dated Oct. 20, 1955, Moses wrote, "I don't personally like either the Museum or what's going into it. . . . I have simply tried at their request to help some good friends in a dubious enterprise because they *are* friends and for no other reason" (Frank Lloyd Wright Correspondence, Box 517, Folder 18, Guggenheim Archives). As one of the public speakers at the museum's opening ceremony on Oct. 21, 1959, Moses said, "I can claim credit here only for successful efforts to keep Cousin Frank close to, if not quite within the law" (Collection of Frank Lloyd Wright, Box 691320, Folder 31, Guggenheim Archives).

162 *By this time, frustrated by the delays* Hession and Pickrel, *Frank Lloyd Wright*.

162 *"an ambitious exemplar"* Letter, Wright to Harry Guggenheim, May 10, 1958, Frank Lloyd Wright Correspondence, Box 518, Folder 23, Guggenheim Archives.

162 *"our precious violin"* Letter, Wright to Harry Guggenheim, May 5, 1958, Frank Lloyd Wright Correspondence, Box 518, Folder 23, Guggenheim Archives.

162 *"would have hated in his guts"* Letter, Wright to Sweeney, Feb. 14, 1958, Frank Lloyd Wright Correspondence, Box 518, Folder 25, Guggenheim Archives.

162 *"not one shred of evidence"* Letter, Harry Guggenheim to Wright, July 8, 1958, Frank Lloyd Wright Correspondence, Box 518, Folder 24, Guggenheim Archives. (There are many such exchanges scattered throughout Box 518.)

163 *"a curving wave"* Quoted in Hession and Pickrel, *Frank Lloyd Wright*, 108.

163 *Out of the 128 works* "Installation of Inaugural Selection," Oct. 24, 1959, Guggenheim Archives. (The document was provided by a curator; it had no folder or file number.)

163 *"20th century art and architecture"* Huxtable, "That Museum: Wright or Wrong."

163 *"is less a museum"* Ibid.

163 *"a war between architecture"* John Canady, "Wright vs. Painting," *New York Times*, Oct. 21, 1959.

163 *or, as she called herself, Peggy* For biographical information, see Mary V. Dearborn, *Mistress of Modernism: The Life of Peggy Guggenheim* (New York: Houghton Mifflin, 2004); Mark Stevens and Annalyn Swan, *de Kooning: An American Master* (New York: Alfred A. Knopf, 2004), 169–171, 207–211; Calvin Tomkins, *Off the Wall: A Portrait of Robert Rauschenberg* (New York: Doubleday, 1980), 39–42, 55–56 (page numbers refer to the 2005 Picador paperback edition).

164 *"the Nazi baroness"* Anton Gill, *Art Lover: A Biography of Peggy Guggenheim* (NY: Harper Collins, 2002), 280.

164 *But she had much broader tastes* Stevens and Swan, *de Kooning*, 169–171.

164 *"the headquarters of surrealism"* Ibid.

164 *One of these friends was James Sweeney* Ibid., 203.

165 *"a real discovery"* Quoted in ibid.

165 *To make money, he was working as a janitor* Tomkins, *Off the Wall*, 40–41.

165 *he once threw up* Stevens and Swan, *de Kooning*, 208.

165 *"Jackson Pollock: Is He"* "Jackson Pollock: Is He the Greatest Living Painter in the United States?" *Life*, Aug. 8, 1949.

166 *"At a certain moment"* Reprinted in Harold Rosenberg, *The Tradition of the New* (New York: Horizon Press, 1959), 23–39 (page numbers refer to the 1994 Da Capo paperback edition).

167 *"the strongest painter of his generation"* Clement Greenberg, "Marc Chagall, Lyonel Feininger, Jackson Pollock," *The Nation*, Nov. 27, 1943.

167 *"American-Type Painting"* Reprinted in Clement Greenberg, *The Collected Essays and Criticism, Vol. 3: Affirmations and Refusals, 1950–1956*, ed. John O'Brian (Chicago: Univ. of Chicago Press, 1999).

167 *The inaugural exhibition*   "Installation of Inaugural Selection."

168 *"the greatest architect"*   Quoted in Hession and Pickrel, *Frank Lloyd Wright*, 77, 133. Johnson later publicly regretted the remark, which he'd circulated widely, and was bowled over by the Guggenheim Museum, which might have been what changed his view of the old man. "In that room," Johnson said of its interior, "museum fatigue is abolished, circulation obvious, simple, direct. It is . . . exciting . . . to be in" (see p. 117).

19. Blurring Art and Life

169 *At the same time that the Guggenheim*   Invoices and delivery notices show that many of the works for the *Sixteen Americans* show were delivered to MoMA in Oct. 1959. See Dorothy C. Miller Papers, Box 1, Folder 15K, Museum of Modern Art Archive, New York. MoMA isn't the Rockefellers' museum in the same sense that the Guggenheim was the Guggenheims', but it was started by Abby Rockefeller, the daughter of Sen. Nelson Aldrich and wife of the oil tycoon John D. Rockefeller, who amassed a vast collection of modern art and donated much of it to the museum that she helped start. Her sons, Nelson and David, succeeded her as very active board members and prodigious collectors themselves.

169 *"simply as individuals"*   *Sixteen Americans*, ed. Dorothy Miller (New York: Museum of Modern Art, 1959), 6.

169 *"combines"*   See *Robert Rauschenberg: Combines*, ed. Paul Schimmel (Los Angeles: Museum of Contemporary Art/Steidl Verlag, 2005). The seven combines in the MoMA show were *Satellite, The Wager, Curfew, Double Feature, Kickback, The Magician*, and *Summer Storm* (*Sixteen Americans*, 58–63).

170 *Jasper Johns's paintings*   They were *Numbers in Color, Tennyson, White Numbers, Large White Flag, Black Target, Target with Four Faces*, and *Green Target* (*Sixteen Americans*, 22–27). Other artists in the show included Ellsworth Kelly, Alfred Leslie, Louise Nevelson, and Frank Stella. For more on Johns, see *Jasper Johns: A Retrospective*, eds. Kirk Varnedoe, et al. (New York: Museum of Modern Art, 2006).

170 *"the boundary of a body"*   *Sixteen Americans*, 22.

170 *"Painting relates to both art"*   Ibid., 58.

170 *Milton Robert Rauschenberg*   Biographical information comes mainly from Calvin Tomkins, *Off the Wall: A Portrait of Robert Rauschenberg*

(New York: Doubleday, 1980, page numbers refer to the 2005 Picador paperback edition); and Mary Lynn Kotz, *Rauschenberg: Art and Life—New Edition* (New York: Harry N. Abrams, 2004).

171 *In the fall of 1948*   Tomkins, *Off the Wall*, chap. 4; and Martin Duberman, *Black Mountain: An Exploration in Community* (New York: E. P. Dutton, 1972). See also chap. 4 of this book.

171 *It was at this show that Rauschenberg met John Cage*   Tomkins, *Off the Wall*, passim, esp. chap. 8; Kotz, *Rauschenberg*, 71ff.

172 *"an affirmation of life"*   John Cage, *Silence: Lectures and Writings* (Middletown, CT: Wesleyan Univ. Press, 1973), 12.

172 *Cage had taught at Black Mountain College*   For several years in the 1950s, and again in the 1960s, Rauschenberg designed the sets and lighting for Cunningham's dance company, while Cage composed the music. Cunningham had the same influence on dance that they had on music and art, respectively: he freed dance from plots, stories, ritual, and even dependence on musical beat. (Tompkins, *Off the Wall*, 92–93. For more detail, see *Robert Rauschenberg: A Retrospective*, eds. Walter Hopps and Susan Davidson [New York: Guggenheim Museum, 1998], 224–287.)

172 *"airports for lights"*   Cage, *Silence*, 102.

172 The White Paintings *inspired him to write* 4'33"   Cage later wrote, in the introduction to an essay about Rauschenberg, "To Whom It May Concern: The white paintings were first; my silent piece came later" (Ibid., 98).

172 *"There is no such thing"*   Cage wrote this in a 1958 lecture on experimental music. Reprinted in ibid., 7.

173 *"There is no poor subject"*   *Sixteen Americans*, 58.

173 *One day at an art store*   Kotz, *Rauschenberg*, 82.

173 *To Rauschenberg, red was just* red   Ibid., 90.

173 *One afternoon, he knocked on de Kooning's door*   Tomkins, *Off the Wall*, 87–88; Kotz, *Rauschenberg*, 82; Mark Stevens and Annalyn Swan, *de Kooning: An American Master* (New York: Alfred A. Knopf, 2004), 359–360. (It was Stevens and Swan who first discovered, from their research, that de Kooning was outraged about the public display of the erased drawing.)

174 *Soon they fell into an intense relationship*   Rauschenberg and Johns were gay (though Rauschenberg had briefly been married and fathered

a son), as were several artists in their circle, but it's a point of some debate whether they created "gay art." The critic Robert Hughes, in *The Shock of the New* (New York: Alfred A. Knopf, 1980), on page 335, called Rauschenberg's *Monogram*—the combine that featured a goat with a tire around its neck—"one of the few great icons of male homosexual love in modern culture: the Satyr in the Sphincter, the counterpart to Meret Oppenheim's fur cup and spoon." Rauschenberg dismissed the interpretation, saying, "A stuffed goat is special in the way that a stuffed goat is special. I wanted to see if I could integrate an object as exotic as that" (quoted in Kotz, *Rauschenberg*, 90). Some note, as part of a psychoanalytical interpretation, that Rauschenberg was emotionally scarred as a child when a pet goat was killed by his father. The art critic Charles Stuckey speculates more prosaically that Rauschenberg may have been inspired by Picasso's bronze sculpture *She-Goat*, which was reproduced in the May 1953 issue of *Magazine of Art* and displayed at the Museum of Modern Art's sculpture garden in 1959. Rauschenberg started *Monogram* in 1955, but didn't figure out how to configure the goat with the canvas until 1959—and he wound up doing it exactly as Picasso did: on top of the wood platform. (Stuckey's essay is in *Rauschenberg: Combines*, 209.) As for the tire, tires were from beginning to end a frequent motif in Rauschenberg's works—an allusion perhaps to Duchamp's bicycle wheel or, more likely, to *Automobile Tire Print*, a 1953 collaboration with John Cage, in which Cage slowly drove his Model A Ford over a connected 22-foot length of drawing paper while Rauschenberg directed him while applying black enamel paint to one of the car's rear tires. It is worth noting that Rauschenberg was never one for metaphor. When a lot of his artist friends were reading Allen Ginsberg's *Howl*, which at one point mentions "a sad cup of coffee," Rauschenberg said, "I've had cold coffee and hot coffee, good coffee and lousy coffee, but I've never had a sad cup of coffee" (Tomkins, *Off the Wall*, 81). He was an artist of found objects; they were what they were. In any case, the basic facts are these: Rauschenberg saw the stuffed goat on sale for $35 in an antique shop during one of his neighborhood walks; he gave the proprietor a $15 down payment and never paid the rest.

174 *"move out"*   Tomkins, *Off the Wall*, 121.
175 *"things," as he put it, "which are seen"*   *Sixteen Americans*, 22.

175 *Many viewers were repelled, many*   Hate mail and accolades can be found in Dorothy C. Miller Papers, Box 1, Folder 15D, Museum of Modern Art Archive.

175 *It marked a departure for the museum*   Oral History Interview with Leo Castelli, Oct. 24, Nov. 16, 1991, pages 22, 24, Museum of Modern Art Archive; Tomkins, *Off the Wall*, 121–122.

175 *"Say what you will"*   Stuart Preston, "Sixteen Americans," *New York Times*, Dec. 16, 1959.

175 *"Nevertheless," he noted, "the most rewarding"*   Stuart Preston, "The Shape of Things to Come?" *New York Times*, Dec. 20, 1959.

176 *Andy Warhol's paintings and screen prints*   Kotz, *Rauschenberg*, 108; Tomkins, *Off the Wall*, 196.

176 *On October 4, 1959*   Allan Kaprow, *18 Happenings in 6 Parts*, ed. Barry Rosen and Michaela Unterdorfer (London & Zurich: Steidl/Hauser & Wirth, 2006).

176 *"events that, put simply, happen"*   Allan Kaprow, "Happenings in the New York Scene," *Art News*, Mar. 1961, reprinted in Kaprow, *Essays on the Blurring of Art and Life—Expanded Edition*, ed. by Jeff Kelley (Berkeley: Univ. of California Press, 2003), 16.

176 *Kaprow, just two years younger*   Biographical information comes mainly from *Allan Kaprow: Art As Life*, eds. Eva Meyer-Hermann, et al. (Los Angeles: Getty Research Institute, 2008); Jeff Kelley, *Childsplay: The Art of Allan Kaprow* (Berkeley: Univ. of California Press, 2004).

177 *"action collages"*   See *Allan Kaprow: Art As Life*. This is the catalogue for a huge exhibition of Kaprow's works, under the same title, at the Museum of Contemporary Art's Geffen Center in Los Angeles. I saw the collages there in the spring of 2008.

177 *"art was more"*   Allan Kaprow, "The Legacy of Jackson Pollock," *Art News*, June 1958, reprinted in Kaprow, *Essays on the Blurring of Art and Life*, 4–9.

178 *Kaprow would later tell*   Tomkins, *Off the Wall*, 138.

178 *"The performance," he wrote in the program*   The program is reproduced in Kaprow, *18 Happenings in 6 Parts*, 1.

178 *In one room, a performer was supposed to say, "Hmmmm!"*   Kaprow's notes were on display at Kaprow exhibit, Geffen Center, Spring 2008.

178 *For a brief spell, Happenings were fashionable*   Tomkins, *Off the Wall*, 139–141.

179 *"half-accepted a sophistry"*   Allan Kaprow, "Preface to the Expanded Edition: On the Way to Un-Art," in Kaprow, *Essays on the Blurring of Art and Life*, xxvii–xxix.

179 *"This is a portrait of Iris Clert"*   Tomkins, *Off the Wall*, 174–175.

179 *"flash mobs"*   See Bill Wasik, "My Crowd, or Phase 5: A Report from the Inventor of the Flash Mob," *Harper's*, Mar. 2006; Maureen Ryan, "All in a Flash: Meet, Mob and Move On," *Chicago Tribune*, July 11, 2003; Otto Pohl, "Berlin Journal: What: Mob Scene. Who: Strangers. Point: None," *New York Times*, Aug. 4, 2003; Caroline Humer, "Oddly Enough: New Yorkers Become a Mob for Fun," Reuters, July 25, 2003. For a video of the Brooklyn Bridge flash, see www.puppiesandflowers .com/archives/2008/06/from_httpwwwimproveverywhereco.html.

20. Seeing the Invisible

181 *In the fall of 1959, after winning*   See chap. 6 of this book.

181 *A French edition of the book,*   Sarah Greenough, the senior photography curator at the National Gallery of Art in Washington, D.C., documents this fact in one of the four essays that she wrote for Sarah Greenough et al., *Looking In: Robert Frank's "The Americans"* (Washington, DC: National Gallery of Art/Steidl, 2009), the catalogue for a Frank retrospective at the NGA beginning in January 2009 and continuing, later in the year, at the Metropolitan in New York. Much of this chapter is based on material in her essays, which she and her superiors at NGA kindly let me read in advance of the book's publication.

181 The Americans *was like no other photo book*   My descriptions come from the newest edition, a beautifully printed facsimile of the original, supervised by Frank himself: Robert Frank, *The Americans* (Washington, DC: National Gallery of Art/Steidl, 2008).

183 *Frank was encouraged in this direction*   Tod Papageorge, *Walker Evans and Robert Frank: An Essay on Influence* (New Haven: Yale Univ. Art Gallery, 1981); Jonathan Green, *American Photography: A Critical History, 1945 to the Present* (New York: Harry N. Abrams, 1984), 82–83.

184 *"to feel the way they do"*   Greenough, *Looking In*. Again, unless otherwise noted, facts and quotations come from this source. Since I read it in manuscript form, I am unable to cite page numbers.

184 *"to see," as he put it, "what is invisible"*   Quoted in Papageorge, *Walker Evans and Robert Frank*.

186 *Gilbert Millstein praised it*   Gilbert Millstein, "In Each a Self-Portrait," *New York Times*, Jan. 17, 1960.

186 *"an attack on the United States"*   Bruce Downes et al., "An Offbeat View of the USA," *Popular Photography*, May 1960.

187 *"a quietly ticking time bomb"*   A. D. Coleman, "Latent Image: Robert Frank," *Village Voice*, May 1, 1969.

187 *More than that, every significant photographer*   Green, *American Photography*, 92.

21. The Off-Hollywood Movie

188 *On the night of November 11*   Ray Carney, ed., *Cassavetes on Cassavetes* (New York: Faber & Faber, 2001), 82; Marshall Fine, *Accidental Genius: How John Cassavetes Invented the American Independent Film* (New York: Hyperion, 2005), 109.

188 *"Hollywood is not failing"*   John Cassavetes, "What's Wrong with Hollywood?" *Film Culture*, Jan. 1959.

189 *In January 1957, during one*   Carney, *Cassavetes on Cassavetes*, 55.

189 *He was especially moved*   Ibid., 60.

189 *"If there can be off-Broadway plays"*   Ibid., 56; Fine, *Accidental Genius*, 79–80. For more on Shepherd, see Eugene B. Bergmann, *Excelsior, You Fathead! The Art and Enigma of Jean Shepherd* (New York: Applause, 2005); the story about *I, Libertine* is recounted on pp. 132ff. Recordings of many of Shepherd's shows from the late 1950s and 1960s (though, as far as I can tell, not of this episode with Cassavetes) are available from Bill Sparks's Old Time Radio CD Store (www.billsparks.com/Jean-Shepherd_c_545-1-0.html).

190 *One of his actors, a part-time cab driver*   Carney, *Cassavetes on Cassavetes*, 62–63.

190 *Largely for that reason, Cassavetes shot a staggering*   Ibid., 68.

191 *Their top choice was Charles Mingus*   Ibid., 77–78.

191 *Near the end of 1958, Cassavetes*   Ibid.,   79–82.

192 *The final version*   Ray Carney, a film-studies professor and the world's most dogged Cassavetes scholar, spent years trying to find a print of the original version of *Shadows*—and, sometime around 2002 (he's vague on the details), he finally did. It was located in a Florida attic belonging to a

child of a woman who had worked on the film. Carney tried to show it at a film festival in 2004, but Gena Rowlands, Cassavetes' widow (he died in 1989), blocked the attempt and several subsequent ones. On his Web site, Carney claims that the first version is not a rough cut but a fully finished film; he also describes the extensive differences between the two and features three minute-long clips from the original. (See http:// people.bu.edu/rcarney/shadows/versions.shtml.)

192 *In the 1930s, as a teenager, Vogel* www.thestickingplace.com/film/ film-as-a-subversive-art/; Carney, *Cassavetes on Cassavetes*, 82; Fine, *Accidental Genius*, 103.

193 *"was able to break out"* Jonas Mekas, "Independent Film Award," *Film Culture*, Jan. 1959; Fine, *Accidental Genius*, 102.

193 *As further celebration* Carney, *Cassavetes on Cassavetes*, 83.

193 *But, once more, Jonas Mekas was in the minority* Cassavetes answered Mekas's blast in a baffled letter published in the *Village Voice*, Dec. 16, 1959.

193 *Meanwhile, as a result of Mekas's rave* Fine, *Accidental Genius*, 119.

194 *In interviews, he even embellished the claim* Carney, *Cassavetes on Cassavetes*, 94–97.

194 *"a landmark in the American cinema"* All blurbs are quoted in Fine, *Accidental Genius*, 119–120.

194 Faces, Husbands Five of his films—*Shadows, Faces, A Woman under the Influence, The Killing of a Chinese Bookie*, and *Opening Night*—are available on DVD, as a boxed set, from the Criterion Collection.

194 *"all of a sudden"* Fine, *Accidental Genius*, 119.

194 *"Nice work"* Peter Biskind, *Easy Riders, Raging Bulls: How the Sex-Drugs-and-Rock 'n' Roll Generation Saved Hollywood* (New York: Simon & Schuster, 1998), 239.

195 *In its style and its attitude* Besides Scorsese and others, Jonas Mekas himself noted, in "Movie Journal," *Village Voice*, Dec. 23, 1971, that the screening of *Shadows* "became an occasion from which the rise of the New American Cinema is usually dated" (though he emphasized "the excitement some of us felt" at the *Paris Theater's* screenings). At the 1989 Sundance Film Festival, held shortly after Cassavetes' death, he was honored posthumously with a retrospective for his role in pioneering the indie movement. See Peter Biskind, *Down and Dirty Pictures: Miramax, Sundance, and the Rise of Independent Film* (New York: Simon & Schuster, 2004).

195 *In Cassavetes' case, it was Kodak's Tri-X* Peter Cowie, *Revolution! The Explosion of World Cinema in the Sixties* (New York: Faber & Faber, 2004), 55–57.

196 *"action film"* Richard Brody, *Everything Is Cinema: The Working Life of Jean-Luc Godard* (New York: Metropolitan Books, 2008), 59–71. Brody also writes that around 1980, Godard wrote, or at least fiddled with, a screenplay based on Kerouac's *On the Road* and that Francis Coppola was interested in filming it until his Zoetrope studio went broke.

196 *But they soon would be* One reason for the heavy trickle (not quite a flood) of foreign films onto American shores in the late fifties was the rise, around this time, of film-loving U.S. importers. The most notable of these was Janus Films, founded in 1956 by Cyrus Harvey and Bryant Haliday. Harvey sailed to France on a Fulbright Scholarship in 1948, ostensibly to study comparative literature at the Sorbonne. He ended up spending most of his time at Henri Langlois's Cinéthèque, which showed films from everywhere and from all periods, three of them a day. (It's conceivable that Harvey sat near the young Truffaut or Godard now and then; they too were skipping school to sit in Langlois's temple, absorbing a comprehensive education in cinema that they put to good use when they turned to making films.) Back in the States, Harvey talked about the Cinéthèque with Haliday, a friend who had recently bought the Brattle Theater in Cambridge. Together, they turned the Brattle into a showcase for foreign films and soon expanded to the Fifty-fifth Street Playhouse in New York. After a while, they ran out of foreign films, so they started an import-distribution company, Janus Films. Among their earliest acquisitions was Fellini's early film *I Vitelloni*, which Harvey had seen in France. It didn't do much business, though Cassavetes saw it and was greatly influenced by it. Harvey discovered Bergman on a subsequent trip to Paris and arranged with the Swedish film industry to gain U.S. rights. The first Bergman Janus showed was *Summer with Monika*, a hit largely because of its nudity. The breakthrough came with *Wild Strawberries*, then *The Seventh Seal* and *The Magician*, all of which played in New York in 1959. Janus came late to the French New Wave films—*The 400 Blows* was imported by Zenith Films, *Breathless* by Films-Around-the-World, Inc. (Neither appears to have lasted for long; Janus acquired *400 Blows* in the mid-sixties.) After that, though, Janus bought the rights to Truffaut's second film, *Jules and Jim*, and to most of the New Wave features after.

Janus never made much money and was on the verge of bankruptcy when Saul Turell and William Becker bought the company in the mid-1960s. Later, their sons, Jonathan Turell and Peter Becker, started the Criterion Collection, which transferred the Janus archive—and, eventually, many other films, as well—first to Laser Disc, then to DVD. (Most of this information comes from an interview with Cyrus Harvey, Apr. 2, 2008.)

22. The Shape of Jazz to Come

198 *On the night of November 17*   Much has been written about the Ornette Coleman Quartet's debut at the Five Spot. See Nat Hentoff, "Biggest Noise in Jazz," *Esquire*, March 1961 (reprinted in Hentoff, *The Jazz Life* [New York: Da Capo Press, 1975], 222–248); Martin Williams, *The Jazz Tradition* (New York: Oxford Univ. Press, 1983), Chap. 22; John Litweiler, *Ornette Coleman: A Harmolodic Life* (New York: Morrow, 1992); A. B. Spellman, *Four Lives in the Bebop Business* (New York: Pantheon, 1966). I also consulted contemporary press coverage. Some information comes from my interviews with Ornette Coleman (Apr. 10, 2008), Paul Bley (Feb. 18, 2008), Sonny Rollins (Feb. 19, 2008), Sy Johnson (April 2008), Gunther Schuller (Apr. 15, 2008), Dan Morgenstern (Apr. 1, 2008), Dick Katz (Apr. 24, 2008), George Schuller (Apr. 4, 2008) and Charlie Haden (August 2002).

198 *His tone was like a yelp*   Whitney Balliett, in the *New Yorker* ("Haymaker," Apr. 16, 1960) called Coleman's sound "anti-aesthetic swaddling," a "concatenation of moans, yelps, frenzied twittering," and sighed that the alto sax "was simply not designed" for his style of playing. John S. Wilson, in the *New York Times* ("The Type of Jazz Recorded Last Year," Jan. 3, 1960) called it "an odd assortment of shrill, harsh cries, swoops and smears." Like many other initial skeptics, who wrote similar snipings, they soon changed their minds.

198 *"the largest collection of VIPs"*   George Hoefer, "Caught in the Act," *downbeat*, Jan. 7, 1960.

199 *Dorothy Kilgallen*   The guest column appeared during his quartet's second stay at the Five Spot. Ornette Coleman, "Modern Jazz Fast Coming of Age," *New York Journal-American*, Aug. 20, 1960. Nat Hentoff reported that it was ghostwritten by the club's publicist (Hentoff, *The Jazz Life*, 228). Mildred Fields is identified as the

publicist in a Five Spot press release, dated Nov. 10, 1959, promoting Ornette Coleman's New York debut (Clippings Files, Ornette Coleman, Jun. 1958–Mar. 1960, 1–24, Institute of Jazz Studies archive, Rutgers University, Newark, NJ).

199 *The next day, he took Coleman backstage*   George Hoefer, "The Hot Box," *downbeat*, Jan. 21, 1960.

199 *"I don't know what he's playing"*   "Beyond the Cool," *Time*, June 27, 1960.

199 *"I know you're up there"*   John Snyder, "Ornette Coleman: Music to Set You Free" (provided to author; Snyder doesn't remember where the piece was published, and I haven't been able to find out). Coleman told me, in my interview with him, that Roach *tried* to punch him in the mouth, but missed when he swung, and that he apologized a few nights later.

200 *But then they heard him warming up backstage*   Interviews with Charlie Haden, Paul Bley, Sy Johnson. See also Williams, *The Jazz Tradition*. In October 1958, Bley recorded a live session at the Hillcrest Club in Los Angeles of his quintet, which consisted of himself and the members of what became the Ornette Coleman Quartet. One of the tunes they played was Parker's "Klack-to-vee-sedstene," which Coleman plays note-perfect, though with his own eccentric touches. Bley later released the tapes on an album, which has gone by various titles on various labels, most notably *Coleman Classics Vol. 1* and *The Fabulous Paul Bley Quintet*.

200 *The next year, during a trip to New York*   Hentoff, *The Jazz Life*, 236.

200 *Ornette couldn't read music well*   There is a dispute, even among musicians who knew and still know him, whether—or how well—he could, or can, read music. Paul Bley has said that Coleman was basically a "primitive" (interview with Bley). Gunther Schuller says that at the Lenox School, he had to guide Coleman, bar by bar, through Herb Pomeroy's big-band arrangements. (Schuller's son, George, confirms that Pomeroy, before he died, confirmed this in a tape-recorded interview that he conducted.) There are also photos of Gunther Schuller showing *something* to Coleman on a score in a practice shed at Lenox. Schuller also says that he gave Coleman informal lessons on musical notation and theory in early 1960 and that, in one session, Coleman panicked and got violently sick when he realized that he'd been misunderstanding transposition (the technique of taking a piece written for an instrument in one key and rewriting it for an instrument in another key). Coleman denies this. However, he also says that he has no memory of ever taking

lessons from Schuller. Yet Hentoff wrote, in his 1960 *Esquire* profile, that Coleman was doing just that: taking lessons on notation and music theory from Schuller. So at least that part of the story is right. On the other hand, the jazz pianist-arranger-photographer Sy Johnson tells a very different story. Johnson says that he met Coleman in October 1958 at the Hillcrest Club. Johnson told him that he had a big band that met informally to rehearse the various players' music. Coleman asked if he could contribute a piece and play in the band. Johnson, of course, said, "Yes." Soon after, Coleman brought him a score—in tiny, squibbly hand-writing, but "readable"—of "Lover, Come Back to Me." It was a "very clever" arrangement, Johnson recalls, in which Coleman had layered a series of augmented-ninth chords on top of the song's regular chords, then written a melody to go with those chord changes, then written a countermelody to go with those. The first thirty-two bars were devoted to a recitation of the theme. In the second thirty-two bars, Coleman, who was playing second alto, took a solo. Then Don Cherry, who also sat in with the band, played the second head. And, Johnson said, the score *was* transposed in the proper keys for the different parts. Coleman later wrote an orchestral symphony called *Skies over America*. The arrangement was idiosyncratic, but it was a proper orchestral arrangement. One possible conclusion from all this is that Coleman could write music (he did study music theory during all those off hours as an elevator operator) but perhaps he couldn't sight-read very well.

200 *One night in 1948* Litweiler, *Ornette Coleman*, 33–34.

200 *Coleman got kicked off bandstands* John Tynan, "Ornette: The First Beginning," *downbeat*, July 21, 1960; Litweiler, *Ornette Coleman*, 44–50; Hentoff, *The Jazz Life*, 234–235; interviews with Ornette Coleman, Sy Johnson.

201 *He wore long hair, a beard* Hentoff, *The Jazz Life*, 237.

201 *Cherry was playing around town* Litweiler, *Ornette Coleman*, 52–53.

201 *"definite maze" of standard chord changes* Ibid., 54–55.

201 *"Why did you end the phrase"* Ibid., 45.

201 *Coleman hadn't read William Carlos Williams* See chap. 4 of this book.

201 *This was also why Coleman sometimes stretched* See Martin Williams, "A Letter from Lenox, Mass," *Jazz Review*, Oct. 1959; and Williams's liner notes on the LP, Ornette Coleman, *The Shape of Jazz to Come* (Atlantic Records, 1959).

201 *In practice sessions, he would sometimes blow*   Darius Brubeck, who
was twelve at the time, recalls hearing Coleman and Cherry doing
this in the practice sheds at the Lenox School of Jazz in August 1959;
Brubeck was there with his father, Dave Brubeck. Darius Brubeck,
"1959: The Beginning of Beyond," in Mervyn Cook and David Horn,
eds., *The Cambridge Companion to Jazz* (Cambridge, UK: Cambridge Univ.
Press, 2002).

202 *"developing your ear"*   Litweiler, *Ornette Coleman*, 148.

202 *Red Mitchell, a prominent jazz bassist*   The story of Coleman's introduc-
tion to Lester Koenig was first recounted in Tynan, "Ornette: The First
Beginning." Some of it also relies on my interview with Koenig's son,
John Koenig, June 26, 2008.

202 *Coleman had given up on a life in music*   Hentoff, *The Jazz Life*, 238.

203 *Before the next date*   Litweiler, *Ornette Coleman*, 65.

203 *Often he would try to break out*   Ibid., 60; Interview with Charlie
Haden.

204 *He was also classically trained*   See Paul Bley and David Lee,
Stopping Time: Paul Bley and the Transformation of Jazz (Montreal:
Vehicule Press, 1999), esp. 22–26, 48, 56–70; Norman Meehan, *Time
Will Tell: Conversations with Paul Bley* (Berkeley, CA: Berkeley Hills
Books, 2003), esp. 4–5, 10, 14–15, 43–51; and interview with Paul Bley.

204 *"I've never heard anything like them"*   Lewis's interview, which took
place in the summer of 1959, was reprinted as Francis Thorne, "An
Afternoon with John Lewis," *Jazz Review*, Mar.–Apr. 1960.

205 *He told Atlantic's owners*   It's unclear who told what to whom first.
I've drawn the most consistent version from information in the previously cited books and articles by Litweiler, Hentoff, and Tynan, as well
as my own interviews with John Koenig and Gunther Schuller.

205 *He and John Lewis were on the board*   Jeremy Yudkin, *The Lenox School
of Jazz: A Vital Chapter in the History of American Music and Race
Relations* (South Egremont, MA.: Farshaw Publishing, 2006); Michael
Fitzgerald's Web site about Lenox (www.jazzdiscography.com/Lenox/
lenhome.htm); interview with Gunther Schuller; interview with George
Schuller, a jazz bassist (and Gunther's son), who helped make a fascinat-
ing, but unreleased, film titled *Music Inn* (produced by Naomi Bombardi-
Wilson, George Schuller, and Ben Barenholtz), which he let me see.

206 *"an idea about the uniqueness"*   Letter, Nesuhi Ertegun to Ornette
Coleman, July 20, 1959, Atlantic Records Archive, "Ornette Coleman,

correspondence with Nesuhi Ertegun" folder, New York City. (Thanks to Grayson Dantzic, Atlantic's archivist, for allowing me access to this and other documents.) After Ertegun suggested the title of *The Shape of Jazz to Come*, Coleman offered a counterproposal: *The Musical Expectations of Jazz*. Ertegun wrote back, in a letter of July 24, 1959, that his proposal means the same thing—"the way things will be in the future." Luckily, Ertegun stuck to his guns, as *Shape* is not only one of the greatest jazz albums, but also one of the greatest jazz album titles.

206 *"I know you've had some very tough"* Letter, Nesuhi Ertegun to Ornette Coleman, June 30, 1959, Atlantic Records Archive.

206 *"Damn it, tune up"* Hentoff, *The Jazz Life*, 239.

207 *George Russell, who had persuaded Miles* George Russell and Martin Williams, "Ornette Coleman and Tonality," *Jazz Review*, June 1960.

207 *"It was as if he opened up something"* Williams, "Letter from Lenox, Mass."

207 *"Just wanted to tell you"* Telephone Message, For Nesuhi Ertegun from Martin Williams, 8/13 [1959], "Ornette Coleman/Don Cherry" folder, Atlantic Records Archive. The word "greatest" is underlined in the message.

207 *"I believe that what"* Martin Williams, liner notes to Ornette Coleman, *The Shape of Jazz to Come*. The liner notes are similar to his "Letter from Lenox" article for *Jazz Review*.

207 *"a shabby cave"* "Beyond the Cool."

208 *The club started out as just another one of thier* Dan Wakefield, *New York in the '50s* (New York: Houghton Mifflin, 1992), 207–212; Hettie Jones, *How I Became Hettie Jones* (New York: Dutton, 1990).

208 *"Man, your poems are weird"* David Lehman, *The Last Avant-Garde: The Making of the New York School of Poets* (New York: Doubleday, 1998), 109.

209 *Norman Mailer was among those* Wakefield, *New York*, 310–311; Mary V. Dearborn, *Mailer* (New York: Houghton Mifflin, 1999), 116. Coleman distinctly remembers Mailer attending several of his sets. "He always made the scene livelier." (Interview with Coleman.)

209 *"Yeah, I'm almost through"* Ginsberg recounts this story in a letter to Jack Kerouac, Sept. 17, 1958. Allen Ginsberg Papers, Box 1, Folder 6, Harry Ransom Research Center, University of Texas, Austin. Ginsberg mentions that his apartment is around the corner from the Five Spot, and that he drops in to hear Monk for "an hour every other night," in a letter to Robert Lavigne, Sept. 10, 1958, Box 1, Folder 7.

209 *Paul Bley, who'd recently moved back*   Bley and Lee, *Stopping Time*, 71.

209 *"I guess I'm out-of-date"*   Hentoff, *The Jazz Life*, 227–228.

210 *"Hell, just listen to what he writes"*   Ibid., 248.

210 *"Well, that must be the answer"*   Coltrane raved about Coleman and his influence on him in an interview with a French magazine; the remarks are translated and quoted in Lewis Porter, *John Coltrane: His Life and Music* (Ann Arbor: Univ. of Michigan Press, 1998), 203. In 2005, Guernsey's held an auction of jazz artifacts at Lincoln Center. It included many items from Coltrane's estate. One of them was Ornette Coleman's practice book, which Coleman apparently gave him in 1960. (A curator flipped through the book at my request; it included—in what appeared to be Coleman's handwriting—page after page of scales, chords, and several standards, including "Embraceable You.")

210 *Much later, Coltrane sent him a check*   Ibid., 204. Porter also quotes Coleman as saying that in the mid-1960s, Coltrane asked him to join his band. Coleman had just been invited to play at the Village Vanguard; had he not been, he would have joined.

210 *In the summer of 1960, he recorded*   The album was called *The Avant Garde*.

210 *As the Black Power movement took off*   Though Coleman was raised amid segregation and experienced much racial discrimination in his life, he never saw free jazz as political. (He has said this in several interviews, including one with me.) Once, in Chicago, Coleman went to hear Elijah Muhammad speak at his Nation of Islam mosque and was totally turned off, telling Nat Hentoff, "I don't see why I should follow what they say when they're not cooled out themselves. I could hardly play for all the hate around me" (Hentoff, *The Jazz Life*, 230–231). Coleman was very much, and very sincerely, into music as "love."

210 *Finally there was the back-and-forth case of Sonny Rollins*   Interview with Sonny Rollins.

211 *"I'm not saying that everybody's"*   Quoted in Leonard Feather, "Blindfold Test: Charles Mingus," *downbeat*, Apr. 28, 1960.

23. Dancing in the Streets

212 *The Edsel had rolled out two years earlier*   Peter Carlson, "The Flop Heard Round the World," *Washington Post*, Sept. 4, 2007.

212 *"an Oldsmobile sucking"*   "The $250 Million Flop," *Time*, Nov. 30, 1959.

212 *"Every Day Something Else Leaks"* Kathleen A. Ervin, *"Failure* Examines the History of the Edsel," *Failure Magazine*, Mar. 2002.

213 *Ford had expected to sell* Carlson, "The Flop."

213 *The Big Three—General Motors, Chrysler, even Ford* "Autos: The New Generation," *Time*, Oct. 5, 1959.

213 *Sales of a squat German car* The ad campaign was conceived by Doyle Dane Bernbach, at the time one of the minor Madison Avenue firms known for its wry campaigns for Jewish clients, such as Orbach's department store, Levy's rye bread, and El Al airlines—doubly ironic, given that the Volkswagen's original design had been supervised by Hitler. The Volkswagen ads, which were headlined "Think Small" and "Lemon," fit well with the rise of irony, *Mad* magazine, sick comics, and the Beats.

213 *"sleeker styling"* Joseph C. Ingraham, "Imports Perk Up for Big Year," *New York Times*, Apr. 5, 1959; see also "The International Auto Show," *Village Voice*, Apr. 1, 1959.

213 *"a hip name for a factory"* Berry Gordy, *To Be Loved: The Music, the Magic, the Memories of Motown—An Autobiography* (New York: Warner Books, 1994), 118.

213 *It would become the first successful* Lars Bjorn with Jim Gallert, *Before Motown: A History of Jazz in Detroit* (Ann Arbor: Univ. of Michigan Press, 2001), 199.

214 *Between 1910 and 1930* Elizabeth Anne Martin, *Detroit and the Great Migration, 1916–1929* (Ann Arbor: Bentley Historical Library, Univ. of Michigan, 1993).

214 *A half million more* Suzanne E. Smith, *Dancing in the Street: Motown and the Cultural Politics of Detroit* (Cambridge, MA: Harvard Univ. Press, 1999), 32.

214 *That summer, race riots erupted* Ibid., 33.

214 *Amid this de facto segregation* Ibid., 10.

215 *The blues were ingrained in Detroit culture* Ibid., 12–13.

215 *During the economic boom of the war years* Nelson George, *Where Did Our Love Go? The Rise and Fall of the Motown Sound* (Urbana: Univ. of Illinois Press, 2007), 16; Gordy, *To Be Loved*, 73; Bjorn, *Before Motown*, 165.

215 *Gordy came from an entrepreneurial* Gordy, *To Be Loved*, 12ff.

216 *3D Record Mart* Ibid., 59–61; George, *Where Did Our Love Go?*, 16–17; Bjorn, *Before Motown*, 198.

216 *So he wrote a song for Green called "Reet Petite"* Gordy, *To Be Loved*, 74ff.

216 *It was in the amount of $3.19*   Ibid., 97; see also 91–107.

216 *That same month he borrowed $800*   A copy of the contract is reproduced in ibid., 108. It's dated Jan. 12, 1959.

217 *His receptionist, Janie Bradford*   Gordy, *To Be Loved*, 120ff.; George, *Where Did Our Love Go?*, 26.

217 *It was only the eighth single*   Gerald Posner, *Motown: Music, Money, Sex, and Power* (New York: Random House, 2002), 46–47.

217 *It rocketed to number two*   Chart rankings are noted in the pamphlet for the CD boxed set, *Hitsville U.S.A.: Motown, 1959–1971* (Motown, 1992).

218 *They called themselves the Funk Brothers*   Allan "Dr. Licks" Slutsky, *Standing in the Shadows of Motown: The Life and Music of Legendary Bassist James Jamerson* (Wynnwood, PA: Dr. Licks Publishing, 1989); George, *Where Did Our Love Go?*, 105–106; Bjorn, *Before Motown*, 163ff. See also the documentary film *Standing in the Shadows of Motown* (Sandy Passman, Allan Slutsky, Paul Justman, producers; Artisan Entertainment, 2002).

218 *The riffs, rhythms, and especially the bass lines*   See esp. Slutsky, *Standing in the Shadows*, 41, 93ff.

219 *Across the Atlantic, in Liverpool*   The Beatles, *The Beatles Anthology* (New York: Chronicle Books, 2002), 198; Walter Everett, *The Beatles As Musicians: Revolver Through the Anthology* (New York: Oxford Univ. Press, 1999), 55, 71, 141; Steven D. Stark, *Meet the Beatles: A Cultural History of the Band That Shook Youth, Gender, and the World* (New York: Harper Paperbacks, 2006), 26–27; Slutsky, *Standing in the Shadows*, 102.

219 *The first portable transistor radio*   George, *Where Did Our Love Go?*, 114; Michael Brian Schiffer, *The Portable Radio in American Life* (Tucson: Univ. of Arizona Press, 1991), especially 189, 191, 209, 212, 221–223.

220 *Norman Mailer's* Advertisements for Myself   See chap. 3 of this book.

24. Andromeda Freed from Her Chains

221 *Toward the end of December*   I have been unable to find an exact date for this meeting. The FDA was not the tight organization that it is today; the hearing seems to have been informal; its archives appear to have no record or transcript. Nor has the archivist at Pfizer, which now owns Searle, been able to track down a document about this meeting.

All the standard histories of this subject—noted below—state only that the meeting took place in "late December." They rely on interviews with the participants, who are now all dead.

221 *Margaret Sanger, a crusader* Biographical material is based mainly on Ellen Chesler, *Woman of Valor: Margaret Sanger and the Birth Control Movement in America* (New York: Simon & Schuster, 1992); James Reed, *From Private Vice to Public Virtue: The Birth Control Movement and American Society Since 1830* (New York: Basic Books, 1978); Bernard Asbell, *The Pill: A Biography of the Drug That Changed the World* (New York: Random House, 1995).

221 *"You caused this"* Asbell, *The Pill*, 20–21.

222 *Diaphragms and condoms* See esp. Reed, *From Private Vice*; Andrea Tone, *Devices and Desires: A History of Contraceptives in America* (New York: Hill & Wang, 2001).

222 *"to look the whole world"* Quoted in Asbell, *The Pill*, 33.

223 *"obscene, lewd, lascivious"* Ibid., 37–38.

224 *A turning point came in 1936* Elizabeth Siegel Watkins, *On the Pill: A Social History of Oral Contraceptives, 1950–1970* (Baltimore: Johns Hopkins Univ. Press, 1998), 14.

224 *McCormick came from a wealthy old family* Asbell, *The Pill*, 9, 31–32, 59, 118; Watkins, ibid., 26–27.

225 *Around this time, at a dinner party* The exact date of this dinner party has never been ascertained; it was probably late 1950 but might have been January or February 1951. See Watkins, *On the Pill*, 21.

225 *She wrote him a check for $40,000* Asbell, *The Pill*, 12, 59, 118.

226 *By the end of the decade* Starting in 1953, beyond the initial $40,000, McCormick gave Pincus' lab $150,000 to $180,000 a year not just through the end of the decade but until she died in 1967 (Watkins, *On the Pill*, 26).

226 *"exhibit, sell, prescribe"* Asbell, *The Pill*, 160.

227 *"Being a good R.C."* Quoted in Reed, *From Private Vice*, 352.

227 *In the winter of 1954–1955* Watkins, *On the Pill*, 28–31.

227 *In 1957, Searle applied* Suzanne White Junod and Lara Marks, "Women's Trials: The Approval of the First Oral Contraceptive in the United States and Great Britain," *Journal of the History of Medicine and Allied Sciences* (Apr. 2002); Asbell, *The Pill*, 164–165.

227 *"that Envoid will inhibit"* Quoted in Junod and Marks, "Women's Trials."

227 *"Of course, this use"* Quoted in Asbell, *The Pill*, 159.

228 *Over the next two years* Ibid., 129.

228 *On July 23, 1959* Many sources put the date as Oct. 29, but documents unearthed by archivists at Pfizer (which now owns Searle) reveal that as the date when the FDA filed the application. (I thank Denise Tindle and Jack Cox of Pfizer for their assistance.) Oct. 29 was also the date when Searle provided the detailed clinical data. See Junod and Marks, "Women's Trials"; Asbell, *The Pill*, 164, 304.

228 *The FDA was a shockingly ramshackle* Junod and Marks, "Women's Trials."

228 *"non-descript thirty-year-old"* Asbell, *The Pill*, 166–167; see also Junod and Marks, "Women's Trials," though they get DeFelice's name wrong.

229 *In the sixties, the birth rate* Asbell, *The Pill*, 63.

229 *"unfettered"* The ad is reproduced in ibid., 73, and in Junod and Marks, "Women's Trials."

230 *"autonomous girls"* Gloria Steinem, "The Moral Disarmament of Betty Coed," *Esquire*, Sept. 1962.

230 *"Is the pill regarded"* "The Pill: How It Is Affecting U.S. Morals, Family Life," *U.S. News & World Report*, July 11, 1966.

230 *Sexual desire pervaded* See Wini Breines, *Young, White, and Miserable: Growing Up Female in the Fifties* (Chicago: Univ. of Chicago Press, 1992); Dan Wakefield, *New York in the '50s* (New York: Houghton Mifflin, 1992), and Wakefield's thinly disguised fictional account of sexual relations in the era, *Going All the Way* (New York: Delacorte Press, 1970).

230 *"A novel, however"* Charles Rembar, *The End of Obscenity: The Trials of Lady Chatterley, Tropic of Cancer, and Fanny Hill* (New York: Harper & Row, 1986), 124. (For more on the trial, see chap. 6 of this book.)

230 *"The first rule of petting"* Quoted in Breines, *Young, White, and Miserable*, 120.

231 *In the mid-fifties a team of sociologists* Ibid., 107ff.

231 *"such as working"* Quoted in Watkins, *On the Pill*, 63.

232 *"magic pill"* Ibid., 140.

25. New Frontiers

234 *On New Year's Day* Kennedy officially announced that he was running on January 2, but his aides leaked it to the press on January 1, so the story would run in the next day's editions. AP, "Kennedy's Hat Ready," *New York Times*, Jan. 2, 1960.

234 *the youngest man ever elected* Teddy Roosevelt was forty-two when, as vice president, he ascended to the office after President William McKinley was assassinated, but he was forty-six when he was *elected* president.

234 *His critics, opponents, and several seasoned* Robert Dallek, *An Unfinished Life: John F. Kennedy, 1917–1963* (New York: Little, Brown, 2003), 210, 230, 236, 302.

234 *"The torch has been passed"* John F. Kennedy, Inaugural Address, Washington, D.C., Jan. 20, 1961.

235 *"a private preserve for Protestants"* Quoted in Dallek, *An Unfinished Life*, 211.

235 *"celebrity"* Ibid., 225.

235 *Kennedy received over 2,500* Ibid., 229, 241.

236 *he mentioned the word "new"* John F. Kennedy, Acceptance Speech, Democratic National Convention, Los Angeles, July 15, 1960.

236 *Years later, Kennedy's speechwriter* Theodore Sorensen, *Counselor: A Life at the Edge of History* (New York: Harper 2008), 218. Sorensen vaguely recalls in the memoir that the phrase was in a packet of suggestions from the historian Allan Nevins, but adds that Nevins had nothing to do with the substantive use of the phrase. Nevins, a famous historian of the day, whose books on the Civil War were greatly admired by Kennedy, was an informal campaign adviser and wrote the introduction to the Inaugural Edition of Kennedy's book, *Profiles in Courage*. On Kennedy's admiration, see Arthur Schlesinger, *Journals 1952–2000* (New York: Penguin Press, 2007), 236.

236 *In January 1959 New York's Hayden* Between January 1959 and just before Kennedy's acceptance speech in July 1960, there were twenty-one articles in the *New York Times* that used the phrase "new frontier." For the examples cited, see the following *Times* stories: "Planetarium Reopens: Its New Show Will Depict Man's Space Exploration," Jan. 10, 1959; John Finney, "Challenge of Lunik Spurs US Effort," Jan. 11, 1959; John Finney, "Record Plans Set at 5.4 Billion," Jan. 20, 1959; "The Oceans—A New Frontier," Feb. 17, 1959; "Men's Minds Seen As New Frontier," May 8, 1959; "M'murray Hails Spur to Housing," Jan. 12, 1959.

236 *The "frontier thesis"* For instance, see in the *New York Times*, "Nation on the Move," Dec. 8, 1959; Austin Wehrwein, "Massive Revision of History Urged," Dec. 29, 1959; "Text of Stevenson's Speech at Parley on World Tensions," May 13, 1960. (For elaboration on the thesis, see chap. 1 of this book.)

237 *earlier that spring, Mailer was at the Five Spot* Peter Manso, *Mailer: His Life and Times* (New York: Simon & Schuster, 1985), 299. No record seems to have been kept of exactly when this fateful encounter occurred. It is tempting to speculate that Ornette Coleman might have been playing at the Five Spot that night. Coleman's quartet did return to the club for an extended run on April 5, 1960. But as of now, no date more specific than "early spring" has been uncovered. (I have checked the *Esquire* archives at the University of Michigan's Bentley Research Library, to no avail.)

237 *Watching Kennedy perform in L.A.* Norman Mailer, "Superman Comes to the Supermart," *Esquire*, Nov. 1960. Mailer was upset that the editor changed his title from "Supermarket" to "Supermart." The original title was restored when it was reprinted in the collection *Smiling Through the Apocalypse: Esquire's History of the Sixties* (New York: Esquire Press/Crown Publishers, 1987).

238 *"may have preferred"* John F. Kennedy, speech, National Press Club, Jan. 14, 1960, Robert Dallek and Terry Golway, eds., *Let Every Nation Know: John F. Kennedy In His Own Words* (Naperville, IL: SourceBooks, 2006), 24.

239 *"S is a much richer"* Schlesinger, *Journals*, 70.

239 *"Stevenson with balls"* David Halberstam, *The Best and the Brightest* (New York: Random House, 1972), 34. (Page number refers to the 1973 Fawcett Crest paperback edition.)

239 *"Why the moon?"* Dallek and Golway, *Let Every Nation Know*, 162.

239 *In his first few months in office, Kennedy had considered* Ibid., 162–163.

239 *a man on the moon as a "stunt"* Dallek, *An Unfinished Life*, 392–393.

239 *"Control of outer space"* Ibid.

240 *"break out of the confines"* Ibid., 237.

240 *fascinated with their theories of counterinsurgency* Fred Kaplan, *The Wizards of Armageddon* (New York: Simon & Schuster, 1983), chap. 23.

240 *"new policies for the US"* Schlesinger, *Journals*, 120.

240 *In fact, though, there was no contradiction* See chap. 14 of this book.

241 *Finally, the Cuban missile crisis* See Sheldon Stern, *"Averting the Final Failure": John F. Kennedy and the Secret Cuban Missile Crisis Meetings* (Palo Alto, CA: Stanford Univ. Press, 2003).

241 *He'd barely heard of King* Taylor Branch, *Parting the Waters: America in the King Years, 1954–63* (New York: Simon & Schuster, 1988), 307.

242 *But President Eisenhower openly rejected it*   Andy Levin, "Eisenhower Wary of Plan to Widen Civil Rights Law," *New York Times*, Jan. 3, 1960.

242 *black voters may have put Kennedy*   Dallek, *An Unfinished Life*, 292–293.

242 *In June 1963, when the Alabama governor George Wallace*   This real-life drama was captured in "Crisis: Behind a Presidential Commitment," an ABC-TV documentary, filmed at the time and originally broadcast soon after. It and two other documentaries—one on the 1960 Wisconsin primary, the other on Kennedy's funeral procession in 1963, all directed by Robert Drew—have been compiled in a two-disc DVD set, *The Robert Drew/Kennedy Films Collection* (DocuDrama Films).

243 *"My pride is that I can explore"*   Quoted in Morris Dickstein, *Leopards in the Temple: The Transformation of American Fiction, 1954–1970* (Cambridge, MA: Harvard Univ. Press, 2002), 154.

Credits

Photos: Fred W. McDarrah: pages 1 top, 7 bottom; John Cohen/Getty Images: page 1 middle; Loomis Dean/Getty Images: page 1 bottom; Emil Cadoo/Janos Gat Gallery: page 2 top left; Julian Wasser/Getty Images: page 2 top right; John Loengard/Getty Images: page 2 bottom; Ed Clark/Getty Images: page 3 top; *New York Times*/Getty Images: page 3 bottom; Hulton Archive/Getty Images: page 4 top; Bob Parent/Getty Images: page 4 bottom; Courtesy Alice Russell: page 5 top; *N.Y. Journal-American* Archive, Harry Ransom Research Center, University of Texas: page 5 bottom; Don Rutledge: page 6 top; Wayne Miller/Center for Creative Photography: page 6 bottom left; Al Ruban/Faces Distribution Corp.: page 6 bottom right; Michael Rougier/Getty Images: page 8 top; DeGolyer Library, Southern Methodist University: page 8 middle; The *New York Times* Photo Archives: page 8 bottom.

Lyrics from "Please, Mr. Foreman," copyright © Joe L. Carter, 1968; Lenny Bruce, "Religions, Inc.," "Christ and Moses," "How to Entertain Colored People at Parties," copyright © Fantasy Jazz/Concord Records.

Index